Essentials of Cont
Business Leadership

Essentials of Contemporary Business Leadership provides contemporary tools for the next generation of aspirational leaders to fully meet their potential and optimise group performance.

The highly experienced authors utilize their own 'Contemporary Leadership Dimensions' model, which provides flexible and creative ways to enhance leadership learning. The book goes through the components of the model sequentially: self-leadership; people leadership, business leadership; client leadership; and finally, community leadership. This progressive approach effectively allows readers to build their knowledge and pull threads of learning into the next component of the unique model. Each chapter also features case studies, multiple interactive exercises and discussion questions which helps complete understanding from theory to practice.

This is an ideal text for students starting their leadership journey, or for practitioners hoping to improve their leadership and management skills.

Online resources will include additional exercises to augment learning.

Amy E. Forbes is the Strategic Director for Custom Executive Education at Cornell University.

Craig A. Talmage is an Associate Professor in Business Management and Entrepreneurship at Hobart & William Smith Colleges.

Essentials of Contemporary Business Leadership

Amy E. Forbes and Craig A. Talmage

Routledge
Taylor & Francis Group
LONDON AND NEW YORK

Designed cover image: AerialPerspective Works / Getty Images

First published 2026
by Routledge
4 Park Square, Milton Park, Abingdon, Oxon OX14 4RN

and by Routledge
605 Third Avenue, New York, NY 10158

Routledge is an imprint of the Taylor & Francis Group, an informa business

British Library Cataloguing-in-Publication Data
A catalogue record for this book is available from the British Library

ISBN: 978-1-032-75583-0 (hbk)
ISBN: 978-1-032-75582-3 (pbk)
ISBN: 978-1-003-47464-7 (ebk)

DOI: 10.4324/9781003474647

Typeset in Berling and Futura
by SPi Technologies India Pvt Ltd (Straive)

Access the Support Material: www.routledge.com/9781032755823

Contents

Figures

Tables

Case Studies

Preface

Bad bosses are a universal problem. They drain morale, stifle creativity, and create workplaces filled with anxiety rather than ambition. "A bad boss is like a disease of the soul" (Bhagat, as cited in Quotement, n.d.). Toxic leadership infects organizations at every level, leaving employees disengaged, dissatisfied, and uninspired. "A bad boss creates a toxic environment where creativity and productivity go to die" (Quotement, n.d.). When leaders fail to support their teams, no amount of perks, salary, or prestige can compensate for poor management. After all, "A good job with a bad boss is still a bad job" (Balmy Quotes, n.d.).

Great leaders inspire engagement and motivation, but bad bosses choose harmful, dark paths. "A bad boss has employees who do their work because they have to; a good boss has employees who do their work because they want to" (QuoteVill, n.d.). The damage caused by bad bosses extends beyond the office. "A bad boss can turn even the best job into a daily grind" (QuoteWords, n.d.), impacting well-being, mental health, and job satisfaction. "Having a bad boss can make you sick" (Green, 2014). Yet, adverse experiences with bad bosses offer much to learn. Alison Green of the *Ask a Manager* blog shares that bad bosses can be seen as "anti-mentors: bosses who were so bad that they unwittingly formed the start of my thinking on management by providing a perfect model of what not to do" (Green, 2016).

The time of bad bosses must end. It is time for the contemporary business leader to rise.

REFERENCES

Balmy Quotes. (n.d.). *40+ quotes on bad boss*. Retrieved from https://balmyquotes.com/quotes-on-bad-boss

Green, A. (2014). *Having a bad boss can make you sick, superstars can struggle to bond with their teams, and more*. Ask a Manager. Retrieved from https://www.askamanager.org/2014/11/having-a-bad-boss-can-make-you-sick-superstars-can-struggle-to-bond-with-their-teams-and-more.html

Green, A. (2016). *Why I'm thankful for the bad managers in my past*. Ask a Manager. Retrieved from https://www.askamanager.org/2016/01/why-im-thankful-for-the-bad-managers-in-my-past.html

Quotement (n.d.). 60 bad boss quotes to help you deal with a lousy manager. Retrieved from https://quotement.com/bad-boss-quotes/

QuoteVill. (n.d.). *93 inspirational bad boss quotes for dealing with office life*. Retrieved from https://quotevill.com/bad-boss-quotes/

QuoteWords. (n.d.). *Quotes for bad bosses*. Retrieved from https://quotewords.com/quotes-for-bad-bosses/

Acknowledgments

This textbook originated from conversations in the Master of Science in Management program at Hobart and William Smith Colleges in Geneva, NY. Both of us teach in this program and were instrumental in its creation. While we had forged respectable careers in leadership and entrepreneurship education, our passion for developing future business leaders began there. We sought one text or one collection of texts to help guide what we wanted to do with our graduate students in the classroom. When we failed to find one, we decided to write it. Here, we acknowledge those who supported this journey.

First, we thank Professor Joyce Jacobson for her vision of initiating the Masters of Science in Management program at HWS. She and Lou Guard shared their experiences with finding a publisher and writing *All the Campus Lawyers* (Guard & Jacobsen, 2024), which kept us going as we sought to find a home for this book. Thanks to Routledge for taking a chance on us.

We thank our friend and colleague, Professor Tom Drennen, for co-creating the Entrepreneurial Studies program, which evolved into the Bachelor of Science in Business Management and Entrepreneurship at HWS. He took a chance on us and continues to support us in our teaching, research, and service. Finally, we thank Associate Provost Susan Pliner for her leadership of the Centennial Center at HWS, which brought us together for co-curricular education. She also offered us morale support as we wrote.

We would not be the professionals we are today without our time at HWS. There, we became colleagues, friends, and now writing partners. At HWS, we were surrounded by exceptional faculty and staff and afforded opportunities to grow and learn as instructors. Thanks to Professor Emeritus Jack Harris for his continuous encouragement throughout the years; he was a role model for us with his book, *The Sixth Level* (Feiner et al., 2023). He supported the Centennial Center and entrepreneurial leadership programs at HWS for years. Our students, too, helped us develop this content and practice the exercises, allowing us to challenge them and ready them for their future roles. We thank President Mark Gearan at HWS, who exemplifies the leadership we emphasized in this book—focus on your people and recruit them for a compelling purpose.

Additionally, Amy thanks her colleagues at Cornell University, who work with her in custom executive education. This role narrowed her lens on what graduate students need to succeed as working professionals and leaders at all levels of organizations. The client often requested: "We want awesome bosses, not mediocre ones." She thanks them and the extraordinary faculty she works with for all their support. She'd also like to thank Wade and Megan (brother and sister-in-law), Owen and Ryan (nephews), and her friends Beth, Cathy, and Michael.

Craig thanks his family, Barb and Steve (parents), Meghan and Todd (sister and brother-in-law), and Benji (nephew) and Lucy (niece). He thanks them for putting up with the laptop being out around the holidays, and for all the fun Mario Kart and Mario Party breaks on Nintendo Switch. He thanks Robinson Murphy for his insights on stakeholder capitalism and sustainability, which served as foundations for two chapters in Community Leadership. He appreciates Robinson's feedback as they co-taught and previewed chapters of this book. Craig thanks Alden Gassert for his friendship and support. He really needed that high five when he told him the book was finished. He also thanks Emily Fisher for showing him the Alison Green's (n.d.) *Ask a Manager* blog. There are still so many bad bosses out there.

We did not want to put out another bad leadership book, and we thank our many friends and family who prompted us to keep going when we had our doubts about what we were creating. Many served as early readers of draft chapters, providing their feedback and offering direction when we got stuck. We especially thank our parents, who have always been our biggest cheerleaders. Amy's mother, Liz, and her late father, Tom, always celebrated her writing and encouraged her to follow her publishing dreams. Finally, we thank Amy's twin seven-year-olds, Addison and Drew, for their unconditional love and for constantly asking us when Craig would come over to write, "When will your book be done?" with much gusto, "You're still writing that book!" Nearly two years later, here it is.

BIOS

I, Amy Forbes, am the Strategic Director for Custom Executive Education at Cornell University. Currently, I design compelling in-person and virtual programs for corporate, government, and nonprofit clients, ranging from senior executives to enterprise employees. As a learning specialist, I make recommendations on content directions, learning journeys, faculty expertise, and assessment measurements. Previously, I was a leadership educator for 11 years at Hobart and William Smith Colleges where I developed content, facilitated classes and programs, and advised students on their career pathways, grounding their understanding of leadership and developing them as leaders. I also supervised a center and all of the talented staff that worked there. I earned a doctorate in educational leadership and policy studies from the University of Vermont in 2011, and although I have transitioned to executive education, I remain focused on developing effective leaders, specifically exceptional supervisors. I have taught classes, workshops, conferences, bootcamps, idealabs, seminars, and trainings. I have expertise in topics such as authenticity, difficult conversations, managing change, innovation, organizational development, strategy and leadership theory, to name a few. Still an adjunct professor at HWS, my current role at Cornell provides a unique lens into the theoretical and applied knowledge that graduate students actually need to succeed as business professionals. Having worked in higher education over 20 years, I am passionate about leading, developing, and designing compelling content that enriches learning experiences.

I, Craig Talmage, am the co-chair of and an associate professor in business management and entrepreneurship at Hobart & William Smith Colleges (HWS) and a faculty associate for the School of Public Affairs at Arizona State University (ASU). I pivoted away from the traditional business school track, earning a business minor at The University of Arizona and a BS in Family Studies and Human Development. I studied industrial/organizational psychology at Minnesota State, Mankato, under Frederick Herzberg's last graduate student, Dr. Daniel Sachau. I sought to understand workplace thought patterns across sectors: Nonprofit, for-profit, and small businesses. This pursuit took me to ASU to earn my PhD. in Community Resources and Development. At HWS, I helped craft our Entrepreneurial Studies minor (2016), our Masters of Science in Management (2021), and a new BS in Business Management and Entrepreneurship (2023). These are the most popular programs at HWS. I teach courses on management science, local development, new venture creation, organizational behavior/development, tourism management, nonprofit management and leadership, conflict resolution, sustainable community development, corporate social responsibility, and social entrepreneurship. I have over 20 years of combined not-for-profit, nonprofit, small business, and public sector research and leadership experience. I founded and operated a research consulting practice for small businesses and nonprofits in Arizona. I have authored over 80 peer-reviewed publications since 2011. I also serve as the editor-in-chief of *Community Development* and associate editor for the *Journal of Social Entrepreneurship*, both published by Routledge.

ACKNOWLEDGMENT OF AI USE

We acknowledge using AI tools in our book, but we limited AI use to a few domains. We used ChatGPT to create summary tables and organize hypothetical case studies and exercises. All AI–generated content was checked for plagiarism, and we used Grammarly to ensure accuracy in spelling, grammar, clarity, engagement, and overall delivery. Grammarly helped us identify and address any AI text patterns and plagiarism concerns. We note in the book that we used AI to create images for examples and exercises. The authors or production team recreated all figures without the use of AI. AI–powered search engines were utilized to find examples, but sources were always provided for any content used.

CONFLICT OF INTEREST STATEMENT

We declare that there are no conflicts of interest related to its publication. We affirm that no financial, professional, or personal affiliations have directly influenced the research, writing, or conclusions presented in this work. We engaged in reflexivity and made notes during our processes (see Lietz & Zayas, 2010). Furthermore, we have not received any external funding, sponsorship, or incentives that could create a potential conflict of interest. We uphold integrity and transparency in the academic and professional discourse with this book. We did our best to ensure all perspectives presented were based on independent analysis, practice, and scholarship.

REFERENCES

Feiner, S., Andreasson, R. W., Overbeke, K. K., & Harris, J. D. (2023). *The sixth level: Capitalize on the power of women's psychology for sustainable leadership*. Amplify Publishing Group.

Green, A. (n.d.). Ask a Manager (blog). https://www.askamanager.org/

Guard, L. H., & Jacobsen, J. P. (2024). *All the campus lawyers: Litigation, regulation, and the new era of higher education*. Harvard University Press.

Lietz, C. A., & Zayas, L. E. (2010). Evaluating qualitative research for social work practitioners. *Advances in Social work, 11*(2), 188–202.

CHAPTER 1

Introduction

CHAPTER OVERVIEW

The introductory chapter outlines the evolving work landscape during COVID-19 by detailing the impact of the global pandemic and then discussing trends, patterns, and lessons learned in the post-COVID professional world. Notably, this chapter emphasizes the role of the business leader as a significant influence on positive workplace experiences for employees, then and now. This chapter discusses the relationship and distinction between leadership and management and further traces who is generally responsible for teaching business leaders. Finally, this chapter details the development model that organizes the overall book and forthcoming chapters in sections on Self Leadership, People Leadership, Organizational Leadership, Client Leadership, and Community Leadership. It concludes with concepts such as the New Normal and the Future of Work and projects what the coming decade will look like for future business leaders.

COVID-19 changed everything. Fear, anxiety, and uncertainty swept sectors of society, causing disruption, upheaval, and shutdowns. Many students' school years were defined by online learning. Similarly, their parents learned to balance virtual work as employers sent their workforces home for extended periods. Furloughs and layoffs decimated other industries, such as retail, hospitality, food services, and travel. Meanwhile, healthcare and other human services workers, the deemed heroes of the pandemic, continued serving community needs despite drastic increases in stress and personal risks in their work environments.

Amanda Hetler (2023) writes, "Employees across multiple sectors realized that they weren't happy with their jobs during the pandemic. People weren't satisfied with their work environment, the industry they were in, or their work-life balance and left their jobs." She notes that Anthony Klotz coined **The Great Resignation** (see also Fox, 2021). His prediction of a mass job exodus due to widespread uncertainty came to be realized; however, its effects remained nuanced and rippled across global economies (Fox, 2021; Hetler, 2023). The ripples are still felt today.

DOI: 10.4324/9781003474647-1

Initially, the Great Resignation's impact was immediate and widespread. "Between April 2021 through April 2022, 71.6 million people separated from their jobs, which averaged 3.98 million people quitting each month" (Hetler, 2023). While specific industries were hit harder than others, professionals across sectors seemed to be reexamining their working lives, opting out for better pay, more apparent paths to advancement, and more inviting cultures with access to flexible hours, more emotional support, stronger supervisors, and essential benefits.

Employers were put on notice. The Great Resignation got so severe that Pew Research Survey observed that one in five non-retired adults left their job by choice in 2021 (Parker & Menasce Horowitz, 2022). Similarly, they observed that the majority of workers who quit a job in 2021 said low pay (63%), no opportunities for advancement (63%), and feeling disrespected at work (57%) were reasons why they quit (Parker & Menasce Horowitz, 2022; Viveros, 2022). Many organizations were at a historical impasse.

Orrell and Cox (2021) write about **The Great America Job Reshuffle** for the Survey Center on American Life. They found, "People's work arrangements and preferences, unemployment experiences, and career aspirations are changing as workers navigate the new post-pandemic labor market." One of the most striking features of the pandemic from a workforce perspective was how it forced American businesses and workers into a national experiment in remote work almost overnight. Orrell and Cox (2021) write, "Eighty-six percent of Americans now say that workplace flexibility is a key factor in choosing a new job. It's especially important for working mothers." This created tension between employers who wanted their workforces in the office and employees who had carved out productive lifestyles while working from home.

With vaccine rollouts, mask mandates were lifted, and a return to work was initiated. The economy came roaring back, and the subsequent movement was named **The Great Rehire** or The Great Rehiring (Partners Personnel, 2022). Employers were looking to fill open positions as hiring and job openings were at record highs (U.S. Bureau of Labor Statistics, 2022). "As of April 2022, there were nearly 11.4 million job openings in the U.S." (Hetler, 2023). Many employers were left scrambling, shifting their attention and resources to staffing, onboarding, and retention. Employers battled a new trend that started on social media called **quiet quitting** (Harter, 2022). Harter (2022) writes for Gallup that "Quiet quitters made up 50% of the workforce" and that it describes the viral idea of millions of workers not going above and beyond while in a job or just meeting the minimum of their job description. This resulted in more headaches for seasoned business leaders with ripple effects today.

Though residual effects from the pandemic remain, today's work climate can be described as steady but still volatile and uncertain. Political polarization, climate change, and global conflicts challenge organizations and communities. The faculty at Cornell University's Industrial Labor and Relations (ILR) School warns of five human resource trends in 2023.

1) **The Boomerang Potential**: With the nation's quit rate still the highest in decades, workers are looking for roles with more compensation and flexibility. "A recent survey from workforce management firm UKG revealed that more than 60% of job-changers have reported dissatisfaction in their new roles" (Anderson, 2022). Many have returned to their former employers, harking deep questions about onboarding effectiveness.

2) **Increased Employee Activism**: No workplace is immune to societal changes. Tight labor markets give employees leverage, "creating opportunities for them to be more outspoken on national and global matters and on what they want from their employers" (Anderson, 2022). This trend has forced senior leaders to examine their organizational cultures and readiness to address employees' needs and values.
3) **Adoption of a "Whole Person" Approach**: The pandemic's toll on workers across industries cannot be ignored. "Research from the McKinsey Health Institute shows that 80% of HR leaders identify mental health as a priority for their companies" (Anderson, 2022). Today's leaders must recognize that relationships with employees have evolved, and they need to pay attention to and support employee health, well-being, and growth.
4) **Coaching Across Generations**: The pandemic's work-from-home conditions placed many managers in new territory. They had to trust their employees' ability to work and deliver without constant supervision. In addition, today, "multigenerational workplaces can present challenges in managing diverse experiences, expectations, and expertise levels" (Anderson, 2022). Authoritarian styles have been sunsetted for more effective approaches, where supervisors favor coaching and mentoring rather than directing.
5) **Retreat from AI**: The latest workforce movement, an expansive chapter that has yet to be entirely written, is automation and its implications for work. Litwin at the ILR School says, "It makes sense that we're blown away when we see the capabilities of AI and other new technologies. But resist the urge to automate away your need to manage" (Anderson, 2022). Most telling is the conclusion that good leaders will never be replaced.

With many factors leading to many contemporary trends, today's organizations are searching for solutions. In 2022, the Massachusetts Institute of Technology Sloan Management School reported that toxic workplace cultures also drove the Great Resignation. Further, "A toxic corporate culture is the single best predictor of which companies suffered from high attrition in the first six months of the Great Resignation" (Sull et al., 2022). Great cultures leverage their organization's unique mission, purpose, and values to strengthen their identity, inspire their employees, and deliver on their brand promise to clients. It is what sets an organization apart from the competition. Yet, most employees do not feel connected to their company's culture.

What is the common denominator? What drives employee engagement, retention of top talent, and successful productivity? Who creates the cultural conditions at an organization? As the economy gradually recovers from the devastation caused by the pandemic, one truth remains evident: people often do not leave their jobs due to dissatisfaction with the work itself, but rather because of poor management. Employees leave bad bosses, not just bad jobs. Kelly (2019) in *Forbes* writes:

> Managing people seems easy from afar. It's actually a difficult skill. It is especially rough when you don't possess any prior management experience and got promoted to this position because you were good at your last job. Excelling at your profession does not necessarily mean that your skills seamlessly transfer over.

The skills required of an employee to be successful are not the same as those required of an effective supervisor. Business leaders equipped with contemporary competencies are needed now more than ever to navigate the tumultuous climate ahead for organizations. This text introduces readers to these new and renewed skills and competencies.

THE SIGNIFICANCE OF THE BUSINESS LEADER

A business leader's central role is to communicate the organization's needs, oversee employee performance, provide support and guidance, identify development needs, and manage the relationship between staff and the organization to ensure mutual success. Sometimes, they are called **managers**. Often, they are described as **supervisors**. More times, they are elevated to leaders. Though this text has content emanating from both the leadership and management fields, as authors, we believe the goalposts have been moved on these significant individuals within an organization. Our essentials offer a contemporary twist on well-trodden topics and brand-new material for future leaders to ponder. Admittedly, we will use manager, supervisor, and even boss throughout this text of essentials, but we believe leader is the most appropriate term for the modern-day business setting.

As authors, we align with Heames and Harvey (2006) in their article "The Evolution of the Concept of the 'Executive' from the 20th Century Manager to the 21st Century Global Leader." We have a clear aspiration in mind for our students. Heames and Harvey (2006) conducted an extensive analysis of executive profiles spanning seventy-five years and concluded that executive requirements have evolved significantly. Evolving from the 20th century to the 21st century, they found that not managers but global leaders are needed to chart the course ahead.

Yet we did not wholly divorce ourselves from management lessons; instead, we incorporated the relevant learnings into a text where management meets leadership on the most contemporary terms. While we agree that both disciplines are nuanced and distinct, we take an "all hands on deck" approach to equipping business leaders with the global skill set and modern tools they will need to succeed in the 21st century.

Being a manager is a role, a place in an institution. Being a leader is an activity and an identity that is not necessarily tied to one's place in a hierarchy. Each has its field of research, scholarship, and teaching. Petriglieri (2020) suggests that separating leadership from management and prioritizing one over the other is overly simplistic, akin to questioning whether the brain or heart is more essential. He emphasizes that removing morality from management and rationality from leadership dehumanizes and disempowers us all. Both roles have value, but leaders will steer their organizations through the eras of uncertainty to come.

According to leadership scholar Warren Bennis (1989):

The manager administers; the leader innovates.
The manager is a copy; the leader is an original.
The manager maintains; the leader develops.
The manager focuses on systems and structure; the leader focuses on people.
The manager relies on control; the leader inspires trust.
The manager has a short-range view; the leader has a long-range perspective.

The manager asks how and when; the leader asks what and why.
Managers have their eyes on the bottom line; leaders have their eyes on the horizon.
The manager imitates; the leader originates.
The manager accepts the status quo; the leader challenges it.
The manager is the classic good soldier; the leader is his own person.
The manager does things right; the leader does the right thing.

The demands on organizations are more significant than ever. The next generation of leaders must be able to reimagine their company's place in the world and transform the organization to live up to a more ambitious purpose. That means a fundamental change in the leaders and how they collectively lead and manage the firm. The term leader accurately fits what contemporary organizations need.

Supervisor is frequently used to describe a person with responsibilities to direct or oversee a person, group, department, organization, or operation. Today, a supervisor is responsible for managing the workflow and training new hires on how to best serve customers and the team of employees. They also create schedules that keep those they supervise busy with deadlines designed to prevent gaps or downtime while giving direction and feedback about improvement. Though straightforward, the popularity of the word is in decline. Further, the etymology of the word leaders, not managers, continues to trend high (Etymology.com, n.d.).

For this reason, this text has chosen to focus on the term **leader**, which includes managers, supervisors, and even bosses. As a leader, one transmits the organizational culture, of which values are one part. Effective leadership often includes optimizing group performance, cultivating exceptional job satisfaction, and delivering unique products and services, the lifeblood of highly functional organizations. One of the leading job sites, Indeed, offers the essential skills for leaders: communication skills, approachability and empathy, management skills, adaptability, confidence and positivity, transparency, teamwork, and a willingness to learn (Herrity, 2023). But frankly, it is not that simple.

Being an effective leader cannot be realized by checklists. Further, it cannot be distilled into one trait, discipline, framework, or methodology. A Google search of "leader" reveals countless titles across many industries. It seems everyone is looking for ways to improve, develop, and produce better leaders in their organization. Whether middle managers or C-suite executives, their roles matter deeply, and individuals must commit to their development when they assume the responsibilities of supervising others. The necessary steps to being a great leader can be learned and taught. We believe that effective leadership development is key to generating successful contemporary business leaders.

Essentials of Contemporary Business Leaders is not a quick fix but rather a path of development for future business leaders that is progressive, reflective of lessons learned during the pandemic caused by COVID-19, a bridge of the best that management and leadership have to offer, and designed to withstand the inevitable turmoil, uncertainty, and rapid change that organizations consistently contend with. This text is a nod to the student who asked one of the authors, "So, is this the class where I learn how to be a boss?" It also captures what a client said during an Executive Education program: "We don't want mediocre leaders; we want awesome leaders." We intentionally selected business leaders as a term throughout as they have an enterprise to run, a vision to build and sell, and work to get done.

Contemporary leaders are clear about their values so they can operate within their environments with authenticity; they care deeply about relationships with people and carefully work within and across differences; they are sound in their fundamentals of contemporary business know-how; further, they cultivate service excellence and understand what drives their clients' behaviors; and last, they value the sense of community they must create with all stakeholders, internally and externally. Modern business leaders are essential to the future of work. They need tools—old, new, and renewed—to be exceptional.

Exercise 1.1 Leadership Timeline

1. Begin by taking out a paper or a slide creation program on your computer.
2. Draw a horizontal line across the page to create your timeline.
3. To frame your journey, mark your birth date on one end of the line and today's date on the other.
4. Note significant leadership high moments as upward stems along the timeline. These represent moments of success, growth, and achievement.
5. Conversely, leadership challenges should be noted as downward stems. These illustrate the difficulties and obstacles you faced along the way.
6. Once you have completed your timeline, share your reflections with a colleague or partner. This exchange is a valuable opportunity for meaningful conversation and insight into your leadership experiences. You can also engage in this exercise at a group meeting or training session.

TEACHING THE ESSENTIALS TO BUSINESS LEADERS

Higher education at the undergraduate level often establishes the formal responsibility for teaching future leaders essential skills. This responsibility is further solidified at the graduate level through various master's programs, especially MBA programs. Additionally, it frequently extends into the professional development industry, where private and academic vendors often provide such training. On-the-ground apprenticeships also offer training grounds for business leadership. Additionally, many local communities host small business incubators and accelerator programs. As the digital future expands, business leadership will be accessed via social media, streaming videos, generative AI queries, and likely in the metaverse. Higher and leadership education must not lose relevance and prominence in the conversation.

Consistently, across mission statements, institutions of higher learning have owned the assertion that they are responsible for shaping and cultivating the next generation of leaders. It is a formidable task at best. Academia, leadership education programs have expanded across colleges and universities over the last several decades. For instance, the International Leadership Association (ILA) lists more than 2000 formal leadership programs, from formal academic programs to certificates and co-curricular programs (ILA, 2017). Some programs allow college students to study leadership broadly, while others are intended to assist in developing students as leaders. These programs are implemented at the curricular and co-curricular level, spanning majors, minors, and certificates, to name a few. The emphasis is that leadership education is inclusive and available to all (HERI, 1996).

Business and management programs are wildly popular across the undergraduate, graduate, and professional/executive education levels. In the last century, both disciplines have analyzed large organizations well and instructed those destined to work in them. However, the focus on bigness has left behind ongoing calls to understand small enterprises and their roles in enhancing society and communities (Drucker, 1985/2006). Today's thought leaders have called for kinder, smaller, conscious, transparent, sustainable, responsible, and community-oriented capitalism, leveraging terms such as corporate social responsibility, triple bottom line, and shared value. These are popular topics of presentations and conversations at TED talks, Aspen Institutes, and other venues where thought leaders gather to problem-solve how to better a world that their enterprises have polluted and harmed (Giridharadas, 2019). This is the fundamental education of the contemporary business leader.

Exercise 1.2 Reflected Best Self

As contemporary business leaders, it is crucial to leverage your strengths to foster an environment of innovation and collaboration. One effective method is the *reflected best-self* exercise (RBSE), developed by researchers at the University of Michigan (Roberts et al., 2005). This exercise empowers you to reflect on your peak performance moments and identify the strengths that led to success. Now, walk through our version:

1. **Identify Your Respondents**: Contact colleagues, mentors, and team members who can provide valuable feedback. Ask them, "What are my strengths, and when have you seen me at my best?" This input is vital for gaining insights into your true capabilities.
2. **Recognize Patterns**: Once you've gathered the feedback, look for common themes. Identify recurring strengths and instances where you excelled. Organize this information into a table, enhancing it with your observations. This will help you spot patterns and understand how your strengths manifest in different scenarios.
3. **Compose Your Self-Portrait**: Craft a self-portrait that weaves together the feedback and your reflections. Write a compelling narrative encapsulating who you are at your best, beginning with, "When I am at my best, I ...." Aim for two to four paragraphs that reflect your unique strengths and contributions.
4. **Design Your Role**: Use your self-portrait to create a personal job description that aligns with your identified strengths. Outline how you can integrate these strengths into your daily work and the impact you wish to make within your organization.

Of the 1.7 million students in the National Research Center for College and University Admissions (NRCCUA) data, 16.8% list business as their top interest. Of those, 49.2% are Black, Indigenous, or people of color (BIPOC), compared to 38% for the entire pool. In contemporary terms, an interdisciplinary, team-taught approach to understanding the challenges and responsibilities business leaders and managers must confront in any **21st-century organization**, including principles of diversity, equity, and inclusion (DEI), ethical decision-making, and sustainability, is vital. By recognizing how past practices continue to afford privilege according to race, as well as ethnicity, religion, gender, sexuality, ability, age, and socioeconomic class, and how current practices threaten the environmental health of the planet, readers will learn how and where change is possible. These essentials are critically important.

Finally, **professional development**, sometimes considered **executive education**, deepens skills, competencies, and abilities as students enter the workforce and become career professionals. Based on the principles of adult learning theory, which stipulate adult learners want content that is (1) relevant to their lives and (2) comes with the opportunity to practice and apply, today's professional education landscape is a fiercely competitive space with vendors from private outfits along with a host of acclaimed academic institutions. Harvard University, Cornell University, Penn's Wharton School, Duke University, and Stanford University, to name a few, all are home to robust executive education programs with compelling asynchronous and synchronous options vying for corporate opportunities against other vendors like Coursera, edX, Linked In Learning, and Google, to name a few. Though solutions vary, the most popular topic continues to be leadership. Or, as one author would say, how to develop "awesome bosses."

This text is for educators at each end of the spectrum who want to provide contemporary tools for the next generation of leaders. Though the learner's developmental stage may change, the core of the content applies to anyone who wants to improve as a business leader. The model proposed here came together after countless classes on leadership and management at the undergraduate and graduate levels, as well as hundreds of Executive Education programs. It is both timely and precise for the contemporary business leader.

THE MODEL

Models are plentiful today, but our model in Figure 1.1 has been used in practice and offers educators tremendous flexibility, creativity, and utility to apply in their classes and

FIGURE 1.1 Contemporary Leadership Dimensions for Contemporary Business Leaders

programming. Each chapter provides compelling content designed to enhance the learning of future business leaders. The book is broken up into each model component, the sequencing of which allows learners to build their knowledge and pull threads through to the next part. Additionally, the sequencing will enable educators to scaffold their lessons using this text as a core reading or a complementary guide.

Self-Leadership

When entrusted to direct or oversee a person, group, department, organization, or operation, individuals must conduct the proper "me search" (akin to research) before engaging. Though *soul* is an enigmatic term, there is little doubt of its place in everyday life. Like leadership, a term used liberally, a definition for soul can be elusive. Still, the public notices when it is present, and further when it is not. The soul tells individuals when moments resonate or when something within ourselves has been moved. It is an inner work. Effective leaders are deeply connected to their soul and the implications it has on their passion and purpose for work. It explicitly relates to their ability to work with others effectively.

This section will offer the following chapters:

A. Chapter 2: Authentic Leadership
B. Chapter 3: Leadership Identity and Style
C. Chapter 4: Emotional and Cultural Intelligence
D. Chapter 5: Identity and Intersectionality

People Leadership

People leadership is a popular term in corporate settings and can mean a new or experienced supervisor. Intrapersonal competencies become key when managing employees or leading others. Essentials like relationship-building, active listening, providing feedback, managing conflict, motivating for performance, collaborating, and creating inclusive environments are the foundational building blocks of positive organizational cultures. Whether in-person, hybrid, or remote, relationship-oriented behaviors lead to more productive, innovative teams. If leadership is defined as "the social process of influencing others in the pursuit of meeting a collective goal" (Yukl, 2006, p. 8), then comprehensive learning and application of these areas is necessary.

This section will offer the following chapters:

A. Chapter 6: Relationship-Building in (In-)Person, Hybrid, and Remote Environments
B. Chapter 7: Motivating Others for High Performance
C. Chapter 8: Leading Collaborative Teams
D. Chapter 9: Creating Inclusive Cultures

Business Leadership

Business leadership refers to how individuals make decisions, set goals, and provide direction in a professional environment. Business leadership can take many forms but usually involves a CEO or higher-level executive guiding and inspiring the rest of the team, which could be a learner's role in reality or an aspiration. Solid strategy, financial acumen, digital savvy, and an entrepreneurial mindset are required for contemporary business leaders to understand and handle real-world organizational situations. It collects general and organization-specific knowledge about how things get done, with whom, and why.

This section will offer the following chapters:

A. Chapter 10: Strategy
B. Chapter 11: Financial Acumen
C. Chapter 12: The Digital Future
D. Chapter 13: Entrepreneurial Mindset vs. Behavior

Client Leadership

Client Leadership is an innovative, unique, solution-oriented approach adopted in all clients' daily services. A great leader will take responsibility for the issues presented to them directly and for every issue their team members encounter. Strong leadership skills require a focus on resolving customer and team member concerns with empathy and efficiency. Lessons in customer service excellence, drivers of client behaviors, managing change, and communicating brand are essential for creating value, competitive advantage, and long-term relationships.

This section will offer the following chapters:

A. Chapter 14: Customer Service Excellence
B. Chapter 15: Drivers of Client Behavior
C. Chapter 16: Managing Change in the Current Client Landscape
D. Chapter 17: Communicating Brand

Community Leadership

Contemporary business leaders increasingly find themselves accountable for managing and guiding internal and external stakeholders. The public closely observes their organization's impact on social, environmental, and political issues, which can significantly affect their reputation and financial performance. To be effective, contemporary business leaders must understand social responsibility, shared value, sustainability, social entrepreneurship, triple bottom line, and meaningful community engagement. These lessons foster positive relationships with communities, generate fruitful collaborations, and ensure long-term success.

A. Chapter 18: Social Responsibility and Multiple Bottom Lines
B. Chapter 19: Shared Value and Sustainability
C. Chapter 20: Social Entrepreneurship
D. Chapter 21: Meaningful Community Engagement

CONCLUSION

As we highlighted in our introduction, the world has been through a lot. Students, workers, educators, communities, and organizations have been through a lot. As a response to the enormous disruption that was COVID-19, the movement of millions of workers, and the conditions now considered a reality in the **New Normal**, scholars have started to focus on the **Future of Work**. This thread is meaningful to us, and our text is on the essentials for contemporary business leaders. Academics, think tanks, and policymakers have fueled rich discussions about the future of work and how we can shape it. As Balliester and Elsheikhi (2018) wrote, "Labour markets in developing and developed countries are likely to undergo major transformations in the next years and decades" (p. v). However, despite a growing body of research in this area, no universally accepted definition exists of what the Future of Work encompasses and the most relevant drivers.

As Balliester and Elsheikhi (2018) describe, "Most publications highlight the impact that the Fourth Industrial Revolution, with its focus on technological developments in robotics, artificial intelligence, and genetics, might have for the labor market" (p. 1). However, they also point out that concurrently with this technological revolution are widespread socio-economic, geopolitical, and demographic changes influencing the future world of work (Balliester & Elsheikhi, 2018). Specifically, they report, "Technology, climate change, globalization, and demography are seen as key megatrends within the context of the world of work and are projected to play a defining role in the upcoming years" (p. 1). Though daunting, we want our readers to understand these dynamics will underpin all chapters going forward.

What does this mean for business leaders? First and foremost, the Future of Work will be the space that our contemporary leaders are operating in. It is not linear, static, or crystal clear. Although our leaders have access to more data than ever, that still does not guarantee they will make all the right decisions when they have it. After being forced into a defensive posture, allegedly caught off guard by the pandemic, many business leaders want to return to the offensive, seeking to be proactive, anticipatory, and aggressive. *But is that even possible in the New Normal when the most powerful analytics can't predict the next disruptor?*

It would seem the Future of Work requires an ambidextrous leader, capable of looking back at the past yet also shaping a new future for the organization. Further, it will be necessary for our business leaders to be sound in their transactional behaviors while demonstrating their ability to be transformational to move their organizations through this next era of change. Finally, the Future of Work will be defined by the modalities of in-person, hybrid, and remote roles, calling for a new look at leadership's "soft skills" to achieve the same old but essential relationships.

In our "all hands on deck" approach, we used leadership and management as vehicles to get to a contemporary place. The essentials we propose here are not an exhaustive list, but are modern. Truth be told, some of the concepts are simple to understand but difficult to execute, especially against the current drivers influencing the Future of Work. This is our attempt at leaving a blueprint for educators to lead discussions that will matter tomorrow. Leadership, after all, is a craft of which there is no mastery—only a lifelong pursuit of learning.

We look forward to hearing how educators, students, and readers tackled this text and our contemporary essentials.

DISCUSSION QUESTIONS

1. How can leaders build self-awareness and resilience during uncertainty?
2. What are the differences between modern and traditional leadership?
3. What proactive strategies can leaders use to predict and deal with changes?
4. How does a "global mindset" boost leadership effectiveness?
5. How do leadership and management differ?
6. How does transparency affect trust and perceptions of authenticity?
7. How is leadership a process and not an innate trait?

Key Terms

- COVID-19
- The Great Resignation
- The Great America Job Reshuffle
- The Great Rehire
- Quiet Quitting
- Manager
- Leader
- Supervisor
- 21st-Century Organizations
- Professional Development
- Executive Education
- New Normal
- Future of Work

CASE STUDY 1.1 LEADING THROUGH UNCERTAINTY AT GLOBALTECH SOLUTIONS

Background: GlobalTech Solutions is a mid-sized technology company that has been a leader in software development for over twenty years. However, it faces significant challenges to differentiate itself from its increasing competition: rapid technological advancements, evolving customer expectations, and industry shifts toward remote work. The leadership team must navigate these disruptions while maintaining productivity, morale, and client relationships.

Situation: Rebecca James, the CEO of GlobalTech, has always taken a hands-on, traditional approach to leadership. She believes in leading from the front and taking quick, decisive actions. However, with the challenges of the pandemic and the rise of remote work, her usual methods seem less effective. The company has faced higher turnover rates, and several key clients have expressed concerns about delayed product development.

Responding to these challenges, Rebecca pivoted her leadership strategy. She adopted a more flexible leadership style, focusing on empowering her team and staying ahead of market shifts. She recognizes the importance of self-awareness and resilience for herself and her employees. She has introduced weekly team check-ins to discuss progress, concerns, and feedback. Rebecca also understands that for GlobalTech to maintain its competitive edge, she must develop a more global mindset and foster cross-cultural collaboration.

Despite her efforts, Rebecca still struggles with transparency issues. The leadership team is divided on how much information should be shared with employees, especially about the company's financial standing and future plans. Some members feel withholding particular info maintains trust, while others argue that more transparency would strengthen cohesion.

Task: Provide four comprehensive recommendations for Rebecca. List what important information this case study offers, and then list what is missing that would help complete the task better. Present to a larger group for feedback and discussion.

REFERENCES

Anderson, T. (2022, November 30). Five trends HR leaders need to leverage in 2023. The ILR School. https://www.ilr.cornell.edu/programs/graduate-degree-programs/blog/emhrm/five-trends-hr-leaders-need-leverage-2023

Balliester, T., & Elsheikhi, A. (2018). *The future of work: A literature review* (ILO Working Paper No. 994987493402676). International Labour Organization. Retrieved from https://www.ilo.org/publications/future-work-literature-review

Bennis, W. (1989). *On becoming a leader*. Addison-Wesley.

Drucker, P. (2006). *Innovation and entrepreneurship* (Reprint of 1985 edition). HarperBusiness.

Etymology.com. (n.d.). *Online etymology dictionary*. Retrieved from https://www.etymonline.com/

Fox, M. (2021, May 10). How to quit your job in the great post-pandemic resignation boom. *Bloomberg*. Retrieved from https://www.bloomberg.com/news/articles/2021-05-10/quit-your-job-how-to-resign-after-covid-pandemic

Giridharadas, A. (2019). *Winners take all: The elite charade of changing the world*. Vintage.

Harter, J. K. (2022, October 6). *Quiet quitters make up half the U.S. workforce, Gallup says*. Gallup. Retrieved from https://careerdesignlab.sps.columbia.edu/blog/2022/10/06/quiet-quitters-make-up-half-the-u-s-workforce-gallup-says/

Heames, J., & Harvey, M. G. (2006). The evolution of the concept of the 'executive' from the 20th century manager to the 21st century global leader. *Journal of Leadership & Organizational Studies, 13*(2), 29–37. https://doi.org/10.1177/10717919070130020301

Herrity, J. (2023). Qualities of a good supervisor (plus 8 skills to develop). *Indeed*. Retrieved from https://www.indeed.com/career-advice/career-development/qualities-of-a-good-supervisor#:~:text=A%20supervisor%20is%20a%20manager,guide%20them%20through%20their%20responsibilities

Hetler, A. (2023, March 1). The Great Resignation: Everything you need to know. *TechTarget*. Retrieved from https://www.techtarget.com/whatis/feature/The-Great-Resignation-Everything-you-need-to-know

Higher Education Research Institute (HERI). (1996). *A social change model of leadership development: Guidebook (Version III)*. Higher Education Research Institute, University of California, Los Angeles.

International Leadership Association. (2017). *Leadership program directory*. Retrieved from http://www.ila-net.org/Resources/LPD/index.htm

Kelly, J. (2019, November 22). People don't leave bad jobs, they leave bad bosses: Here's how to be a better manager to maintain and motivate your team. *Forbes*. Retrieved from https://www.forbes.com/sites/jackkelly/2019/11/22/people-dont-leave-bad-jobs-they-leave-bad-bosses-heres-how-to-be-a-better-manager-to-maintain-and-motivate-your-team/?sh=c69184f22b90

Orrell, B., & Cox, D. A. (2021, July 15). *The great American jobs reshuffle*. Survey Center on American Life. Retrieved from https://www.americansurveycenter.org/research/the-great-american-jobs-reshuffle/

Parker, K., & Menasce Horowitz, J. (2022, March 9). Majority of workers who quit a job in 2021 cite low pay, no opportunities for advancement, feeling disrespected. *Pew Research Center*. Retrieved from https://www.pewresearch.org/

Partners Personnel. (2022). *The Great Rehire: 6 ways to retain talent in 2022*. Partners Personnel. Retrieved from https://www.partnerspersonnel.com/the-great-rehire-6-ways-to-retain-talent-2022/

Petriglieri, G. (2020). Leading with heart: The moral imperative of leadership. *Harvard Business Review*, *98*(3), 58–67.

Roberts, L. M., Dutton, J. E., Spreitzer, G. M., Heaphy, E. D., & Quinn, R. E. (2005). Composing the reflected best-self portrait: Building pathways for becoming extraordinary in work organizations. *Academy of Management Review*, *30*(4), 712–736.

Sull, D., Sull, C., & Zweig, B. (2022, January 11). Toxic culture is driving the great resignation. *MIT Sloan Management Review*. Retrieved from https://sloanreview.mit.edu/article/toxic-culture-is-driving-the-great-resignation/

U.S. Bureau of Labor Statistics. (2022, April 12). *Job openings reach record highs in 2022 as the labor market recovery continues*. Monthly Labor Review. Retrieved from https://www.bls.gov/opub/mlr/2023/article/job-openings-reach-record-highs-in-2022-as-the-labor-market-recovery-continues.html

Viveros, S. (2022, December 23). Get loud, not quiet: The importance of employee engagement for mitigating quiet quitting and firing. *Forbes*. Retrieved from https://www.forbes.com/councils/forbescommunicationscouncil/2022/12/23/get-loud-not-quiet-the-importance-of-employee-engagement-for-mitigating-quiet-quitting-and-firing/

Yukl, G. (2006). *Leadership in organizations* (6th ed.). Pearson Education.

PART 1

Self Leadership

This section offers not an exhaustive collection of competencies but a highly contemporary pathway toward **Self Leadership**. Authenticity, leadership identity and style, emotional and cultural intelligence, social identity, and intersectionality are essential cornerstones to modern business leaders. We hope this section will drive aspiring leaders out of their comfort zones and catalyze profound "aha moments" as each chapter takes the reader back to a moment when they felt alive when it resonates deeply. Additionally, as the business world opens up to global markets and workplaces grow exponentially diverse, future leaders must understand how their actions are shaped by their backgrounds and their ability to make meaning and behaviors in the face of uncertainty and change.

Self Leadership as a concept bore out of countless classes and sessions where we centered the education of the self, readied the individuals, and prepared leaders for all that would be asked of them. Solid foundation footing, interpersonal grounding, and role clarity within the organizational system are essentials for contemporary business leaders. Sometimes dismissed or overlooked as mere "soft skills," as authors, we would caution any organization to skip this commitment at their peril, less they want to be led by individuals who lack self-awareness, are unsure of their values, or are low in human-centric competencies. Exceptional leaders work hard to cultivate their sense of self and know that their innate abilities are not enough to confront today's challenges. Self Leaders recognize that personal development is a lifelong process.

DOI: 10.4324/9781003474647-2

CHAPTER 2

Authentic Leadership

CHAPTER OVERVIEW

This opening chapter on Self Leadership describes the process of authentic leadership. After considering where the distrust of leaders comes from, the authors offer authenticity as a core quality for effective leaders to cultivate and nurture. Meaning-making and self-authorship are essential for gaining self-awareness and an increased understanding of one's purpose. Authentic leadership is a disciplined and lifelong learning process. If ignored or misaligned, leaders risk falling into toxic traits and destructive habits. The toxic triangle is described as a destructive leader and susceptible followers, along with a conducive environment. Future business leaders need tools for critical self-reflection, such as scholarly personal narrative writing that calls for personal accounts and universal application.

Most college admissions brochures will offer how their institution is commissioned to develop the next generation of global leaders. Modern leaders will address ethnocentrism, economic threats, geopolitical unrest, climate change, and globalization. Yet Barbara Kellerman (2012), a professor at Harvard's Kennedy School of Government, believes those responsible have not reached the point where leadership education produces leaders that meet the public's needs. Skepticism regarding the readiness of modern leadership education to address the needs of today and tomorrow prevails across the board.

We, the authors, have been frequently asked: *What do you think about the void of good leaders today? What are we doing to confront the public's distrust of today's leaders?* Another favorite: *How can we have so many leadership development opportunities and this many bad leaders?* Indeed, all are provoking. Some would even categorize this period as a crisis of leadership. We tend to think one of the biggest culprits is an authenticity deficit in today's leaders. This chapter outlines authentic leadership, pathways to authenticity, the consequences if not developed, and a power instrument for applying it to become an effective contemporary leader.

DOI: 10.4324/9781003474647-3

AUTHENTIC LEADERSHIP

A mental thread that would often run throughout our classes was: *Do we have fewer authentic leaders or more barriers to being authentic today? What does it mean to be authentic?* If one considers the checklists that state the ideal attributes or characteristics for leaders, **authenticity** is nearly always present. It is, perhaps, a buzzword needing a concrete definition and, even more so, a precise pathway for its foundation. Without recounting each scandalous public malady, the clamor for authentic leaders could not be more conspicuous. Students, undergraduate and graduate alike, crave experiences that build on their authentic reserves and want to engage in work that precipitates authenticity. Leadership education offers an extraordinary repository to steer students toward transformative personal growth but too often misses the mark.

We recommend **authentic leadership**, which has emerged as a critical contemporary framework. Bill George and Peter Sims (2007) have offered one of the most influential contributions with *True North,* which still serves as a guide after its thoughtful insights derived from 125 different leaders, many of whom are household names. David Gergen concludes in the foreword, "What ultimately distinguishes the great leaders from the mediocre are the personal, inner qualities—qualities that are hard to define but are essential for success" (George & Sims, 2007, p. vvii). More so, George and Sims use true north, an internal compass that "pulls you towards the purpose of your leadership" (p. xxii), as a central metaphor. They define authentic leaders as those who "not only inspire those around them, they empower them to step up and lead" (George & Sims, 2007, p. xxxi). They explain that authentic leaders are engaged with a purpose, lead with heart, establish enduring relationships, practice their values, and maintain steady self-discipline, never mincing words that it is a lifetime commitment (George & Sims, 2007). These are core essentials for authentic leaders.

Authentic leadership exploration equates to intensive self-reflection. Self Leaders are willing to undergo self-clarification that can sometimes be tremendously uncomfortable. The immediate implications may serve their current leadership roles or understanding of leadership in general. Yet, meaning-making is valuable for sustaining a connection to their core self. This is the primary discipline of authentic leaders.

Exercise 2.1 Checking Your Values

1. **Write down ten things you value on slips of paper**: (Make sure you do not rank them in order of importance.) The values can be tangible (e.g., parents, food), intangible (e.g., God, sleeping), or concepts (e.g., honesty, integrity).
2. **Let go of some values**: Choose two values to eliminate from your life by "discarding" them. You should now have eight values left. Reflect on which values you let go of and why.
3. **Editing**: Identify your top five from your remaining values and "remove" three that didn't make the cut. You should now have five values left. Consider which values you chose to keep and the reasons behind your choices.

4. **Seek input from others**: With someone you know, discuss which value you think reflects you best and which value reflects you least. Choose one value to discard for each other. Each of you should now have four values. Share what value was taken from you and how you felt about it.
5. **Quick decision time**: After counting to ten, hold one of your values in the air and then "let it go." You should now have three values left. Reflect on how it felt to be rushed into giving up a value and discuss which value you chose to give up and why.
6. **Exchange among peers**: Switch one of your values with another person. You should still have three values. Share what you traded and the reasoning behind your choice. Also, check if anyone ended up with matching values and discuss the commonality of shared values.
7. **Reassess your choices**: Release another value, so you'll be left with just two. Reflect on which one you chose to let go of and why.
8. **Explore the discarded values**: Look through the values you've set aside and decide if you want to swap one of your remaining values with any from the list of discarded values. You should have two values at the end. Share your reasoning on whether you chose to switch or stay.
9. **Final elimination**: Let go of one more value, leaving you with just one. Reflect on what value you have left and why you consider it your most important.
10. **Discussion**: Engage in a conversation about your experiences during this exercise. What was challenging about it? What was the purpose of this activity? How did it feel to give up your values? How confident are you in the single value you retained?

In *Helping College Students Find Purpose: The Campus Guide to Meaning-Making* (2010), Nash and Murray (2010) describe the process of meaning-making, which is gaining a following. This is precisely where the field can gain ground if it aims to fill the authenticity deficit.

MEANING-MAKING

Meaning-making has constructivist principles, meaning learners construct knowledge rather than passively take in information, along with inquiry activities that can steer leaders toward transformative, self-generated learning. Under the umbrella of spiritual development, meaning-making pedagogy requires learners to analyze complex narrative-grounded questions to author an authentic vision of self. Like meaning-making, **self-authorship** is integrated learning activities that steer students toward epistemological, interpersonal, and intrapersonal maturity (Hodge et al., 2009, p. 18). As the authors of *Engaged Learning* write, "Self-authorship enables learners to evaluate information critically, form their own judgments, and collaborate with others to act wisely. It is, however, necessary to adopt increasingly complex meaning-making structures" (Hodge et al., 2009, p. 18).

Although **spirituality** suggests a religious connotation that is not the intention, it aptly describes an inner movement toward a state of wholeness, fullness, or excellence. Indeed, individuals have long sought organized religion in hopes of realizing a personal transformation, but any activity that offers episodes of mood-elevating meaning can lead to transformative personal growth.

To many, leadership initially feels abstract, subjective, and complex. Similarly, defining meaning can be particularly challenging. An operational definition should be more straightforward than muddled in a scientific context, but such blurriness is often more realistic. Nash and Murray (2010) describe meaning as a guiding force that assists individuals in uncovering their core values, such as connections, commitments, joys, and love. This definition represents just one perspective among many. The mystery of the human experience does not fit into tidy categories or conceptual frameworks, and new elements of the experience continue to be discovered (Nash & Murray, 2010). Modern Self Leaders must embrace, despite inherent complexity and vagueness, that meaning hinges on experience through a blend of intuition and context.

Humans are intrinsically inclined toward contemplating existence (Nash & Murray, 2010). Such contemplation existentially questions rationales for pain, death, and suffering, often connected to others. Life is marked by deep anguish and extraordinary joy, pleasure, and fulfillment. The persistent struggle with existential dilemmas becomes even more poignant in this light. While humans experience moments of happiness and satisfaction, they are often tinged with awareness of life's transience and the suffering that is an inescapable part of the human experience. This juxtaposition is vital as modern business leaders continuously seek answers whilst navigating a world rich with joy and sorrow (Nash & Murray, 2010). When meaningful inquiries are embedded in pedagogical approaches and framed as questions within leadership education, a critical touchstone for authenticity can be reached. Meaning-making is thus a precursor for purpose, shaped by values and fueled by an understanding of self. This aptly describes self leadership's aims, a critical first building block for contemporary business leaders.

With leadership, experts tend to sort into classic skills, traits, or behaviors because they lack the vocabulary to describe the phenomena. Yet, when examined, leadership reflects "an innate tendency for self-transcendence" (Cooper, 1998, p. 26) and a compelling struggle for inner balance. Leadership development can underscore a profound search for a personal understanding of self when it collides with traditional college student or adult developmental shifts. Further, "meaning-making is an interdisciplinary activity," and it "requires the appropriate cultivation and refinement of consciousness" (Cooper, 1998, p. 3).

Rooted in constructivist theory, particularly the work of Jean Piaget (1950), the idea is that individuals actively interpret their experiences, thus crafting perceived reality. This dynamic process centers around stable changes and patterns that help humans make sense of the world. These patterns and changes are boxed into frameworks, rules, heuristics, or guides to shape future interactions and perceptions (Dantley & Rogers, 2001). Modern business leaders recognize that other humans undergo the interpretation process and synthesize different results. At times, modern business leaders will feel the conflict when their perceived reality does not align with the perceived realities of their employees, supervisors, clients, and communities.

Modern business leaders lean into interconnectedness to address such conflicts. As Sean Gehrke (2008) states, "A search for more meaning is apparent in the lives of many people as modern science suggests an interconnectedness of every aspect of our being to everything else, 'an unbroken wholeness'" (p. 351). While some fail to tether to the fundamental mystery of human existence (Nash & Murray, 2010), theoretical frameworks have merit.

THEORETICAL FRAMEWORKS FOSTERING PURPOSE IN SELF

> Most people require purpose to provide coherence and focus to their lives … having no purpose is to assume that the present is … a solution to life's problems. It is also to be disoriented and possibly discontented. Purpose carries people to a future state of fulfillment that may be personal growth, enlightenment, salvation, or the maintenance of important social relationships with people who have similar or compatible goals and purposes.
>
> (Michael Hughes, 2006, p. 623)

Questions concerning identity remain at the heart of most life inquiries. Arthur Chickering and Linda Reisser (1993) offered seven vectors, which substantially enhanced Erikson's (1968) theory within student affairs practice by elaborating on specific tasks associated with identity development in young adults (see also Boyle et al., 2019). The seven vectors are:

- Establishing identity
- Developing purpose
- Fostering integrity
- Managing emotions
- Developing competence
- Moving from autonomy to interdependence
- Developing mature interpersonal relationships.

Modern business leaders should note these concepts as they will be explored in-depth across this book's chapters beyond self leadership to community leadership.

During young adulthood, aspiring leaders must actively develop strategies to achieve purpose. These strategies generally encompass vocational goals, personal interests, and relationship commitments. They can build their capacity and equip themselves with tools to find purpose and lead with a deep connection to their motivations. Drawing from psychosocial and cognitive-structural theories, Robert Kegan's (1983) theory of meaning-making and self-authorship emphasizes the importance of understanding the self and the world (Murray, 2005). Kegan (1983) asserts that individuals organize their comprehension of themselves, others, and the broader world in increasingly complex ways.

As individuals pass through five distinct orders, seen in Figure 2.1, they illustrate progressively more advanced thought patterns, which emerge in sequence (Murray, 2005). The first order is where knowledge forms independent elements, mainly shaped by child impulses and desires with no clear distinction between fantasy and reality. The second order is when durable categories are created with defining characteristics, which, independent of the individual's wishes, are a sign that the child has started to mature. Ultimately, an independent point of view is the defining characteristic of the college student stage.

The third order constitutes cross-categorical meaning-making, where a higher mental organization emerges due to maturation. The individual understands and can manage the complexities of the various relationships among the durable categories. In the fourth order,

Developmental Stage/ Order of Mind (typical ages)	1st Order: Impulsive Mind (~2–6 years-old)	2nd Order: Instrumental Mind (~6 years-old through adolescence)	3rd Order: Socialized Mind (post-adolescence)	4th Order: Self-Authoring Mind (variable, if achieved)	5th Order: Self-Transforming Mind (typically > ~40, if achieved)
What can be seen as *object* (the content of one's knowing)	one's reflexes	one's impulses, perceptions	one's needs, interests, desires	interpersonal relationships, mutuality	self-authorship, identity, ideology
What one is *subject* to (the structure of one's knowing)	one's impulses, perceptions	one's needs, interests, desires	interpersonal relationships, mutuality	self-authorship, identity, ideology	the dialectic between ideologies
Underlying Structure of Meaning-Making	Single Point 	Categories 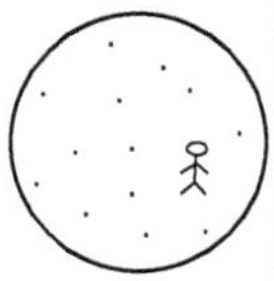	Across Categories 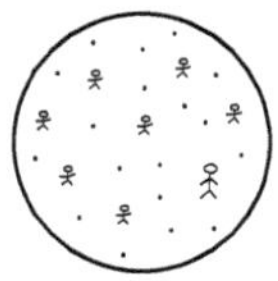	Systemic 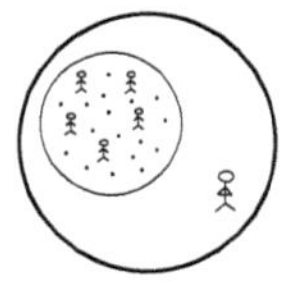	System of Systems 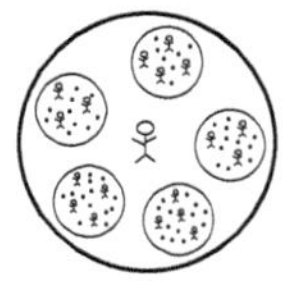

Adapted from Robert Kegan, *In Over Our Heads: the Mental Demands of Modern Life* (Cambridge: Harvard University Press, 1994), pp. 314–315 by Peter W. Pruyn, peterpruyn.medium.com. May be used for non-commercial purposes with this attribution.

FIGURE 2.1 Order of Mind and Meaning-Making

an individual gains the capacity to manage multiple relationships within larger systems and reconcile discrepancies in values within the relationships. Finally, in the fifth order, an individual's meaning-making is further refined when they can recognize where potential changes may be needed within them. This order is where many adult learners fall.

Yet stages can be misleading. Nash and Murray (2010) write, "If carried to an extreme, developmental ages and stages can often become tight little boxes that slot and plot students throughout their college experience—and, sadly, long afterward" (p. 9). Thus, Nash and Murray offer the term cycle, which

> indicates the somewhat repetitive nature of meaning-making. Meaning develops in spiraling layers over time, and we want to allow for the likelihood that quarter-lifers will find themselves revisiting one or another cycle on their way to becoming more fully themselves.
>
> (Nash and Murray, 2010, p. 9)

This is helpful when working with college students.

When meaningful inquiries are embedded in leadership education and framed as questions within life cycles, critical touchstones for leadership learners can be reached. These encounters with learners come in a diverse array of opportunities, along with many identities and perspectives, but what they share in common is an innate enthusiasm for transformative growth experiences. The catalyst of leadership education should be helping students grow in their authenticity. These are the early seeds of producing great leaders.

PATHWAYS TO AUTHENTICITY

The etymology of the word authentic can be traced to the Greek word *authento*, "to have full power" (Trilling, 1972), reflecting the notion of authentic functioning whereby an individual is "the master of his or her own domain" (Kernis & Goldman, 2006). Former head of Medtronic Bill George (2003) states, "We need leaders who lead with purpose, values, and integrity; leaders who build enduring organizations, motivate their employees to provide superior customer service, and create long-term value for shareholders" (p. 9, see also Copeland, 2014). Thus, authentic leadership remains the foundational construct for all positive forms of leadership and its development. While not a new concept, its relevance persists, if not holds a more considerable outcry as a skill of modern business leaders today.

Authentic leaders require a substantial commitment to self-awareness, cultivated through years of self-exploration, to differentiate a leader's inner values from societal influences (Avolio & Wernsing, 2008). They also highlight the importance of understanding that team members may be at various stages of their personal self-awareness and ability to embrace complex ideas presented by authentic leaders. Therefore, contemporary leaders must focus on personal growth and create opportunities for those they lead to develop into their most authentic selves.

Business leaders can engage in the long-term practice of authentic leadership, modeled after Bill George (2003), by focusing on five key dimensions, as shown in Table 2.1.

TABLE 2.1 Five Dimensions of Authentic Leadership

Leadership Principle	*Description*
Pursue Purpose with Passion	Leaders must relentlessly chase an explicit purpose. This drive parallels leaders balancing personal ambitions and job searches.
Practice Solid Values	Education helps solidify values, and adversity tests leaders' ability to stay true to their values, ensuring authentic decisions.
Lead with Heart	Authentic leadership is best observed when leaders can express their true selves and build personal connections for mutual inspiration.
Establish Connected Relationships	Building meaningful relationships in various work settings is critical for authentic leadership and team engagement.
Demonstrate Self-Discipline	Authentic leaders commit to lifelong reflection and transformation, maintaining discipline to develop themselves and others effectively.

Adapted from George (2003).

Contemporary business leaders exploring the merits of authentic leadership and its pathways must sunset some traditional notions of leadership in favor of what begets authentic forms. Instead of a singular focus on goals, authentic leaders envision a purpose. As opposed to a selfish agenda, authentic leaders transfer their team's collective values into the organization. Additionally, where ego once resided, authentic leaders are unafraid to engage with their heart, personalizing their message and relationships with others. Previously, business leaders were evaluated by their ability to accumulate transactions, but as contemporary leaders leading authentically, they need to cultivate long-term internal and external relationships. Finally, positions of authority and power have been replaced by methods that model excellence through self-discipline, a contiguous quality that can cascade throughout an organization.

The Consequences

The next generation of leaders possesses the qualities of discovery and exploration and the desire and intention to impact the world. As professionals advance in the business world, the complexities of compensation, authority, power, and ownership develop barriers to the pursuit of authenticity. Leadership can be toxic and contain dark, destructive sides.

Destructive leadership encompasses behaviors that negatively impact followers and the organization (Kellerman, 2004). Such leaders employ detrimental methods of influence, compelling their followers to act in ways that can lead to harmful consequences. Contemporary business leaders must act vigilantly against this type of leadership in today's context, especially given rising concerns regarding misguided populism and gravitation toward those who speak the loudest (Mounk, 2019). Later in this book, leaders will read about the darker, shadier, and more nuanced sides of entrepreneurship and community development (Talmage et al., 2022, 2024).

Destructive leadership does not exist within a vacuum; it takes root due to complex interactions between the leader, the followers, and the context. To explain what fosters destructive leadership, Padilla et al. (2007) created the **Toxic Triangle** model (see Figure 2.2), outlining the key components that make destructive leadership possible. The toxic triangle includes destructive leaders, susceptible followers, and conducive environments. When we ask our students to give an example of the Toxic Triangle, they most often cite Adolf Hitler and the conditions that allowed for Nazi Germany in the 1930s. However, many more recent examples exist, such as Elizabeth Holmes and her unethical conduct surrounding her company, Theranos, where she misled investors and patients who used

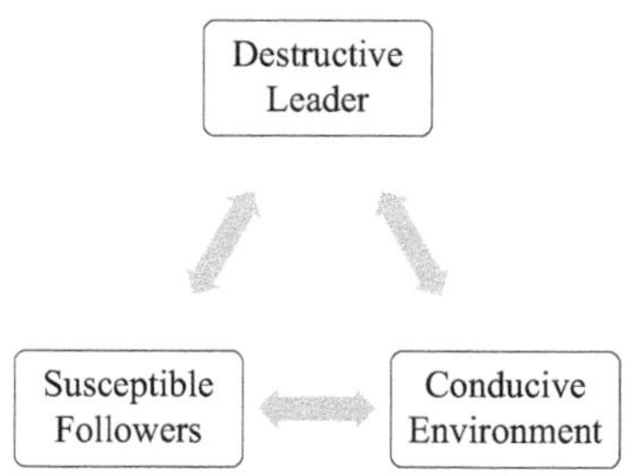

FIGURE 2.2 Toxic Triangle Model

her erroneous blood tests. She also lied about the scale of the company's profits. Both examples would fit within the Toxic Triangle. Sam Bankman-Fried and the FTX Scandal are other apt examples. These scandals are discussed in the later chapters of the book.

To avoid becoming toxic leaders, contemporary business leaders must prioritize self-discovery and self-examination, essential aspects of authentic leadership. Followers rely on leaders for direction and stability, particularly during crises. However, some leaders may exploit the situation for personal gain when organizational structures are unclear. Later chapters explore mission drift, self-interest, and the Fraud Triangle (Chapter 11).

Integrity involves doing what is right despite challenges, and **ethics** move beyond compliance, falling within the fibrous essence of leaders as persons. These topics are discussed at length within and across each book chapter. Modern business leaders embrace authenticity and meaning-making. By prioritizing these values, leaders can foster a healthier workplace culture while effectively navigating today's business landscape. With authentic leadership at the core of content for self-leadership, tools such as Scholarly Personal Narrative (SPN) become a powerful instrument for avoiding the dark sides of leadership and bolstering integrity and authenticity.

Scholarly Personal Narrative

Scholarly Personal Narrative (SPN) writing serves as a valuable resource for emerging leaders, encouraging them to explore critical questions that arise throughout their experiences, before and during their leadership journeys. As Nash (2004) observes, "the researcher becomes the main research instrument as he or she observes, asks questions, and interacts with the research participants" (p. 18). By distilling personal experiences into analytical insights, SPN empowers leaders to understand their journeys better. As emphasized by Nash (2004), "The best analysis and prescription come out of the scholar's efforts to make narrative sense of personal experience. All else is commentary—significant, to be sure, but commentary nonetheless" (p. 18). This form of inquiry is not merely academic; it is a reflective exercise that allows individuals to process their experiences in their distinct voices while linking personal stories to broader themes.

SPN draws from the social sciences, humanities, oral history, and autobiography. Individuals weave personal narratives into a scholarly framework, facilitating connections with readers. This approach resonates with autoethnography. It invites researchers to *restory* their experiences, ultimately universalizing the lessons learned for a wider audience. As Nash (2004) asserts, "The ultimate intellectual responsibility of the SPN scholar is to find a way to use the personal insights gained to draw larger conclusions for readers, possibly even to challenge and reconstruct older political or educational narratives" (p. 18). SPN can yield profound learning outcomes for leaders, direct reports, clients, and communities, fostering a culture of introspective inquiry.

Self Leaders will grapple with deeply personal questions and challenging contexts using the SPN model (Nash, 2004). While the culmination of this inquiry may feel like an individual achievement, the journey itself is filled with enriching insights that tap into our innate desire to share stories. Nash (2004) explains the essence of this research paradigm to illustrate the unique methodological approach of SPN and provide a glimpse into its classroom implementation. He notes that his intellectual endeavors focus on speculation and questioning instead of testing empirical data: "I look for hidden subtexts and pretexts inside assigned readings and inside colleagues' and students' assumptions about their lives and professions" (Nash, 2004, p. 17). Nash (2004) emphasizes the importance of "clarity, simplicity, and spiritedness" (p. 9). These principles enrich authentic leadership and help Self Leaders face challenges head-on.

Exercise 2.2 "This I Believe" Exercise

For years, National Public Radio (NPR) hosted a beloved program called "This I Believe," where individuals from all walks of life shared their deeply held beliefs through heartfelt narratives (Allison & Gediman, 2005–2009). Inspired by this powerful tradition and guided by Robert J. Nash's Scholarly Personal Narrative (SPN) approach, this exercise invites you to explore the experiences that have shaped your worldview. Follow the process outlined in Table 2.2 to articulate core beliefs that resonate personally and beyond.

Once the steps in Table 2.2 are completed. Explore the following questions below.

- What experience or lesson has fundamentally shaped your view of the world? Feel free to look back at your leadership timeline in Exercise 2.2.
- Do you hold a guiding principle, mantra, or value that informs your decisions? What cultural, social, or spiritual truths resonate profoundly with you, and why?
- How have experiences of joy, struggle, or transformation influenced your beliefs about leadership, community, or relationships?

TABLE 2.2 "This I Believe" Exercise Steps

Step	*Description*
Anchor in Your Lived Experience	Reflect on the pivotal moments, relationships, challenges, or joys shaping your perspective. Draw from personal insights and select a story or memory that serves as the foundation for your belief.
Connect the Personal to the Universal	Consider how your personal experiences connect to universal themes. Reflect on how your beliefs resonate beyond your life, aligning with broader societal, cultural, or spiritual truths.
Use the Cadence of "This I Believe"	Use the phrase "this I believe" to anchor your statement, guiding the narrative and emphasizing key points. This rhythm helps structure your reflection and invites deeper contemplation.
Be Bold, Authentic, and Reflective	Write with vulnerability and authenticity, embracing the passion behind your beliefs. Challenge conventional ideas and express your unique perspective openly and honestly.
Infuse Meaning-Making	Explore their significance in shaping your identity and actions beyond recounting events. Explain why these experiences hold meaning for you and others and how they inform your worldview.
Prepare to Share	Prepare to share your "This I Believe" statement. Sharing requires courage and fosters connection, reinforcing how personal stories can promote understanding among diverse audiences.

CONCLUSION

We, the authors, practitioners, and educators, are dedicated to developing the next generation of leaders and find that revealing experiences are critical to this cause. Deborah Stone (2004) writes, "Even more important than the explicit stories numbers tell are the implicit ones" (p. 172). The implicit stories are intimate. When they are personal, they take courage to write and investigative instincts to unearth. Vivian Gornick (2001) writes, "Penetrating the familiar is by no means a given. On the contrary, it is hard, hard work" (p. 9).

This chapter reflects time spent helping students and leaders as they work on their core selves. As the protagonist, the SPN researcher reports "to others from foreign territory: the territory of the writer, of the self, of an *I*" (Roorbach, 2008, p. 14). In discussing authenticity, Nash (2004) notes environments must be personally honest, engaging, and inclusive, particularly for non-specialists. Modern business leaders balance how to fulfill human needs, in the short and long term, while also having intrinsic value through enlightenment, entertainment, or inspiration.

One of the central goals of SPN involves recognizing and sharing personal stories with enthusiasm while also understanding their significance for both the storyteller and the audience. Such storytelling can reaffirm the belief that leadership, as a field, is progressing toward a more authentic approach. We, the authors, find students often display a deeper understanding of authenticity than what is commonly depicted in media narratives as flippant critiques of this next generation that does not "get it," which equips them with the conviction to lead with their values. This commitment has the potential to instigate meaningful change in the world.

Though this chapter may have explored many often-used terms like *spirituality* or *meaning*, we wrote with gusto to showcase the essentiality of authenticity in leadership. Authenticity is essential for any leader who wants to connect with their teams. To achieve this, aspiring leaders can measure success in increments of meaning. Authentic leadership development is a lifelong journey. Few argue that leaders require a steely sense of self to work in business, across politics, or within politically charged environments.

Modern business leaders must foster transformative experiences to bolster authenticity (see our later chapters on motivation and client leadership). Authenticity is fundamental to the human experience and should be a cornerstone in any institution. This focus on authenticity is vital for cultivating effective leaders during pivotal formative years and beyond.

Corporations increasingly appreciate the cultivation of *soft skills* that make fantastic leaders. Time, money, and energy spent tying leaders back to their sense of self, purpose, and work's meaning can have an immediate return on investment. Contemporary leaders embrace meaning-making as a lifelong commitment because their impact on others matters. Frequently, scholars are turning to the study of toxic or destructive leaders and finding that those who have not undergone this fundamental self-examination can have a predominantly negative effect on those they manage. Additionally, during times of turmoil or challenge, business leaders must stay connected to their values and what they believe. Authenticity in the face of adversity is essential for all leaders, whether team leaders, middle managers, or senior executives. As aspiring leaders continue through this book, we hope they find themselves personally and professionally challenged the further they move.

DISCUSSION QUESTIONS

1. What are the barriers to being authentic in today's business environments?
2. What sort of "me search" do you still need to do?
3. What do you still need to know about your purpose to lead?
4. What are your five core values?
5. Do we have fewer authentic leaders today than in the past?
6. What practices help us as a society to avoid the authenticity deficit?
7. How can followers confront toxic leaders?
8. Why do business leaders need authentic leadership development?

Key Terms

- Authenticity
- Authentic Leadership
- Meaning-Making
- Spirituality
- Self-Authorship
- Destructive Leadership
- Toxic Triangle
- Integrity
- Ethics
- Scholarly Personal Narrative

CASE STUDY 2.1 INNOVATEX AND AN AUTHENTICITY DILEMMA

Authentic leadership is increasingly recognized as vital in today's organizations. It emphasizes self-reflection, genuine relationships, transparency, and ethical decision-making. This case study explores Maya Nguyen, founder and CEO of InnovateX, a rapidly growing tech startup focused on transforming data analytics in healthcare.

Maya started InnovateX five years ago with a small team, which has since expanded to over 50 employees, bolstered by significant funding and partnerships with leading healthcare providers. Central to her leadership is authenticity; she leads by example and fosters strong connections with her team, maintaining openness and a commitment to ethical practices.

Maya's focus on transparency and open dialogue has created a supportive workplace culture that drives growth and sets a benchmark for leadership in the tech startup ecosystem. As InnovateX continues to expand, she remains dedicated to these values, though challenges inevitably arise.

CHALLENGES AND QUESTIONS

1. Maya must navigate the complexities of scaling InnovateX from a small startup to a mid-sized company while striving to maintain its innovative culture. As the organization expands, hiring the right talent and ensuring new employees

embrace the company's core values are critical. *How can InnovateX seize expansion opportunities while staying true to its mission?*

2. In the competitive tech landscape, Maya will frequently face ethical dilemmas. The pressure to meet growth targets will conflict with her commitment to ethical practices. *How could she guard against corruption and unethical behavior in this challenging environment?*
3. As InnovateX grows, maintaining open communication becomes more challenging. Maya wants to uphold her open-door policy but needs to balance formal and informal communication. *Which practices would best foster authenticity within the company?*
4. Maya recognizes that authentic leadership requires ongoing growth and self-reflection. Balancing her duties with personal development will be difficult. *How can she maintain her commitment to growth while meeting job demands?*

Task: Reflect on the preceding questions and provide four comprehensive recommendations for Maya. Make sure to connect the recommendations to the chapter's key concepts. Present the recommendations to a larger group for feedback and discussion.

REFERENCES

Allison, J., & Gediman, D. (Producers). (2005–2009). *This I believe* [Radio series]. National Public Radio. Retrieved from https://www.npr.org/series/4538138/this-i-believe

Avolio, B. J., & Wernsing, T. S. (2008). Practicing authentic leadership. In C. Hickman (Ed.), *Leading organizations: Perspectives for a new era* (2nd ed., pp. 331–338). Sage Publications.

Boyle, J., Halpin, R., & Ji Hyland, C. (2019). Best practice in designing groupwork for first year students. Retrieved 20 February 2025 from https://arrow.tudublin.ie/cgi/viewcontent.cgi?article=1024&context=ltcpgdprp.

Chickering, A. W., & Reisser, L. (1993). *Education and identity* (2nd ed.). Jossey-Bass.

Cooper, A. (1998). *Playing in the zone: Exploring the spiritual dimensions of sport* (pp. 2–3). Shambhala Publications.

Copeland, M. K. (2014). The emerging significance of values based leadership: A literature review. https://core.ac.uk/download/48617327.pdf

Dantley, J. L. R. M. E., & Rogers, J. L. (2001). Invoking the spiritual in campus life and leadership. *Journal of College Student Development, 42*, 589–603.

Erikson, E. H. (1968). *Identity: Youth and crisis*. W. W. Norton & Company.

Gehrke, S. J. (2008). Leadership through meaning-making: An empirical exploration of spirituality and leadership in college students. *Journal of College Student Development, 49*(4), 351–359.

George, B. (2003). *Authentic leadership: Rediscovering the secrets to creating lasting value*. Jossey-Bass.

George, B., & Sims, P. (2007). *True north*. Jossey-Bass.
Gornick, V. (2001). *The situation and the story*. Farrar, Straus, and Giroux.
Hodge, D. C., Baxter Magolda, M. B., & Haynes, C. A. (2009). Engaged learning: Enabling self-authorship and effective practice. *Liberal Education, 95*(4), 16–23.
Hughes, M. (2006). Affect, meaning, and quality of life. *Social Forces, 85*(2), 611–629.
Kegan, R. (1983). *The evolving self: Problem and process in human development*. Harvard University Press.
Kellerman, B. (2004). *Bad leadership: What it is, how it happens, why it matters*. Harvard Business Press.
Kellerman, B. (2012). *The end of leadership*. HarperCollins.
Kernis, M. H., & Goldman, B. M. (2006). A multicomponent conceptualization of authenticity: Theory and research. *Advances in Experimental Social Psychology*, 38, 283–357. https://doi.org/10.1016/S0065-2601(06)38006-9
Mounk, Y. (2019). *The people vs. democracy: Why our freedom is in danger and how to save it*. Harvard University Press.
Murray, J. L. (2005). *Theory & practice in student affairs*. Student Affairs Program in Higher Education, Bucknell University.
Nash, R. J. (2004). *Liberating scholarly writing: The power of personal narrative*. Teachers College, Columbia University.
Nash, R. J., & Murray, M. C. (2010). *Helping college students find purpose*. Jossey-Bass.
Padilla, A., Hogan, R., & Kaiser, R. B. (2007). The toxic triangle: Destructive leaders, susceptible followers, and conducive environments. *The Leadership Quarterly, 18*(3), 176–194. https://doi.org/10.1016/j.leaqua.2007.03.001
Piaget, J. (1950). *The psychology of intelligence* (M. Piercy & D. E. Berlyne, Trans.). Routledge & Kegan Paul. (Original work published 1947).
Roorbach, B. (2008). *Writing life stories*. Writer's Digest Books.
Stone, D. (2004). *Policy paradox: The art of political decision making* (Rev. ed.). W. W. Norton & Company.
Talmage, C. A., Boyl, K., & Gassert, T. A. (2022). Toward a theory of misfit entrepreneurship: Insights from alternative enterprises and misfit entrepreneurs. In Mars, M. M., & Schau, H. J. (Eds.), *How alternative is alternative? The role of entrepreneurial development, form, and function in the emergence of alternative marketscapes* (Advances in the Study of Entrepreneurship, Innovation and Economic Growth, Vol. 29) (pp. 1–27). Emerald Publishing Limited. https://doi.org/10.1108/S1048-473620220000029001
Talmage, C. A., Mars, M. M., Hains, B. J., Hains, K. D., & Ashdown, B. K. (2024). Pushing against a future dark side for community development: An editorial call to action. *Community Development, 55*(3), 310–324.
Trilling, L. (1972). *Sincerity and authenticity*. Harvard University Press.

CHAPTER 3

Leadership Identity and Style

CHAPTER OVERVIEW

The next chapter within the Self Leadership section is about leadership identity and style. Both play a substantial role in a leader's sense of self and ability to be effective. Identity and style can be learned and developed over time, meaningfully contributing to the elusive "it factor" of leadership. Although leadership is a highly social process, it is key for leaders to identify as leaders and, in turn, be motivated to lead. This chapter outlines several constructs for identity development. Further, it discusses leadership style and offers the continuum of transformational and transactional leadership as a valuable tool for business leaders to situate themselves within. Leaders must cultivate their identity and lean into their unique style.

Identity and style play a substantial part in a sense of self in leadership. Like authentic leadership, contemporary business leaders must comprehend the complex dimensions of *being* a leader. Such notions of identity and style have improved and evolved with new research over the last few decades. Still, as noted in Chapter 1, nuanced and overly academic concepts often fall short in their bridges to practice and staying relevant in today's context.

In Fall 2024, we, the authors, asked our graduate students whether they saw themselves as leaders, and nearly 95% said they did. *Why?* As we unpacked their responses, anecdotally, we found that most had had an experience where an obstacle challenged them. Yet, through hard work and discipline, they had earned their way, with others, to success, most of whom had experienced this during their formitive years. This is not a surprise when a definition of leadership is working with others toward a collective goal. *But is it essential for individuals to identify as leaders? And what are the ingredients that lead some to see themselves as leaders and others do not?* Finally, *how does one's leadership style impact leaders' effectiveness in business environments?* This chapter will explore the implications of identity and style on leadership.

DOI: 10.4324/9781003474647-4

LEADERSHIP IDENTITY

Leadership identity is multifaceted, involving how individuals perceive themselves as leaders or followers. According to Scott DeRue and Ashford (2010), this identity encompasses three key components: personal internalization, relational acknowledgment, and collective affirmation. **Personal internalization** refers to the process by which individuals begin to see the roles of leader or follower as integral to their self-concept. Effective, authentic leadership is resonant in individuals with strong self-awareness (see Chapter 2), displayed through emotional intelligence (Chapter 4), and connected to their identity as a leader (Chapter 5). These elements are showcased as "me as a leader" internalized identity and expressions of that identity (Haslam et al., 2021a, 2022). *How does this internationalization evolve in Self Leaders?*

Socialization is crucial in shaping leadership identity. In their research, Haslam et al. (2021a, 2022) highlight that effective leadership is vital for driving social progress and bringing about change. Haslam et al. (2021a, 2022) emphasize that leadership is a fundamental mechanism through which individuals come together to enact significant societal transformations across sectors. Historically, even when the complexities of leadership were not fully understood, communities have consistently trained their children to assume leadership roles essential for the future. Experiences, challenges, adversities, communities, and relationships with others strongly influence self-identity as a leader (McCarron et al., 2023). Consequently, many individuals are motivated to pursue leadership roles due to their profound impact on their organizations and society (Guillén et al., 2015; Haslam et al., 2021b).

While each leader's journey is uniquely personal, modern business leaders must acknowledge that leadership fundamentally relies on social dynamics. Haslam et al. (2021a, 2022) argue that effective leadership involves a collective process where leaders foster and promote a shared identity among their teams, creating a cohesive sense of "us as a group." Scott DeRue and Ashford (2010) also highlight that **relational recognition** is vital in shaping leadership identity. Leadership is a process of mutual influence that transcends formal roles and hierarchies, distributing responsibility among all social system members (Scott DeRue and Ashford, 2010). This view highlights the importance of recognizing contributions over titles and aligning the self-concepts of both leaders and followers.

In Scott DeRue and Ashford's (2010) framework, **collective endorsement** is vital for contemporary business leaders. They discuss how individuals, such as leaders or followers, are perceived concerning their group roles. This visibility ensures that roles are recognized and endorsed publicly. Their work emphasizes integrating individual, relational, and collective identity theories, noting that leadership identity differs significantly from more commonly analyzed social identities (see Chapter 5). Lastly, the definitions and characteristics that distinguish leaders from followers are subject to change and influenced by the context in which they operate.

Contemporary business leaders should understand identity complexity to foster effective leadership styles. As defined by Hoang and Gimeno (2010), **identity complexity** refers to the diversity of roles an individual perceives as central to their self-concept. For example, founders may identify as entrepreneurs in various roles, such as parents, mentors, or community members. This concept underscores that leadership is not solely about how leaders view themselves; it is equally important to recognize how others attribute identities to them. Research suggests that leaders with high identity complexity—those who embrace multiple significant roles—can better navigate transitions and maintain persistence in their entrepreneurial and leadership journeys (Hoang & Gimeno, 2010). Modern business leaders recognize that dynamic social processes shape leadership identities. Self Leaders reflect on the multifacetedness and intersectionality of identities (Chapter 5) and their influences on individuals, teams, supervisors, clients, and communities.

A Closer Look at Identity

The leadership industry is dynamic (a term we continue to use throughout this chapter), often chasing the latest innovations. Still, we recommend focusing on the enduring elements that have shaped the field over the past several decades (Haslam et al., 2021a, 2021b, 2022); hence, why we wrote this text in the first place (see Introduction). Notably, Haslam et al. (2022) identify two key constants: (1) an increase in research dedicated to leadership and (2) a growing understanding of leadership as a process rooted in the unique psychology of exceptional individuals (Haslam et al., 2021a, 2022). From the philosophical inquiries of Plato to contemporary studies, the quest to uncover the elusive *it factor* distinguishing effective and ethical leaders from their followers remains a central theme in leadership discourse.

Barbara Kellerman (2016) argues that bias has beset the leadership industry. This bias has been directed toward leaders and away from two other equally pertinent variables that further explain the trajectory of human history. The first is **followers** or other group members involved in the leadership process, even if passively. The second is **contexts**, the specific situations where leaders and followers are necessarily embedded. In her classic, "Leadership—It's a System, Not a Person!" Kellerman (2016) presents leadership as a **system** that includes leaders, followers, and contexts.

Kellerman (2016) cautions not to fixate on leaders or their so-called mystique at the expense of the other elements equally essential to creating the leadership process. We are especially interested in minding her commentary, "This fixation on learning leadership–in particular on learning how to lead, as opposed to learning about leadership–ripples across American curricula as it does across corporate America" (Kellerman, 2016, p. 84). Kellerman continues to be a voice of reason in an overtly tilted industry. Further, her leadership system can help explain leadership identity more fully.

We agree with Kellerman (2016) when she asks, seemingly incredulously,

> Is there anything about the leadership industry to which one can reasonably point that could be fixed, improved, or changed to make the process of leadership learning richer, fuller, deeper, and therefore more likely to yield more obviously positive results?
>
> (p. 85)

Indeed, exploring leadership as a system and spending time on each of its parts can make a substantial difference, but, just perhaps, recent developments designed to decipher the identity of leaders are noteworthy and hardly superficial. Leaders are often researched as individuals who identify as leaders or leaders of groups, which can be tied to identity (Haslam et al., 2021a).

Modern business leaders must understand their roles as group members, which are heavily influenced by the Social Identity Model of Identity Change (SIMIC). This model suggests that, in various social and organizational settings, individuals primarily define themselves as unique individuals through their affiliation with specific groups (Haslam et al., 2021a). Chapter 5 discusses further the balance of being in and distinct from a group (i.e., deindividuation). Table 3.1 highlights the key concepts in the SIMIC model, complemented by three elaborated shoutouts to compatibility, maintenance, and entrance into groups (see also Dong et al., 2022).

Modern business leaders must recognize that when individuals define themselves through a specific social identity (for example, as a feminist), they should also understand what that identity truly means (such as the values and beliefs associated with being a feminist) and behave congruently with that understanding. However, these meanings can be challenging to identify in an unpredictable world. As a result, people often seek information from others within their social group to make sense of their environment and role in it. This reliance on group communication has critical implications for leaders' self-perception and their leadership effectiveness.

A thread that often runs throughout our classes is: *how has leadership changed from past to present?* Time and time again, over and over from students, our discussions note that leaders of the past were once primarily wealthy, educated white men. Today, however, leaders come from all walks of life and backgrounds—albeit there is still much progress to be made. Indeed, other research inspired by social identity theory has shown that being

TABLE 3.1 Augmented SIMIC Model with Examples

Concept	*Definition*	*Example*
Social Identity Continuity	Maintaining consistent group memberships to provide stability, a sense of self, and support during change, helping leaders navigate and guide others.	A seasoned leader guides a company through a merger by leveraging existing relationships and their experience to maintain stability and build employee trust.
Social Identity Gain	Expanding one's social identity by joining new groups, bringing fresh perspectives and resources that enhance leadership adaptability.	A leader joining an industry consortium to gain new perspectives and strategies that enhance their adaptability in a rapidly changing market.
Compatibility	Aligning with the values, norms, and practices of teams, ensuring effective collaboration, influence, and leadership within groups.	A leader whose values of transparency and collaboration align with their team's culture, ensuring trust and fostering a productive work environment.
Maintenance	The ongoing effort to sustain meaningful relationships and participate in groups, ensuring leaders remain active, valued members.	A leader continuously mentors others, reinforcing their role and ensuring they are a valued participant in the company's culture and development.
Entrance into Groups	Adapting to new groups by aligning leadership style with the team's culture, helping leaders integrate and build stronger connections.	A leader transitioning into a new industry, adapting their leadership style to fit the new group's values, fostering collaboration, and driving team success.

perceived as "one of us" is as important as leaders being seen as doing "it for us" through their work with followers (Haslam et al., 2001). The two most problematic items for leaders' effectiveness are the perception that they are either acting for themselves or, worse, for outsiders (Hogg et al., 2012). Another large body of research shows that leaders will be more effective when they are also seen to act in ways that advance group interests (Giessner et al., 2013). This is a critical lesson for contemporary leaders.

The foregoing analysis assumes, however, that in any given situation, there will always be a pre-existing social identity for leaders to represent and advance (Haslam et al., 2021a, 2022). Moreover, the process envisioned here is relatively passive, and leaders can only be successful if circumstances place the mantle of the group on their shoulders. *How can leaders be creative drivers of change if they always need to represent and advance the interests of others?* Social identities are not set in stone but on a moveable spectrum (Haslam et al., 2021a, 2022). Therefore, a hallmark of effective leadership is taking advantage of this flexibility. More specifically, work by Reicher and Hopkins (2001) suggests that leaders need to be entrepreneurs of social identity who work not only to create a sense of shared group membership amongst would-be followers but also to shape their understanding of identity.

Where research on identity leadership zeroes in on leaders' "we-ness," research on leader identity focuses firmly on their "I-ness" (Haslam et al., 2022), an equally compelling strand of research. This focus means "that it sees leadership as a process that is facilitated and furthered by individuals who have a well-developed personal understanding of themselves as leaders and who also succeed in getting others to accept this understanding" (Haslam et al., 2022). Leadership identity is central to self-leadership and effective leadership.

To sustain the reciprocal nature of the leadership identity process, the claims and grants between leaders and followers must be of sufficient quality. **Identity construction** implicitly assumes that social interaction between leaders and followers is free, fluid, and without interruption (Scott DeRue & Ashford, 2010). The more members of these groups that have internalized leadership identities, which are mutually recognized and collectively endorsed, the more successful distributed and shared forms of leadership will be. Modern leaders must communicate values that speak to followers' identities and exemplify them as models that serve as a basis for their self-regulation (Scott DeRue & Ashford, 2010). Kellerman's (2016) leadership as a system supports this.

Exercise 3.1 Exploring Your Leadership Identity through Peer Interviews

Objective: This activity encourages Self Leaders to explore their leadership identities by conducting peer interviews to gain diverse perspectives on effective leadership practices.

Preparation: Generate a list of tailored interview questions to guide your discussions. Feel free to use Generative AI like ChatGPT, Gemini, Co-Pilot, or others to help you. Some sample questions/prompts to consider include:

- What personal experiences have significantly shaped your leadership identity in a business context?
- How do your core values influence your leadership style in the workplace?

- Share when you faced a leadership challenge in your career and describe how you addressed it.
- Who do you view as a leadership role model in the business world, and what qualities make them stand out?
- In what ways does your unique personal background inform your approach to leadership in modern business?

Conducting Interviews: You should pair up to conduct interviews, with each of you taking turns as interviewer and interviewee.

- Allocate approximately 15 minutes for each interview session, and practice active listening and thoughtful questioning.
- Taking notes or recording your conversations for future reflection is a good idea.

Reflection: After completing the interviews, take some time to write a reflective piece on your own leadership identity, considering the following:

- What insights did you gain about your leadership style through the process?
- How did understanding your partner's experiences and values reshape your perceptions of leadership?
- What new ideas can you adopt to enhance your approach to leadership in your professional journey?

Discussion and Sharing Insights: Generate key takeaways from your interviews in a group discussion. Focus on:

- Any surprising or enlightening aspects of your partner's leadership identity.
- How your perspectives on leadership have evolved due to this exercise.
- Commonalities or notable differences between your leadership identities and your peers.

Discuss how leadership identities can significantly enhance modern leadership practices, improve collaboration, activate diversity, bolster inclusivity, and strengthen relationships.

IDENTITY FORMATION AND MOTIVATION

Effective leadership involves gaining recognition from followers and entails leaders perceiving themselves as such. Haslam et al. (2022) emphasize that when individuals adopt a leadership identity—integrating it into their self-concept—they feel more compelled to act more indicatively of strong leadership. For instance, leaders who see themselves as motivators may proactively encourage team collaboration, fostering an environment where innovation thrives.

The **leadership identity development** (LID) framework describes how leaders grow into their leadership identities. This framework acknowledges the influence of the surrounding environment or ecosystem (Komives et al., 2009). Its primary goal is not to label individuals as leaders but to better understand their lived experiences and how they perceive their roles in various contexts (Komives et al., 2009). For example, a student in a student club may face challenges and successes shaping their leadership approach, influenced by interactions with peers, advisors, and the community.

The LID framework remains highly relevant in modern business leadership discussions, as it illustrates how leaders are shaped by their social experiences over time. This view is supported by the research of Scott DeRue and Ashford (2010) and Kellerman (2016), which underscores the relational dynamics and systemic factors in leadership emergence. Contemporary business leaders must understand that leadership is a fluid process shaped by interactions and social contexts. This understanding allows leaders to appreciate the developmental journey of emerging leaders and the importance of cultivating supportive environments that nurture their growth.

As Figure 3.1 demonstrates, leaders form their identity through their environment and experiences. The society in which they live influences the values, norms, and expectations of leadership. In addition, cultural, social, and organizational influences play a role. Social and environmental factors can positively and negatively affect identity. The first phase is to become aware that they can lead, often encouraged by a trusted role model. The second phase is where they see themselves as a leader as reinforced by followers and contexts. In the third phase, generativity is understood as the focus on nurturing and guiding the development of future generations (Erikson, 1950). In the fourth phase, a complex, dynamic, and cyclical process, individuals move from fundamental awareness of leadership identity to integrating leadership into their core being (Komives et al., 2005, 2009).

Scholars have also noted that knowing one is a leader is not enough to make one effective (Guillén et al., 2015); a modern business leader must also be genuinely motivated to

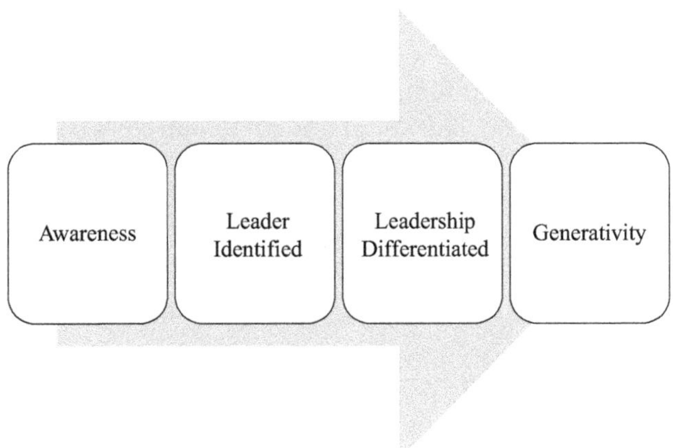

FIGURE 3.1 The Leadership Identity Development Framework. *Foundational Categories: (1) Changing Views of Self as Leader; (2) Expanding Views of Leadership; (3) Influences; (4) Meaningful Involvement; and (5) Reflective Learning*

(Adapted from Komives et al., 2009)

TABLE 3.2 MTL Component Breakdown

MTL Component	*Description*	*Example*
Affective-Identity	Reflects an intrinsic enjoyment of leadership roles and fosters a strong personal identity as a leader.	A CEO who is passionate about guiding their company through transformative change.
Social-Normative	Characterized by a sense of duty or obligation to lead, shaped by societal expectations and norms.	A supervisor who mentors younger professionals to give back to the community.
Non-Calculative	Captures the motivated desire to lead without weighing personal costs or rewards, focusing on leadership despite potential downsides.	A social entrepreneur dedicating time to lead initiatives in underserved communities, fully aware of challenges.

persist despite the challenges leaders face. Therefore, it is unsurprising that an increasing number of studies have recently focused on understanding the motivation to lead. **Motivation to lead** (MTL) (Chan & Drasgow, 2001) is the willingness to engage in leadership training activities and assume leadership roles.

MTL comprises three key components that shape an individual's motivation to lead. Table 3.2 outlines the three components of MTL and provides examples of modern Self Leaders. Together, these components provide a comprehensive understanding of what drives individuals to take on leadership roles (Chan & Drasgow, 2001). Guillén et al. (2015) focus on the affective component for theoretical and practical reasons. As seen in Table 3.2, examples across the components are evident; however, modern Self Leaders may show all three.

Theoretically, the affective component has been related to the intrinsic motivation to lead (Chan & Drasgow, 2001). In contrast, those who score high on the other two components of MTL would lead for different reasons—either a high sense of duty or responsibility or beliefs about the costs and benefits associated with leading. From a practical standpoint, research has consistently shown that among the MTL components, the affective component is the strongest predictor of leadership outcomes such as ratings of leadership potential made by supervisors (Chan & Drasgow, 2001), leadership emergence (Hong, 2005), and overall team effectiveness (Hendricks & Payne, 2007). Identity scholars suggest that incorporating leadership into the sense of self motivates individuals to seek leadership opportunities (Ibarra et al., 2010). This has now shown to be especially important if a leader is to be effective within the leadership system.

Exercise 3.2 Motivation Map

Begin by exploring what motivation means to you as a modern business leader. Consider what drives you to take on leadership roles or responsibilities in today's dynamic environment. Introduce the idea of creating a "motivation map" to help you visualize and reflect on these driving forces.

Identifying Your Motivational Factors: Grab some sticky notes and a pen. Write down the various factors that motivate you to lead. Consider the following categories:

- *Personal Values* include the principles guiding you, such as integrity and empathy.
- *Career Goals* include a position, promotion, or meaningful project or initiative.
- *Influences* encompass those who inspire you, including mentors and role models.
- *Experiences* consist of the past moments that have shaped your leadership, whether successes or challenges.
- *Interests and Passions* highlight what drives you, like innovation or service.

Creating Your Motivation Map: Take a large sheet of paper or a poster board. In the center, draw a circle labeled "My Leadership Motivation." Start grouping your sticky notes into categories surrounding this central circle. Create clusters representing different types of motivation (e.g., values, goals, influences). Use lines or colors to connect related notes, forming a visual map of your motivations. Feel free to enhance your map with colors, symbols, or illustrations to highlight connections between different motivational factors.

Reflection: Once your map is complete, take some time to write a brief reflection regarding:

- What are the main categories of motivation that drive you as a leader?
- How do these motivations align with your leadership actions and decisions?
- Were there any surprises or new insights about what motivates you to lead?
- How can understanding your motivations assist you in your current or future roles?

Discussion: Share your motivation map in small groups or with the larger class. Discuss:

- What key motivations did you uncover, and how did you discover them?
- How might your motivation map influence your leadership approach?
- What similarities and differences did you notice among your peers' motivations?

Action Planning: Knowing your motivations can help you become a more genuine leader. Based on what you've learned, create a plan of action. List specific steps to connect your leadership style with your motivations. This might include finding a mentor, setting career goals, or getting involved in projects that match your core values.

LEADERSHIP STYLE

Leadership identity is the extent to which someone sees him or herself as a leader. It reflects values, beliefs, mindsets, actions, and situation responses. Additionally, leadership identity includes one's attitude and readiness to impact an organization. In contrast, a leadership style refers to a leader's methods, characteristics, and behaviors when directing, motivating, and managing their followers. A **leader's style** is shaped by various factors, including personality, values, skills, and experiences, and can significantly impact the effectiveness of his or her leadership. Leaders must find their identity and lean into their style (for more, check out Jackson, 2024; Mamchii, 2023).

Some individuals have an unusual talent for spinning their failures into tales of prowess as if they were the stars of their comedy show. "It's not that I made poor choices," they'll assert, "it's just that my pioneering leadership style is too ahead of its time for this team to grasp fully." Or another favorite: "The real issue was that this organization wasn't ready to embrace the groundbreaking brilliance of my epic three-hour brainstorming sessions." It remains fascinating to us, whether in classes or in organizations, how what they call "visionary leadership" often seems to morph into "selective memory" when the feedback rolls in, revealing just how vital genuine interpersonal relations and sound decision-making are. Furthermore, leadership style is not an online personality quiz, like which *Harry Potter* house (Rowling, 1997) you fit in, but your role in Kellerman's (2016) system.

Leadership identity style refers to differences in the way individuals construct, revise, or maintain their sense of identity. Recently, Kennett wrote on LinkedIn (2022) that "Identity can be minimized, but they have found that one of the most effective ways to change our behavior long term is to do so by changing or upgrading our identity." Further, she writes, "You need to see, own, and step into your leadership identity before consciously choosing and practicing a leadership style" (Kennett, 2022). We wholeheartedly agreed with Kennet that the best leadership style for today's business environments is the agile one.

In a text that incorporates both management and leadership, we cannot help but mention the transformational and transactional spectrums, which offer two distinct styles and outline their nuances. As we explain to students, it's crucial to appreciate the spectrum and not make it one versus the other. **Transactional leadership** constitutes an exchange between leader and followers, described by the following tasks: budgeting, controlling, coordinating, scheduling, and other detail-oriented planning.

Transactional leadership involves exchanging tangible rewards for work and followers' loyalty. It is responsive to environmental events and seeks to work within the organization's culture. Transactional leaders also aim to motivate followers through rewards and punishments and by appealing to their self-interest. They largely maintain the status quo and stress correct actions to improve performance.

At the other end of the spectrum, first introduced by James McGregor Burns in 1978, **transformational leadership** implies a leader who changes and inspires. According to Burns, transformational leadership is a process in which "leaders and followers help each other to advance to a higher level of morale and motivation" (Burns, 1978). Transformational leaders engage followers, focusing on higher-order intrinsic needs and raising consciousness. This highly proactive style shifts the organizational culture by executing new ideas. Additionally, they motivate followers by encouraging them to put group interests first. Further, this style takes individualized consideration, behavior directed to each individual to express respect and support.

Often in class, students ask: *Do I show up as a transformational or transactional leader? What are my strengths, and where must I expand my repertoire?* Further, *do organizations today need more transformational or transactional leadership?* There is no one correct

TABLE 3.3 Benefits of Transformational Leadership

Leadership Attribute	*Description*
Encourages Team Members	Inspires employees to endure obstacles while nurturing a positive and encouraging workplace environment.
Defines Clear Objectives	Communicates a clear vision and defines team objectives, offering simple direction to reach those goals effectively.
Supports Employees	Fosters solid connections with team members and acknowledges their accomplishments to boost their sense of worth.
Leads by Example	Exhibits honesty and strong moral principles, acting as a model for ethical conduct among team members.
Promotes Positivity	Maintains a hopeful perspective, aiding in overcoming obstacles and fostering a positive environment among team members.
Inspires Achievement	Inspires and empowers team members to achieve their individual and career aspirations, contributing to their overall success.

answer. Without the transactional style, there is chaos, disorganization, and dysfunction. Core functions like supply chain, operational processes, human resources, or project management can fail. Transactional vitality is frequently associated with management and must persist in most organizations.

Yet, the transformational style is needed in today's contemporary business environments. Seminal conversations like retention, employee satisfaction, positive morale, and healthy cultures all lead back to the presence and actions of transformational leaders who inspire, mentor, and guide meaningful change. McGregor Burns (1978) outlined the importance of four factors for transformational leadership: idealized influence, inspirational motivation, intellectual stimulation, and individual consideration (see also Indeed Editorial Team, 2023). The Indeed Editorial Team (2023) noted the benefits of these components (see Table 3.3).

We often guide students in identifying their positions on the transactional and transformational spectrum. They should blend both styles in their future leadership roles. Healthy and effective organizations require a mix of these approaches, whether by a single leader or a leadership team. A key aspect of leadership agility is the ability to assess the context of a situation (again, see Kellerman's (2016) system). Modern Self Leaders apply the appropriate style from the spectrum to address new challenges effectively. Identity differs from style but is tethered (see Table 3.3).

CONCLUSION

With today's constant disruptions, it is less about organizational leaders' technical or functional expertise and more about how effectively they lead. Leadership, frankly, matters more than ever. Self-awareness has tremendous power. Leaders should study themselves instead of chasing charisma, a long-lauded leadership quality inherited by the select few and questionable how much it serves in substance. The presence or mystique of leaders that attracts others to follow is a solid sense of self and passion for what one pursues. The steady self-discipline of inner work takes an individual to the level required of today's contemporary leaders.

This chapter emphasizes that leaders must adopt an identity incorporating leadership into their self-schema. New research deciphers identity leadership, which zeroes in on leaders' "we-ness," versus leader identity, which focuses firmly on their "I-ness." We will continue to look at both in the coming chapters as we explore the social process of leadership, the relationships with followers, and the critical need to step into a fully actualized version of self as a leader. Further, being motivated to do so is complex, nuanced, and essential to the cause.

Finally, identity and style are critical to a leader's effectiveness. When a leader has a solid identity and is endorsed by followers, their style can align with the context. Transactional and transformational leadership styles still have relevance today. When leaders calibrate their style along this spectrum based on the context, they exude the agility required for contemporary business environments. Authenticity, identity, and style are key conversations that will help build a foundational sense of self within future business leaders.

DISCUSSION QUESTIONS

1. What is required for an individual to identify as a leader?
2. What is the difference between identity leadership and leadership identity?
3. How does the social process impact the leadership system?
4. How does motivation impact an individual's effectiveness as a leader?
5. Do I show up as a transformational or transactional leader?
6. What are my strengths, and where must I expand my repertoire?
7. Do organizations today need more transformational leadership or transactional leadership?

Key Terms

- Leadership Identity
- Personal Internalization
- Relational Recognition
- Collective Endorsement
- Identity Complexity
- Followers
- Leadership System
- Contexts
- System
- Social Identity Continuity
- Social Identity Gain
- Identity Construction
- Leadership Identity Development
- Motivation to Lead
- Affective-Identity MTL
- Social-Normative MTL
- Non-Calculative MTL
- Leadership Identity Style
- Transactional Leadership
- Transformational Leadership

CASE STUDY 3.1 TECHNOCORE

This case study explores the leadership journey of James Reynolds, CEO of TechnoCore, a prominent global technology firm focused on artificial intelligence and machine learning solutions. James's leadership identity and style significantly influence TechnoCore's strategic direction, organizational culture, and overall market success.

Background: James is an experienced entrepreneur and technologist who co-founded TechnoCore a decade ago after identifying a gap in the market for scalable AI–driven solutions tailored for enterprise settings. With a strong foundation in computer science and prior leadership roles in various tech startups, he successfully guided TechnoCore from its inception to becoming a key player in the global technology landscape.

Before co-founding TechnoCore, James held positions in several Silicon Valley startups, gaining essential experience in product development and market strategy while navigating the tech industry's complexities. His entrepreneurial spirit and passion for innovative technology motivated him to build a team of forward-thinking innovators at TechnoCore, focusing initially on developing robust AI algorithms for data analytics.

James's hands-on leadership identity was shaped by his ability to inspire and motivate his team to pursue ambitious goals. He envisioned TechnoCore as a provider of advanced technological solutions and a transformative force within the industry. This vision influenced his leadership style, combining transformative qualities and strategic foresight with a strong commitment to nurturing a culture of creativity and excellence within the organization. However, he faces several key challenges.

1. **Technological Disruption**: James must keep up with rapid technological advancements, focusing on AI and machine learning while balancing innovation with market needs.
2. **Cultural Adaptation**: As TechnoCore expands globally, it faces challenges related to differing cultural norms and business practices, requiring sensitivity and adaptability to align strategies with local markets.
3. **Talent Acquisition**: Attracting and retaining skilled professionals is critical for innovation. James emphasizes creating a strong workplace culture to retain top talent in a competitive market.
4. **Strategic Partnerships**: Alliances must align with TechnoCore's goals for growth. James needs strategic insight and diplomacy to manage these relationships effectively.

Task: Provide four comprehensive recommendations for James. Make sure to connect the recommendations to key chapter concepts. Present the recommendations to a larger group for feedback and discussion.

REFERENCES

Burns, J. M. (1978). *Leadership*. Harper and Row.

Chan, K., & Drasgow, F. (2001). Toward a theory of individual differences and leadership: Understanding the motivation to lead. *Journal of Applied Psychology, 86*(3), 481–498. https://doi.org/10.1037/0021-9010.86.3.481

Dong, Y., Xu, L., Xu, L., Wu, S., Wu, S., Qin, W., Hu, F., Li, M., & Xu, Y. (2022). The mediating effect of perceived social support on mental health and life satisfaction among residents: A cross-sectional analysis of 8500 subjects in Taian City, China. *International Journal of Environmental Research and Public Health, 19*(22), 14756.

Erikson, E. H. (1950). *Childhood and society*. W. W. Norton & Company.

Giessner, S. R., van Knippenberg, D., van Ginkel, W., & Sleebos, E. (2013). Team-oriented leadership: The interactive effects of leader group prototypicality, accountability, and team identification. *Journal of Applied Psychology, 98*(4), 658–667. https://doi.org/10.1037/a0031779

Guillén, L., Mayo, M., & Korotov, K. (2015). Is leadership a part of me? A leader identity approach to understanding the motivation to lead. *The Leadership Quarterly, 26*(5), 802–820. https://doi.org/10.1016/j.leaqua.2015.02.003

Haslam, C., Haslam, S. A., Jetten, J., Cruwys, T., & Steffens, N. K. (2021a). Life change, social identity, and health. *Annual Review of Psychology, 72*(1), 635–661.

Haslam, S. A., Gaffney, A. M., Hogg, M. A., Rast III, D. E., & Steffens, N. K. (2022). Reconciling identity leadership and leader identity: A dual-identity framework. *The Leadership Quarterly, 33*(4), 101620.

Haslam, S. A., Platow, M. J., Turner, J. C., Reynolds, K. J., McGarty, C., Oakes, P. J., Johnson, S., Ryan, M. K., & Veenstra, K. (2001). Social identity and the romance of leadership: The importance of being seen to be 'doing it for us'. *Group Processes and Intergroup Relations, 4*(3), 191–205. https://doi.org/10.1177/1368430201004003001

Haslam, S. A., Steffens, N. K., Reicher, S. D., & Bentley, S. V. (2021b). Identity leadership in a crisis: A 5R framework for learning from responses to COVID-19. *Social Issues and Policy Review, 15*(1), 35–83. https://doi.org/10.1111/sipr.12076

Hendricks, J. W., & Payne, S. C. (2007). Beyond the big five: Leader goal orientation as a predictor of leadership effectiveness. *Human Performance, 20*(4), 317–343. https://doi.org/10.1080/08959280701521983

Hoang, H., & Gimeno, J. (2010). Becoming a founder: How founder role identity affects entrepreneurial transitions and persistence in founding. *Journal of Business Venturing, 25*(1), 41–53. https://doi.org/10.1016/j.jbusvent.2008.07.002

Hogg, M. A., Van Knippenberg, D., & Rast, D. E. (2012). Intergroup leadership in organizations: Leading across group and intergroup boundaries. *Academy of Management Review, 37*(2), 232–255. https://doi.org/10.5465/amr.2010.0458

Hong, Y. (2005). Motivation to lead: Antecedents and resulting leader emergence (Master's thesis, Saint Mary's University). Saint Mary's University Repository.

Ibarra, H., Snook, S., & Guillén Ramo, L. (2010). Identity-based leader development. In R. Khurana & N. Nohria (Eds.), *Leadership: Advancing an intellectual discipline* (pp. 657–678). Harvard Business Press.

Indeed Editorial Team. (2023, February 3). *The 4 key components of transformational leadership*. Indeed.com. Retrieved from https://www.indeed.com/career-advice/career-development/key-components-of-transformational-leadership

Jackson, R. (2024, January 12). *The campfire leadership style*. Magnovo Training Group. https://magnovo.com/the-campfire-leadership-style/

Kellerman, B. (2016). Leadership—It's a system, not a person! *Daedalus, 145*(3), 83–94. https://doi.org/10.1162/DAED_a_00386

Kennett, J. (2022, October 3). Leadership identity gaps and leadership styles. *LinkedIn*. Retrieved from https://www.linkedin.com/pulse/leadership-identity-gaps-styles-jody-kennett/

Komives, S. R., Lucas, N., & McMahon, T. R. (2005). *Exploring leadership: For college students who want to make a difference* (1st ed.). Jossey-Bass.

Komives, S. R., Lucas, N., & McMahon, T. R. (2009). *Exploring leadership: For college students who want to make a difference* (3rd ed.). Jossey-Bass.

Mamchii, O. (2023, May 29). *Leadership identity: 10 ways to cultivate your own in 2025*. Best Diplomats. Retrieved from https://bestdiplomats.org/leadership-identity/

McCarron, G. P., McKenzie, B. L., & Yamanaka, A. (2023). Leadership identity development. *New Directions for Student Leadership, 2023*(178), 31–43. https://doi.org/10.1002/yd.20552

Reicher, S. D., & Hopkins, N. (2001). *Self and nation: Categorization, contestation and mobilisation*. Sage.

Rowling, J. K. (1997). *Harry Potter and the sorcerer's stone*. Scholastic.

Scott DeRue, D., & Ashford, S. J. (2010). Who will lead and who will follow? A social process of leadership identity construction in organizations. *The Academy of Management Review, 35*(4), 627–647. https://doi.org/10.5465/AMR.2010.53503267

CHAPTER 4

Emotional and Cultural Intelligence

CHAPTER OVERVIEW

The composition of business environments is changing due to accelerated globalization, increased immigration, and changing demographics. Developing the next generation of global leaders is critical for modern business leaders to gain a competitive advantage. Emotional (EI) and cultural intelligence (CQ) are core to leading effectively globally. They are distinct intelligences but overlap when applied in business settings. Much like the previous work in Self Leadership, EI and CQ can be learned. When taught together, EI and CQ help contemporary leaders execute situational competencies for interpersonal business conduct. Mastering both is no longer optional—leaders must harness EI and CQ in tandem to create inclusive workplaces, build resilient teams, and drive innovation in an era of complexity and change.

As described in the introduction, the composition of business environments is changing. *What factors are driving this?* As Clark and Polesello (2017) write, "Globalization, increased immigration, and technological change have resulted in increased diversity in organizations, placing new demands with respect to the contemporary workplace" (p. 337). *What new skill sets does this require for individuals and organizations?* Further, *how can organizations leverage this diversity for competitive advantage?*

The COVID-19 pandemic and global challenges underscore the urgent need for modern business leaders to adapt into global leaders. Business leaders today must cultivate global cultural and emotional competencies. Bryan et al. (1999) predicted that by 2029, 80% of world output would be in global markets. As reported by the World Bank in 2023, the ratio of global trade to GDP was 58.51% (Trading Economics, 2023). Engaging with global customers, competitors, suppliers, and employees is commonplace, even for medium and small firms in post–COVID-19 pandemic (Alon & Higgins, 2005; Chanyasak et al., 2022). Thus, modern leaders must recognize the relationship between managerial competencies and global leadership.

Increasingly, scholars are turning to emotional and cultural intelligence as essential skills for developing global leaders. Specifically, they are teaching them together to counteract the changes taking place in the workplace. Clark and Polesello (2017) write, "We view emotional intelligence (EI) and cultural intelligence (CQ) as a means of creating the

DOI: 10.4324/9781003474647-5

skills and resulting behaviors needed to create inclusive organizational cultures and environments that truly recognize the benefits and challenges associated with diversity" (p. 337). According to Crowne (2009), the goal is to demonstrate the relationship between EI and CQ while also clarifying how these two concepts are both distinct and interconnected components of social intelligence. We argue that this will significantly aid organizational outcomes, specifically in creating more globally competent leaders and truly leveraging these increasingly diverse workforces.

Modern business leaders must be highly skilled in interpersonal conduct in addition to their function area (Alon & Higgins, 2005; Osland, 2017). This interpersonal conduct includes deep self-awareness and a steadfast consciousness of a leader's impact on others. When leaders flex social intelligences like EI and CQ, they execute the (soft) skills and behaviors needed to excel in global environments. We increasingly see these as essentials for today's business leaders.

Technical expertise alone is insufficient, as noted in our earlier chapters. Modern business leaders must bridge the **intelligence divide**—the gap between analytical ability and interpersonal competencies to navigate diverse, interconnected workplaces. This term is borrowed from others who have summarized and synthesized work beyond cognitive intelligence and technical expertise (MSCEIT, n.d.; Roy, 2015). EI and CQ are the twin pillars of this bridge, equipping leaders with the ability to connect, empathize, and adapt in a rapidly globalizing world. Those who master EI foster trust and engagement within their teams, while those skilled in CQ navigate cultural differences with strategic insight, ensuring their organizations remain competitive across international markets (Alon & Higgins, 2005; Bratianu & Paiuc, 2025).

Yet, despite their growing importance, EI and CQ remain underdeveloped in many leadership pipelines. This chapter explores the intersection of these intelligences, examining how they shape leadership effectiveness and organizational success. Mastering both is no longer optional—leaders must harness EI and CQ in tandem to create inclusive workplaces, build resilient teams, and drive innovation in an era of complexity and change. The question for today's business leaders is not whether these intelligence forms matter, but rather: *Are leaders and firms able and willing to close the intelligence divide?*

WHAT IS EMOTIONAL INTELLIGENCE?

The term **emotional intelligence** (EI) was first introduced in the literature by Salovey and Mayer (1990), who defined EI as a subset of social intelligence that represents three individual abilities related to feelings: (1) appraisal and expression of emotions of self and others, (2) regulation of emotions for adaptive and reinforcing mood states, and (3) utilization of emotions for solving problems. Emotions are organized responses to external or internal events that will produce a positive or negative meaning to the individual (Clark & Polesello, 2017). They are characterized as adaptive because they can transform personal and social interactions (Salovey & Mayer, 1990). Gardner (1998) extended the discussion of EI to specifically include two areas of intelligence, namely, interpersonal (the ability to read other people's moods, motives, and other mental states) and intrapersonal (the ability to access one's feelings and draw on them to guide behavior). He believed EI should focus more on cognition and understanding than feelings (Gardner, 1998). EI rose to prominence as a determiner of success and became frequently measured by EI assessments (Alon & Higgins, 2005).

As the academic research on EI advanced, there was some debate about what is encompassed and how to operationalize it (Cartwright & Pappas, 2008). Some believe EI encompasses delayed gratification, impulse control, and mood regulation (Goleman, 1997). Others refer to it as an ability to perceive, express, understand, use, and manage emotions accurately and adaptively (Salovey & Pizarro, 2003). Still, others have examined EI as a competency that can lead to or cause effective performance (Boyatzis & Sala, 2004). Yet others see EI as a personality trait (Smith et al., 2008). Some definitions describe EI as a range of noncognitive abilities, skills, and competencies that impact an individual's capacity to effectively manage the demands and pressures of their environment (Matthews et al., 2002). Frankly, all EI definitions contribute to the argument for why EI is essential in contemporary workplaces.

EI has become one of the most sought-after interpersonal skills in the workplace. Harvard Business School noted that 71% of employers value EI more than technical skills when evaluating candidates (Landry, 2019). This growing emphasis stems partly from the work of Daniel Goleman (1997, 2020), who brought EI into mainstream leadership discourse. While technical skills and intelligence are foundational, they are merely prerequisites for leadership roles. Successful leaders can navigate interpersonal dynamics, manage emotions effectively, and foster collaboration. In practice, technical expertise may help individuals secure a position, but their EI enables them to advance, influence, and lead effectively.

Many misconceptions about EI persist, often reducing it to simply being nice or avoiding conflict. Goleman (2020) argues EI is far more nuanced and includes self-awareness, self-management, social awareness, and relationship management competencies. A common misunderstanding is that emotionally intelligent individuals prioritize harmony at the expense of difficult conversations. Instead, EI equips leaders to navigate conflicts effectively, balancing assertiveness with empathy. Additionally, some leaders misuse EI to manipulate others, leveraging cognitive and emotional empathy without genuine concern for their well-being. This selective application can lead to toxic workplace cultures, prioritizing short-term productivity over sustainable employee engagement. Recognizing the full scope of EI allows leaders to foster authentic relationships, make strategic decisions, and create inclusive environments where people feel supported and challenged (Goleman, 2020). We will get into these dark sides of leadership in our future chapters, especially those about entrepreneurship.

How specifically does EI allow leaders to interact with diversity in the workplace? The definitions of EI focus on recognizing and understanding emotions in oneself and others and effectively using this emotional information in thought processes and appropriate actions (Crowne, 2009). As the composition of contemporary work environments continues to shift, this intelligence becomes increasingly important. Leaders must manage themselves in high-pressure arenas and accurately interpret the emotions of others to build the sustaining relationships necessary for the interpersonal conduct of business.

The benefits of evaluating EI to leverage the construct to address diversity issues were also reflected in studies that established a connection between EI and CQ. For example, Jonck and Swanepoel (2015) stated, "Combining cultural and emotional intelligence will significantly increase organizational effectiveness and increase cost and time effectiveness" (p. 82). Lillis and Tian (2009) suggested that leaders with a high EI are more likely to adjust their behavior in a cross-cultural interaction because one may effectively perceive context-driven emotion patterns. Moreover, Aslam et al. (2016) investigated the impact of many types of intelligence on managerial effectiveness and career success in Pakistan. They concluded that EI is one of the stronger predictors of leader effectiveness. We intend to explore this connection further.

Exercise 4.1 Concentric Circles

Divide into two groups from a larger group. One group will be the outer ring. The other group will be the inner ring. Each person should be lined up facing a partner within concentric circles.

The outer ring partner will have one minute to respond to each prompt while the other listens. Then, the paired individuals will switch, and the inner partner will have one minute to respond while the other listens. After each prompt, ask the outer ring to step one person to their left to change partners. Each person should have a new partner for every new prompt. Try out the prompts listed in Table 4.1 as starters. Each is mapped onto different components of EI.

TABLE 4.1 Reflective Prompts Related to EI

#	*Prompt*	*EI Component(s) Addressed*
1	How do you typically react under stress?	Self-awareness, self-management
2	How well do you understand your own emotions?	Self-awareness
3	How do you handle disagreements or conflicts with others?	Relationship management, self-regulation
4	How do you perceive and respond to the emotions of others?	Social awareness, empathy
5	What triggers a negative emotion from you?	Self-awareness, impulse control
6	Do you have difficulty saying no, even when you want to? Why or why not?	Boundaries, self-management
7	How do you generally release your emotions?	Self-regulation, stress management
8	Do you generally read others well? Why or why not?	Social awareness, empathy
9	What do you need from others when you feel exposed or vulnerable?	Emotional expression, trust-building
10	Can you think of a time when your emotions influenced a significant decision? What was the outcome?	Emotional reasoning, decision-making

TABLE 4.1 (Continued)

#	Prompt	EI Component(s) Addressed
11	How should you shift your communication style based on others' emotions?	Social intelligence, adaptability
12	Have you ever misread someone's emotions? What happened, and what did you learn from it?	Social awareness, self-reflection
13	How do you handle receiving constructive criticism?	Self-management, growth mindset
14	Describe a time when you had to manage emotions in a professional setting. What strategies did you use?	Emotional regulation, workplace EI
15	How do you balance empathy with assertiveness under challenging conversations?	Relationship management, leadership

WHAT IS CULTURAL INTELLIGENCE?

Contemporary business leaders with interpersonal capabilities and stress management skills will effectively respond to opportunities and challenges in a socially diverse work environment, showing a higher multicultural competence (Chrobot-Mason & Leslie, 2012). *Why is this critical today?* Leaders face increasingly complex and subtle differences among employees reflected in team compositions, professions, individual business units, and corporate identities, to name a few (Earley & Mosakowski, 2004; Granow & Asbrock, 2021; Stahl & Maznevski, 2021). Today's contemporary leaders must understand how work differs across cultures, how diverse teams function, how business is conducted across national borders, and how to be agile (Granow & Asbrock, 2021). This is the challenge of modern global leaders.

Modern business leaders must navigate diverse cultural landscapes in today's globalized environment. **Cultural intelligence** (CQ), introduced by Earley (2002) and grounded in Sternberg and Detterman's (1986) framework on multiple loci of intelligence, refers to an individual's capacity for cultural adaptation, which leverages cognitive, motivational, and behavioral competencies (Earley, 2002). Research highlights that CQ is primarily an individual-level capability, yet its impact extends across organizations, influencing how leaders and teams effectively interact with people from different backgrounds. For business leaders, CQ is essential for managing diverse teams and excelling in expatriate assignments and long-term international engagements. Understanding and applying CQ is integral to self-leadership, ensuring leaders can engage across cultures with agility, confidence, and strategic insight.

Earley and Mosakowski (2004) noted two major CQ types. The first is organizational CQ, which matters most when leaders move into or interact with new organizations. When faced with a new organizational culture, a lack of organizational CQ can contribute to individual and corporate failures (Alon & Higgins, 2005). The second type of awareness is related to geographic and ethnic culture (Earley & Mosakowski, 2004). This is the focus of our self-leadership section.

Hofstede (1984) outlined the various cultural indicators commonly associated with CQ that modern business leaders should comprehend. Schermerhorn and Bachrach (2017) further described these indicators. Hofstede (1984) identified five cultural dimensions: **power distance**, **uncertainty avoidance**, **individualism-collectivism**, **masculinity-femininity**, and **time orientation**. The five dimensions are explained in Table 4.2.

These cultural dimensions contribute to CQ, but Schermerhorn and Bachrach (2017) caution against generalizing entire countries, as micro-cultures exist within regions. Today's business leaders must intentionally navigate cultural differences within their global organizations or international customer bases, demonstrating the interpersonal awareness required for modern business success.

CQ encompasses the skillful navigation of cultural elements with readiness, openness, and adaptability. Rosen and Digh (2001) introduced the concept of **global literacy** as a critical leadership competency for business success. Global literacy involves seeing, thinking, acting, and mobilizing in culturally mindful ways (Rosen & Digh, 2001; Shliakhovchuk, 2021). This perspective aligns closely with the principles of CQ, emphasizing the importance of cultural awareness and adaptability to effective leadership.

TABLE 4.2 Cultural Dimensions and Business Implications

Cultural Dimension	*Description*
Power Distance	Societal acceptance of unequal power distribution varies across cultures. High-power distance cultures emphasize respect for age and status, while moderate cultures embrace informality. This difference can confuse visitors from more casual environments.
Uncertainty Avoidance	Societal tolerance for risk and change varies. High uncertainty-avoidance cultures favor structure and predictability, while lower uncertainty-avoidance cultures embrace flexibility and openness to change.
Individualism-Collectivism	Societal values of individual accomplishments and self-interest differ, with the United States ranking highest in individualism, while collectivist cultures prioritize group success over personal recognition.
Masculinity-Femininity	Societal values of assertiveness and material success (masculinity) over relationships and quality of life (femininity) differ. Conservative cultures may emphasize traditional gender roles, posing challenges for those used to more progressive attitudes.
Time Orientation	Societal prioritization of short-term versus long-term goals. Some cultures emphasize immediate results and instant gratification, while others value persistence, patience, and strategic planning for long-term success.

COMBINING EI AND CQ

Since the clamor for more global leaders began decades ago, globalization has only accelerated, increasing the dynamics that leaders in today's workplaces face. For example, Riggio, Murphy, and Pirozzolo (2002) presented a strong case that global leaders must possess more than high intelligence quotients. **Intelligence Quotient** (IQ) is a standardized measure to assess human intelligence through various cognitive tasks, including reasoning, problem-solving, and memory (Kovacs & Conway, 2019). Riggio et al. (2002) asserted that intelligence is a multidimensional construct with several types, and, most importantly, different kinds of intelligence are needed for effective situational leadership, which we have already discussed.

Similarly, Alon and Higgins (2005) describe the three intelligences shown in Table 4.3 as the core of global leadership and further explain that the development of global leaders includes these intelligences. While the latter two are still emerging, substantial evidence indicates that the interdependence of EI and CQ will increase for future leaders. Scholars are increasingly critical and mindful that the hope of CQ is not overhyped (Fang et al., 2018).

EI and CQ as Keys to Success

EI is crucial to success in both work and life (Alon & Higgins, 2005). A popular EI assessment tool, the Mayer-Salovey-Caruso Emotional Intelligence Test or MSCEIT (MSCEIT, n.d.), can quantify this emphasis on emotions. The MSCEIT measures emotional intelligence in a way similar to an IQ test. It utilizes emotional problem-solving instead of a

TABLE 4.3 Three Forms of Intelligence for Modern Self Leaders

Form of Intelligence	*Description*	*Example Leadership Action*
Rational and Logic-Based Intelligence (IQ and Cognition)	Verbal and quantitative intelligence, measured by traditional IQ tests or tests of problem-solving and analytical thinking.	A CEO uses quantitative analysis to drive business strategies, relying on data-driven decisions to forecast growth and risk management.
Emotional Intelligence (EI)	The ability to recognize, understand, and manage one's own emotions and the emotions of others.	A supervisor fosters a team environment by actively listening to employee concerns, showing empathy, and managing conflicts constructively, which boosts team morale and performance.
Cultural Intelligence (CQ)	The capacity to interact effectively with people from different cultural backgrounds, involving adaptability and awareness of cultural differences.	The manager of a global marketing team adapts campaign strategies to resonate with local cultures by incorporating diverse cultural perspectives into the advertising process.

self-reported inventory. Participants are asked to solve several EI problems. Caruso (2005), co-author of the MSCEIT, indicates that the test examines four different but related emotional intelligence abilities:

1. **Perceiving emotions**—the ability to accurately recognize how you and those around you are feeling;
2. **Using emotions**—the ability to generate emotions and use emotions in cognitive tasks such as problem-solving and creativity;
3. **Understanding emotions**—the capacity to comprehend intricate emotions and the connections between them, including how feelings evolve from one state to another; and
4. **Managing emotions**—the ability to intelligently integrate the data of emotions in yourself and others to devise effective strategies to help you achieve positive outcomes.

These abilities are often called interpersonal and intrapersonal or, more generally, referred to as "soft skills." Nonetheless, the competency of leaders today cannot be overstated. The connection between leaders with a high EI and their success in diverse workplaces is clear. As Kamps and Engelbrecht (2011) observed in their empirical study, there is a positive relationship between EI and attitudes toward diversity. Antonakis et al. (2009) explained that emotionally intelligent employees can effectively manage diverse interactions and value individual differences. Further, the insights from EI studies also seem appropriate for addressing issues of conflict associated with a diverse workplace. EI can reduce conflict in diverse work groups (Lillis & Tian, 2009). Lillis and Tian (2009) found that EI has a more significant positive impact on the performance of gender-diverse teams than homogenous work groups (see also Clark & Polesello, 2017). According to Ayoko and Konrad (2012), leaders of diverse work groups should manage emotions to assist with diverse teams' performance and conflict resolution.

Relatedly, CQ allows individuals to read and navigate emotions across cultures and cultural differences. Scholars note CQ's three key components: knowledge, mindfulness, and behavioral skills (Thomas & Inkson, 2004). CQ enables individuals to understand and act appropriately across various cultures, requiring the ability to gather, process, and respond effectively to emotions in each situation (Thomas, 2006; Mammadov & Wald, 2025). EI, which involves perceiving, using, understanding, and managing emotions, extends into CQ when leaders navigate culturally diverse individuals, situations, and environments (Mammadov & Wald, 2025). Recent research indicates the interdependence of EI and CQ is persistent, which is notable for future leaders (Mammadov & Wald, 2025). Combining EI and CQ into global mindsets is tied to positive outcomes (Mammadov & Wald, 2025).

Research-based consulting firms like the Center for Cultural Intelligence have helped corporations like McDonald's, Coca-Cola, and Walmart improve employee CQ by offering diagnostic tools, training, and development (Center for Cultural Intelligence, 2025). They are working to assess and develop cultural intelligence, intercultural effectiveness, and cultural competency in businesses worldwide. These organizations understand the importance of building bridges and removing barriers to working and relating effectively across cultures. Leaders should understand how to interact effectively with co-workers, and supervisors must understand how to use emotions to motivate employees (see Chapter 7) and understand clients (see Chapter 15), especially across cultures (Crowne, 2009). These competencies are crucial in global or multinational organizations.

In summary, EI remains highly relevant today when paired with CQ. Binsaeed et al. (2023) suggest that the nexus of emotional and cultural intelligence is a strong pathway toward achieving innovative performance. EI and CQ are part of global mindsets (Mammadov & Wald, 2025) and innovation mindsets (Binsaeed et al., 2023). The work of Binsaeed et al. (2023)bolsters resiliency and adaptability to technological advancements (see also Chapter 12).

These constructs are distinct and do not always overlap. CQ is focused on aspects of an interaction that are specifically related to culture (Earley & Ang, 2003; Ang et al., 2004), which are not always associated with emotions. Furthermore, some elements of EI are not facets of CQ. For example, perceiving and understanding one's own emotion is an intrapersonal process that one's CQ will not likely influence because it involves accurately recognizing aspects of oneself (Crowne, 2009). How an individual generates an emotion is also an intrapersonal component that CQ does not likely influence because this is an individually based process.

Yet, many scholars state the CQ contains a "heart or emotional" component (Westby, 2007), indicating that EI is very much a part of CQ. Despite conflicting research, we look toward the future and see where, in cross-cultural interactions, adapting emotions to what is most appropriate in the situational context is a skill not only of an emotionally intelligent person but also of a culturally intelligent individual. As CQ requires individuals to develop and expand their ideas about appropriate behaviors (Earley & Peterson, 2004), this also applies to emotional events. Thus, similar competencies are involved in EI and CQ.

These two intelligences will be linked in the changing workplace, and their power will be realized when leaders can effectively manage their emotions and appreciate the depths of emotions in their frequent interpersonal interactions. Today's business leaders will experience a barrage of cultural differences that beget positive and negative emotions, which they must resolve with courage and perseverance. Building the muscles that work EI and CQ requires resilience and experience.

Developing and Training to Build EI and CQ in Tandem

In the coming decades, the new workforce will increasingly comprise people of color, immigrants, the disabled, and women (Hewins-Maroney & Williams, 2013; Flores et al., 2021). Such changes suggest that future workplaces will look dramatically different than they have in the past. The implications of these changes extend to individuals, teams, organizations, and customers. This is consistent with Chen et al.'s (2012) statement that "the dramatic increase of residents from different cultural profiles in the United States should result in not only a more diverse workforce but also a culturally diverse customer base" (p. 94, see also Clark & Polesello, 2017). We consider this again in the Business (Part 3) and Client Leadership (Part 4) sections.

As Clark and Polesello (2017) point out in their research findings, too often diversity tends to focus on a few hot-button issues. Further, studies seem predisposed to examine diversity issues related to age, sex, and race, typically in US contexts (Shore et al., 2009; Davaei et al., 2022). This has translated into reactive performative corporate training, emphasizing diversity to avoid legal issues (Clark & Polesello, 2017). We are pushing for a more proactive approach. The work of developing global leaders with these two intelligence forms will not only allow organizations to achieve a universal sense of belonging for all employees, which we focus on more in upcoming chapters, but also leverage diverse workforces for a strong competitive advantage.

Organizations that embrace EI and CQ will be rewarded with compelling performances from business leaders on this highly global stage and within their culturally dynamic and diverse workplaces. These interpersonal and intrapersonal competencies need to be developed for internal interactions with supervisors, colleagues, and key stakeholders, as well as externally for countless exchanges and necessary relationship-building with an increasingly diverse customer base. The adjustments to a post-COVID world and growing mental health concerns should compel all business leaders to grapple with their role in creating a just and welcoming community regardless of where they are in the world and workplace. This new normal requires mindfulness, awareness, and emotional, social, and cultural intelligence more centrally in their work lives (Watson, 2023).

Exercise 4.2 Global Leadership Role Play

Preparation: Explain the importance of EI CQ in the workplace. Discuss how understanding and managing emotions and navigating cultural differences are crucial for effective global leadership.

Scenario Distribution: Divide into small groups (3–4 members each). Provide each group with a role-play scenario card. Scenarios should involve emotional and cultural elements. To deepen learning, we offer five example scenarios/roles to try out before crafting new scenarios.

Scenario 1: A diverse team is working on a project, and Alex needs to provide constructive feedback to Mei. Alex comes from a culture that values straightforward communication, while Mei comes from a culture where criticism is often conveyed indirectly to preserve harmony and save face. As Alex prepares to give feedback, he must navigate Mei's cultural norms to ensure the conversation is productive and respectful. Mei, in turn, may find Alex's direct approach uncomfortable and could struggle to respond openly. Observers will analyze the interaction, noting how effectively Alex adjusts his communication style and how Mei reacts to the feedback.

Scenario 2: Sara and Raj work together on a collaborative project but misunderstand deadlines due to their different communication styles. Sara comes from a high-context culture, where messages are often implied rather than explicitly stated. In contrast, Raj comes from a low-context culture, where clarity and direct communication are expected. Sara may assume that indirect cues are enough to indicate her concerns, while Raj expects firm and clearly defined deadlines. As they discuss the project timeline, observers will assess how well they bridge their communication gap and whether they find a mutual understanding.

Scenario 3: Hana has recently joined a team that makes decisions independently, but she comes from a culture where collective decision-making is the norm. As she tries to integrate into the team, she finds it difficult to adapt to the expectation of making decisions autonomously. Meanwhile, James, an established team member, is accustomed to working independently and may see Hana's preference for group consensus as inefficient. Their interaction will highlight the challenges of reconciling different decision-making styles, and observers will evaluate how well they adapt to each other's approaches to foster collaboration.

Scenario 4: Emily is experiencing personal issues affecting her work, but she comes from a culture where discussing personal matters in a professional setting is uncommon. Her colleague, Marcus, notices her struggles and wants to offer support but is uncertain how to do so in a way that respects her cultural norms. As Marcus approaches Emily, he must balance sensitivity with genuine concern, while Emily may struggle to open up or maintain professional distance. Observers will assess how Marcus navigates this delicate situation and whether the interaction produces a productive outcome for both colleagues.

Scenario 5: Due to their contrasting leadership styles, Maria and Tom face challenges while managing a project. Maria comes from a culture that values hierarchical decision-making, where authority and structure guide the process. Tom, however, comes from a culture that emphasizes egalitarianism and collaborative decision-making, favoring open dialogue and shared leadership. Their differing approaches lead to tension as they determine how best to structure the project. Observers will analyze their interactions to see if they can find a balance between structure and collaboration while maintaining efficiency and mutual respect.

Role-Play Performances: Each group should perform their role-play. Encourage each other to fully engage with the scenarios and demonstrate their emotional and cultural intelligence. After each role-play, facilitate a brief discussion to reflect on:

- What strategies effectively managed the scenario's emotional and cultural aspects?
- How did the role-play enhance understanding of the situation?
- What could be improved in handling similar real-life situations?

Debrief and Reflection: After the role-plays are complete, lead a debriefing session to share insights and experiences connected to this chapter's lessons and the role-plays. Discuss:

- Key takeaways about handling emotional and cultural challenges in the workplace.
- Any new understanding of cultural norms and emotional responses.
- Strategies for applying these insights to improve workplace interactions and conflict resolution.

Positive associations between EI skills and effective managerial performance are verified across multiple studies, highlighting the importance of selecting candidates with strong EI attributes, particularly for leadership roles (Alon & Higgins, 2005; Dasborough et al., 2022). While progress has been made in integrating CQ into leadership development (Dasborough et al., 2022), there remains a pressing need for more CQ assessments tailored to specific industries, customer bases, and organizational contexts. Prioritizing EI and CQ in hiring can give organizations a competitive advantage over industry peers who overlook these competencies. However, hiring for EI and CQ alone is insufficient—businesses must also foster these competencies across leadership levels to fully leverage diverse workforces and excel in today's globalized business landscape. Corporate training programs should incorporate EI, CQ, and motivation into global leadership development initiatives, equipping leaders with the skills necessary for domestic and international business success. We will discuss this incorporation and motivation in future chapters. These elements enhance managerial effectiveness and drive long-term organizational resilience and agility in an increasingly interconnected world.

Finally, CQ and EI are crucial in shaping employees' perceptions of their supervisors. Research shows that when employees perceive their leaders as emotionally intelligent, they are more likely to feel satisfied that their needs are being met and aligned with organizational values (Zadel, 2008). Since perception strongly influences satisfaction, CQ is expected to impact employee engagement and overall workplace morale (Crowne, 2009; Fujimoto & Presbitero, 2022). Given the significant costs associated with training programs, organizations that invest in EI and CQ development can expect their leaders and employees to benefit, leading to more decisive leadership, improved job satisfaction, and a more cohesive organizational culture.

CONCLUSION

As we close this chapter, we offer that these two subsets of EI and CQ deserve the appropriate levels of hype to close the intelligence divide. Social intelligence is contemporary and calls for more research, and we have not been able to cover the many dimensions posited by scholars and educators over the years (e.g., Gardner, 1998). As outlined, EI and CQ are distinct constructs, but it is decidedly evident that their growing interdependence is compelling and valuable for leaders and organizations in today's tremendously diverse workplaces. We hope more scholars will help us unlock the secrets beyond the tethering of EI and CQ in practice.

We positioned this discussion of EI and CQ within our Self Leadership section as we seek to shift mindsets and grasp firmly the essentials individuals will need to learn and develop in contemporary business environments. Like the discipline of authentic leadership and the pursuit of one's leadership identity and style, EI and CQ are competencies that take nurturing, experience, and time. Like so many concepts under the phenomenon of leadership, there is rarely any mastery as conflicts, tensions, and failures are a constant part of the interpersonal conduct of business, particularly when engaged in the nuances of difference. Yet, with steadfast commitment, each of these abilities can mature in an individual so that time and time again, they will execute the appropriate action for the given situation. That action, grounded in this chapter's insights, exemplifies effective leadership.

As authors, we would be remiss if we did not highlight vital skill sets for business environments and life. EI and CQ can help an individual grow into a competent global leader who is poised and ready for dynamic interactions within the interconnectedness of the world's economics. Still, they also can benefit individuals in their relationships with family, friends, and partners. As long-time instructors of undergraduate and graduate students, we cannot help but appreciate them as whole persons and root for them to succeed in their future professions and personal lives. Much of our section on Self Leadership is our effort to achieve these goals twofold.

This chapter has outlined how EI and CQ equip leaders with different but related skills and mindsets to operate across diverse geographies, problems, teams, and markets. Together, these intelligences form a critical foundation for inclusive leadership, organizational agility, and sustainable competitive advantage. However, their impact depends on more than individual aptitude; organizations must intentionally develop and embed EI and CQ into their leadership training, talent management strategies, and corporate culture. Those who fail to close the intelligence divide risk stagnation in an era where diversity, adaptability, and human-centered leadership define success. The challenge for modern business leaders is clear: *Are you actively cultivating these essential skills or allowing outdated leadership models to limit your individual or organization's potential?*

DISCUSSION QUESTIONS

1. What factors are influencing the changing work environments?
2. What is emotional intelligence, and how can it build our reserves when we're faced with these changes at work?
3. What is the intrapersonal conduct of business all about?
4. What is cultural intelligence, and why is it growing in prominence in business?
5. How are EI and CQ connected?
6. How do EI and CQ competencies contribute to developing global leaders?
7. What are their weaknesses?
8. How do EI and CQ contribute to one's understanding of oneself?

Key Terms

- Intelligence Divide
- Emotional Intelligence
- Cultural Intelligence
- Power distance
- Uncertainty Avoidance
- Individualism-Collectivism
- Masculinity-Femininity
- Time Orientation
- Global Literacy
- Intelligence Quotient
- Perceiving Emotions
- Using Emotions
- Understanding Emotions
- Managing Emotions

CASE STUDY 4.1 NEXUS SOLUTIONS, A HYPOTHETICAL GLOBAL COMPANY

Introduction: This case study explores the leadership journey of Dr. Mei Ling, Chief Global Officer at Nexus Solutions, a multinational corporation specializing in renewable energy solutions. Dr. Mei Ling's success as a global leader is attributed to her exceptional EICQ, which have been instrumental in navigating diverse cultural landscapes and fostering a collaborative, inclusive work environment.

Background: Dr. Mei Ling's journey to becoming Chief Global Officer at Nexus Solutions reflects a career dedicated to sustainable development. She is a highly skilled professional with a PhD in Environmental Engineering and an MBA in International Business. Her career began in renewable energy research, where she worked with international teams and industry leaders, gaining valuable insights into global sustainability and cross-cultural collaboration.

Before joining Nexus Solutions, she held executive roles in multinational corporations focused on clean energy initiatives, honing her leadership abilities in strategic planning and stakeholder engagement. Known for her innovative solutions and strong ethical standards, Mei Ling has earned recognition in the renewable energy sector.

Mei Ling's leadership style is distinguished by her emphasis on EI and CQ. She believes successful global leadership requires technical expertise, understanding, and empathy for diverse perspectives. This holistic approach has enabled Mei Ling to foster a collaborative and inclusive organizational culture at Nexus Solutions, where innovation thrives amid cultural diversity. Yet, she faces challenges (see Table 4.4).

TABLE 4.4 Leadership Challenges for Nexuxs Solutions

Challenge	*Description*	*Key Question*
Navigating Complex Global Markets	Mei Ling must navigate varying global market regulations, cultural norms, and business practices. Success hinges on customized strategies for market entry, partnerships, and compliance with environmental laws.	How can modern business leaders develop strategies that incorporate cultural dimensions?
Cultural Integration & Team Cohesion	Mei Ling must unite diverse teams internationally, bridge cultural gaps, enhance cross-cultural communication, and foster a shared purpose.	How can modern business leaders leverage EI to strengthen diverse teams?
Stakeholder Engagement & Relationship Building	Mei Ling must build lasting trust with government officials, community leaders, and business partners, which requires cultural sensitivity, adaptability, and strong interpersonal skills.	How can modern business leaders combine EI and CQ to align stakeholder relationships?

TABLE 4.1 (Continued)

Challenge	*Description*	*Key Question*
Emotional Resilience in Leadership	Mei Ling must manage stress, regulatory challenges, and market fluctuations while maintaining composure and sound decision-making in her global organization.	How does resilience factor into emotional intelligence?

Task: Provide four comprehensive recommendations for Mei Ling. Make sure to connect the recommendations to key chapter concepts. Present the recommendations to a larger group for feedback and discussion.

REFERENCES

Alon, I., & Higgins, J. M. (2005). Global leadership success through emotional and cultural intelligences. *Business Horizons, 48*(6), 501–512. https://doi.org/10.1016/j.bushor.2005.04.003

Ang, S., Van Dyne, L., Koh, C., & Ng, K. Y. (2004). The measure of cultural intelligence. *Academy of Management Meeting Proceedings, 2004*, 1–5.

Antonakis, J., Ashkanasy, N. M., & Dasborough, M. T. (2009). Does leadership need emotional intelligence? *The Leadership Quarterly, 20*(2), 247–261. https://doi.org/10.1016/j.leaqua.2009.01.006

Aslam, U., Ilyas, M., Imran, M. K., & Ur Rahman, U. (2016). Intelligence and its impact on managerial effectiveness and career success: Evidence from the insurance sector of Pakistan. *Journal of Management and Development, 35*(4), 505–516.

Ayoko, O. B., & Konrad, A. M. (2012). Leaders' transformational, conflict, and emotion management behaviors in culturally diverse workgroups. *Equality, Diversity and Inclusion: An International Journal, 31*(8), 694–724. https://doi.org/10.1108/02610151211277581

Binsaeed, R. H., Yousaf, Z., Grigorescu, A., Condrea, E., & Nassani, A. A. (2023 July 13). Emotional intelligence, innovative work behavior, and cultural intelligence reflection on innovation performance in the healthcare industry. *Brain Sciences, 13*(7), 1071. https://doi.org/10.3390/brainsci13071071

Boyatzis, R. E., & Sala, F. (2004). The emotional competence inventory (ECI). In G. Geher (Ed.), *Measuring emotional intelligence* (pp. 147–180). Nova Science Publishers, Inc.

Bratianu, C., & Paiuc, D. (2025). Emotional and cultural intelligence impact on multicultural leadership. In Veronica Grosu, Anatol Melega, and Anamaria Bores (Eds.), *Emotional intelligence and networking competencies: Implications for effective leadership* (pp. 15–34). Springer Nature Switzerland.

Bryan, L., Rall, W., Fraser, J., & Oppenheim, J. (1999). *Race for the world: Strategies to build a great global firm*. Harvard Business School Press.

Cartwright, S., & Pappas, C. (2008). Emotional intelligence, its measurement and implications for the workplace. *International Journal of Management Reviews, 10*(2), 149–171. https://doi.org/10.1111/j.1468-2370.2007.00220.x

Caruso, D. (2005). A practical guide to the MSCEIT. Retrieved February 8, 2005, from http://www.emotionalintelligencemhs.com/1APractical.asp?GUID=&#MSCEIT

Center for Cultural Intelligence. (2025, July 16). CQ certification (July 16–17, 2025).

Chanyasak, T., Koseoglu, M. A., King, B., & Aladag, O. F. (2022). Business model adaptation as a strategic response to crises: Navigating the COVID-19 pandemic. *International Journal of Tourism Cities, 8*(3), 616–635.

Chen, X. P., Liu, D., & Portnoy, R. (2012). A multilevel investigation of motivational cultural intelligence, organizational diversity climate, and cultural sales: Evidence from U.S. real estate firms. *Journal of Applied Psychology, 97*(1), 93–106. https://doi.org/10.1037/a0024697

Chrobot-Mason, D., & Leslie, J. B. (2012). The role of multicultural competence and emotional intelligence in managing diversity. *The Psychologist-Manager Journal, 15*(4), 219–236. https://doi.org/10.1080/10887156.2012.730442

Clark, J. M., & Polesello, D. (2017). Emotional and cultural intelligence in diverse workplaces: Getting out of the box. *Industrial and Commercial Training, 49*(7/8), 337–349. https://doi.org/10.1108/ICT-06-2017-0040

Crowne, K. A. (2009). The relationships among social intelligence, emotional intelligence and cultural intelligence. *Organization Management Journal, 6*(3), 148–163.

Dasborough, M. T., Ashkanasy, N. M., Humphrey, R. H., Harms, P. D., Credé, M., & Wood, D. (2022). Does leadership still not need emotional intelligence? Continuing "The Great EI Debate". *The Leadership Quarterly, 33*(6), 101539.

Davaei, M., Gunkel, M., Veglio, V., & Taras, V. (2022). The influence of cultural intelligence and emotional intelligence on conflict occurrence and performance in global virtual teams. *Journal of International Management, 28*(4), 100969.

Earley, P. C. (2002). Redefining interactions across cultures and organizations: Moving forward with cultural intelligence. *Research in Organizational Behavior, 24*, 271–299. https://doi.org/10.1016/S0191-3085(02)24008-3

Earley, P. C., & Ang, S. (2003). *Cultural intelligence: Individual interactions across cultures*. Stanford Business Books.

Earley, P. C., & Mosakowski, E. (2004). Cultural intelligence. *Harvard Business Review, 82*(10), 139–140.

Earley, P. C., & Peterson, R. S. (2004). The elusive cultural chameleon: Cultural intelligence as a new approach to intercultural training for the global manager. *Academy of Management Learning & Education, 3*(1), 100–115.

Fang, F., Schei, V., & Selart, M. (2018). Hype or hope? A new look at the research on cultural intelligence. *International Journal of Intercultural Relations, 66*, 148–171.

Flores, L. Y., Settles, I., McGillen, G. G., & Davis, T. M. (2021). Critical contributions to scholarship on women and work: Celebrating 50 years of progress and looking ahead to a new decade. *Journal of Vocational Behavior, 126*, 103490.

Fujimoto, Y., & Presbitero, A. (2022). Culturally intelligent supervisors: Inclusion, intercultural cooperation, and psychological safety. *Applied Psychology, 71*(2), 407–435.

Gardner, H. (1998). A multiplicity of intelligences. *Scientific American Presents, 9*(4), 18–23.

Goleman, D. (1997). *Emotional intelligence*. Bantam Books, Inc.

Goleman, D. (2020, December 22). *What people (still) get wrong about emotional intelligence*. Harvard Business Review. Retrieved from https://hbr.org/2020/12/what-people-still-get-wrong-about-emotional-intelligence

Granow, M., & Asbrock, F. (2021). A framework for culturally diverse teams and the importance of agility: Findings from a qualitative study. *International Studies of Management & Organization, 51*(1), 47–68.

Hewins-Maroney, B., & Williams, E. (2013). The role of public administrators in responding to changing workforce demographics: Global challenges to preparing a diverse workforce. *Public Administration Quarterly, 37*(3), 456–490. Retrieved from www.jstor.org.ezp3.lib.umn.edu/stable/24372115

Hofstede, G. H. (1984). *Culture's consequences: International differences in work-related values*. SAGE Publications.

Jonck, P., & Swanepoel, E. (2015). Exploring the theoretical link between cultural and emotional intelligence: A system analysis for human resource management. *South African Journal of Business Management, 46*(4), 1–9. https://doi.org/10.4102/sajbm.v46i4.111

Kamps, J. M., & Engelbrecht, A. S. (2011). The influence of emotional intelligence on diversity complexity cognition and the attitude towards diversity. *South African Journal of Business Management, 42*(3), 37–48. http://hdl.handle.net/10019.1/19256

Kovacs, K., & Conway, A. R. (2019). What is IQ? Life beyond "general intelligence". *Current Directions in Psychological Science, 28*(2), 189–194.

Landry, L. (2019). Why emotional intelligence is important in leadership. *Harvard Business School Online*. https://online.hbs.edu/blog/post/emotional-intelligence-in-leadership.

Lillis, M. P., & Tian, R. G. (2009). Cross-cultural communication and emotional intelligence: Inferences from case studies of gender diverse groups. *Marketing Intelligence & Planning, 27*(3), 428–438. https://doi.org/10.1108/02634500910955272

Mammadov, A., & Wald, A. (2025). The role of cultural intelligence and emotional intelligence in the internationalization of SMEs: Does global mindset matter? *Management International Review*. Advance Online Publication. https://doi.org/10.1007/s11575-024-00561-5

Matthews, G., Zeidner, M., & Roberts, R. D. (2002). Introduction. In G. Matthews, M. Zeidner, & R. D. Roberts (Eds.), *Emotional intelligence: Science and myth* (pp. 3–29). MIT Press.

Osland, J. S. (2017). An overview of the global leadership literature. In J. S. Osland (Ed.), *Global leadership* (pp. 57–116). Routledge.

Riggio, R. E., Murphy, S. E., & Pirozzolo, F. J. (Eds.). (2002). *Multiple intelligences and leadership*. Lawrence Erlbaum Associates.

Rosen, R., & Digh, P. (2001). Developing globally literate leaders. Retrieved January 3, 2004, from http://www1.sim.edu.sg/sim/pub/mag/sim_pub_mag_list.cfm?ID=961

Roy, S. R. (Ed.). (2015). *Promoting trait emotional intelligence in leadership and education*. IGI Global.

Salovey, P., & Mayer, J. D. (1990). Emotional intelligence. *Imagination, Cognition & Personality, 9*(3), 185–211.

Salovey, P., & Pizarro, D. (2003). The value of emotional intelligence. In R. J. Sternberg, J. Lautrey, & T. I. Lubart (Eds.), *Models of intelligence: International perspectives* (pp. 263–278). American Psychological Association.

Schermerhorn, J. R. Jr., & Bachrach, D. G. (2017). *Exploring management* (6th ed.). Wiley.

Shliakhovchuk, E. (2021). After cultural literacy: New models of intercultural competency for life and work in a VUCA world. *Educational Review, 73*(2), 229–250.

Shore, L. M., Chung-Herrera, B. G., Dean, M. A., Ehrhart, K. H., Jung, D. I., Randel, A. E., & Singh, G. (2009). Diversity in organizations: Where are we now and where are we going? *Human Resource Management Review, 19*(2), 117–133. https://doi.org/10.1016/j.hrmr.2008.10.004

Smith, L., Heaven, P. C. L., & Ciarrochi, J. (2008). Trait emotional intelligence, conflict communication patterns, and relationship satisfaction. *Personality & Individual Differences, 44*(6), 1314–1325.

Stahl, G. K., & Maznevski, M. L. (2021). Unraveling the effects of cultural diversity in teams: A retrospective of research on multicultural work groups and an agenda for future research. *Journal of International Business Studies, 52*(1), 4.

Sternberg, R. J., & Detterman, D. K. (1986). *What is intelligence: Contemporary viewpoints on its nature and definition*. Ablex.

The Mayer-Salovey-Caruso Emotional Intelligence Test (MSCEIT). (n.d.). Consortium for Research on Emotional Intelligence in Organizations. Retrieved March 29, 2023, from https://www.eiconsortium.org/measures/msceit.html

Thomas, D. C. (2006). Domain and development of cultural intelligence: The importance of mindfulness. *Group & Organization Management, 31*(1), 78–99.

Thomas, D. C., & Inkson, K. (2004). *Cultural intelligence: People skills for global business*. Berrett-Koehler.

Trading Economics. (2023). United States imports by country. Retrieved June 22, 2025, from https://tradingeconomics.com/united-states/imports-by-country

Watson, L. W. (2023). *How to leverage emotional, social, and cultural intelligence to enhance professional lives*. Advice & News.

Westby, C. (2007). Being smart in a diverse world. *Communication Disorders Quarterly, 29*(1), 7–13.

Zadel, A. (2008). Do emotionally intelligent leaders have more satisfied employees? *International Journal of Management & Enterprise Development, 5*(5), 590–608.

CHAPTER 5

Social Identity and Intersectionality

CHAPTER OVERVIEW

The final chapter in the Self Leadership section focuses on social identity (the parts) and intersectionality (the whole). Business leaders who understand who they are and their impact on others from a power, privilege, and system perspective are better equipped to lead effectively in diverse workplaces. Social identity constitutes membership to one or more groups, profoundly affecting a leader's self-schema. Further, their understanding of intersectionality is essential, allowing them to examine social identities more explicitly by placing them within a macro-level analysis during a particular social or historical period within larger, interlocking systems of advantage and access.

Before wrapping up Self-Leadership, readers should revisit the previous chapter on authentic leadership. Authentic leadership demands deep self-examination and a lifelong commitment to self-discovery. Modern business leaders must prioritize uncovering their authenticity and empowering their team members to express their true selves at work. This is critical for fostering employee satisfaction, cultivating a positive company culture, retaining top talent, and building healthy organizational cultures.

Social structures create differential opportunities for individuals to express their true self in the workplace. As workplaces become more diverse, contemporary business leaders must recognize that systems favor some and exclude others. In our classes, we often ask students: *Who are privileged? Who are marginalized? How does power impact leadership? How are power structures kept in balance?* Further, *who am I within this complex power, privilege, and identity system? What is my role in addressing power?* These core inquiries are essential.

Today's business leaders must understand social identities (the parts) and the framework of intersectionality (the whole). To be effective, modern leaders must develop their identities and styles as leaders and cultivate their social intelligences, such as emotional intelligence and cultural intelligence. The previous chapter covered these concepts and their power when leveraged together. Modern business leaders must delve into social identity and intersectionality and understand who they are within a diverse tapestry of differences to be better colleagues, professionals, and leaders.

DOI: 10.4324/9781003474647-6

SOCIAL IDENTITY

The term **social identity** has its roots in social psychology. It was coined by Tajfel (1982), who emphasized the role of intergroup dynamics and the perception of group membership regarding identity. Tajfel (1982) defined social identity as "that part of an individual's self-concept that derives from their knowledge of their membership in a social group (or groups) together with the value and emotional significance attached to that membership" (1982, p. 2). These groups are socially constructed; they are designed and accepted by the people in a particular society and create categories, such as class, race, sex, gender identity, sexual orientation, ability, religion, age cohorts, and socio-economic status.

Membership in one or more groups is foundational to one's identity. Weber (2010) writes,

> At the individual level, race, class, gender and sexuality are fundamental sources of identity for all of us: how we see ourselves, who we think we are. They are, in fact, so fundamental that to be without them would be like being without an identity at all. (p. 119)

Social identity groups are based on individuals' physical, social, and mental characteristics. They are sometimes overt and transparent, and just as often not; sometimes, they are described as visible versus invisible identities. They can be self-claimed and frequently ascribed by others.

In Beverly Tatum's (2000) seminal article "The Complexity of Identity: 'Who am I?'" she analyzes the factors that contribute to one's identity and the societal factors that influence identity. She explains that combined individual traits, family connections, previous encounters, and the societal and political environment shape our identity. The amalgamation of our past, present, and future experiences molds who we are. The development of social identities happens throughout one's lifetime and is a process of naming and accepting critical aspects of who one is as an individual. Identity development and acceptance are influenced by messages received in an individual's environment. Research has unearthed many social identity development models, each with nuance, depth, and layers.

Exercise 5.1 Mapping Social Identities

Social identity consists of various aspects, including personal, cultural, and social characteristics. This activity will help you visualize and reflect on these elements using digital tools.

Materials and Digital Tools Needed: For this exercise, you will need computers or tablets with internet access and digital mapping tools (e.g., Canva, MindMeister, Google Slides, Miro, etc.). You will use a digital mapping tool to represent your social identity visually. Look for or listen to a brief tutorial on creating and customizing a digital map using the tool. You will learn to add text, images, and links to enhance your map.

Identifying Social Identity Factors: Think about the different components that make up your social identity. These may include:

- **Personal Identity**—Interests, values, personality traits
- **Cultural Identity**—Ethnicity, religion, language, cultural practices
- **Social Identity**—Gender, socioeconomic status, occupation, roles within family or community
- **Relational Identity**—Relationships, social networks

Make a list of these factors for your digital map.

Creating Your Digital Social Identity Map (Should take about 30 minutes)

1. Open the digital mapping tool and create a new project.
2. Start by creating a central node labeled "My Social Identity."
3. Add branches or nodes for each social identity category (e.g., Personal, Cultural, Social, Relational). Populate these nodes with the factors you identified.
4. Use images, icons, colors, and text to represent the different aspects of your identity visually. Add links to relevant articles, personal documents, or videos.

Reflection and Analysis: Once you've completed your digital map, write a reflection addressing the following prompts:

- What did you discover about yourself through creating your digital social identity map?
- How do different aspects of your social identity intersect and influence your experiences and interactions?
- Did you notice any surprising insights or patterns in your map?
- How does your social identity impact your perspective and behavior in various situations?

Sharing and Discussion: Share your digital maps with your peers, which is especially effective in small groups. Consider:

- What common themes or differences do you observe in your peers' maps?
- How can understanding your and others' social identities enhance empathy and collaboration?

If you have time, culminate smaller group discussions into larger ones with your peers.

INGROUPS AND OUTGROUPS

Tajfel and Turner (1979) wrote of group conflict early in forming their concept of social identities. Their idea of **ingroup** and **outgroup** refers to forming identities through a process of differentiation that is relative and flexible, depending on one's engagements. This theory anticipates specific intergroup behaviors based on perceived group status differences, the perceived legitimacy and stability of those differences, and the perceived ability to move from one group to another (Benwell & Stokoe, 2006). In essence, while acknowledging the positive aspects of defining one's social identities, business leaders must recognize the tensions arising from differences are just one part of a complex and multifaceted social landscape.

Ingroup favoritism (ingroup bias) is an effect in which people give preferential treatment to others when perceived as being in the same ingroup (Turner & Reynolds, 2001). Ingroup favoritism occurs because of a psychological need for positive distinctiveness. It happens when people perceive their group to have high status, legitimacy, stability, and permeability (Ellemers & Barreto, 2001). How this plays out in the workplace is that individuals may identify strongly with their ingroup members and, thus, be more inclined to align with people who are similar in age, gender, ethnicity, or other characteristics and spend less time with people who are different from them, inevitably leading to outgroups (Tajfel et al., 1971).

According to Northouse (2021), an outgroup member does not consider themselves (i.e., identify with) a part of the larger group. Outgroup members are usually uninterested in pursuing the same goals as the ingroup for multiple reasons. Outgroups can often be subject to prejudice and discrimination from members of the ingroup. Outgroups may report a lack of understanding, unfair treatment, and feeling undervalued. Outgroups are marked by a sense of difference and frequently, though not always, by some degree of antagonism. In other words, outgroups are those within an organization who do not feel they belong.

Hogg (2001) describes the **social identity theory of leadership** as a group process generated by social categorization and prototype-based processes associated with social identity. Social categorization divides the social world into groups individuals belong to (ingroups) and groups individuals do not belong to (outgroups); these groups are prototypes (Hogg, 2001). These prototypes are context-specific, multidimensional attributes that prescribe attitudes, feelings, and behaviors that characterize and distinguish one group from others (Hogg, 2001, p. 187). This process is called **depersonalization** because people are not viewed as unique and multifaceted individuals but as matches to the relevant ingroup or outgroup prototype. Depersonalization refers to the change in the perception of others toward group members (Hogg, 2001; Anjewierden et al., 2024).

These ideas were initially integrated and formalized by a large body of research, which shows that people are more receptive to more prototypical leaders, which means that they represent the usual or quintessential version of a relevant group (Hogg, 2001). In particular, this relationship was confirmed in two meta-analyses. The first included 35 independent studies with over 6,000 participants; the second included 128 studies with over 30,000 participants (Steffens et al., 2021). Notably, their later study confirmed this relationship was also present in the subset of studies that used experimental designs and were able to establish the causal impact of prototypicality (Steffens et al., 2021). They confirmed that more prototypical leaders are more favorably evaluated. This study showed leaders' group prototypicality predicted their behavioral impact—whether their leadership translated into others following (Haslam et al., 2022).

People tend to like members of their own group more than those outside their group. This could be because they see ingroup members as like themselves or similar to a positive image of the group or relate to them as extensions of themselves (Hogg, 2001; Anjewierden et al., 2024). Within the ingroup, members are more likely to appreciate those who are more prototypical than those who are less prototypical; modern business leaders must recognize this social attraction gradient.

Leveraging the metaphor of punk rock, Talmage et al. (2017) offer **individuation** and **deindividuation** as alternative terms. Individuation is how people find a balance between being themselves and being part of a larger group. It highlights the importance of self-expression and distinctness while still being connected to others. Individuation celebrates nonconformity, rebellion, and individual uniqueness to challenge power. Individuation allows individuals to express their true selves while contributing to community well-being. Deindividuation occurs when individuals feel they have lost their identity in a group and must conform. They can feel invisible; this can restrict self-expression and stifle actions that challenge the norm. As a result, it strengthens group unity but limits diversity. These notions are essential given today's news stories about scandals, often noting persons afraid to stand up for ethics (e.g., whistleblow) or stop bad behavior before and while it occurs.

Individuation empowers marginalized individuals to embrace their unique identities through self-expression and elite-challenging action (Talmage et al., 2017). Self-leaders must find and foster environments that promote personal expression and build community to counteract the adverse effects of deindividuation, exclusion, and outgrouping. They must also encourage individuation to foster a more inclusive community that celebrates diverse perspectives.

Gender Inequality and Prototypicality

Focusing on a better business world, a microcosm of society, organizations have long had prototype-based ingroups and outgroups. For example, we can trace today's gender inequality in the workplace back to ingroups of white men who were portrayed as the prototypical professionals in corporate America by a system that lacked women in leadership positions, had biases against mothers, enforced traditional gender roles and occupational segregation, and discriminated against women in hiring and promotion. In 2013, the Pew Research Center reported that while women were achieving more educationally and participating more in the workforce than before, polls indicated a widespread perception that full equality between men and women remained an elusive goal.

Women have made notable progress in education and the workforce, now comprising 51% of the US college-educated workforce; however, their labor force participation has plateaued, and they remain underrepresented in high-paying jobs and leadership roles (Schaeffer, 2024). Despite increasing representation in top occupations like medicine and law, women still earn only 82 cents for every dollar men earn, and they are underrepresented in leadership positions, holding only 11% of Fortune 500 CEO roles. Public opinion on whether being a woman makes it harder to succeed reflects clear ingroup and outgroup dynamics. Women are more likely than men to perceive gender as a barrier, with 58% of women versus 40% of men saying that being female hinders their ability to advance. In the workplace, this disparity continues, as 34% of women believe being a woman makes success more complex, compared to 21% of men. These views reinforce women's collective identity as an ingroup facing systemic challenges, while men, as the dominant outgroup, are less likely to see gender as a significant obstacle (Schaeffer, 2024). This should alarm business leaders.

As the name implies, ingroup members receive benefits not afforded to the outgroup members. In business environments, these benefits include tangible rewards such as better offices, newer equipment, more ideal assignments, and promotions/advancement and intangible rewards such as meaningful friendships at work and mentoring by senior leaders. Johnson (2022) writes that the ingroup/outgroup phenomenon remains alive in the workplace. Even when leaders build a team, they are more likely to select individuals who are similar in appearance, thinking, decision-making, and problem-solving (Johnson, 2022). These practices are discriminatory and harmful to organizational productivity, as research shows diverse teams are more innovative than homogeneous ones (Lyon, 2021). Unfortunately, instinct still triumphs over reason.

For leaders to intervene or, for that matter, to effectively change their organizations, they must understand the dimensions of power, privilege, and identity and how these dimensions play out in the workplace. Next, the ingroup/outgroup concepts are positioned alongside a framework called intersectionality. Intersectionality is designed to understand social identities at the multifaceted and systems levels. Business leaders must discover how intersectionality can help manage ingroups and outgroups and establish cultures celebrating differences. Authentic leadership (see Chapter 2) with effective styles (see Chapter 3) and high CQ and EI (see Chapter 4) also grasp intersectionality as a competitive advantage.

INTERSECTIONALITY

Moreover, Kimberlé Crenshaw (1989) introduced the concept of intersectionality to illustrate how interlocking power systems disproportionately impact marginalized individuals. Power dynamics within this framework are prevalent in organizations and society today. Modern Self Leaders must understand their intersectional positionalities and be prepared to work with clients, direct reports, supervisors, and community members who hold different positionalities.

Intersectionality examines social identities more explicitly by placing them within a macro-level analysis that tethers individual experience to membership in social groups during a particular social or historical period within larger, interlocking systems of advantage and access (Charmaine & Jones, 2014; Núñez et al., 2020). This complex view of identity describes how individuals, as members of social groups constructed and affected by more extensive systems, experience their lives within various contexts (Zambrana & Dill, 2009; Holvino, 2012). Modern business leaders comprehend intersectionality, recognize the interconnectedness of various forms of discrimination, and foster more equitable, diverse, and inclusive workplaces.

Richardson and Loubier (2008) established two compelling reasons to consider intersectionality when studying leadership. First, they explain that intersectionality aims to uncover leaders' multiple identities and personas, exposing the connections between those points (Richardson & Loubier, 2008). Second, they describe, "it suggests that analysis of complex social situations should not reduce understanding to a singular category; rather, it should facilitate the understanding of substantively distinct experiences from the effects of inextricably connected roles and situations" (p. 143). In short, leaders need to understand who they are within the complex schema of privilege and marginalized identities and the systems that distribute power to some but not others to lead effectively.

Intersectionality has immense currency with leaders because the multiple social identities of individuals are seen, thus creating a more complete portrayal of the whole person. While Dill et al. (2007) noted that "to a large extent, intersectional work is about identity" (p. 630), it is not *only* about identity (Jones & Abes, 2013). Although Nash (2008) referred to "intersectionality's theoretical dominance as a way of conceptualizing identity" (p. 3), intersectionality is not a catch-all framework for understanding a single person or individual identity narratives (Collins, 2009). Instead, intersectionality highlights how people, as members of multiple groups of individuals, experience privilege and marginalization, even in organizations promoting inclusion and belonging. Intersectionality influences how safe individuals feel to express themselves and their motivations (see Chapters 7 and 8).

Intersectionality complicates identity (Zambrana & Dill, 2009) because it highlights the intricacies of individuals' experiences when simultaneously embodying multiple identities. In addition, intersectionality acknowledges the diversity within social groups, often overlooked in earlier social identity development models that described experiences based on a single identity (Charmaine & Jones, 2014). Given this complexity and diversity, the question arises as to whether new social identity models can legitimately attend to one Black experience or a single experience of queer employees since individuals who share one common social identity (such as race, gender, or sexuality) may differ across several others. Those differences often include multiple locations of privilege and marginalization (Weber, 2010) that must be acknowledged and integrated into interventions that create inclusion and belonging in organizations. Table 5.1 contains four critical concepts that modern business leaders must understand to better comprehend and leverage intersectionality as Self Leaders.

Sylvia Duckworth's (2020) Intersectionality Wheel of Privilege/Power provides examples of unique circumstances, aspects of identity, discrimination impacting identity, and more significant structural forces that can inform an intersectional framework (see Figure 5.1). The wheel visually represents how identity and intersectionality combine at the individual and system levels. Table 5.2 summarizes our interpretation of each part of the wheel with examples.

The wheel (Figure 5.1) is ever moving, and when one locates themselves within the various circles, it might look different each time. Some identities are permanent, and others are fluid. As instructors, we often offer identity **salience**, which refers to the probability that a social identity will be invoked in a given situation; the higher the identity salience, the greater the likelihood of identity-related behavioral choices (Stryker & Burke, 2000). Additionally, **positionality** is helpful here; positionality encompasses personal values, views, and locations in time and space that impact interactions and understandings of

TABLE 5.1 Four Critical Concepts for Comprehending Intersectionality

Key Concept	*Description*	*Example*
Privilege	Privilege is intersectional, meaning individuals experience advantages and disadvantages based on unique aspects of their identity. It encompasses race, gender, religion, socioeconomic status, ability status, sexuality, age, and education level (Charmaine & Jones, 2014).	White, male, and economically advantaged individuals may receive unearned benefits from their social identities that offer them advantages in organizational settings (Charmaine & Jones, 2014).
Marginalization	Marginalization treats individuals or groups as insignificant, isolating and disempowering them within an organization, often resulting in limited access to resources and opportunities (Livingston & Rosette, 2020).	Marginalized groups often face systemic exclusion, limiting access to resources and opportunities, and experience discrimination from dominant groups (Livingston & Rosette, 2020).
Stigmatization	Stigmatization occurs when a group is perceived as a significant threat despite low interdependence, often leading to negative scrutiny from dominant groups, especially when members display behaviors associated with leadership (Livingston & Rosette, 2020).	Assertive Black male executives may be misinterpreted as aggressive, while similar behaviors from White males are viewed as effective leadership, showing societal bias (Livingston & Rosette, 2020).
Power	Power refers to the ability to influence, lead, dominate, or significantly impact others. Social identities and group privilege play a critical role in wielding power, often leading to an unequal distribution of resources and opportunities (Power, n.d.).	Leaders from privileged social groups may exert disproportionate influence and control within organizations, contributing to systemic inequality and reinforcing group-based biases (Power, n.d.).

reality. Positionality intertwines the elements from Table 5.1. For example, one's gender, race, class, and other aspects of social identities influence and inform how one interacts with the world, what knowledge one values, and the biases through which one thinks and does are filtered, intentionally or otherwise.

Intersectionality encourages a culture of inclusion and belonging for all employees, specifically diverse employees. When individuals from various backgrounds with different lived experiences work together, an intersectional perspective supports effective collaboration by valuing each participant's unique contributions. Self Leaders build teams of diverse thinkers who tackle challenges from all angles, fueled by nuanced lived experiences. They create environments and introduce extraordinary solutions. That is what intersectional leadership enables.

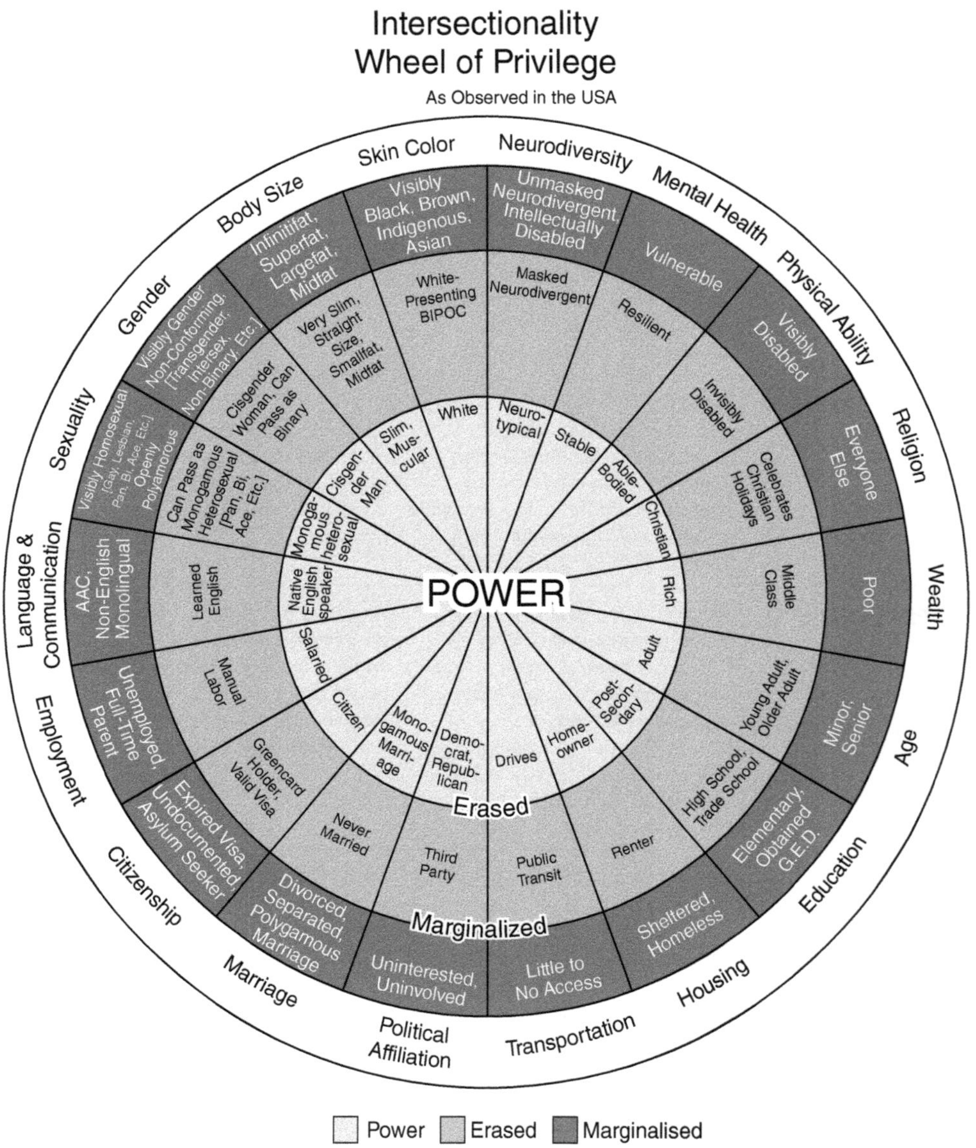

FIGURE 5.1 Intersectionality Wheel of Privilege
(Original from CCR, n.d.)

Before one can do this, leaders must traverse their path of discovery, allowing intersectionality to complicate their identity development. Locating oneself in the interlocking systems of the intersectionality framework provides life-changing understanding, awareness, and the tools to articulate one's lived experience. As authors, our years of teaching students these concepts remind us that individuals can have any number of emotions—validation, sadness, anger, triumph, confusion, belonging, mattering, resilience, and curiosity—when navigating social identities and intersectionality. Intersectionality, positionality, and social identity require lifelong self-reflection and inquiry so individuals can transform into authentic Self Leaders.

TABLE 5.2 Wheel of Privilege Components with Examples

Circle	*Description*	*Example*
Innermost Circle: Unique Circumstances of Power, Privilege, and Identity	Represents the intersection of individual identities and their access to power, privilege, and societal positioning.	A highly educated, able-bodied individual from a privileged socioeconomic background may have more opportunities compared to others with marginalized identities.
Second Circle: Aspects of Identity	Refers to specific aspects of identity that contribute to one's experience of privilege or oppression, such as gender, age, or income.	A transgender person may experience different levels of privilege or oppression depending on their gender, sexuality, class, or race.
Third Circle: Types of Discrimination Impacting Identity	Describes the various forms of discrimination that impact individuals based on their identity, such as racism, sexism, or homophobia.	An individual from a racialized background may experience racism or discrimination based on their ethnicity or skin color.
Outermost Circle: Largest Forces and Structures Reinforcing Exclusion	Broad societal forces and structures that shape systems of exclusion and privilege, such as capitalism, globalization, and colonization.	Global economic policies and systems of colonialism reinforce social hierarchies and perpetuate inequality on a worldwide scale.

Exercise 5.2 Intersectionality Wheel to You

In this exercise, you learn about yourself, your salient social identities, and how they interact with our society's systems of power and marginalization. Think about your social positions on the Intersectionality Wheel (see Figure 5.1) and the intersecting identities that shape your ways of being within your organizations. *How are these similar and different to your colleagues, peers, and leaders? How has business favored those with identities closer to the center of power and reinforced unjust power dynamics?*

Look at the Intersectionality Wheel and consider how you define yourself and where your salient social identities are on the wheel. Get curious about:

- *How close or far away from the center are you?*
- *How does your level of power shift as you locate in different identity categories?*
- *Where do you experience bias, privilege, or marginalization?*
- *How does this affect how you interact with others?*

CONCLUSION

Modern business leaders appreciate social identities and abhor injustice experienced because of social identity, actively working to bridge differences effectively. Of all the challenges today's leaders face, perhaps none is more central to sustained success and the growing list of must-haves, such as retention of top talent, positive company morale, employee productivity, and innovative breakthroughs, than having the capacity to leverage differences into a competitive advantage at an organization. Leaders who can do this are marketable, unique cultural assets in step with today's increasingly diverse workforces. Further, intersectionality recognizes that identities do not exist in isolation; they interact and overlap, creating unique and often complex experiences of privilege and marginalization.

Today's business world is volatile and uncertain. It's as critical as ever for leaders to understand themselves. Indeed, this section has covered several essentials, but more is needed for leaders to be aware of their capabilities, motivations, and values. Frameworks like intersectionality illuminate social identities and the explicit contexts with which they reside, better informing our leaders and allowing them to establish cultures that embrace differences. These frameworks are a nice bedrock for the next book sections.

DISCUSSION QUESTIONS

1. What is social identity, and how does it impact one's sense of self?
2. What does effective leadership look like for both ingroups and outgroups?
3. Why is intersectionality a crucial concept for contemporary business leaders?
4. How do privilege, marginalization, stigmatization, and power inform intersectionality?
5. How does one engage in intersectional leadership?
6. How does knowledge of social identities and intersectionality help one lead effectively?

Key Terms

- Social Identity
- Ingroup
- Outgroup
- Depersonalization
- Individuation
- Deindividuation
- Intersectionality
- Privilege
- Marginalization
- Stigmatization
- Power
- Salience
- Positionality

CASE STUDY 5.1 MARIA'S DILEMMA

Introduction: Maria is a 28-year-old Latina software engineer at a mid-sized tech company in California. She holds a master's degree in computer science and has been with the company for three years. Maria's workplace experiences reflect the complexities of social identities and intersectionality, influencing her interactions, opportunities, and sense of belonging.

Background: Maria faced numerous challenges in her academic career, balancing schoolwork and part-time jobs to support her family. Despite these obstacles, she excelled, driven by a desire to prove herself and create opportunities for her community. Her experiences reflect the complexities of social identities and intersectionality that impact her professional interactions and sense of belonging.

As a Latina woman in a male-dominated industry, Maria encounters stereotypes about her abilities and experiences gender bias, often feeling unheard in meetings. Being one of the younger employees, she sometimes feels underestimated by older colleagues, which affects her authority. As a first-generation college student, she also grapples with her family's expectations, which influence her confidence and decision-making. Explore Table 5.3.

TABLE 5.3 Challenges Faced and Key Leadership Actions Regarding Social Identity

Challenges	*Description*	*Key Leadership Actions*
Stereotyping	Maria faces stereotypes about her ethnicity and gender, leading colleagues to underestimate her expertise and disrespect her ideas.	Leaders should actively challenge stereotypes by advocating for Maria's expertise, ensuring fair discussion contributions, and implementing bias training.
Gender and Ethnic Microaggressions	Maria faces microaggressions, like being interrupted and having her ideas taken by male colleagues, which undermine her confidence and sense of belonging.	Leaders should implement structured speaking protocols to ensure equitable participation, recognize and credit contributions, and address microaggressions.
Lack of Representation and Mentorship	Maria faces challenges finding mentors in a predominantly male and white industry, which hinders her career growth and networking.	Leaders should establish mentorship programs that connect women and minorities with experienced mentors, fostering professional growth and career opportunities.

TABLE 5.3 (Continued)

Challenges	*Description*	*Key Leadership Actions*
Career Advancement Barriers	Maria observes that despite her strong performance, male colleagues are often promoted over her, revealing systemic bias that hinders career advancement for minority women.	Leaders should ensure transparent promotion criteria, conduct bias audits in advancement decisions, and actively support diverse talent through leadership training.
Workplace Culture and Inclusion	The workplace culture is unwelcoming, with a lack of diverse voices and an emphasis on homogeneity, making it hard for Maria to feel accepted.	Leaders should cultivate an inclusive culture by amplifying diverse voices, fostering employee resource groups, and implementing inclusive workplace policies.
Work-Life Balance Struggles	Maria feels pressure to excel at work while managing family obligations, resulting in stress, anxiety, burnout, and job dissatisfaction.	Leaders should offer adequate work arrangements, promote a healthy work-life balance, and support employees through mental health resources and policies.

Task: Provide four comprehensive recommendations for Maria. Connect the recommendations to key chapter concepts. Present the recommendations to a larger group for feedback and discussion.

REFERENCES

Anjewierden, B. J., Syfers, L., Pinto, I. R., Gaffney, A. M., & Hogg, M. A. (2024). Group responses to deviance: Disentangling the motivational roles of collective enhancement and self-uncertainty reduction. *Group Processes & Intergroup Relations*, *27*(5), 1170–1187. https://doi.org/10.1177/13684302241247030

Benwell, B., & Stokoe, E. (2006). *Discourse and identity*. Edinburgh University Press. https://www.jstor.org/stable/10.3366/j.ctt1r2356

Canadian Council for Refugees [CCR]. (n.d.). Anti-oppression. https://ccrweb.ca/en/anti-oppression

Charmaine, L. W., & Jones, S. R. (2014). *Intersectionality & higher education: Theory, research, & praxis*. Peter Lang.

Collins, P. H. (2009). Emerging intersections: Building knowledge and transforming institutions. In R. E. Zambrana & B. T. Dill (Eds.), *Emerging intersections: Race, class, and gender in theory, policy, and practice* (pp. vii–xiii). Rutgers University Press.

Crenshaw, K. (1989). Demarginalizing the intersection of race and sex: A Black feminist critique of antidiscrimination doctrine, feminist theory, and antiracist politics. *University of Chicago Legal Forum, 1989*(1), 139–167.

Dill, B. T., McLaughlin, A. E., & Nieves, A. D. (2007). Future directions of feminist research: Intersectionality. In S. N. Hesse-Biber (Ed.), *Handbook of feminist research* (pp. 629–637). Sage.

Duckworth, S. (2020, October 18). Wheel of power/privilege [Infographic]. Flickr. https://flic.kr/p/2jWxeGG

Ellemers, N., & Barreto, M. (2001). The impact of relative group status: Affective, perceptual and behavioral consequences. In S. L. Brown & M. Gaertner (Eds.), *Blackwell Handbook of social psychology: Intergroup processes* (Vol. 3, pp. 324–343). Blackwell. https://doi.org/10.1002/9780470693421.ch16

Haslam, S. A., Gaffney, A. M., Hogg, M. A., Rast III, D. E., & Steffens, N. K. (2022). Reconciling identity leadership and leader identity: A dual-identity framework. *The Leadership Quarterly, 33*(4), 101620.

Hogg, M. A. (2001). A social identity theory of leadership. *Personality and Social Psychology Review, 5*(3), 184–200.

Holvino, E. (2012). The 'simultaneity' of identities: Models and skills for the 21st century. In C. L. Wijeyesinghe & B. W. Jackson (Eds.), *New perspectives on racial identity development* (pp. 161–191). New York University Press.

Johnson, N. (2022). Leadership and the in-group/out-group phenomenon. *Blanchard.com*.

Jones, S. R., & Abes, E. S. (2013). *Identity development of college students: Advancing frameworks for multiple dimensions of identity*. John Wiley & Sons.

Livingston, R. W., & Rosette, A. S. (2020). Stigmatization, subordination, or marginalization?: The complexity of social disadvantage across gender and race. In S. R. Jones (Ed.), *Inclusive leadership* (pp. 39–59). Routledge.

Lyon, S. (2021). The benefits of creating a diverse workforce. *Forbes.com*.

Nash, J. C. (2008). Re-thinking intersectionality. *Feminist Review, 89*(1), 1–15.

Northouse, P. G. (2021). *Leadership: Theory and practice* (9th ed.). Sage.

Núñez, A. M., Rivera, J., & Hallmark, T. (2020). Applying an intersectionality lens to expand equity in the geosciences. *Journal of Geoscience Education, 68*(2), 97–114.

Pew Research Center. (2013). On pay gap, millennial women near parity – For now. Despite gains, many see roadblocks ahead. https://www.pewresearch.org/social-trends/wp-content/uploads/sites/3/2013/12/gender-and-work_final.pdf

Power. (n.d.). *Encyclopaedia Britannica*. Retrieved from https://www.britannica.com/topic/power-political-and-social-science

Richardson, A., & Loubier, C. (2008). Intersectionality and leadership. *International Journal of Leadership Studies, 3*(2), 142–161.

Schaeffer, K. (2024, February 27). For Women's History Month, a look at gender gains – and gaps – in the U.S. *Pew Research Center*. https://www.pewresearch.org/

Steffens, N. K., Munt, K. A., van Knippenberg, D., Platow, M. J., & Haslam, S. A. (2021). Advancing the social identity theory of leadership: A meta-analytic review of leader group prototypicality. *Organizational Psychology Review, 11*(1), 35–72.

Stryker, S., & Burke, P. J. (2000). The past, present, and future of an identity theory. *Social Psychology Quarterly, 63*(4), 284–297. https://doi.org/10.2307/2695840

Tajfel, H. (Ed.). (1982). *Social identities and intergroup relations*. Cambridge University Press.

Tajfel, H., Billig, M., Bundy, R., & Flament, C. (1971). Social categorization and intergroup behavior. *European Journal of Social Psychology, 1*(2), 148–178.

Tajfel, H., & Turner, J. C. (1979). An integrative theory of intergroup conflict. In W. G. Austin & S. Worchel (Eds.), *The social psychology of intergroup relations* (pp. 33–47). Brooks/Cole.

Talmage, C. A., Peterson, C. B., & Knopf, R. C. (2017). Punk rock wisdom: An emancipative psychological social capital approach to community well-being. In R. Phillips & C. Wong (Eds.), *Handbook of community well-being research* (pp. 11–38). Springer.

Tatum, B. D. (2000). The complexity of identity: "Who am I?" In M. Adams, W. J. Blumfield, R. Castañeda, H. W. Hackman, M. L. Peters, & X. Zúñiga (Eds.), *Readings for diversity and social justice: An anthology on racism, antisemitism, sexism, heterosexism, ableism, and classism* (pp. 9–14). Routledge.

Turner, J. C., & Reynolds, K. H. (2001). The social identity perspective in intergroup relations: Theories, themes, and controversies. In S. L. Brown & M. Gaertner (Eds.), *Blackwell Handbook of social psychology: Intergroup processes* (Vol. 3, pp. 133–152). Blackwell. https://doi.org/10.1002/9780470693421.ch7

Weber, L. (2010). *Understanding race, class, gender, and sexuality* (2nd ed.). Oxford University Press.

Zambrana, R. E., & Dill, B. T. (2009). Future directions in knowledge building and sustaining institutional change. In R. E. Zambrana & B. T. Dill (Eds.), *Emerging intersections: Race, class, and gender in theory, policy, and practice* (pp. 1–21). Rutgers University Press.

PART 2

People Leadership

The second dimension of our model, **People Leadership**, could also be called "Leading Others." People Leadership is a nod to the corporate role that describes a supervisor with a team of employees, often called direct reports. The competencies included here are required to lead others in today's contemporary environments. A blend of classic theory and modern strategy, this section outlines what leaders must do to shape a highly functioning, collaborative team.

As authors, we used "people" in this section's title because it recognizes that organizations are powered by their people, flying in formation with direction and purpose. People Leaders are the architects behind relationship-building, motivational techniques, collaborative processes, and inclusive cultures in which teams thrive. While teams operate in a new era of modalities across vast geographies, their ability to produce and deliver is still a critical mandate for businesses. Fostering new elements such as psychological safety, belonging, and autonomy considers a multigenerational workforce with modern needs, desires, and expectations.

People leader roles are often the aspirational goals of our students, a pathway to promotion and advancement at an organization. What matters for new People Leaders to remember is that the skills that allow them to succeed as contributors are not the same as the ones they will need to lead others. Like the Self Leadership concept, People Leadership requires discipline, learning, and development, considering constant change, disruption, and innovation. Leading others calls for focus, intention, and ongoing engagement with the humans we work with.

Much like most chapters within this text, this section attempts to build concrete understanding and offers much-needed time to practice. Skills like active listening and providing feedback are easy to grasp but much more complicated to execute. Taken together as a whole, the People Leadership section allows students to pursue with courage and ambition the supervisor roles they want while, at the same time, readies them to be the bosses that others want to work for. We want our students to be the contemporary leaders who will inspire, retain, and develop their employees, recruiting them to a vision for the team and the organization.

DOI: 10.4324/9781003474647-7

CHAPTER 6

Relationship-Building in (In-)Person, Hybrid, and Remote Environments

CHAPTER OVERVIEW

This first chapter of People Leadership focuses on relationship-building as a critical practice for modern business leaders. Workplace modalities have shifted to include in-person, hybrid, or remote options. Leaders must adapt their methods for building relationships essential for enhancing overall productivity, retaining employees, motivating individuals, and fostering team cohesion. The relational leadership model is shared with readers. It focuses on empowerment, ethics, inclusion, purpose, and process. The mode still applies in workplaces despite newer modalities. Leaders can still have positive relationships with employees and coworkers across modalities. This chapter also examines frameworks like Level 5 Leaders and servant leadership as impactful approaches to developing professional relationships across modalities.

In the introduction of this text, we reviewed the impact on the workplace due to the global pandemic caused by COVID-19. Categorically, COVID-19 changed the trajectory of **work modalities**, which refers to how work is coordinated, performed, and compensated over time and space. The COVID-19 pandemic spawned roles deemed **essential** or **nonessential**, dictating whether an employee was required to be in the office or otherwise could work from home. COVID-19 has also changed the physical and virtual spaces preferred or utilized for collaboration. In the post-COVID world, **in-person**, **hybrid**, and **remote** shifted job positions, locations, times, tasks, and cooperation within and across the organization.

Why have so many employers opted to keep these alternative ways of working long after the COVID-19 restrictions? First, it brought more benefits for individuals and companies than initially imagined. Many companies saw productivity increases, less absenteeism, and loyalty and retention from top talent. For the individuals, the most noted benefits are greater flexibility, less stress due to commutes, and higher work satisfaction. Second, hybrid and remote modalities lowered operation costs, such as renting or leasing buildings. Third, it prevented some high-performing, talented individuals from leaving their positions for others that offered work-from-home options.

DOI: 10.4324/9781003474647-8

The advantages of in-person work environments cannot be ignored. Two key items stand out when employees interact within a traditional office space, namely, (1) ease of communication and (2) opportunity for relationship-building. The switch to remote work initially harmed these essential team-oriented behaviors tremendously. Ron Carucci (2021) noted:

> Over the past 18 months, most organizations have experienced some degree of fracturing as social connections and cultural cohesion have been strained. The challenges of remote work, dramatic uncertainty, the clumsy process of figuring out what returning to the office could look like, and the mass exodus of workers fed up with cultures that make them feel devalued have all served to threaten a sense of community.
>
> (para 4)

Yet some companies are making these alternative modalities work. Today, corporations such as Amazon have embraced a structured hybrid modality approach. Famously, in a 2023 letter from CEO Andy Jassy, Amazon announced they'd begin their return-to-office efforts on May 1st of that year, which caused some stir among those who worked from home full-time. Still, this mandate only applies to three days of the week, and employees are free to work from anywhere the other two days. Amazon's policy change clearly showed the value they place on face-to-face collaboration. According to Jassy, "Teams tend to be better connected to one another when they see each other in person more frequently" (Ketter, 2024).

Further, the leading job search site Indeed rated companies for their fully remote policies and found that noteworthy names such as Intuit, Microsoft, Yahoo, IBM, Johnson & Johnson, and Fidelity Investments were finding success (Eads, 2025). These companies scored well on Indeed's Well-Being rating, which measures how people feel at work, focusing on the primary outcomes of work well-being like happiness, purpose, satisfaction, and stress. It also measures work well-being's key drivers: accomplishment, appreciation, belonging, energy, fair pay, flexibility, inclusion and respect, learning, support and encouragement, trust, and being well-managed (Eads, 2025). Employee well-being can be raised in non–in-office environments.

We recommend contemporary leaders focus on rebuilding relationships and enhancing the foundational elements of organizational culture while effectively embracing each modality's advantage within their teams. Leadership is inherently a relational, communal process. "Leadership is always dependent on the context, but the context is established by the relationships we value" (Wheatley, 1992, p. 144). Although a person could exert leadership of ideas through persuasive writings or making speeches, most leadership happens in an interactive context between leaders and followers.

The global shift from traditional offices to hybrid and remote setups offers notable opportunities and formidable challenges. Ron Carucci (2021) notes that the disrupted connections of recent years have shattered workplace culture, eroded social bonds, and diminished the sense of community once prevalent in offices. With the hurdles of remote work, uncertainty around office returns, and an escalating demand for flexibility, leaders are compelled to urgently reevaluate their approach to relationship cultivation, as the media note strong perceptions of disconnection, if not loneliness, across the world (Ortiz-Ospina, 2019).

Contemporary business leaders must grasp that leadership transcends a mere title or position—it is a vital relational process anchored in trust, commitment, and a shared mission (Ciulla, 2014). Modern business leaders demonstrate effective leadership by cultivating meaningful, inclusive, resilient relationships across various modalities. This chapter teaches leaders to navigate these challenges, focusing on the relational leadership model. It outlines actionable strategies to enhance communication, trust, and collaboration in in-person, hybrid, and remote contexts. After reading this chapter, leaders can improve team performance and foster a workplace culture that values, empowers, and connects employees to their work and colleagues.

RELATIONAL LEADERSHIP MODEL

We frequently start our class or professional development sessions with several core questions:

1. *How do our current office relationships shape the overall culture and climate within the organization?*
2. *How do strong interpersonal connections enhance teamwork and productivity among our staff?*
3. *What practices can we implement to cultivate and nurture healthy, meaningful relationships in our workplace?*
4. *What behaviors or practices have been observed that undermine trust and weaken colleague relationships?*

In practice, the responses are often mixed. Many remote workers comment that they had never felt more connected because the post-COVID ways of work had brought them back into the company's fold through the heavy use of video conferencing through Zoom, WebEx, or Microsoft Teams. Meanwhile, some in-person workers still felt the fractions that Carucci (2021) referred to, noting how frayed relationships had negatively impacted organizational cultures because of these alternative work modalities. The relationship leadership model (see Figure 6.1) helps discern where and what to tackle to build relationships and bolster team performance.

The **relational leadership model** emphasizes the relationships among people when leading an organization. Relational leadership values are inclusion, empowerment, purposefulness, ethical behaviors, and process orientation. Leaders using this model consider everyone's viewpoint and experiences when making decisions. Further, relationship-oriented leaders prioritize the welfare of everyone in the group and will place time and effort into meeting the individual needs of everyone involved. By fostering relationships with all team members, leaders can establish trust with their employees on a personal level. Trusting a leader builds loyalty to the company and creates a healthy work environment for employees.

The relational leadership model (see Figure 6.1 adapted from McMahon et al., 2013) has merit in these evolving work environments where relationships must be a leader's priority. Developing relationships across an organization at all levels leads to more

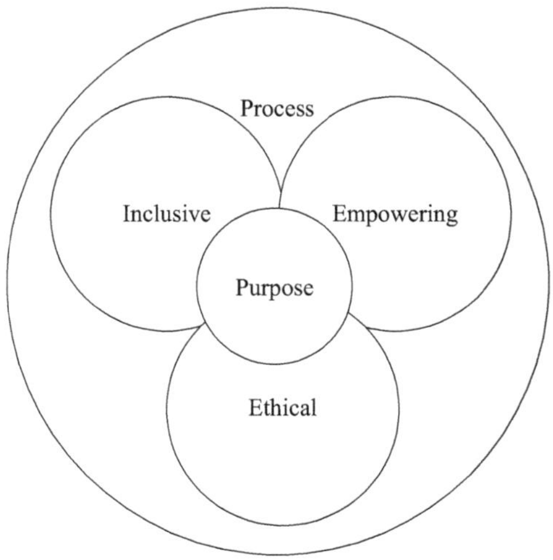

FIGURE 6.1 Relationship Leadership Model

efficient and effective working practices, with sharing and collaboration occurring frequently and naturally. It has to start from the top and cascade throughout the enterprise to reach this stage. To that end, strong companies depend on strong relationships, and fostering those relationships among employees keeps people satisfied, engaged, and productive at work. Although this might sound like a simple goal, relationship-building can be a complex process to implement and even further to sustain.

Relational leadership focuses on five primary components (see Figure 6.1). As McMahon et al. (2013) outline, this approach to leadership is purposeful, builds a commitment toward positive practices that empower, are inclusive of diverse viewpoints, are ethical, and recognize that all four elements are accomplished by being process oriented. The components are nuanced, especially in today's environments with many modalities. However, the model reflects how the organization's purpose influences the components of being inclusive, empowering, and ethical, which are key drivers of successful relationships.

Other signature qualities of this model include (1) how the purpose is achieved (the process) is just as important as the outcome; (2) how the goals are accomplished and how others' involvement in the process matters; and (3) the purpose is vision-driven and not position-driven (McMahon et al., 2013). Small, mid-size, or large companies benefit from contemporary leaders who clearly understand how to execute this model. Next, we unpack each component.

Purpose

Purpose means committing to a goal or activity. In business, this should include the bottom line but also extend into outlining an aspirational vision and pointing the people within the organization toward it. Here, leaders need the ability to collaborate and to find common ground with others to facilitate the many positive outcomes required to reach an ambiguous vision. Very often, purpose includes working hard toward resolving differences among colleagues, generating buy-in for key directions, and building a shared sense of "we're in this together" where everyone is needed to contribute to meet our objectives. All employees in the organization must be able to articulate the purpose and use it as a driving force (McMahon et al., 2013).

Collective purpose is the heartbeat of functional organizations, taking both compelling relationships and dynamic leadership to achieve. "Effective leaders don't just impose their vision on others. They recruit others to a shared vision. Especially in our digital age, when power tends to coalesce around ideas, not positions, leadership is a partnership" (Bennis & Thomas, 2002, p. 137). This component is a key part of the process and, in our rapidly changing work environments, can often get skipped, confused, or perceived as coming from top-down measures. The contemporary leader should ask their team members: *What is our shared purpose? What is our process in getting to this shared purpose? How does our process seek involvement and engagement from all organization members?*

Exercise 6.1 Start, Stop, and Continue

To further conversations about shared purpose with your team, try the start, stop, and continue exercise. Each team member should consider (1) what they should start doing more, (2) what they should stop doing altogether, and (3) what they should continue doing. Team members can write this down or create short presentation slides. Items can be professional or personal. Reflect on what activities serve you well, what is getting in the way of you being productive, and what new practices might generate a positive change. Give each team member 5–8 minutes to share with the group. After everyone has presented, work to draw connections about what the team shares in common. Questions to consider:

1. *What could we start doing collectively that would serve our overall purpose?*
2. *What should we immediately stop doing because it no longer serves our purpose?*
3. *What habits, practices, or activities must we continue to fulfill our purpose?*

Inclusiveness

Inclusiveness means understanding, valuing, and actively engaging with diverse views, approaches, styles, and aspects of individuality, such as sex, race, or culture, which add many perspectives to an organization's goals. Additionally, inclusiveness describes how different groups or individuals might approach issues from various perspectives or frames. Maintaining respect for differences is paramount, and equity and involvement are of tremendous value.

McMahon et al. (2013) suggest that inclusiveness means thinking of networks and webs of connection instead of seeing issues and problems as isolated and discrete. Further, being inclusive as an organization means embracing the steps to develop the talent of all members so they can be readily involved. This component requires listening with empathy, communicating with civility, and other communication skills that facilitate the inclusion of others.

People Leaders intentionally foster inclusiveness, inspiring new leaders reflected as a positive long-term cycle. They recognize that each individual is vital, as they represent and shape the whole. Further, the whole's purpose, vision, and values come to life as each member describes and applies them. McMahon et al. (2013) state that the goal is not to overcome variations and differences among individuals but to build a shared purpose. Leaders should ask: *What practices block inclusiveness in our organizational climate? Where are we strengthened by multiple perspectives or diverse points of view? Where are we challenged?*

Empowering

Change "demands the empowerment of every person in the organization—no ifs, ands, or buts" (Peterson, 1989, p. xiv). Authoritarian and directive leadership styles have replaced more contemporary coaching and mentoring forms. Research suggests that attracting and retaining new generations of workers, such as Millennials and Gen Z, will call for **empowering** approaches from leaders. Recently, Deloitte (2023) surveyed Millennials and Gen Z workers across 44 countries and found that "they want their employers to support and empower them to make more sustainable decisions in their own lives and to develop the skills needed to succeed."

McMahon et al. (2013) highlight two dimensions of empowerment business leaders should embrace: (1) fostering a personal sense of ownership and active expectation of involvement among team members and (2) creating an environment that encourages full participation by removing barriers to individual talent and engagement. Recognizing these dimensions is crucial for building strong relationships between leaders and their teams. Effective leaders understand influence originates from followers (Kouzes & Posner, 1987; Olley, 2021).

Power dynamics in organizations can vary from power "over" (autocratic) to power "with" (collaborative) or power "alongside" (collegial) (McMahon et al., 2013). Leaders use power (Bolman & Deal, 2003) and navigate power dynamics (Surakhmat et al., 2024). Modern business leaders, as People Leaders, distribute power to empower team members to express their opinions and feel valued. These approaches foster a sense of justice and meaning, which we call **mattering**, within the organization.

Furthermore, McMahon et al. (2013) explain that empowerment is claimed ("I have a legitimate right to be here and share my thoughts") and shared ("You should be involved too; your input is important"). Leaders who implement empowering strategies actively mitigate environmental factors hindering meaningful participation. Modern business leaders ensure individuals feel integral to organizational success instead of marginalized or overlooked, reinforcing the concept of mattering (McMahon et al., 2013).

Mattering has grown in popularity and has a long history. Notably, "Mattering is a motive: the feeling that others depend on us, are interested in us, are concerned with our fate…[which] exercises a powerful influence on our actions" (Rosenberg & McCullough, 1981). McMahon et al. (2013) suggest that individuals may feel excluded or unimportant in new situations, roles, or when interacting with new people. This feeling often arises unless the group actively welcomes them and encourages their meaningful participation. In contrast, mattering is the feeling that individuals are significant to others and the process, and this is essential to building and sustaining meaningful relationships. Contemporary business leaders should ask: *How does the organization tell each member they matter? Where might this be improved?*

Ethics

The relational leadership model emphasizes **ethics**, meaning leadership driven by values, standards, and morals. The derivation of ethics is from ethos, from the Greek word for "character" and "sentiment of the community" (Toffler, 1986, p. 10). Ethical means "conforming to the standards of a given profession or group. Any group can set its ethical standards and then live by them or not" (Toffler, 1986, p. 10). For this model, ethics are defined as "rules or standards that govern behavior" (Toffler, 1986, p. 10). This is essential for healthy relationships.

Leadership is values-driven. Stephen Covey's (1989) *The 7 Habits of Highly Effective People* uses the metaphor of "leadership by compass" to illustrate principle-centered leadership (p. 19). Principles like values, ethics, standards, and morals "provide 'true north' direction to our lives when navigating the 'streams' or our environments" (p. 19). Ethical leadership should steer organizations, particularly as they implement practices conducive to healthy cultures while navigating rapidly changing conditions. In our chapters focusing on social responsibility and entrepreneurship, we will get further into ethics and values.

Again, leadership is a relational and ethical process of people working together and attempting to accomplish positive change (McMahon et al., 2013). Using this philosophy, leaders and followers act out of a sense of shared value—the desire to cause real change and a commitment to mutual purposes. Further, the actions of leaders and followers emanate from a set of values, which should be congruent and derived from the collective. These are the ingredients of successful organizations that thrive on meaningful relationships. Today's organizational leaders should ask: *What are our shared organizational values? How could we communicate these values to new members or external stakeholders?*

Process

Finally, **process** is critical to relationships. This component can be tension-laden, as contemporary business leaders operating in fast-paced environments often need to make quick, urgent decisions without soliciting feedback or input. Still, the relational leadership model encourages leaders to slow down, involve their teams, seek perspectives, and incorporate divergent views whenever possible. Being process-oriented requires a specific discipline. Modern business leaders look forward and backward, thinking fast and slow, soliciting rapid data-driven feedback to ensure short-term and long-term success, even in the face of big change.

Many employees worldwide express concerns about organizational changes across global systems (see Chapter 16). Such changes include leadership shifts, restructuring efforts, mergers, acquisitions, political upheaval, and regulatory modifications (Galbraith, 2018). Modern business leaders must navigate a climate of ongoing uncertainty in the workplace. A survey of more than half a million U.S. employees highlighted that a third of employees do not fully understand why changes in their organizations are happening (Galbraith, 2018). To manage change well, modern business leaders must leverage transparent communication. Contemporary leaders should actively engage employees. When individuals feel integral to planning and executing change, they are committed and enthusiastic about its successful implementation.

Process underpins the model's elements of purpose, inclusiveness, empowerment, and ethics. Today's leaders need to be clear and resolute in their process because including others is central to building relationships with the employees they manage. These leaders should ask: *What are the principles of our decision-making process? How does change impact our process? What does it take for us to reach full participation and engagement?*

Mentoring and Coaching with the Relationship Leadership Model

Mentoring and coaching are essential leadership practices that foster professional and personal development. Modern business leaders focus on developing future talent and fostering an inclusive workplace culture. **Mentoring** involves an experienced individual supporting a less experienced colleague, offering insights and guidance for career advancement (Early, 2020). **Coaching** zeroes in on performance, providing structured feedback and skills development to enhance specific task effectiveness (Holder & Pursley, 2024). Through mentoring and coaching, modern business leaders create supportive environments where employees feel valued.

The relational leadership model emphasizes that leadership is a dynamic, people-centered process rather than merely a hierarchical position (McMahon et al., 2013). Mentoring and coaching enable leaders to empower employees to navigate career pathways, sharpen problem-solving skills, build trust, enrich engagement, and boost their leadership capabilities. These practices strengthen teams and cultivate a culture of lifelong learning, constructive feedback, and resilient adaptability in the face of substantial change.

Exercise 6.2 Mentor or Coach? Making the Right Choice for Leadership Growth

This exercise helps contemporary business leaders determine whether they need a **mentor** or a **coach** based on their professional development goals and how to ensure these relationships align with McMahon et al.'s (2013) and is adapted from other sources (Rolfe, 2016; U of MI, n.d.).

SELF-ASSESSMENT—DO YOU NEED A MENTOR OR A COACH?

Read the following statements in Table 6.1 and check (✔) those that resonate with your current situation. *You likely need that relationship if you check more than 3 in either column.*

TABLE 6.1 Mentoring or Coaching Self-Assessment

Mentor	*Coach*
I need **long-term career guidance** from someone who has been where I want to go.	I need **short-term, skill-based improvement** for a current challenge.

Mentor	*Coach*
I seek **wisdom, life lessons, and big-picture insights** on leadership.	I want **structured feedback** to improve my performance on a specific task.
I want **a sounding board for career decisions** and work-life balance.	I need **an accountability partner** to push me toward specific goals.
I need **help navigating organizational culture and politics**.	I am looking for **practical tools and techniques** to apply immediately.
I value **relationship-based learning over time**.	I am comfortable with a **transactional, results-driven approach**.
I prefer **guidance from an experienced leader** in my field.	I want **an expert in leadership development** regardless of industry.

REFLECTION—ENSURING A STRONG RELATIONSHIP THROUGH THE RELATIONAL LEADERSHIP MODEL

Reflect on how you can make the most of a coaching or mentoring relationship by considering:

1. *What is the explicit goal of this relationship? Ensure you and your mentor/coach define your objectives and success criteria early.*
2. *How will this relationship embrace diverse perspectives? Choose someone who challenges your thinking and brings a different viewpoint.*
3. *Does this relationship encourage your growth?* A strong mentor or coach helps you take ownership of your development and doesn't just provide answers.
4. *Are both parties committed to honesty, integrity, and confidentiality in discussions?*
5. *Are you committed to the ongoing learning process rather than just seeking quick solutions?* Build a relationship that evolves rather than seeking only immediate answers.

ACTION PLAN—FINDING AND ENGAGING THE RIGHT MENTOR OR COACH

1. **Identify a potential mentor or coach—**use your professional network, industry groups, or leadership development programs.
2. **Reach out clearly—**explain why you seek guidance and what you hope to gain.
3. **Structure the relationship**—decide on meeting frequency, format (virtual/in-person), and discussion topics.
4. **Stay engaged**—be proactive, ask insightful questions, and reflect on feedback to maximize learning.
5. **Reassess the relationship periodically**—ensure it continues to meet evolving needs.

BUILDING RELATIONSHIPS IN ALTERNATIVE WORK MODALITIES

In today's corporate landscape, a **people leader** is a supervisor responsible for one or more team members. The ability to cultivate and sustain relationships has never been more crucial. Modern people leaders must actively develop extensive networks of employees to meet organizational objectives, deliver value, and gain competitive edges.

Modern business leaders recognize that effective relationship-building extends beyond immediate teams to include stakeholders, clients, colleagues, and external partners, discussed in greater detail in later chapters. Today's contemporary leaders must foster strong connections to drive engagement, collaboration, inclusivity, resilience, and success. Leadership has become more decentralized and democratic, evolving from a focus on results and authority to prioritizing team development and collective impact. While traditional leadership emphasizes measurable outcomes and respect, modern People Leaders dedicate themselves to team empowerment, relationship-building, and shared visions (Ernst, 2019). The author, Jim Collins (2001), initiated a new look at leadership that scholars, educators, and practitioners have built upon in this light.

Level 5 and Servant Leadership

Level 5 leadership is the pinnacle of effective leadership, merging personal humility with a strong professional drive (Collins, 2001). Level 5 leaders exhibit modesty and selflessness with an unwavering determination to secure long-term organizational results. Level 5 leaders often place the institution's advancement above their recognition or professional advancement. Level 5 leaders are willing to "look out the window, not in the mirror," giving credit to their teams for achievements while accepting accountability for shortcomings (Collins, 2001, p. 85). Level 5 leadership encompasses servant-like humility and a steadfast commitment to results, setting it apart from other leadership approaches (Reid et al., 2014; Zorlu et al., 2021).

Servant leadership, first proposed by Greenleaf (1977), resonates with Level 5 leadership. Servant leaders focus on follower growth, development, and well-being. Servant leaders leverage purpose-driven approaches rather than ego-driven ambition or remarkability. They demonstrate stewardship, empathy, active listening, and ethical decision-making (Greenleaf, 1977; Reid et al., 2014; Zorlu et al., 2021). Reid et al. (2014) identified similarities between Level 5 leaders and servant leaders, noting both highlight humility, integrity, and a long-term perspective while slightly differing in their focus on professional determination and organizational goals.

Modern business leaders grasp these leadership models to balance results-oriented approaches with relational leadership. Level 5 and servant leadership underscore selflessness, ethical practices, and resilience as tantamount to success. These styles of People Leaders pursue success and foster sustainable, inclusive, people-centric organizational cultures that will help teams and organizations flourish (Reid et al., 2014; Zorlu et al., 2021).

Ernst's (2019) Principles and Practices

Ernst (2019) reports that, according to Gallup, "bad managers cost businesses billions of dollars each year." This further illustrates that individuals do not quit their jobs; they quit their bosses. Ernst (2019) contends that nearly anyone can become a people leader by implementing effective leadership practices, as shown in Table 6.2.

While this book section will go over these practices in more depth in forthcoming chapters, such guidance can help modern People Leaders establish healthy relationships. But they must be constantly vigilant. If they are operating in an in-person environment, such practices can appear natural, organic, or, in some cases, conventional. Many companies have had bold returns to workplace policies mainly because they know that in-person time matters to relationships.

According to Goldberg (2023), The U.S. Labor Department saw a notable reduction in remote work, with 72.5% of businesses reporting that their employees seldom or never teleworked in the past year. This figure reflects a significant increase from 60.1% in 2021 and is comparable to the 76.7% of businesses that did not utilize remote work before the pandemic; however, these findings are not ubiquitous.

Remote work growth and stabilization have become notable trends for contemporary business leaders to consider. A monthly survey conducted by Stanford University and the Census Bureau further shows that remote work continues to be significant, representing

TABLE 6.2 Effective Leadership Practices

People Leadership Practices	*Examples*
Maintain a team-first mentality	Encourage collaboration over competition, recognizing team success over individual wins.
Set high standards of excellence	Set clear performance benchmarks and continuously encourage professional development.
Communicate, communicate, communicate	Hold regular one-on-one check-ins, team meetings, and transparent updates to align goals.
Follow through on commitments	Deliver on promises, ensuring accountability and modeling reliability for the team.
Give public recognition	Celebrate employees' contributions in meetings, newsletters, or social media spotlights.
Remove barriers	Address inefficiencies, advocating for necessary resources and simplifying bureaucratic processes.
Have tough conversations	Provide constructive feedback and address conflicts directly but empathetically.
Inspire and motivate	Share a compelling vision, leading by example, and recognizing employees' intrinsic motivations.

Aadapted from Ernst, 2019

over a quarter of paid full-time workdays in the United States, slightly down from 33% in 2021. The survey indicates that 12% of workers are fully remote, around 60% are entirely on-site, and 28% follow a hybrid model (Goldberg, 2023). The percentage of employees working remotely (most or all of the time) has increased significantly since 2015. The figure reached 28% in 2023 (PayScale, 2024a). Beyond a clear spike in remote work during the COVID-19 pandemic, remote work persists globally (PayScale, 2024a). People Leaders recognize this shift and adapt strategies accordingly.

Different industries have varied in their adoption of remote work, with some embracing it far more than others. As of 2023, sectors like technology, at 67.75%, agencies and consultancies, at 50.56%, and finance and insurance, at 48.72%, led in remote work adoption (PayScale, 2024b). Healthcare, construction, and food and accommodation report much lower proportions (PayScale, 2024b). Industry trends and differences are crucial data for leaders to know the context and competition when planning workforce strategies and shifts.

Despite its advantages, remote work is challenged by reported struggles with loneliness, difficulty unplugging, staying motivated, and issues with collaboration (Buffer, 2023). Notably, 27% of remote workers reported distractions at home in 2023, 25% faced challenges with communication and cooperation, and 21% were concerned about career advancement (Buffer, 2023). Hybrid models may evolve as the more prominent work approach, requiring flexible leaders. Adaptability remains crucial for effective modern business leadership, given the varying attitudes toward work modalities and employee reluctance to return to in-person settings.

Modern People Leaders go beyond being aware of these challenges, remain vigilant and flexible to new challenges and modalities, and face them head-on.

Lessons for Meetings and Communication in Diverse Modalities

Do Ernst's (2019) *principles still apply in environments with multiple modalities?* Hybrid or remote work brings significant challenges to building relationships with others. It is much harder to create authentic connections when individuals are not face to face. A substantial amount of communication is lost without body language, facial expressions, and gestures, and telephone and email can be a poor substitute for in-person contact (Building Careers, 2023). Remote work allows teams to assemble across geographies quickly (Torres, 2022). While time zones remain challenging to navigate, remote options lessen the barriers and pose opportunities to enhance communication and foster meaningful, enduring cross-cultural relationships (Torres, 2022).

Bonding and trust among team members are still essential for remote teams. People Leaders prioritize creating opportunities for members to relax and share personal experiences, hobbies, and thoughts. This can be achieved through regular, meaningful, and strategically planned in-person gatherings throughout the year (Torres, 2022). A regular meeting cadence utilizing video rather than just audio facilitates more meaningful engagement, allowing team members to experience facial expressions and body language to build community and reduce isolation. Remote work can easily relegate to focus on daily tasks and objectives at the cost of nurturing relationships, undermining shared goals, values, and trust. People Leaders showcase relationship-forward approaches, moving beyond goal-only orientations to ensure team success.

CONCLUSION

As we open this section on people leadership, we consider how leaders, managers, and supervisors must cultivate and nurture relationships with their team members. While this is pressing, the residual effects from the COVID-19 pandemic continue to circulate, most notably in how an overnight experiment with remote work continues to persist—launching today's modern workplaces into the various dynamics of in-person, hybrid, and remote modalities. As authors, we frequently prepare our students to work professionally and on teams amidst this new reality. Similarly, we have updated our leadership content to include all modalities, particularly when preparing contemporary leaders for their respective positions.

The relational leadership model continues to serve as a tool for leaders supervising others. It is values-driven and applies across all modalities. Recruiting others to a purpose, committing to inclusiveness, empowering employees, and operating with ethical principles, all within a consistent process, resonates with workers, whether in person, hybrid, or remote, because it begets critical relationships. While this chapter has shared the nuances of building relationships for each modality, we advocate that effective teams are founded on healthy and productive relationships, driving business productivity.

This lens will tie into the forthcoming chapters of this section. Much like the essentials for Self Leadership, these contemporary times have required leaders to re-orient their approach to a compelling set of challenges that constitute a revisit to traditional 'soft skills' but with a modern twist. As this text explores, motivating others, collaborating with teams, and creating inclusive climates are now set against globalization, emerging technologies, and disruption from climate change, the COVID-19 pandemic, and geopolitical unrest. Today, people leaders must influence their teams through compelling relationships in these dynamic contexts and across all modalities.

DISCUSSION QUESTIONS

1. How is this new era of work modalities affecting relationships at work?
2. What are the advantages and disadvantages of each modality?
3. Why are relationships key to effective leadership?
4. What makes the relational leadership model a unique tool for leaders?
5. How can you apply the relational leadership model across each modality?
6. What practices should People Leaders use to build relationships on in-person, hybrid, or remote teams?
7. What barriers get in the way of relationship-building?

Key Terms

- Work Modalities
- Essential
- Nonessential
- In-Person
- Hybrid
- Remote
- Relational Leadership Model
- Purpose
- Inclusiveness
- Empowering
- Mattering
- Ethics
- Process
- Mentoring
- Coaching
- People Leader
- Level 5 Leadership and Leaders
- Servant Leadership and Leaders

CASE STUDY 6.1 GLOBALTECH SOLUTIONS AND MULTIMODAL CHALLENGES

GlobalTech Solutions is a multinational software development corporation headquartered in New York. It employs over 10,000 people in its offices in North America, Europe, and Asia. Since the onset of the COVID-19 pandemic, GlobalTech has adopted a hybrid work model, allowing employees to work remotely and in the office. This transition has presented unique challenges in maintaining effective leadership and team dynamics across diverse cultures and time zones.

As GlobalTech adapted to hybrid work, leadership recognized the need for a framework to enhance collaboration among dispersed teams. To strengthen relationships and ensure productivity, they implemented the relational leadership model, aligning with the company's values of inclusivity and empowerment. However, senior leaders encountered challenges in fostering better connections across teams.

CHALLENGES FACED AND QUESTIONS

1. **Time Zone Differences**—With team members spread across multiple continents, scheduling meetings accommodating everyone's availability proved difficult. This often led to essential discussions without full participation from all team members, resulting in feelings of exclusion and disconnection. *How should senior leaders develop the necessary cadence of meetings with all team members around time zones?*
2. **Feelings of Isolation**—Some remote workers expressed feelings of isolation, particularly those in locations far from major offices. This isolation negatively impacted their motivation and commitment to the team. *How can the organization re-engage these remote workers and get them better connected?*

3. **Trust and Relationship Building**—Building trust among team members who rarely interacted face to face was a significant challenge. The absence of informal interactions, which often happen in physical offices, hindered relationship development. *How can people leaders build the trust essential to relationships in remote environments?*
4. **Performance Management and Accountability**—Tracking team performance and individual contributions become more complex in a hybrid environment. With members working in various locations, it was challenging to assess accountability and ensure everyone was meeting their responsibilities. *How can People Leaders create a positive culture of accountability, with all team members executing their responsibilities without becoming micro-managers?*

Task: Answer the preceding questions above provide four comprehensive recommendations for GlobalTech's leaders. Connect the recommendations to key chapter concepts. Present the recommendations to a larger group for feedback and discussion.

REFERENCES

Bennis, W. G., & Thomas, R. J. (2002). *Geeks and geezers: How era, values, and defining moments shape leaders*. Harvard Business School Press.

Bolman, L. G., & Deal, T. E. (2003). *Reframing organizations: Artistry, choice, and leadership* (3rd ed.). Jossey-Bass.

Buffer (2023, April). Struggles with working remotely worldwide from 2020 to 2023. *State of Remote Work Report 2023*. https://buffer.com/state-of-remote-work

Building Careers. (2023, January 19). *How to work well with remote coworkers*. Building Careers. Retrieved from https://buildingrecareers.com/2023/01/19/how-to-work-well-with-remote-coworkers/

Carucci, R. (2021, November 15). Rebuilding relationships across teams in a hybrid workplace. *Harvard Business Review*. Retrieved from https://hbr.org/2021/11/rebuilding-relationships-across-teams-in-a-hybrid-workplace

Ciulla, J. B. (2014). *Ethics: The heart of leadership* (3rd ed.). Praeger.

Collins, J. (2001). *Good to great: Why some companies make the leap... and others don't*. HarperCollins

Covey, S. R. (1989). *The seven habits of highly effective people: Restoring the character ethic*. Simon & Schuster.

Deloitte. (2023). *Deloitte 2023 Gen Z and Millennial Survey*. Retrieved from https://www.deloitte.com/global/en/issues/work/content/genzmillennialsurvey.html

Eads, A. (2025). Best remote work companies in 2025. *Indeed.com*.

Early, S. L. (2020). Relational leadership reconsidered: The mentor–protégé connection. *Journal of Leadership Studies, 13*(4), 57–72. https://doi.org/10.1002/jls.21671

Ernst, R. (2019, March 15). What does it mean to be a people leader? *Forbes Magazine*. Retrieved from https://www.forbes.com/sites/forbeshumanresourcescouncil/2019/03/15/what-does-it-mean-to-be-a-people-leader/

Galbraith, M. (2018, October 22). Don't just tell employees organizational changes are coming: Explain why. *Harvard Business Review*. Retrieved from https://hbr.org/2018/10/dont-just-tell-employees-organizational-changes-are-coming-explain-why

Goldberg, E. (2023, March 30). Do we know how many people are working from home? *The New York Times*. Retrieved from https://www.nytimes.com/2023/03/30/business/economy/remote-work-measure-surveys.html

Greenleaf, R. K. (1977). *Servant leadership: A journey into the nature of legitimate power and greatness*. Paulist Press.

Holder, C., & Pursley, D. (2024). Centering relationships in collegiate leadership curricula. *New Directions for Student Leadership, 2024*(180), 49–59. https://doi.org/10.1002/yd.20580

Ketter, M. (2024). Top 13 companies with hybrid and remote work models in 2024. *Officespace.com*.

Kouzes, J. M., & Posner, B. Z. (1987). *The leadership challenge: How to get extraordinary things done in organizations*. Jossey-Bass.

McMahon, T. R., Komives, S. R., & Nance, L. (2013). *Exploring leadership: For college students who want to make a difference* (3rd ed.). Jossey-Bass.

Olley, R. (2021). A focussed literature review of power and influence leadership theories. *Asia Pacific Journal of Health Management, 16*(2), 7–17.

Ortiz-Ospina, E. (2019). Is there a loneliness epidemic? *Our World in Data*.

PayScale (2024a, January). Percentage of employees who work from home all or most of the time worldwide from 2015 to 2023. https://www.payscale.com/research-and-insights/remote-work/

PayScale (2024b, January). Percentage of employees who work fully or mostly remote worldwide in 2023 by industry. https://www.payscale.com/research-and-insights/remote-work/

Peterson, R. R. (1989). Empowering an organization. *Public Management, 71*(1), 2–3.

Reid III, W. A., Bud West, G. R., Winston, B. E., & Wood, J. A. (2014). An instrument to measure level 5 leadership. *Journal of Leadership Studies, 8*(1), 17–32.

Rolfe, A. (2016). Do I need a mentor or a coach? *Korean Journal of Medical Education, 28*(4), 397–399. https://doi.org/10.3946/kjme.2016.45

Rosenberg, M., & McCullough, B. C. (1981). Mattering: Inferred significance and mental health among adolescents. *Research in Community & Mental Health, 2*, 163–182.

Surakhmat, A., Hapsari, R. D., & Arta, E. B. (2024). The Nexus of Leadership Models, Influence Tactics, and Power in Shaping Organizational Outcomes. *Digital Innovation: International Journal of Management, 1*(2), 31–39.

Toffler, B. L. (1986). *Tough choices: Managers talk ethics*. Wiley.

Torres, J. (2022, March 28). How to build meaningful relationships within a remote team. *Forbes Magazine*. Retrieved from https://www.forbes.com/sites/forbestechcouncil/2022/03/28/how-to-build-meaningful-relationships-within-a-remote-team/

University of Michigan [U of MI]. (n.d.). *Coaching, mentoring, and feedback*. Michigan Medicine Human Resources. Retrieved February 2, 2025, from https://hr.medicine.umich.edu/hr-services/hr-resources/performance-management/coaching-mentoring-feedback

Wheatley, M. J. (1992). *Leadership and the new science: Learning about organization from an orderly universe*. Berrett-Koehler Publishers.

Zorlu, Ö., Baytok, A., Avan, A., & İnci, E. (2021). How servant leaders psychologically empower their followers: The case of five-star hotels. *Tourism: An International Interdisciplinary Journal*, 69(4), 505–526.

CHAPTER 7

Motivating for High Performance

CHAPTER OVERVIEW

The next chapter in the People Leadership section is about motivating employees. Here, classic theories in motivation are paired with very contemporary models. Motivation has long been linked to employee productivity and performance and is essential for business leaders to understand when leading a team. Tools like the root cause analysis and performance analysis quadrant allow leaders to diagnose employee motivation challenges and implement practical solutions for each case. Modernization of motivation techniques is key as well, and including concepts like employee voice and career development are much needed. This chapter helps People Leaders wrestle with the paradox of balancing employee well-being while also ensuring that organizational performance metrics are met.

What motivates anyone to do anything? This question has perplexed humans since the dawn of psychology, or perhaps intelligence. Social, behavioral, and psychological scientists have long been fascinated with what leaders must do to improve **employee performance**: how well individuals complete work. Across studies, **motivation**—the why of doing something—and **employee productivity**—how much is done—remain inextricably linked.

People Leaders still find themselves in a paradox today where, on the one hand, they must address employee well-being by adhering to their wants, needs, and desires to keep them satisfied. On the other hand, People Leaders must still make decisions based on employee performance, such as whether or not their employees are producing. Motivating employees is a critical priority so they experience **job satisfaction**, which is contentment with a job and likely organization. Furthermore, scholars and practitioners may look beyond satisfaction, exploring **employee engagement**, which amounts to the effect of positive behaviors enacted at work. Employee engagement can be seen as the tip of an iceberg where employees are observed doing impactful positive things at work; however, there is great depth in their attitudes, perceptions, and motivations below the surface (Saks, 2006). Satisfaction and engagement connect to higher employee performance and productivity.

This chapter explores employee motivation and how to be a better supervisor (remember our introductory chapter). In our opening, we noted the shortfalls of bad supervisors and their notable influence on employee and organizational performance. We revisit

DOI: 10.4324/9781003474647-9

classic motivation theories, citing foundational concepts that shape managerial practices today. We examine contemporary strategies around employee voice, autonomy, and career development in enhancing job satisfaction and employee engagement. Through tools like root cause analysis andperformance analysis quadrant, we provide People Leaders with essential tools to diagnose and address challenges. The timeless theories and modern approaches offer a comprehensive toolkit for leaders seeking to inspire their teams, boost productivity, and foster thriving workplace cultures.

MOTIVATION THEORY CLASSICS

Modern business leaders must understand human motivation to navigate challenges like quiet quitting, employee stress, low morale, and burnout. Classic theories, such as Maslow's hierarchy of needs, highlight the importance of belonging and purpose, while Herzberg's two-factor theory emphasizes intrinsic motivators like meaningful work over mere financial compensation. Self-determination theory further examines autonomy, competence, and relatedness to bolster employee engagement. These theories, along with others, are tools for modern business leaders to enrich the lives of their employees and workplaces.

Herzberg's Two-Factor Theory

Herzberg's motivation-hygiene theory, the two-factor theory, has stood the test of time for People Leaders. While the scholarly merit of Herzberg's two-factor theory is heavily methodologically dependent on the critical incidents approach, where individuals report on the highest and lowest moments at work, the theory, even as a metaphor, has high utility for contemporary business leaders (Robbins & Judge, 2013; Sachau, 2007; Ser & Webber, 2024). Herzberg's theory comes from a generation of theories of management rooted in **human capital** (Schultz, 1961, 1975) that focus on humans as more than tools in the workforce but unique individuals that, as an engaged and growing collective, can be a powerful organizational force.

Herzberg's theory argues that job satisfaction and dissatisfaction are distinctly different. The theory asserts that separate sets of mutually exclusive factors in the work environment cause job satisfaction or dissatisfaction (Herzberg, 1966, 1982; Herzberg et al., 1959). Herzberg and his colleagues (1959) elucidated factors influencing job satisfaction, categorizing them as hygienic or motivational. Motivators increase job satisfaction, while hygiene prevents job dissatisfaction. Generally, motivators encourage job satisfaction and relate to self-growth and self-actualization, the influence of Maslow's classic hierarchy of needs (another human capital theory discussed later) being very evident (Nickerson, 2023). Motivators bolster job satisfaction, while poor hygiene leads to job dissatisfaction.

As noted, the motivation-hygiene theory explores critical incidents. Critical incident approaches ask employees to describe situations where they felt good about their jobs. Participants note factors intrinsic to their work. In contrast, those describing situations where they felt bad about their jobs cite extrinsic factors. This approach renders distinct factors; thus, the highs and lows usually have different thematic commonalities (Robbins & Judge, 2013; Herzberg et al., 1959).

Hygiene and motivators are distinct when using this approach. To Herzberg (1966), the opposite of job satisfaction was not job dissatisfaction but no job satisfaction (which might be best conceptualized as boredom or stagnation, but not necessarily unpleasant). Conversely, the opposite of job dissatisfaction is no job dissatisfaction (which might be best conceptualized as short-lasting positive feelings at its highest extreme). These continua are shown in Figure 7.1.

These concepts of job satisfaction and dissatisfaction support the possibility that people can be content with certain aspects of their jobs but discontent with others (Herzberg et al., 1959; Kacel et al., 2005; Sachau, 2007). This understanding has been vital for scores of leaders in positions where they must manage employees.

Herzberg et al. (1959) argue that **motivators** are necessary to improve job satisfaction, and these factors tend to be more intrinsic, which we will discuss later. **Hygiene** encompasses factors that decrease **job dissatisfaction**, that is, discontent with a job and likely organization. Herzberg et al. (1959) used the term hygiene, connoting a more medical or hazard-based connection, suggesting negative hygiene should be mitigated, avoided, or removed (Alshmemri et al., 2017; Herzberg, 1966). Table 7.1 offers each of the modernized factors and their components.

Herzberg's critics argue that if hygiene and motivators are equally important, both should be capable of motivating employees (Robbins & Judge, 2013). Herzberg's research emerged during a time of rigid, bureaucratic organizational structures. As companies transitioned from mass production to a focus on innovation, new motivational theories (discussed later) developed (Bassett-Jones & Lloyd, 2005). Contemporarily, hygiene in the context of the developed world may be seen as a baseline expectation employers must provide for employees, or they will not attract and retain them. Poor salaries and hostile and unsafe work environments, especially in the age of social media and company review sites like Glassdoor, now showcase greater transparency regarding what employees might expect on day one.

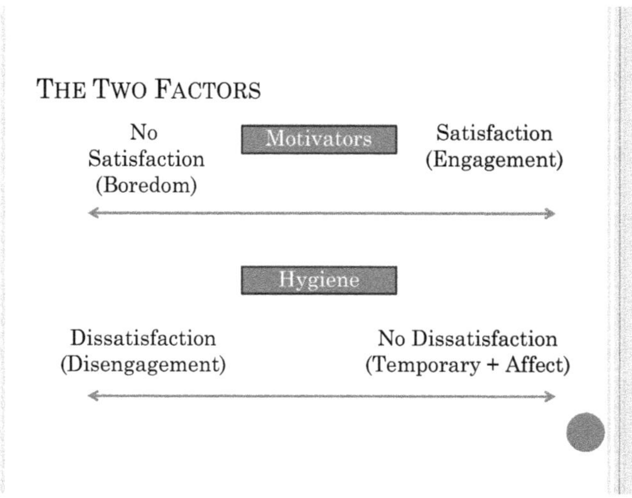

FIGURE 7.1 Two Spectrums of Job Dissatisfaction and Job Satisfaction

TABLE 7.1 Motivators and Hygiene

Motivators (Job Satisfaction)	*Hygiene (Job Dissatisfaction)*
Achievement—Completing meaningful work leads to motivation.	**Salary**—Compensation must be fair, but high pay alone does not motivate.
Recognition—Employees feel valued when acknowledged for their contributions.	**Company Policies & Administration**—Clear policies reduce frustration but do not inspire motivation.
The Work Itself—Engaging, meaningful tasks increase satisfaction.	**Supervision**—Supportive and competent managers prevent dissatisfaction but do not drive engagement.
Responsibility—Empowering employees with autonomy enhances motivation.	**Interpersonal Relations**—Positive relationships create pleasant work environments.
Advancement—Career growth opportunities encourage long-term motivation.	**Working Conditions**—A comfortable, safe workspace reduces dissatisfaction but does not enhance motivation.
Growth—Professional development fosters long-term engagement.	**Job Security**—Stability prevents anxiety but does not necessarily increase enthusiasm.

Daniel Sachau (2007), a former student of Herzberg, revisited and challenged the two-factor theory's oversimplification. While acknowledging its significance, he noted that modern work environments often blur the lines between hygiene and motivators. For instance, salary—traditionally a hygiene factor—can be motivating when linked to performance-based incentives. Sachau also highlighted that job enrichment and autonomy are vital components that bridge the gap between motivators and hygiene. Nevertheless, Herzberg's work remains relevant, as motivators and hygiene aid People Leaders in addressing performance issues.

Business leaders must balance hygiene and motivators to apply Herzberg's insights in contemporary workplaces effectively. Ensuring robust hygiene, such as competitive compensation and favorable working conditions, minimizes employee dissatisfaction. Modern business leaders invest in motivators that inspire engagement and enrich jobs. **Job enrichment** strategies enhance engagement by assigning meaningful responsibilities and advancement opportunities. Job enrichment mitigates dissatisfaction and promotes intrinsic motivation and engagement, boosting productivity, engagement, innovation, and retention (Sachau, 2007).

Maslow's Hierarchy of Needs

People Leaders must grasp what motivates employees to retain talent, enhance performance, and foster innovation. Building on Herzberg's distinctions between job satisfaction and dissatisfaction, **Maslow's hierarchy of needs** (1943, 1954) provides a timeless perspective identifying the core factors influencing human behavior. While Herzberg focused on intrinsic versus extrinsic motivators (discussed by Deci and Ryan in the next section), Maslow's (1943, 1954) framework illustrates how employees advance to achieve their full potential.

For People Leaders, the task extends beyond eliminating dissatisfaction to cultivating engagement. People Leaders do not allow their direct reports to feel stuck, undervalued, or disconnected from purpose. They understand the evolving needs of their workforce and tailor engagement and retention strategies that harmonize individual goals with team objectives.

Maslow's theory suggests individuals strive to meet their needs sequentially, starting from basic survival requirements and moving toward higher levels of personal satisfaction. When leaders neglect to address needs across the hierarchy, it can lead to employee disengagement, quiet quitting, and turnover. Table 7.2 outlines how Maslow's needs can be observed in the workplace and offers strategies for leaders to address them effectively. Please note that while Maslow's hierarchy is often depicted as a pyramid, that is not how he initially presented it.

Maslow's model of motivation offers valuable insights for contemporary business leaders, but its rigid hierarchy requires reevaluation in today's dynamic work environments. Employees often prioritize purpose-driven work alongside financial security, especially in high-skilled industries (Tay & Diener, 2011). Younger generations, particularly Millennials and Gen Z, favor meaningful work over salary (Twenge, 2017). Organizations emphasizing a strong mission and corporate social responsibility (discussed in our later chapters) help employees achieve self-actualization more rapidly, leading to higher engagement levels.

TABLE 7.2 Maslow's Needs with Approaches

Level	*Description*	*Strategic Leadership Approach*
Physiological	The most basic human requirements and survival concerns include food, water, shelter, and rest.	Competitive compensation, work-life balance, paid leave, healthy office conditions, flexible work arrangements, and wellness programs.
Safety	Employees seek job security, financial stability, and a workplace without physical and emotional harm.	Transparent job security policies, health insurance, fair wages, workplace safety initiatives, and financial wellness programs.
Social Belonging	Employees crave connection, collaboration, and a sense of inclusion in their teams and organizations.	Strong team dynamics, mentorship programs, networking opportunities, social events, and company culture initiatives.
Esteem	Recognition, status, and achievements drive motivation.	Public recognition, performance incentives, career progression pathways, leadership opportunities, and conferences.
Self-Actualization	The desire to achieve one's full potential, embrace creativity, and find purpose in work.	Opportunities for leadership, project autonomy, personal and professional growth, and meaningful work.

People Leaders should recognize that individuals may seek to fulfill multiple needs simultaneously.

Many companies conduct engagement surveys of their organizations and departments, examining concepts from Maslow's and Herzberg's theories. Professional development programs can build esteem and self-actualization through leadership pathways, lifelong learning, mentorship, coaching, and stretch assignments. A psychologically safe environment, which we will cover in a future chapter, encourages open communication, feedback, representation, and inclusion in leadership. Our community leadership chapters emphasize helping employees see the bigger picture. Still, a strong culture of **work-life balance** needs investment from leaders and employees to meet mental health and well-being support, flexibility, and other needs. Maslow's hierarchy advocates for a flexible leadership framework instead of a strict sequence, where leaders can better adapt their motivation strategies to meet workforce needs.

Intrinsic and Extrinsic Motivation

In the 1980s, psychologists Edward Deci and Richard Ryan developed the **Self-Determination Theory (SDT)**, substantially shifting the motivation literature (Deci & Ryan, 1980, 1983, 1985). Their findings contested the conventional behaviorist perspective that external incentives such as bonuses or promotions drive performance. Instead, Ryan and Deci posited that intrinsic motivation, a person's inherent desire for personal and psychological growth, is the cornerstone of lasting success and fulfillment. For modern business leaders facing intricate and swiftly changing workplace dynamics, SDT offers insights into motivation beyond monetary rewards. It builds upon Maslow's and Herzberg's foundations, examining how motivation is undermined.

A crucial concept within SDT is that poorly managed extrinsic rewards can diminish intrinsic motivation, a phenomenon known as the **overjustification effect** (Deci et al., 1999). Employees prioritizing external rewards like bonuses may lose sight of their intrinsic motivation, shifting from autonomy to control and undermining their engagement. For example, an employee who enjoys problem-solving may focus on the number of problems solved to obtain financial rewards, sacrificing the quality of their work for quantity.

People Leaders are cautious not to overemphasize external rewards, creating a transactional work culture. Failing work environments persist, where employees only engage in the minimum required for compensation rather than pursuing excellence and fulfillment. This aligns with Herzberg's framework, which posits that while adequate compensation prevents dissatisfaction, it is insufficient to foster long-term engagement. People Leaders ensure extrinsic rewards complement, rather than overshadow, employees' intrinsic motivations. People Leaders motivate their teams to excel through meaning, recognition, and achievement, not temporary extrinsic benefits. These distinctions resonate with transactional and transformational leadership, which we previously discussed.

The Three Pillars: Deci and Ryan (2000) identified three fundamental psychological needs that drive intrinsic motivation. Employees are more engaged, resilient, and productive when these needs are fulfilled. When neglected, employees may fall into patterns of burnout, disengagement, or even quiet quitting (discussed later), which affects productivity. When the three pillars of SDT are leveraged well, and intrinsic motivation is not undermined, People Leaders can foster cultures where employees recommend their workplaces to others, demonstrate strong commitment and engagement, and want to do more beyond their job roles (Table 7.3).

Autonomy makes employees more innovative, engaged, and accountable, increasing job satisfaction and productivity. Autonomy fosters a sense of ownership, which enhances intrinsic motivation and commitment to the organization (Reisinger & Fetterer, 2021). Companies that embrace principle-based hybrid work strategies, where employees are encouraged to choose the best work environment for their tasks, experience greater productivity and engagement than rigid policy-based approaches. For example, firms that imposed strict return-to-office mandates, such as Apple, faced backlash and resignations as employees perceived these policies as limiting their autonomy (Reisinger & Fetterer, 2021).

Competence is another critical factor in growth and retention. Competence comes from skill mastery, which is supported by practice over time and solid feedback (Deci & Ryan, 2000). Modern business leaders invest in employee development that enriches individual capabilities and strengthens organizational commitment. A recent report on LinkedIn.com found that 94% of employees say they would stay at a company longer if it invested in their learning and development (Cai, 2023). Organizations that offer autonomy and competence-building opportunities, such as professional development programs, foster more engagement, reduce burnout, and encourage long-term employee commitment (Bakker & van Woerkom, 2017).

Relatedness is paramount in today's flexible work environments. Organizations that promote strong interpersonal relationships through mentoring, collaboration, and a shared mission tend to experience heightened job satisfaction among their workforce (Dweck, 2006). For instance, companies implementing team-building exercises and proper communication channels create a sense of community that encourages employees to remain committed. We covered the advantages of mentoring and coaching in a previous chapter.

When organizations apply SDT within their leadership practices, they can expect elevated levels of innovation, employee satisfaction, and retention. Research indicates that employees who enjoy greater autonomy, competence, and relatedness report reduced stress levels and greater employee engagement. People Leaders pursue organizational

TABLE 7.3 Three Pillars of SDT

Component	*Definition*	*Workplace Application*
Autonomy	Needing to feel in control of one's actions and decisions rather than micromanaged or externally controlled.	Flexible work arrangements, decision-making authority, and opportunities for employees to take ownership of projects.
Competence	Needing to feel capable, effective, and skilled in one's work.	Professional development programs, clear performance feedback, and skill-building opportunities that foster mastery.
Relatedness	Needing to feel socially connected and valued by others in the workplace.	Team-building initiatives, mentorship programs, and organizational cultures that promote collaboration and belonging.

cultures that support self-determination, ensuring engaged and productive employees do not leave (Deci et al., 2017).

Workplace Stress, Emotional Labor, and Burnout

Quiet Quitting is a trend in which employees do the minimum required without going above and beyond, which can be linked to a lack of meaningful work or engagement. **Burnout** is characterized by chronic stress, leading to emotional exhaustion and diminished feelings of accomplishment. Both terms have become more prevalent in organizational leadership, requiring more holistic approaches to motivation and work-life balance (Harter, 2022; Urban et al., 2024).

Emotional labor refers to how employees manage emotions to align with organizational expectations, particularly in customer-facing or supervisory roles. It involves regulating internal emotions to present an externally consistent emotional expression, which can be emotionally taxing for employees (Peng & Li, 2023). This emotional regulation can lead to emotional exhaustion, especially when employees engage in **surface acting** (pretending to feel emotions they do not genuinely experience) rather than **deep acting** (modifying internal feelings to match the required emotional display). **Emotional exhaustion** results from persistent and intense emotional labor and can contribute to work **withdrawal behavior**. **Absenteeism** is the most overt form of withdrawal; however, disengagement from social outings, tardiness to meetings, and lack of communication are other indicators. Withdrawal behavior, fueled by burnout, reflects a coping mechanism for dealing with the emotional demands of the job (Peng & Li, 2023). People Leaders have emotional labor and must effectively manage the emotional labor of others.

MOTIVATIONAL TOOLS

Root Cause Analysis

Root Cause Analysis (RCA) is helpful in motivating employees (James-Ward et al., 2012; Okes, 2019). Similar to critical incidents used by Herzberg, RCA provides notable benefits to improve a People Leader's understanding of the problem and its implications on job performance by finding the underlying factors influencing employee motivation, satisfaction, and productivity. RCA helps leaders assist their direct reports to develop more effective solutions to prevent recurrence or any worsening of problems, enhancing job performance and team productivity.

RCA systematically asks why a problem occurs and traces it back to its origin (James-Ward et al., 2012; Okes, 2019). The objective is to identify and address the root cause of a problem, aiming to eliminate or reduce it. RCA can be applied to various technical, operational, or organizational challenges. It assists modern leaders in avoiding superficial or quick-fix solutions that do not truly resolve the underlying issue and may even lead to additional problems.

When People Leaders suspect low morale in their teams, they must first define the problem clearly and objectively. For example, they may observe low engagement, turnover, poor communication, or low quality of work. They must then quantify the problem by collecting data, evidence, and feedback. For example, they could use surveys, interviews, performance reviews, or other job metrics to assess the level and impact of this low morale.

Next, People Leaders must identify possible causes of the problem and organize them into groups. For example, they could categorize the causes into factors associated with leadership, culture, work environment, responsibility, recognition, or advancement opportunities. Herzberg's motivators and hygiene could certainly be helpful here. Maslow's needs and SDT are helpful to leverage as well. People Leaders must verify the root causes by testing their assumptions and gathering evidence. They may conduct more interviews, observations, or experiments to support or debunk their hypotheses. They must also co-create the process with their stakeholders.

Finally, People Leaders develop and implement solutions that address the root causes and carefully monitor the results. They properly utilize their resources to design and execute action plans that involve coaching, mentoring, professional development, or organizational changes. People Leaders also set goals or key performance indicators to measure the effectiveness and sustainability of their solutions, consistent with goal-setting theory (Locke & Latham, 2006).

Applying RCA for low morale offers several benefits, including improving a leader's understanding of the problem, its root causes, and its impact. This information helps address employee motivation, satisfaction, and performance, developing more effective solutions to prevent the recurrence or worsening of the problem and enhancing communication and collaboration within the team. RCA can establish credibility and improve morale, engagement, and productivity. People Leaders who are perceived as practical problem solvers are considered competent at their jobs and often regarded as supervisors for whom others want to work.

Exercise 7.1 Root Cause Analysis Tree

Instructions: Split into several small groups of 3–4 members. Assign each group a typical scenario (Table 7.4). Each group should draw the trunk of a tree on their newsprint. In the trunk, write the scenario or the problem. Next, by drawing "branches" to the tree, group members should detail the potential causes of the problem. Branches can join or split from one reason to another related cause. Allow for ample time to brainstorm possible causes. Finally, below the ground of the trunk, groups should draw "roots" to demonstrate the potential solutions to the problem. Roots should reflect the causes and attempt to address them. Each group should present and explain their RCA tree to the larger group.

TABLE 7.4 Typical Scenarios Needing Motivational Interventions

#	*Scenario*	*Background*
1	Declining Team Morale	Team morale has declined over the past few months, with increased complaints about work conditions and decreased enthusiasm during team meetings.

#	Scenario	Background
2	Frequent Product Returns	A company has experienced a significant increase in product returns over the last quarter. Customers cite quality issues as the primary reason for returns.
3	Low Employee Engagement in Training Programs	A company has rolled out new training programs, but employee participation and engagement have been lower than expected.
4	Customer Service Response Delays	The customer service department is experiencing delays in response times, leading to increased customer frustration and dissatisfaction.
5	Project Budget Overruns	Several projects have been exceeding their budgets, causing financial strain and delays in project completion.

Performance Analysis Quadrant

One effective RCA technique is the **performance analysis quadrant** (PAQ) (Jones, 1993, see Figure 7.2). This quadrant is a four-quadrant, double-axis visual tool developed at Delta Airlines to discuss team member performance and potential. This tool can determine whether the root cause of a problem is employee motivation, resources or environment, employee selection, or employee training. The variables are to collect evidence or observe are the employee's knowledge and attitude or desire to perform the job.

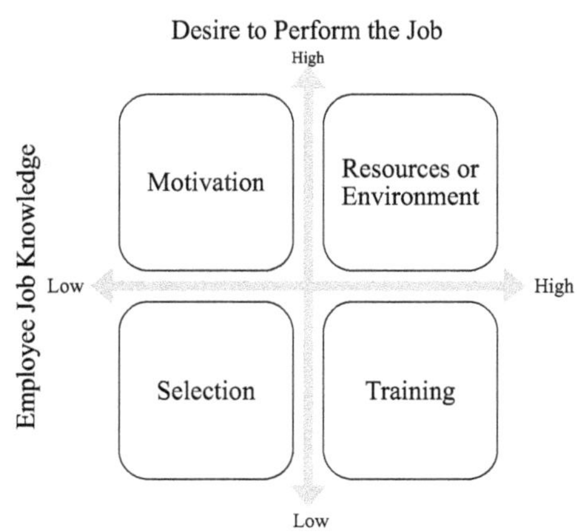

FIGURE 7.2 PAQ

(Adapted from Jones, 1993)

For a People Leader facing low morale or employee disengagement, such understanding can mean investing strategically in an employee or moving on from an employee.

Complex or multifaceted problems with various interrelated causes can lead to resistance from team members who disagree with the identified root cause or the proposed action plan. Implementing solutions requires behavioral, cultural, or structural changes, which can create employee tensions and inadvertently lower job performance if the RCA is poorly executed. People Leaders take extra care in gaining buy-in for the process, especially when employees or teams may already be low in morale or disengaged.

RCA and PAQ approaches have been established for some time and remain relevant in today's business environment. These techniques are effective across modalities. People Leaders must first master Self Leadership before leading others. They recognize that what motivates leaders may not necessarily motivate employees, as these factors can differ significantly. They acknowledge many employees today are driven by higher purposes discussed in our community leadership section. We continue by offering some additional approaches.

Exercise 7.2 Practicing the Performance Analysis Quadrant

You are a leader in the marketing department of a mid-sized company. The team has been working on a new product launch campaign crucial to the company's success. Last month's performance reviews and recent feedback have raised concerns about individual contributions and team dynamics. Use the PAQ to assess and address your team members' concerns better.

- **Alex**—Consistently delivers high-quality work and contributes innovative ideas. Shows strong leadership potential but has not yet been given formal leadership responsibilities.
- **Taylor**—Produces excellent work and meets all deadlines but shows little interest in taking on new challenges or responsibilities.
- **Jordan**—Struggles with meeting deadlines and producing work up to the team's standards. However, Jordan is highly motivated and eager to learn and grow.
- **Riley**—Frequently misses deadlines and delivers work that does not meet expectations. Shows little initiative or interest in improving performance.

Assessment and Categorization. Divide into small groups, decide on each team member's quadrant, and develop a strategy based on their performance analysis. For each quadrant, develop targeted strategies to address the specific needs and opportunities associated with the team members in that quadrant. Strategies should improve performance, maximize potential, and align with organizational goals. Present strategies for each member, explaining the rationale, connecting with the PAQ, and highlighting each member's potential.

MODERNIZING MOTIVATION

People Leaders must maintain high employee motivation and engagement levels. While classic theories like Herzberg's two-factor theory, Maslow's hierarchy of needs, and SDT provide essential insights into motivation, contemporary frameworks such as the job demands-resources model (JD-R), psychological capital (PsyCap), expectancy theory, goal-setting theory, and the theory of planned behavior introduce new dimensions to leaders (see Table 7.5).

Modern business leaders must understand that motivation goes beyond competitive salaries and benefits to engage employees effectively. Vital insights from these theories highlight the necessity of autonomy, meaningful work, and psychological well-being. Herzberg emphasizes that factors like achievement, recognition, and responsibility foster job satisfaction, while hygiene factors prevent dissatisfaction. Maslow's framework finds that higher-order needs better fuel engagement. SDT shows intrinsic motivation as more promising for employees to flourish.

Modern theories build on the classics by exploring how organizational and psychological factors influence motivation. The JD-R model suggests leaders balance job demands with sufficient resources to reduce burnout and disengagement. PsyCap emphasizes optimism, resilience, and self-efficacy to boost motivation and retention. Expectancy theory notes the importance of transparent expectations and rewards to drive performance.

For People Leaders, the goal is to select a single theory and synthesize multiple frameworks into a flexible motivation strategy. Recognizing employees' diverse generational expectations and personal aspirations, such as those of Millennials and Gen Z, and prioritizing purpose over traditional incentives allows leaders to tailor engagement strategies effectively. Classic and contemporary perspectives offer People Leaders approaches to meet individual needs aligned with organizational objectives. These approaches sustain motivation and productivity and ensure employees feel valued and invested in their work, driving long-term business success.

Flow Theory

Flow theory, formulated by Mihaly Csikszentmihalyi (1975), encapsulates a mental state where individuals find themselves deeply engrossed, genuinely enjoying their tasks, and performing at their best in response to challenges that align with their capabilities. Achieving this flow state occurs when tasks are appropriately matched with a person's skills, fostering total immersion in their work and cultivating intrinsic motivation and high productivity (Csikszentmihalyi, 1997; Bakker, 2008). Flow is essential to employee well-being, engagement, and performance, especially as organizations strive to create environments conducive to innovation and sustained productivity (Bakker & van Woerkom, 2017).

People Leaders can cultivate flow by establishing conditions that harmonize challenge with skill, granting employees autonomy, and providing meaningful work experiences. This state is inherently linked to intrinsic motivation, which is more enduring than external rewards like monetary incentives (Deci & Ryan, 2000). Modern business leaders can leverage **job crafting**, allowing employees to tailor their roles to their strengths and

TABLE 7.5 More Motivational Theories That People Leaders Must Know

Theory	*Key Concept*	*Application*	*References*
Job Demands-Resources (JD-R) Model	Balancing job demands (stressors) with job resources (support, autonomy) prevents burnout and increases engagement.	Helps manage workload, reduce burnout, and enhance employee well-being through supportive policies and flexible work arrangements.	Bakker and Demerouti (2007)
Psychological Capital (PsyCap) Theory	Employees with high levels of hope, efficacy, resilience, and optimism (HERO) are more engaged and motivated.	Encourages organizations to invest in resilience training, mental health initiatives, and employee coaching to enhance performance and retention.	Luthans et al. (2007)
Expectancy Theory	Employees are motivated when they believe effort leads to performance, and performance leads to rewards.	Helps design performance-based incentives like commission structures, equity-based pay, and goal-based bonuses.	Vroom (1964)
Self-Efficacy Theory	Belief in the ability to succeed increases motivation and perseverance.	Applied development, training programs, and mentorship initiatives to boost confidence and competence.	Bandura (1986)
Drive Theory & Purpose-Driven Motivation	Intrinsic motivation is fueled by autonomy, mastery, and purpose rather than external rewards.	Helps rethink employee engagement strategies by fostering meaningful work, skill-building, and decision-making autonomy.	Pink (2009)
Goal-Setting Theory	Specific, challenging, and clear goals drive motivation and performance.	Many businesses use SMART goals and OKRs (objectives and key results) to enhance accountability and productivity.	Locke and Latham (2006)
Equity Theory & Fair Process Effect	Employees compare their efforts and rewards to others; perceived unfairness leads to disengagement.	Supports pay transparency, DEI initiatives, and fair promotion policies to improve retention and morale.	Adams (1963) and Colquitt et al. (2001)
Theory of Planned Behavior / Reasoned Action Model	Employee decision-making is based on attitudes, subjective norms, and perceived behavioral control that shape behavioral intentions.	Helps predict employee behavior, design effective change management strategies, and enhance participation in training programs, ethical initiatives, and diversity efforts.	Ajzen (1991) and Fishbein and Ajzen (1975)

increase their propensity toward flow (Bakker, 2005; Demerouti, 2006). Employees experiencing flow report elevated job satisfaction, lower levels of burnout, and enhanced creativity (Stavrou et al., 2015).

People Leaders can embrace these concepts to create motivating environments that promote deep concentration, effective problem-solving, and personal accomplishment. Digital tools, flexible conditions, and psychologically safe environments enable employees to experience flow, despite physical divides. People Leaders can leverage flow theory to bolster employee satisfaction, engagement, and productivity so long as they listen to employee needs.

CONCLUSION

Effective leadership development can unleash an organization's full potential by nurturing capable individuals. Motivation is vital in influencing employee productivity, as demonstrated in this chapter. People Leaders wrestle with the paradox of balancing employee well-being while also ensuring that organizational performance metrics are met.

Job satisfaction and engagement are just the tip of the iceberg; a wealth of underlying attitudes and motivations are tied to performance and productivity (Saks, 2006). Classic motivation theories provide foundational insights to enhance employee motivation. Maslow emphasizes the importance of belonging and purpose, and Herzberg distinguishes between intrinsic factors that lead to job satisfaction (motivators) and extrinsic factors that can prevent dissatisfaction (hygiene). Furthermore, SDT and flow theory connect autonomy, competence, and relatedness as essential elements that foster employee engagement. Tools like root cause analysis and performance analysis quadrants are helpful aids to People Leaders. Still, People Leaders must recognize that the voice of employees and their career aspirations offer essential contexts for optimizing motivational tactics and building relationships.

Employee voice refers to the extent to which employees feel free to express their opinions, concerns, and suggestions regarding their workplace (Morrison, 2011; Visser, 2020). Encouraging employee voice can foster a sense of ownership and demonstrate to employees that their contributions are valued, enhancing motivation and engagement. Employees should feel they can voice their desires for autonomy or paint a picture of what achievement, advancement, and recognition look like to them. They are invested in their career development.

Career development emphasizes the importance of providing opportunities for employees to grow professionally within the organization, helping them acquire new skills and advance their careers (Greenhaus et al., 2010). This investment in career development by employees and leaders fosters greater employee satisfaction and loyalty, as individuals perceive their organization as committed to personal growth. People Leaders are key players in the career development of their direct reports.

People Leaders play a crucial role in their career development and that of their team members. Essentially, they need to motivate themselves and others through meaningful work, appreciate the contributions of everyone involved, avoid micromanaging, and offer autonomy to foster growth. Motivation goes beyond perks and extrinsic rewards; it is fundamentally relational and linked to higher purposes.

DISCUSSION QUESTIONS

1. What is the linkage between motivation and employee job satisfaction?
2. Why do People Leaders need a repertoire of strategies for motivating their employees?
3. How could you adjust the motivators for this employee?
4. How could you adjust the hygiene for this employee?
5. As a People Leader, when you suspect a motivation problem with an employee, how could you apply the Root Cause Analysis?
6. As a People Leader, when you suspect a motivation problem with an employee, how could you apply the Performance Analysis Quadrant?
7. How could you increase the opportunity for meaningful employee voice in in-person, hybrid, or remote environments?
8. What are the tensions associated with providing autonomy to employees in in-person, hybrid, or remote environments?
9. Why is co-creating a career development plan with a People Leader and their employee critical to employee performance?

Key Terms

- Employee Performance
- Employee Productivity
- Motivation
- Job Satisfaction
- Employee Engagement
- Herzberg's Motivation-Hygiene Theory
- Human Capital
- Motivators
- Hygiene
- Job Dissatisfaction
- Job Enrichment
- Maslow's Hierarchy of Needs
- Work-Life Balance
- Self-Determination Theory (SDT)
- Overjustification Effect
- Autonomy
- Competence
- Relatedness
- Quiet Quitting
- Burnout
- Emotional Labor
- Surface Acting
- Deep Acting
- Withdrawal Behavior
- Root Cause Analysis
- Performance Analysis Quadrant
- Flow Theory
- Job Crafting
- Employee Voice
- Career Development

CASE STUDY 7.1 GREENTECH SOLUTIONS

GreenTech Solutions, established in 2015, is a leading provider of innovative renewable energy technologies, focusing on solar and wind solutions. Despite a strong product lineup and growing customer base, the company faced significant challenges with employee motivation. This resulted in a 30% turnover rate by 2022, decreased project completion rates, and lowered morale. Acknowledging the urgent need to enhance motivation and performance amid a rapidly evolving industry, senior leaders initiated multiple initiatives to address these issues.

Sarah Thompson is an innovative People Leader at GreenTech. She is committed to fostering a thriving workplace culture and understands employee dynamics. She has significantly influenced the company's people strategy, advocating for initiatives that support employee well-being and professional growth. Known for her empathetic leadership style, Sarah actively listens to her team's concerns, promoting trust and open communication to ensure every employee feels valued. Despite her efforts to enhance personal engagement, she has encountered various challenges in her role.

CHALLENGES FACED AND QUESTIONS

1. **Burnout and Workload Imbalance**—Many employees, like Jake, reported feeling overwhelmed by excessive workloads and tight deadlines, which can lead to burnout. The pressure to meet ambitious project goals often results in long hours and high stress, diminishing job satisfaction. *What can Sarah do to better manage employees like Jake?*
2. **Lack of Clear Vision and Alignment**—Employees felt disconnected from the company's mission and objectives. Many struggled to find purpose in their work without clearly understanding how their roles contributed to the broader goals. *What can Sarah do to clarify intent and better motivate employees?*
3. **Inconsistent Communication**—The communication between leaders and employees was often top-down, leaving employees excluded from meaningful conversations and decision-making processes. This created a divide between leadership and the workforce. What can People Leaders like Sarah do to open channels for employee voice?
4. **Limited Growth Opportunities**—Many employees expressed concerns about career advancement within the company. Because the company focused on immediate project needs, there were few structured opportunities for professional development, leading to stagnation and frustration. *What can People Leaders like Sarah do to enhance employee growth and development opportunities?*

Task: Answer the preceding questions and provide four comprehensive recommendations for Sarah. Make sure to connect the recommendations to key chapter concepts. Present the recommendations to a larger group for feedback and discussion.

REFERENCES

Adams, J. S. (1963). Toward an understanding of inequity. *Journal of Abnormal and Social Psychology, 67*(5), 422–436.

Ajzen, I. (1991). The theory of planned behavior. *Organizational Behavior and Human Decision Processes, 50*(2), 179–211

Alshmemri, M., Shahwan-Akl, L., & Maude, P. (2017). Herzberg's two-factor theory. *Life Science Journal, 14*(5), 12–16.

Bakker, A. B. (2005). Flow among music teachers and their students: The crossover of peak experiences. *Journal of Vocational Behavior, 66*(1), 26–44.

Bakker, A. B. (2008). The work-related flow inventory: Construction and initial validation of the WOLF. *Journal of Vocational Behavior, 72*(3), 400–414.

Bakker, A. B., & Demerouti, E. (2007). The Job Demands-Resources model: State of the art. *Journal of Managerial Psychology, 22*(3), 309–328.

Bakker, A. B., & van Woerkom, M. (2017). Flow at work: A self-determination perspective. *Occupational Health Science, 1*(1), 47–65.

Bandura, A. (1986). *Social foundations of thought and action: A social cognitive theory*. Prentice Hall.

Bassett-Jones, N., & Lloyd, G. C. (2005). Does Herzberg's motivation theory have staying power? *Journal of Management Development, 24*(10), 929–943.

Cai, L. J. (2023, February 15). *2023 Workplace Learning Report: Building the agile future*. LinkedIn Talent Blog: Data Insights. https://www.linkedin.com/business/talent/blog/learning-and-development/workplace-learning-report-2023

Colquitt, J. A., Conlon, D. E., Wesson, M. J., Porter, C. O., & Ng, K. Y. (2001). Justice at the Millennium: A meta-analytic review of 25 years of organizational justice research. *Journal of Applied Psychology, 86*(3), 425.

Csikszentmihalyi, M. (1975). *Beyond boredom and anxiety: Experiencing flow in work and play*. Jossey-Bass.

Csikszentmihalyi, M. (1997). *Finding flow: The psychology of engagement with everyday life*. Basic Books.

Deci, E. L., Koestner, R., & Ryan, R. M. (1999). A meta-analytic review of experiments examining the effects of extrinsic rewards on intrinsic motivation. *Psychological Bulletin, 125*(6), 627–668.

Deci, E. L., Olafsen, A. H., & Ryan, R. M. (2017). Self-determination theory in work organizations: The state of a science. *Annual Review of Organizational Psychology and Organizational Behavior, 4*(1), 19–43.

Deci, E. L., & Ryan, R. M. (1980). Self-determination theory: When the mind mediates behavior. *The Journal of Mind and Behavior, 1*(1), 33–43.

Deci, E. L., & Ryan, R. M. (1983). The basis of self-determination: Intrinsic motivation and integrated internalizations. *Academic Psychology Bulletin, 5*(1), 21–29.

Deci, E. L., & Ryan, R. M. (1985). The general causality orientations scale: Self-determination in personality. *Journal of Research in Personality, 19*(2), 109–134.

Deci, E. L., & Ryan, R. M. (2000). The "what" and "why" of goal pursuits: Human needs and the self-determination of behavior. *Psychological Inquiry, 11*(4), 227–268.

Demerouti, E. (2006). Job characteristics, flow, and performance: The moderating role of conscientiousness. *Journal of Occupational Health Psychology, 11*(3), 266–280.

Dweck, C. S. (2006). *Mindset: The new psychology of success*. Random House.
Fishbein, M., & Ajzen, I. (1975). *Belief, attitude, intention, and behavior: An introduction to theory and research*. Addison-Wesley.
Greenhaus, J. H., Callanan, G. A., & Godshalk, V. M. (2010). *Career management*. Sage.
Harter, J. K. (2022, October 6). *Quiet quitters make up half the U.S. workforce, Gallup says*. Gallup. Retrieved from https://careerdesignlab.sps.columbia.edu/blog/2022/10/06/quiet-quitters-make-up-half-the-u-s-workforce-gallup-says/
Herzberg, F. I. (1966). *Work and the nature of man*. World Publishing.
Herzberg, F. I. (1982). *The managerial choice: To be efficient and to be human* (2nd ed., Rev.). Olympus.
Herzberg, F. I., Mausner, B., & Snyderman, B. (1959). *The motivation to work* (2nd ed.). John Wiley & Sons.
James-Ward, C., Frey, N., & Fisher, D. (2012). Root cause analysis. *Principal Leadership, 13*(2), 57–61.
Jones, B. (1993). The four domains affecting job performance. Internal Document, Delta Air Lines. Atlanta, GA. As found in, Mancuso, V. (1995). *Moving from theory to practice: Integrating human factors into an organization*. Annual Flight Safety Foundation Conference. http://www.crm-devel.org/ftp/mancuso.pdf
Kacel, B., Miller, M., & Norris, D. (2005). Measurement of nurse practitioner job satisfaction in a Midwestern state. *Journal of the American Academy of Nurse Practitioners, 17*(1), 27–32.
Locke, E. A., & Latham, G. P. (2006). New directions in goal-setting theory. *Current directions in psychological science, 15*(5), 265–268.
Luthans, F., Avolio, B. J., Avey, J. B., & Norman, S. M. (2007). Positive psychological capital: Measurement and relationship with performance and satisfaction. *Personnel Psychology, 60*(3), 541–572.
Maslow, A. H. (1943). A theory of human motivation. *Psychological Review, 50*(4), 370–396.
Maslow, A. H. (1954). *Motivation and personality*. Harper & Row.
Morrison, E. W. (2011). Employee voice behavior: Integration and directions for future research. *Academy of Management Annals, 5*(1), 373–412.
Nickerson, C. (2023, January 5). Herzberg's two-factor theory of motivation-hygiene. *Simply Psychology*. https://www.simplypsychology.org/herzbergs-two-factor-theory.html
Okes, D. (2019). *Root cause analysis: The core of problem-solving and corrective action*. Quality Press.
Peng, P., & Li, X. (2023). The hidden costs of emotional labor on withdrawal behavior: The mediating role of emotional exhaustion, and the moderating effect of mindfulness. *BMC psychology, 11*(1), 342. https://doi.org/10.1186/s40359-023-01392-z
Pink, D. H. (2009). *Drive: The surprising truth about what motivates us*. Riverhead Books.
Reisinger, H., & Fetterer, D. (2021). Forget flexibility: Your employees want autonomy. *Harvard Business Review*. Retrieved from https://hbr.org/2021/10/forget-flexibility-your-employees-want-autonomy
Robbins, S. P., & Judge, T. A. (2013). *Organizational behavior* (15th ed.). Pearson.
Sachau, D. A. (2007). Resurrecting the motivation-hygiene theory: Herzberg and the positive psychology movement. *Human Resource Development Review*, 6(4), 377–393.

Saks, A. M. (2006). Antecedents and consequences of employee engagement. *Journal of Managerial Psychology, 21*(7), 600–619.

Schultz, T. W. (1961). Investment in human capital. *The American Economic Review, 51*(1), 1–17.

Schultz, T. W. (1975). The value of the ability to deal with disequilibria. *Journal of Economic Literature, 13*(3), 827–846.

Ser, E. M. & Webber, J. K. (2024). Herzberg's motivational factors applied to generational influencers, *Journal of Management History*, Advanced Online Publication. https://doi.org/10.1108/JMH-01-2024-0002

Stavrou, N. A. M., Psychountaki, M., Georgiadis, E., Karteroliotis, K., & Zervas, Y. (2015). Flow theory–goal orientation theory: Positive experience is related to athlete's goal orientation. *Frontiers in Psychology, 6*, 1499.

Tay, L., & Diener, E. (2011). Needs and subjective well-being around the world. *Journal of Personality and Social Psychology, 101*(2), 354–365.

Twenge, J. M. (2017). *iGen: Why today's super-connected kids are growing up less rebellious, more tolerant, less happy and completely unprepared for adulthood and what that means for the rest of us*. Simon and Schuster.

Urban, A., Agus, M., Aru, N., Corona, F., Cantone, E., Cortese, C. G., & Nonnis, M. (2024). Double-duty caregiving, burnout, job satisfaction, and the sustainability of the work-life balance among Italian healthcare workers: A descriptive study. *Sustainability, 17*(1), 39.

Visser, C. (2020, December 14). *Humble leadership and employee performance*. Progress-focused. Retrieved from https://www.progressfocused.com/2020/12/humble-leadership-and-employee.html

Vroom, V. H. (1964). *Work and motivation*. Wiley.

CHAPTER 8

Leading Collaborative Teams

CHAPTER OVERVIEW

This next chapter in People Leadership focuses on the know-how to lead high-performing and collaborative teams. First, the chapter grounds the reader in the foundational Tuckman group development model and then explains the critical concept of psychological safety in teams. Additionally, this chapter covers "soft skills," such as active listening and providing feedback, using frameworks that are easy to grasp but challenging to execute. Finally, this chapter steps into conflict, which is evitable on teams, examining a model that frames conflict as crucial conversations that invite the opportunity to be candid, transparent, and expert at mastering the mutual purpose. People Leaders must lay the foundational building blocks described here to shift a team from cooperation to collaboration.

This section now broadens the scope of responsibility for People Leaders. At the core, they must lead and sustain a high-functioning, collaborative team. While previous chapters have discussed relationship building across workplace modalities and motivating employees for high performance, other prosocial behaviors are essential to managing a team effectively. We did not want to get caught up in the debate over what terms like "soft skills" really mean. The truth is that these skills can be incredibly intricate to master. What matters is that today's People Leaders need to be able to put these soft skills into action effectively. We frequently warn our students to be prepared to be challenged regarding the forthcoming content.

The benefits of **collaborative teams** seem apparent, but they should be stated. Teams with differing perspectives and diverse backgrounds generally benefit from rigorous debate of ideas, products, processes, and outputs. Consequently, their innovations experience the necessary development, vetting, iteration, and challenges before going to market. Collaborative teams work efficiently and productively to meet goals, deliver projects on time, and produce for organizations. Collaborative teams benefit from strong communication and solid working relationships, whether in-person, hybrid, or remote. When they achieve success, it is shared and often fulfills a sense of purpose where there is an intense belonging to a team. Collaborative teams know the sum is greater than the parts, and team members put collective goals before self-interests. This, of course, is the ideal.

DOI: 10.4324/9781003474647-10

Yet dysfunction is common, conflict is inevitable, and team performance can be inconsistent. Indeed, collaborative teams are more creative than lone individuals, but a main caveat is that they must be healthy, functioning, and motivated to collaborate as a team. As authors, we have found that most of our students, community members, and workshop participants have experienced being on high-performing and dysfunctional teams by the time they reach college. Within these conversations, we often ask: *What needs to be present for a team to be collaborative and high-performing? What is missing when a team is dysfunctional?* This chapter focuses on the work of People Leaders when it comes to leading collaborative teams. This chapter amends Tuckman's (1965) group development model and offers vital skills to foster psychological safety, active listening, providing feedback, and positive conflict resolution.

FOUNDATIONAL GROUP THEORY

Bruce Tuckman (1965) introduced a foundational **model for group development** that remains relevant to modern business leaders. The model's simplicity allows undergraduate and graduate students and professionals to seamlessly apply it to their sports teams, clubs, campus organizations, and workplaces. The Forming, Storming, Norming, and Performing stages have become synonymous with effective teamwork (Williams et al., 2016).

In Tuckman's original model (1965), the stages of Forming, Storming, Norming, and Performing are foundational. Later, Tuckman and Jensen (1977) introduced the Adjourning stage to address team disbandment, which adds a vital dimension for modern leaders to consider. Additionally, it is crucial to acknowledge that teams can regress to earlier stages, necessitating leaders to remain vigilant and responsive to their team's evolving dynamics. Tuckman's (1965) model shows leaders should adapt and support their teams as they develop, focusing on observable behaviors and key milestones. We summarize our adaptation of those stages in Table 8.1 and Figure 8.1.

Tuckman observed that groups evolve through distinct stages, even if group members are unaware of these stages (see Table 8.1 and Figure 8.1). His model illustrates how a team can mature, enhance its skills, and deepen interpersonal relationships while navigating various leadership dimensions required at each stage. The real takeaway for leaders is identifying where their team is in this developmental process and facilitating their transition to the next stage using prosocial behaviors and effective leadership techniques. It is essential to recognize that a team's progression is not always linear; as teams form and undergo changes, they may regress to previous Tuckman's (1965) stages (see Adapting in Figure 8.1). For example, a team might function effectively in the Norming or Performing stage, but introducing a new member could trigger a return to Storming. Leaders must guide their teams back on track toward Performing.

Each stage of Tuckman's (1965) model provides valuable opportunities for leaders to reflect on observable behaviors, team dynamics, and the necessary leadership strategies. In the **Forming** stage, leaders must establish the team's structure. During this time, team members often feel uncertain and unclear about their roles and avoid conflict due to their desire for acceptance. Forming requires a meaningful orientation grounded in clear mission-based values. People Leaders play a vital role by providing direction and guidance and

TABLE 8.1 Tuckman's Adapted Stages of Group Development

Stage	*Description*	*Observable Behaviors*	*Milestone or Crisis*	*Leadership Strategies*
Forming	The team is newly assembled, and members are uncertain about roles, expectations, and group dynamics. There is a strong desire for acceptance, and conflict is avoided.	- Politeness and cautious interactions - Uncertainty about roles and objectives - Reliance on the leader for direction	Establishing clear structure, goals, and expectations prevents confusion and lays the foundation for collaboration.	- Define mission, vision, and objectives - Clarify roles and responsibilities - Facilitate team bonding activities - Provide strong leadership and direction
Storming	The team begins to express differing opinions, personalities emerge, and conflicts arise. Struggles over leadership, roles, and power dynamics dominate this stage. Resistance to authority may occur.	- Conflicts and disagreements emerge - Challenges to leadership and decision-making - Frustration and resistance to roles	Navigating interpersonal conflicts and power struggles while reinforcing team unity and psychological safety.	- Encourage open communication and set conflict resolution protocols - Foster psychological safety by allowing constructive dissent - Provide mediation and coaching - Reinforce team norms and accountability
Norming	Team members develop shared working methods, build trust, and align around common goals. Collaboration increases, and constructive feedback improves performance.	- Increased teamwork and problem-solving - Greater trust and cohesion - Constructive feedback and shared leadership	Shifting from leader-driven to shared leadership where team members trust each other and take ownership of their roles.	- Empower collaborative decision-making - Strengthen team norms and accountability - Recognize and celebrate progress - Promote knowledge-sharing and cross-training

(*Continued*)

TABLE 8.1 (Continued)

Stage	*Description*	*Observable Behaviors*	*Milestone or Crisis*	*Leadership Strategies*
Performing	The team operates at a high-efficiency level with strong collaboration, adaptability, and self-sufficiency. Members trust and support one another while handling complex challenges.	- High engagement and innovation - Effective conflict resolution - Team self-manages and adapts to new challenges	Maintaining momentum and resilience, ensuring the team sustains high performance even when facing new challenges.	- Empower the team to lead itself and encourage continued growth - Foster innovation and continuous improvement - Support well-being and prevent burnout through balance and recognition
Adapting (Regression to Earlier Stages)	Due to external changes (turnover, restructuring, leadership shifts), teams may revert to earlier stages. Leaders must help teams re-establish stability and cohesion.	- Uncertainty or disengagement - Decrease in trust and performance - Resistance to change	Helping the team reconnect with its purpose and adjust to new realities.	- Assess team needs and realign expectations - Provide guidance and reassurance through change - Rebuild trust and reinforce team cohesion
Adjourning	The team completes the task and disbands. Members reflect on their accomplishments and may experience mixed emotions, including a sense of loss or fulfillment.	- Recognition of goal completion - Mixed feelings about disbanding - Reflection on successes and challenges	Facilitating closure and ensuring team members can transition effectively to new roles or projects.	- Celebrate achievements and provide recognition - Conduct debrief sessions to capture lessons learned - Offer support for future endeavors and transitions.

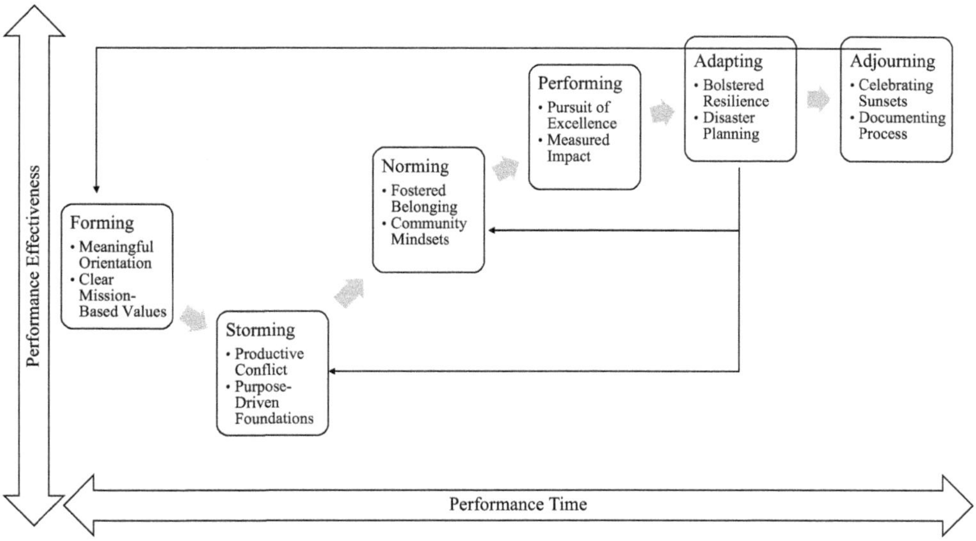

FIGURE 8.1 Adapted Tuckman's (1965) Model

facilitating the establishment of mission and vision, objectives, responsibilities, roles, ground rules, and team expectations.

As team elements become established, they frequently progress into **Storming**, the stage characterized by interpersonal conflicts stemming from task and process disagreements. Leadership dynamics, power struggles, and structural issues often arise during this phase. The purpose of self, team, and organization should already be ingrained in the team so conflict can be resolved productively and resistance to change may be overcome. Leaders must leverage transparent communication strategies, focused objectives, active listening, constructive feedback, and conflict management skills to foster psychological safety.

Following the Storming stage is **Norming**. In this stage, team members find ways to work together, establish rules and boundaries, and get to know each other better. Shared leadership emerges as team members learn to trust and leverage each other's strengths. In the Norming stage, a sense of belonging arises, confidence soars, constructive critique flourishes, and team members collectively engage in decision-making, staying on target toward outlined project goals.

Time and wins at projects help teams advance to the **Performing** stage, where proper interdependence forms. The teams pursue excellence by utilizing feedback on how to improve performance. In this stage, team members' commitment is exceptionally high; they build tight bonds, experience synergy, and tackle challenging tasks together. Successful collaborative teams that reach the Performing stage gain momentum. They learn to handle conflict constructively, practice shared leadership, offer mutual support, and adapt readily to new challenges.

Teams may revert to earlier stages of development, which we call **Adapting**. This reversion can come from external changes like turnover, restructuring, or leadership shifts. This regression can disrupt established dynamics and efficacy, so leaders need to recognize these signs and intervene proactively. Adapting is successful when resilience has been built into the team through focusing on community and purpose, and disasters must be planned for where possible. Leaders help their teams adjust to changes by communicating transparently, clarifying roles, and realigning goals. They foster adaptability and resilience to overcome new challenges.

In the **Adjourning** stage, tasks are completed and disbandment begins. Leaders should ask their members to reflect on their achievements and contributions during this stage. Adjournment can be emotional, ranging from loss to fulfillment. Leaders should help their team members celebrate their successes and encourage the members to stay connected as the team sunsets. Leaders should keep good records so that future teams can learn from past experiences and not have to recreate the wheel. This approach allows team members to share insights and lessons learned, which helps to foster a positive transition and encourages future collaborations.

Though it continues to be a model with applicability for People Leaders, today's contemporary work environments offer plenty of disruption, change, and turmoil that once again can send a team back to an earlier stage, whether caused by team member turnover, new leadership, company restructuring, or complex problems that are either internal or external to the team. Tuckman's (1965) foundation allows leaders to visualize where their team is and where it needs to go. More importantly, it encourages competencies that team members need to nurture and demonstrate if a team is to pass from Forming to Performing. We authors consider these competencies essential and plan to cover them next.

PSYCHOLOGICAL SAFETY

First coined by Harvard Professor Amy Edmondson, **psychological safety** has gained widespread traction in business environments and is now considered a fundamental building block for collaborative teams. While in hospitals researching for her PhD, Edmondson studied the relationship between error-making and teamwork. She expected to find that more effective teams made fewer mistakes. Instead, she found that the teams who reported better teamwork seemed to experience more errors (Gallo, 2023). When she examined the data, she began to suspect that better teams might be more willing to report their mistakes because they felt safe doing so. She referred to this as "team psychological safety." She defined it as a shared belief held by team members that it is essential to take risks, express their ideas and concerns, speak up with questions, and admit mistakes without fear of negative consequences (Gallo, 2023). Edmondson explained that this phenomenon operates at the group level, influencing the learning behaviors within the team, which subsequently impacts both their performance and the performance of the organization as a whole (Gallo, 2023). We would consider psychological safety essential in contemporary life and necessary to the future of leadership.

First, psychological safety makes team members feel more engaged and motivated because they feel that their contributions matter and that they can speak up without fear of retribution (Gallo, 2023). Second, it can lead to better decision-making as team members feel more comfortable voicing opinions and concerns, often leading to more diverse perspectives being heard and considered. Third, it can foster a culture of continuous learning and improvement as team members feel safe sharing their mistakes and learning from them (Gallo, 2023). People Leaders must actively cultivate this essential skill within their teams.

In his excellent book *The Four Stages of Psychological Safety*, Timothy Clark (2020) describes **four stages of psychological safety**. Teams need to get to the last stage to achieve groundbreaking innovation. Clark (2020) highlights the importance of fostering a safe environment where team members feel free to question existing practices without the risk of being embarrassed, sidelined, or penalized. We would offer that an essential update to Tuckman's (1965) conventional group model would be that the foundational tenets of psychological safety need to be established in the Forming stage for teams to truly realize the emotional trust, sense of belonging, ability to challenge, and capacity to leverage diverse perspectives and backgrounds to achieve creative outcomes or breakthrough success.

Clark (2020) expanded psychological safety to include four dimensions: (1) **inclusion safety**, (2) **learner safety**, (3) **contributor safety**, and (4) **challenger safety**. Inclusion safety means each team member is accepted and genuinely feels they belong. Members sense they are a part of a purposeful social collective and that they matter for the team to work effectively. Second, learner safety allows team members to ask each other questions, try new things, experiment, and make mistakes. This is critical as the team takes on tasks, sets goals, and develops projects. Third, contributor safety means team members can fully deploy their skills and expertise. Responsibilities are more prominent, and team members experience confidence when encouraged to perform their roles with autonomy. Finally, challenger safety invites team members to disagree, challenge one another, pitch novel ideas, and creatively dissent without fear of retribution (Clark, 2020). People Leaders bolster psychological safety and look for signs of erosion (see Table 8.2).

TABLE 8.2 Indicators of Psychological Safety and Signs of Erosion

Dimension	*Definition*	*Psychological Safety Indicators*	*Signs of Erosion*
Inclusion Safety	Team members feel accepted, valued, and part of the group.	- Open collaboration - Encouraging diverse perspectives - Respectful dialogue	- Cliques and exclusion - Employees feel isolated or unseen - Lack of diversity in decision-making
Learner Safety	Team members can ask questions, make mistakes, and experiment without fear.	- Encouraging trial and error - Constructive feedback - Willingness to seek help	- Fear of asking questions - Blame culture - No opportunities for skill development
Contributor Safety	Team members feel confident applying their skills and knowledge.	- Autonomy in roles - Recognition of contributions - Ownership of tasks	- Micromanagement - Fear of making independent decisions - Lack of recognition

(Continued)

TABLE 8.2 (Continued)

Dimension	*Definition*	*Psychological Safety Indicators*	*Signs of Erosion*
Challenger Safety	Team members can question the status quo and voice concerns.	- Encouragement of dissenting views - Leaders invite feedback - Open debate on ideas	- Employees fear retaliation - Suppression of concerns - No platform for feedback

The Boeing 737 MAX crisis is a stark example of the erosion of psychological safety within an organization. Leading up to two tragic crashes of the 737 MAX aircraft, Boeing faced serious internal cultural issues. Internal reports and employee interviews revealed that engineers felt pressured to keep quiet about safety concerns due to a corporate environment that discouraged speaking out. The company prioritized meeting tight deadlines and cutting costs over discussing potential design problems (Kitroeff et al., 2019).

One Boeing employee lamented, "This airplane is designed by clowns, who in turn are supervised by monkeys" (Gelles et al., 2020). This statement highlights employee frustration and lack of trust, creating a psychologically unsafe culture regarding voicing concerns. This failure contributed to two major crashes, subsequent heavy regulatory scrutiny, financial losses, and damage to Boeing's reputation. This erosion of psychological safety is resonant with Table 8.2.

Introducing psychological safety and establishing the dimensions as team norms is now a best practice for contemporary People Leaders. Once again, in a blending of traditional theory with modern concepts, team psychological safety should happen in Tuckman's (1965) Forming stage, and if practiced consistently, it can help teams navigate the Storming stage, improve during the Norming Stage, and achieve high functioning status in the Performing stage. Teams with a culture of psychological safety can maintain momentum through the inevitable change, turmoil, and disruption inherent to modern business environments. Organizations that systematically tackle this concept can guard against toxic workplace cultures, which this text has named as one of the single biggest reasons professionals leave a company.

ACTIVE LISTENING AND PROVIDING FEEDBACK

While psychological safety is a new essential for successful teams, there are more "soft skills" vital to establish early in the group development process to have a collaborative team. Further, surviving the Storming stage requires additional competencies from People Leaders and team members. While active listening and providing feedback are hardly new concepts, a scholar or practitioner always seems to be giving them a fresh design, reestablishing their importance in contemporary business settings. With models plentiful, we often wonder why active listening or providing feedback is done so poorly or not at all.

Unfortunately, the higher a leader ascends in an organization, the less time they appear to have to listen or provide feedback to their people. This is a terrible detriment to the organization.

Active Listening

The previous chapter on Motivating for High Performance discussed motivation strategies like employee voice, autonomy, and career development. None of these can be achieved without a People Leader who practices **active listening**. People Leaders must pay close attention to their team members, comprehend their message, respond thoughtfully, and retain the information for future reference. This process engages the listener and the speaker together, reifying mindsets focused on teamwork and collaboration.

Active listening is essential to strengthen relationships, boost collaboration, and enhance employee well-being. Active listening increases workplace satisfaction through just procedures and helping members identify with their teams (Lee et al., 2024). Active listening improves interactional competence, especially in cross-cultural business communication, where appropriate listener responses are crucial for understanding and engagement (Gao & Wang, 2024). These findings emphasize that leaders who actively listen are more capable of motivating their teams, embracing diverse perspectives, and cultivating psychologically safe workplaces.

Julian Treasure (2011), sound expert, TedTalk speaker, and author, proposes the **RASA active listening method**. RASA is an acronym for receive, appreciate, summarize, and ask. RASA is a simple but effective practice that encourages deep, empathic listening between a listener and a speaker. R stands for **receive**, which is to hear the speaker. A is to **appreciate**, providing visual or verbal cues affirming that the listener has listened to the speaker. S is to **summarize**, allowing the listener to reflect on what they have heard. A is to **ask**, which is to encourage follow-up questions for clarification, greater understanding, and additional insights. The challenge is frequently executing this method naturally and with genuine intention.

Exercise 8.1 Practicing RASA

This exercise will allow individuals to practice the RASA method. Break the class into groups of three. One role is the listener. One role is the speaker. One role is the observer. The speaker should discuss a problem they are having, which could be personal or professional, large or small. The listener should work through the RASA method (receive, attend, summarize, and ask), attempting to be natural. Once the listener and speaker are finished, allow the observer to reflect on what they saw regarding the RASA method. The facilitator should keep time and switch roles so that each group member can take a turn as a listener, speaker, and observer.

GROUP DISCUSSION QUESTIONS

1. What step in the RASA method is the easiest?
2. What step in the RASA method is the most challenging?
3. Observers, what did you notice, and where could there be improvement?
4. Listeners, what scenarios might be more challenging to apply the RASA method?
5. What tensions might surface for People Leaders as they try to use the RASA method with their team members?

Feedback Is Given and Heard

Similarly, there is no shortage of methods for **providing feedback**. What's essential is that People Leaders adopt a technique that allows for candid, constructive critique, and honest assessment. Giving feedback is vital for employee engagement, morale, productivity, and performance. People Leaders must provide feedback regularly, not only at annual performance reviews; they should do so often and continuously so that team members have a clear view of expectations and how they perform. Feedback on goals, projects, key performance indicators, and other job-related metrics is critical for employee growth and development.

The **DESC script** was developed by Bower and Bower (2009) and is discussed more fully in their book *Asserting Yourself*. DESC stands for describe, express, specify, and consequences. **Describe** means to outline the behavior or situation objectively using facts and evidence. **Express** includes stating the leader's feelings or thoughts about the behavior or situation. It is recommended that the leader use "I" statements as "You" statements can put the team member on the defensive. **Specify** is the leader's opportunity to outline the behavior or outcome they would prefer to happen and do so collaboratively, where they are co-creating the steps to change the behavior, leading to optimal results. **Consequences** entail describing what will happen, positive or negative, if no change is made. Strikingly similar to the RASA method, the challenge with the DESC script is in executing it naturally and applying it in one's leadership style without sounding like a robot.

This chapter outlined the RASA method and DESC script based on the premise that People Leaders use them with their employees. Yet, collaborative teams have individuals demonstrating both competencies with one another on the peer-to-peer level. As Tuckman's group development model suggests, **shared leadership** where power, responsibility, and decisions are distributed is the most effective way for teams to achieve the Performing stage. Active listening and feedback among team members within each workplace interaction are essential for healthy communication, project management, strong relationships, onboarding new members, and producing breakthrough innovations. People Leaders must ensure these interpersonal skills are nurtured and developed consistently among their team members for a collaborative team.

Exercise 8.2 Practicing the DESC Script

Break into groups of three. One role is the People Leader. One role is a team member reporting to the People Leader. One role is the observer. The scenario is that the People Leader has noticed multiple times how the team member has had a negative attitude in team meetings when tasks are assigned or project responsibilities are discussed. This is impacting team meetings and overall team collaboration. The People Leader should work through the DESC script (describe, express, specify, and consequences) to address this behavior with the team members. After the People Leader and team member have completed their conversation, allow the observer to reflect on what they noticed. Keep time and switch roles so that all group members get a turn as the People Leader, team member, and observer. Discuss the following questions to debrief.

1. What element of the DESC script is the easiest?
2. What element of the DESC script is the most challenging?
3. Observers, what did you notice, and where could we improve?
4. People Leaders, what scenarios might be more challenging to apply the DESC script?
5. What tensions might surface for People Leaders as they try to use the DESC script with team members?

MANAGING CONFLICT THROUGH CRUCIAL CONVERSATIONS

As the Tuckman model indicates, team storming, disagreement, or conflict is inevitable. As authors, we often teach the **crucial conversations** (2021) model (Grenny et al., 2021). Conflicts should be reframed into crucial interactions in that they are conversations that "transform people and relationships. They are anything but transacted" (Grenny et al., 2021, p. x). Further, "They produce what Buddhism calls 'the middle way—not a compromise between two opposites on a straight-line continuum, but a higher middle way, like the apex of a triangle" (Grenny et al., 2021, p. x). Such conversations are essential for collaborative teams.

Grenny et al. (2021) boldly state that "dramatic improvements in organizational performance were possible if people learned the skills routinely practiced by those who have found a way to master these high-stakes, 'crucial' moments" (Grenny et al., 2021, p. xiii). Crucial conversations are interactions where opposing opinions are expressed under high stakes and emotions. Individuals often avoid these conversations, or they handle them poorly when they finally face them. According to Grenny et al. (2021), conversations that take a wrong turn can have serious and widespread consequences. Their research indicates that the strength of relationships, careers, organizations, and communities relies heavily on the capacity to engage openly in discussions about challenging, emotional, and controversial subjects. Fortunately, it is a competence that can be learned and improved with experience. Grenny et al. (2021) assert that becoming skillful at crucial conversations can benefit workplace relationships and employee well-being.

Their model is based on the power of **dialogue**, which they describe as the free flow of meaning between two or more people (Grenny et al., 2021). Further, "When it comes to risky, controversial, and emotional conversations, skilled people find a way to get all relevant information (from themselves and others) out into the open" (Grenny et al., 2021, p. 23). Leaders should stay alert to recognize when a conversation shifts from routine to contentious or crucial. *What are the physical signs? What are the emotional signs? What are the behavioral signs?*

Approaching a crucial conversation can benefit from the following before dialogue begins:

1) What do I really want for myself?
2) What do I really want for others?
3) What do I really want for the relationship?

This model is helpful in contemporary business environments, as its authors caution leaders to learn to look for **safety problems**, similar to the tenets of psychological safety. Grenny et al. (2021) assert that leaders gifted at dialogue stay vigilant regarding safety. They pay attention to the content and watch for signs that people are becoming fearful. When team members move away from healthy dialogue, skillful communicators focus on who is forcing their opinions or purposefully keeping their ideas out.

Grenny et al. (2021) are clear about techniques designed to disengage from dialogue, such as silence, which consists of any act to withhold information from the dialogue process purposefully. Other behaviors like **masking**, which consists of understating or selectively withholding genuine opinions (sarcasm, sugarcoating, or couching), can upend attempts at dialogue. Also, **avoiding** involves steering altogether away from sensitive subjects. Team members might talk, but without addressing the real issues. Finally, **withdrawing** means pulling out of the conversation altogether. Team members either exit the conversation or the room.

When safety is violated, Grenny et al. (2021) describe it as similar to violence. This forcefulness through particular techniques during dialogue is unproductive and undermines meaning and purpose. **Controlling** consists of coercing others to the team member's way of thinking. **Labeling** is putting a label on people or ideas so team members can dismiss them under a general stereotype or category. **Attacking** is when a team member moves from winning the argument to making the other person suffer. Grenny et al.'s (2021) model emphasizes looking for one's style under stress and becoming a vigilant self-monitor to then alter one's strategy if necessary to avoid violence and undermining psychological safety.

The model encourages People Leaders to make it safe to talk about anything. Essential goals for crucial conversations are as follows:

1) **Mutual purpose** means that others perceive that team members are working toward a common outcome in the conversation and that each member cares about their goals, interests, and values. This is the entry condition of dialogue.
2) **Watch for signs that mutual purpose is at risk**: When mutual purpose is at risk, team members end up in debate and try to win the conversation. Other signs include defensiveness, hidden agendas, accusations, and circling back to the same topic.

Much like active listening and providing feedback, countless methods exist for managing conflict or navigating difficult conversations. Establishing an adequate model, a team norm, and consistent practice for all team members is essential. People Leaders must remain effective during crucial moments and address conflict as opportunities to enhance mutual purpose, team communication, and relationship building. With these skills and approaches, People Leaders can reap the benefits of diverse perspectives, unique backgrounds, differing points of view, and a range of lived experiences.

Exercise 8.3 Official Truth vs. Ground Truth

With origins from the military, this exercise allows team members to generate scenarios that could call for a crucial conversation. First, team members should think of an organization they are part of, including school, sports, clubs, jobs, or internships. At nearly every organization, leaders proclaim what would be described as the official truth. This information can be found on websites, in official communication, heard from senior leaders, and shared publicly. In contrast, information is always shared at lower levels of the organization between colleagues, team members, and peers. This information offers reality and is generally meant to be kept private so that outsiders are unaware of it. Ask team members to write down the official truth of their organization. Then, ask them to write down the ground truth about the organization.

Divide into groups of 3–4 members. Have each team member share their organization's official and ground truths. Then, bring them back for a more extensive group discussion. Discuss:

1. What did you notice about the difference between an official and ground truth?
2. What tension points might this create between leaders and members of the organization?
3. What crucial conversations must occur at your organization based on these truths?

CONCLUSION

Deloitte's recent future of work research found that 65% of the C-level executives surveyed have a strategic objective to transform their organization's culture and turn toward a focus on connectivity, communication, and collaboration (Goman, 2017). One of the challenges with this is the current reality of today's large multinational organizations assembling large global teams to tackle challenging tasks. The more complexity teams face, the more collaborative practices are needed (Gratton & Erickson, 2007).

Gratton and Erickson (2007) looked carefully at 55 large teams and identified those demonstrating high levels of collaborative behavior despite their complexity. In doing so, they identified four general categories that support collaborative practices in teams: executive support, HR practices, team leader strength, and team structure (Gratton & Erickson, 2007). Simply put, executives need to model the collaborative behavior they want to see in their teams and make themselves available to coach and mentor these teams (We discuss executive presence in Chapter 17). Additionally, organizations need to allow human resources departments, many with learning and development units, to implement the essential competencies programs that enrich teams with skill work like psychological safety, active listening, providing feedback, and managing conflict.

Gratton and Erickson (2007) also found that the proper leader led these collaborative teams. Their research indicates that the most productive and innovative teams tend to be led by individuals who balance task- and relationship-oriented approaches. Additionally, these leaders adapt their leadership style throughout a project (Gratton & Erickson, 2007).

As discussed when examining the Tuckman model, leaders need to be task-oriented early to clarify roles, determine objectives, and construct work plans. Yet, as the team develops, leaders must shift to a relationship-orientation (Gratton & Erickson, 2007). People Leaders should take note.

Gratton and Erickson (2007) highlight that new teams, particularly those composed of members unfamiliar with each other, struggle more to collaborate than teams with established relationships. Building trust within these new teams takes considerable and intentional time. Collaboration improves when roles are clearly defined and understood. Without clarity, team members may spend excessive energy negotiating roles rather than concentrating on tasks. While historical factors can hinder collaboration, team challenges are compounded by the need for greater diversity and long-distance cooperation.

People Leaders must adopt adaptable team models to thrive and bolster team member strength and team structure. They distinguish between cooperation and collaboration. Generally, both terms emphasize the importance of teamwork. Collaboration involves team members working together for a common purpose, while cooperation works with others to help others achieve goals. To shift a team from cooperation to collaboration, People Leaders need to motivate and lay the foundational building blocks described here. This is the challenge of leading collaborative teams, which we covered in this chapter. The quest for inclusion is not easier than collaboration and is discussed in the next chapter.

DISCUSSION QUESTIONS

1. What are the competitive advantages of developing collaborative teams?
2. What are the responsibilities of People Leaders at each stage of the Tuchman group development model?
3. How can People Leaders implement psychological safety among in-person, hybrid, or remote teams?
4. What are the benefits of the RASA method? Where could it be improved?
5. What are the benefits of the DESC script? Where could it be improved?
6. Why is managing conflict central to leading collaborative teams?
7. What outcomes are possible when People Leaders shift conflict into crucial conversations?
8. What do People Leaders need to be vigilant about to get the most from their collaborative team?

Key Terms

- Collaborative Teams
- Tuckman's Model of Group Development
- Forming
- Storming
- Norming
- Performing
- Psychological Safety

- Four Stages of Psychological Safety
- RASA Method
- DESC script
- Shared Leadership
- Crucial Conversations
- Dialogue
- Safety Problems
- Masking
- Avoiding
- Withdrawing
- Controlling
- Labeling
- Attacking
- Mutual Purpose

CASE STUDY 8.1 MEDISYS SOLUTIONS

MediSys Solutions is a leading innovator in healthcare technology. It is dedicated to revolutionizing patient care through advanced medical software and digital health solutions. MediSys emphasizes integrating cutting-edge technology with clinical expertise. It serves healthcare providers globally and empowers them to deliver efficient, high-quality care. The company operates in a dynamic industry characterized by rapid technological advancements and stringent regulatory requirements.

By 2023, MediSys Solutions recognized a pressing need to enhance collaboration to foster innovation within its workforce. Despite employing highly skilled professionals across various disciplines, team members hesitated to voice new ideas or challenge established practices. This lack of psychological safety hindered creativity, innovation, and achieving optimal team performance in a competitive market.

A pivotal aspect of enhancing collaboration at MediSys Solutions was the proactive involvement of People Leaders, who played a crucial role in supporting and motivating their teams. MediSys invested substantial professional development in its People Leaders, implementing psychology safety and collaborative practices such as active listening, providing feedback, and managing conflict. Still, People Leaders faced challenges when they returned to their teams to build on these skills.

CHALLENGES FACED AND QUESTIONS

1. **Resistance to Change**—Some team members initially hesitated to embrace new communication norms and participate in open discussions. There were existing tensions and a lack of trust among team members with differing communication styles and preferences. *What can People Leaders do to establish the norms of psychological safety?*
2. **Managing Conflicting Personalities and Work Styles**—Team members with diverse backgrounds, personalities, and work styles sometimes clash, leading to communication breakdowns and interpersonal conflicts. This hindered collaboration, impacted team cohesion, and created tension. *What can People Leaders do to build competencies in teams around managing conflict?*
3. **Dealing with Virtual Team Challenges**—With the rise of remote work, managing virtual teams presents unique challenges, such as building trust, maintaining

communication, and ensuring accountability. Virtual teams can experience isolation, miscommunication due to technology issues, lack of in-person connection, and difficulties in building rapport. *What can People Leaders do to ensure remote teams are still collaborative?*

4. **Handling Rapidly Changing Priorities and Deadlines**—In dynamic industries or projects, teams often face shifting priorities and tight deadlines, impacting their ability to collaborate effectively. Stress, burnout, and decreased morale arise among team members trying to manage competing demands and deliverables. *What must People Leaders stay vigilant about when they are leading a team in this type of environment?*
5. **Encouraging Innovation While Maintaining Stability**—Balancing the need for innovation with the requirement for stability and consistency in processes and outcomes can be challenging. Teams may struggle to take calculated risks and explore new ideas while maintaining operational efficiency and meeting organizational goals. *How can People Leaders balance this while pushing their teams to reach the Performing stage?*

Task: Answer the preceding questions and provide four comprehensive recommendations for the leaders at MediSys. Make sure to connect the recommendations to key chapter concepts. Present the recommendations to a larger group for feedback and discussion.

REFERENCES

Bower, S. A., & Bower, G. H. (2009). *Asserting yourself: A practical guide for positive change* (Updated ed.). Da Capo Lifelong Books.

Clark, T. R. (2020). *The four stages of psychological safety: Defining the path to inclusion and innovation*. Berrett-Koehler Publishers.

Gallo, A. (2023). What is psychological safety? *Harvard Business Review*. Retrieved from https://hbr.org

Gao, W., & Wang, M. (2024). Listenership always matters: Active listening ability in L2 business English paired speaking tasks. *International Review of Applied Linguistics in Language Teaching*. https://doi.org/10.1515/iral-2023-0258

Gelles, D., Kitroeff, N., Nicas, J., & Schmidt, M. S. (2020, January 9). Boeing employees mocked fAA and 'clowns' who designed 737 MAX. *The New York Times*. Retrieved from https://www.nytimes.com

Goman, C. K. (2017). Six crucial behaviors of collaborative leaders. *Forbes*. Retrieved from https://www.forbes.com

Gratton, L., & Erickson, T. J. (2007). Eight ways to build collaborative teams. *Harvard Business Review, 85*(11), 100–109.

Grenny, J., Patterson, K., McMillan, R., Switzler, A., & Gregory, E. (2021). *Crucial conversations: Tools for talking when stakes are high* (3rd ed.). McGraw-Hill.

Kitroeff, N., Gelles, D., & Nicas, J. (2019, March 23). Boeing was 'go, go, go' to beat Airbus with the 737 MAX. *The New York Times*. Retrieved from https://www.nytimes.com

Lee, G. C., Platow, M. J., & Cruwys, T. (2024). Listening quality leads to greater working alliance and well-being: Testing a social identity model of working alliance. *British Journal of Clinical Psychology, 63*(4), 573–588. https://doi.org/10.1111/bjc.12489

Treasure, J. (2011). *5 ways to listen better* [Video]. TED Conferences. https://www.ted.com/talks/julian_treasure_5_ways_to_listen_better.

Tuckman, B. W. (1965). Developmental sequence in small groups. *Psychological Bulletin, 63*(6), 384–399.

Tuckman, B. W., & Jensen, M. A. C. (1977). Stages of small-group development revisited. *Group & Organization Studies, 2*(4), 419–427.

Williams, D., Kahn, L., & Whitley, C. (2016). The Basics of developing effective teams. *AMLE Magazine, 4*(1), 44–45.

CHAPTER 9

Creating Inclusive Cultures

CHAPTER OVERVIEW

This chapter focuses on creating inclusive cultures within organizations. People Leaders shape team dynamics and overall workplace climate. This chapter explores how an organizational culture influences individual and team effectiveness. People Leaders are encouraged to establish clear structures to reduce chaos, enrich communication, and clarify roles and responsibilities. This chapter outlines four factors—providing structure, modeling norms, building cohesiveness, and promoting standards of excellence—that contributes to healthy cultures. It also highlights the vitalness of developing an environment where team members feel a sense of belonging; they feel included and valued, which is a competitive advantage.

This section covered several interpersonal competencies that People Leaders must possess and model for their teams' effectiveness. Beyond the mechanics of building and sustaining high-performing teams, People Leaders profoundly influence an abstract but decidedly essential phenomenon in an organization: its culture. This chapter takes this nebulous concept and makes it concrete for future leaders so that they can move toward inclusiveness.

Climate refers to the overall atmosphere within a team or organization, typically understood as the shared perceptions of its members about how things operate. Shared perceptions shift over time, and modern leaders must track when they are in upswings and downswings. Favorable climates reflect individuals as supported, appreciated, and encouraged in their roles. Unfavorable climates indicate complacency, disengagement, fear, hostility, and toxicity. Favorable climates push satisfied employees to achieve their full potential (Culture Partners, 2024).

Prevalent team beliefs, values, and traditions shape climate. **Culture** develops gradually through various interactions over time. It is reinforced by members who establish collaboration patterns to address challenges and coordinate their efforts effectively. These shared values and assumptions are passed on to newcomers regarding *how things are done here* (Laker, 2024).

Healthy, functional cultures are essential in contemporary organizations and successful team environments. Today's People Leaders must create inclusive cultures where team

DOI: 10.4324/9781003474647-11

members feel a sense of belonging. They can leverage inclusive cultures as a competitive advantage and, finally, shift their units into models that elevate the goals of a multicultural organization.

ESTABLISHING HEALTHY CULTURES

First, since the concept of culture can be abstract, we want to provide clear guidelines for constructing the foundational building blocks that lead to healthy cultures. Leaders should consider four factors when establishing culture: providing structure, modeling norms, building cohesiveness, and promoting standards of excellence (Middlebrooks et al., 2020). We will examine each one.

Leaders who offer **structure** to their teams benefit from decreasing chaos and providing clarity and meaning to group objectives. Establishing structure within the organization gives individuals a sense of security, direction, and stability, helping them understand their roles and the goals they need to achieve (Middlebrooks et al., 2020). Table 9.1 shares examples of structure for teams.

Along with the structure of the team, leaders must clarify group **norms**. Norms are the shared behavioral rules established by group members. Social psychologists have long argued that norms significantly impact a group's performance and effectiveness (Middlebrooks et al., 2020). They serve as a roadmap for navigating expected behaviors within the group, indicating what is considered appropriate or inappropriate, right or wrong, and what is permissible or not. Norms do not develop independently; they result from the thousands of interactions among group members and their engagement with the leader. Some examples of healthy group norms that lead to functional workplace culture are in Table 9.2.

Cohesiveness embodies a sense of "we-ness" as the glue that binds a team around shared values, mission, purpose, and goals. Cohesiveness enables members to share their views, give and receive feedback, embrace differing opinions, and feel comfortable engaging in meaningful work (Middlebrooks et al., 2020). In a cohesive group, members experience a strong connection with one another and the group as a whole. They value their group and, in return, feel valued by it. Members identify with the group's goals and derive satisfaction from being accepted as part of the team. Table 9.3 offers ways that leaders can develop group cohesion.

Researchers have found that **standards of excellence** are crucial to team success (Middlebrooks et al., 2020). These standards are the expressed and implied expectations for performance that exist within a group or an organization. In essence, standards of excellence refer to the established benchmarks of desired performance for a group. Middlebrooks et al. (2020) stress the "**Three R's**": (1) Require results, (2) Review results, and (3) Reward results. As we have discussed in previous chapters, giving constructive feedback is a must for a leader if he or she is going to help group members reach and maintain standards of excellence. Examples of standards of excellence that People Leaders might implement to establish a healthy culture are in Table 9.4.

TABLE 9.1 Structures in Modern Workplaces

Strategy	*Description*	*Examples in Modern Business Leadership*
Clear Communication Channels	Creating channels for open communication by holding regular meetings, implementing feedback mechanisms, and utilizing digital platforms fosters an environment where everyone feels acknowledged and well-informed.	- Weekly team meetings with open Q&A sessions - Slack or Microsoft Teams for real-time communication - Anonymous suggestion boxes for employee input
Defined Roles and Responsibilities	Clearly outlining team members' roles and responsibilities reduces confusion and empowers individuals to take ownership of their work.	- Job descriptions with clear expectations - Using project management tools like Asana or Trello to track tasks - Regular one-on-one check-ins to clarify roles
Regular Training and Development	Offering ongoing training opportunities fosters personal and professional growth, demonstrating the organization's employee investment.	- LinkedIn Learning or Coursera courses provided by employers - Leadership development programs for high-potential employees - Internal mentorship programs pairing junior and senior staff
Employee Recognition Programs	Implementing systems to acknowledge and reward achievements boosts morale and encourages a culture of appreciation.	- Monthly employee awards or shout-outs in company newsletters - Performance-based bonuses and incentives - Peer-to-peer recognition programs
Flexible Work Arrangements	Providing options for remote work or flexible hours promotes work-life balance and demonstrates trust in employees.	- Hybrid work models - Four-day workweeks or compressed schedules - Asynchronous work policies supporting different time zones

Team-Building Activities	Organizing regular team-building events helps strengthen relationships among team members and fosters collaboration.	- Virtual happy hours or in-person retreats - Escape rooms or problem-solving activities - Volunteering as a team for social impact initiatives
Wellness Initiatives	Supporting mental and physical well-being through programs like gym memberships, mindfulness sessions, or mental health days creates a healthier work environment.	- Employee assistance programs (EAPs) providing mental health support - Subsidized fitness memberships or on-site yoga - "No meeting Fridays" to reduce burnout
Conflict Resolution Mechanisms	Implementing clear procedures for addressing conflicts helps maintain a respectful and productive workplace.	- Mediation programs with trained HR personnel - Open-door policies for conflict resolution - Training on constructive feedback and difficult conversations
Feedback and Evaluation Processes	Regular performance reviews and feedback sessions encourage continuous improvement and align individual goals with organizational objectives.	- 360-degree feedback reviews involving peers, managers, and direct reports - Quarterly performance check-ins instead of annual reviews - Continuous feedback tools like Lattice or 15Five

TABLE 9.2 Examples of Group Norms

Norm	*Description*	*Examples in Modern Business Leadership*
Open Communication	Encouraging team members to share ideas, concerns, and feedback openly fosters transparency and trust.	- Open-door policies for leadership - Regular all-hands meetings with Q&A sessions - Anonymous employee surveys for honest feedback
Respectful Disagreement	Promoting a culture where differing opinions are valued and discussed respectfully helps to create a psychologically safe environment for collaboration.	- Structured debates in meetings to explore multiple viewpoints - Conflict resolution training for managers - Encouraging "challenge meetings" where dissenting ideas are welcomed
Accountability	Establishing a norm where team members hold themselves and each other accountable for their responsibilities enhances reliability and commitment.	- Using Key Performance Indicators to track progress - Implementing shared project management tools like Jira or Trello - Peer accountability groups for goal setting
Support and Encouragement	Creating an atmosphere where team members actively support and encourage one another boosts morale and teamwork.	- Buddy or mentorship programs for new hires - Recognizing supportive behaviors in performance reviews - Creating Slack channels for peer shout-outs and encouragement
Constructive Feedback	Emphasizing the importance of providing and receiving feedback encourages growth and improvement.	- Hosting regular 360-degree feedback sessions - Using tools like Lattice or 15Five for structured feedback - Training employees on delivering feedback effectively

Work-Life Balance	Valuing and respecting personal time reinforces the importance of maintaining a healthy work-life balance.	- Enforcing "no after-hours emails" policies - Offering mental health and personal days - Implementing flexible working hours
Celebrating Successes	Making it a norm to recognize and celebrate both individual and team achievements promotes a positive and motivating culture.	- Monthly team award ceremonies or shout-outs - Sharing success stories in company newsletters - Celebrating milestones with office events or virtual parties
Continuous Learning	Encouraging a mindset of constant improvement and learning helps team members adapt and grow in their roles.	- Providing tuition reimbursement for professional development - Encouraging participation in industry conferences and workshops - Creating internal learning platforms with curated content
Collaboration Over Competition	Prioritizing teamwork and collaboration rather than individual competition enhances cohesion and collective success.	- Rewarding team achievements over individual performance metrics - Encouraging cross-departmental projects - Using collaborative software like Miro or Notion for brainstorming sessions

TABLE 9.3 Approaches to Building Cohesion

Strategy	*Description*	*Examples in Modern Business Leadership*
Build Trust	Establish trust by being transparent, honest, and consistent in communication and actions.	- Leaders openly sharing company updates in town halls - Transparent decision-making processes - Encouraging vulnerability in team discussions
Set Clear Goals	Define shared objectives the team can rally around, ensuring everyone understands their role in achieving them.	- Objectives and key results to align team goals - Visual goal tracking on dashboards (e.g., Monday.com, Asana, Trello, etc.) - Weekly goal-setting meetings
Model Positive Behavior	Demonstrate the behaviors and attitudes you want to see in the team, such as respect, collaboration, and support.	- Leaders openly recognize and appreciate employees - Encouraging peer mentorship and knowledge sharing - Leading by example in conflict resolution
Foster a Sense of Purpose	Help team members understand how their work contributes to the organization's larger goals, instilling a sense of shared mission.	- Sharing customer success stories in company meetings - Aligning personal and team objectives with company mission - Leadership reinforcing company values through storytelling
Organize Social Events	Arrange informal gatherings, such as team lunches or outings, to strengthen relationships outside of work-related tasks.	- Virtual happy hours for remote teams - Team-building retreats or off-site activities - Monthly coffee chats with leadership
Mentorship Programs	Implement mentorship initiatives where experienced members support newer ones, fostering connections and knowledge sharing.	- Formal mentorship programs pairing junior and senior employees - Reverse mentoring for generational learning - Shadowing opportunities within the organization

Regular Check-Ins	Schedule one-on-one and team check-ins to discuss progress, challenges, and feelings, showing that everyone's voice matters.	- Weekly stand-ups to share challenges and wins - One-on-one career development meetings - Employee engagement surveys to track team sentiment
Create a Shared Workspace	Design a physical or virtual workspace that encourages collaboration, such as open offices or collaborative online platforms.	- Slack channels dedicated to cross-team collaboration - Open-concept office spaces with flexible seating - Project management tools like Notion for shared knowledge
Empower Decision-Making	Involve team members in decision-making processes, giving them a sense of ownership and investment in outcomes.	- Employee advisory boards providing input to leadership - Team-led innovation challenges or hackathons - Consensus-building discussions before major decisions
Share Personal Stories	Encourage team members to share their backgrounds or experiences, fostering empathy and connection.	- "Storytelling sessions" where employees share personal journeys - Diversity and inclusion panels highlighting different perspectives - Team bonding exercises like "Two Truths and a Lie"
Establish Rituals	Create team rituals, such as weekly check-ins or end-of-project celebrations, reinforcing group identity and continuity.	- "Wins of the Week" celebration emails - End-of-quarter recognition events - Daily stand-up meetings for agile teams

TABLE 9.4 Example Standards for Excellence

Standard	*Description*	*Examples in Modern Business Leadership*
Integrity and Transparency	Promote honesty and openness in all communications and actions, encouraging trust among team members.	- Publicly sharing company financials and strategic goals - Open Q&A sessions with executives - Whistleblower protection policies to encourage ethical reporting
Respect and Inclusivity	Establish standards prioritizing respect for all individuals, fostering an inclusive environment where diverse perspectives are valued.	- Diversity, equity, and inclusion (DEI) training programs - Employee resource groups (ERGs) supporting underrepresented communities - Inclusive hiring practices with bias-reducing interview techniques
Collaboration and Teamwork	Set expectations for collaborative behavior, emphasizing the importance of working together to achieve common goals.	- Cross-functional teams working on major initiatives - Recognition of team achievements over individual accomplishments - Collaboration tools like Miro, Asana, or Slack to enhance teamwork
Excellence in Service	Establish high standards for customer service and responsiveness, reinforcing the importance of meeting the needs of clients and colleagues.	- Implementing Net Promoter Score tracking for customer satisfaction - Customer service training for all employees - Response time Service Level Agreements to ensure quick client resolution

Innovation and Creativity	Encourage a culture that values creative thinking and experimentation, allowing employees to propose new ideas and solutions without fear of failure.	- Google's "20% time" policy allows employees to work on passion projects - Hackathons or innovation challenges to generate new ideas - Encouraging "fail-fast" learning through rapid prototyping
Empowerment	Promote autonomy by empowering team members to make decisions within their roles, fostering a sense of ownership and responsibility.	- Delegating decision-making authority to employees - Allowing teams to set their work schedules and methods - Leadership development programs that prepare employees for growth roles
Adaptability and Resilience	Encourage a culture that embraces change and promotes flexibility, helping employees navigate challenges with a positive mindset.	- Implementing agile work methodologies - Change management training for employees - Mental health and stress management resources to support resilience
Community Engagement	Set standards for social responsibility, encouraging team participation in community service and charitable initiatives to foster a sense of purpose.	- Offering paid volunteer days for employees - Partnering with nonprofits for corporate social responsibility programs - Employee donation matching programs to support charitable causes
Clarity of Vision and Values	Communicate the organization's vision and core values, ensuring all team members understand and align with them.	- Publishing company values on internal and external platforms - Leadership reinforcing values in all-hands meetings - Embedding values in performance evaluations and hiring criteria

Exercise 9.1 **Constructing Positive Cultures**

This exercise helps aspiring leaders explore strategies to foster positive organizational cultures.

Breakout Groups: Form groups of 3–4 members each.

Role Play: Assume the roles of senior leaders discussed across this book so far, focusing on how to guide our People Leaders in effectively managing their teams.

Task: Each group will create four slides addressing key areas. First, provide structure. Discuss establishing clear roles, responsibilities, and processes to enhance team functionality. Second, develop positive norms. Identify specific behaviors and attitudes that promote a supportive and inclusive environment. Third, build cohesiveness. Share strategies to strengthen team unity and collaboration, ensuring everyone feels valued and connected. Fourth, craft ways to promote standards of excellence. Outline how to reach and sustain high-performance standards.

Presentation and Reflection: After creating the slides, each group will present its strategies to the larger group. Then, the groups should discuss their insights, challenges, and best practices for constructing a positive culture within this chapter.

CREATING INCLUSIVE CULTURES

The modern workforce is increasingly diverse, and People Leaders must recognize that inclusion and intersectionality are ethical imperatives for future success. *The 2025 Skills Horizon* (Peter et al., 2024) outlines substantial workforce transformations. To address complex, multidimensional challenges, People Leaders must prioritize diversity and inclusion, essential for cultivating innovative and resilient workplaces. Diverse perspectives meet societal expectations and enhance problem-solving, decision-making, and team performance.

Inclusion extends beyond mere representation, ensuring everyone feels valued and belonging within a team. The *2025 Skills Horizon* identifies "**working across difference**" (p. 7) as a core leadership competency for the coming decade (Peter et al., 2024). People Leaders must embrace **intersectionality**, which understands overlapping social identities and their effects on workplace experiences (see Chapter 5). People Leaders must foster environments where multiple voices (see Chapter 7) contribute to decision-making, psychological safety is prioritized (see Chapter 8), conflict is productive (see Chapter 8), and leadership styles adapt to meet needs (see Chapter 3).

Integrating **inclusive leadership** practices enhances team cohesion, drives meaningful engagement, and fosters sustainable and innovative work environments. People Leaders navigate cultural, generational, and ideological differences to compete (Peter et al., 2024). People Leaders must prioritize cultivating inclusive environments at all levels.

Diversity reflects variety and differences in backgrounds, geographies, positionalities, and beyond (Hunt et al., 2015). Diversity goes beyond teams to organizational policies and practices (Herring & Henderson, 2014). This understanding implies the need for an organizational culture that values and integrates the contributions of all its members.

Inclusion involves bringing diverse individuals into a group and fostering a climate where everyone feels they belong, regardless of their differences. Minority perspectives are heard and amplified, not overlooked. Booysen (2014) asserts that in inclusive workplaces, "all people from diverse backgrounds will feel valued, respected, and recognized," ensuring that no one questions their place within the organization (p. 299). Furthermore, Ferdman (2014) emphasizes that inclusion is experienced through individual treatment and respect for identity groups.

Equity is an equally important aspect of this discourse, which addresses the historical inequalities that have restricted access to programs, financial resources, and employment opportunities for certain groups, particularly racial minorities. Unlike **equality**, which provides the same resources to everyone, equity recognizes that individuals have disparate starting points due to discrimination and systemic inequalities linked to societal disparities (Streitmatter, 1994).

Inclusive leadership requires an intentional approach to diversity, inclusion, and inclusiveness across workplace policies, development, and enrichment. Talmage and Knopf (2017) argue that diversity should be treated as a community resource, inclusion as a process, and inclusiveness as a desired outcome. This framing is highly relevant to ensure psychological safety and move beyond mere representation. People Leaders must actively develop inclusive cultures.

In Table 9.5, we integrate the four stages of psychological safety (Clark, 2020) into Talmage and Knopf's (2017) conceptual framework. Organizations can move beyond token representation and foster environments where employees feel safe contributing, challenging, and innovating. This connection underscores the importance of building inclusion into the earliest stages of team formation, reinforcing that psychological safety is a prerequisite for high-performing and socially responsible organizations. People Leaders who champion development and enrichment will improve workplace well-being and drive long-term innovation and resilience in an era of rapid social and technological change.

Diversity acknowledges differences as an asset, inclusion leverages those assets, and equity ensures proper access to resources. Myers (2011) encapsulates this metaphorically by stating that diversity is "being invited to the party," while inclusion is "being asked to dance" (p. 13). If we extend the metaphor, equity allows everyone to take dance lessons. While leaders often recognize the importance of diversity, they face the challenge of fostering inclusive cultures, ensuring that each individual feels included and empowered to contribute fully.

Fostering a Sense of Belonging

Diversity, equity, and inclusion (DEI) are widely recognized as assets to companies; however, equity can be more contentious to discuss depending on political persuasion and substantially impact today's business landscape. An additional asset is a strong sense of **belonging** within the workplace. Given the current political rhetoric and critiques of the merits of DEI initiatives, we propose belonging may be a better avenue for gaining buy-in across stakeholder groups.

The idea is quite simple: when individuals feel connected to a larger purpose, they cultivate a sense of belonging that directly relates to their work environment.

TABLE 9.5 Policy, Development, and Enrichment Through Diversity, Inclusion, and Inclusiveness

Dimension	*Definition*	*Application in Leadership & Organizations*	*Connection to Psychological Safety*
Diversity (Resource)	The presence of varied identities, backgrounds, and perspectives within a group.	Policy-driven diversity initiatives (e.g., recruitment, hiring, quotas, anti-discrimination laws).	Leaders create structures that value and sustain diverse talent, ensuring *inclusion and safety*.
Inclusion (Process)	The active engagement of diverse individuals in decision-making, teamwork, and leadership.	Community development and organizational practices that create space for authentic participation (e.g., mentorship programs, inclusive team meetings).	Supports *learner and contributor safety*, fostering an environment where employees feel valued and encouraged to contribute.
Inclusiveness (Outcome)	The complete integration and belonging of diverse members ensure long-term equity and access.	Enrichment efforts include recognition programs, leadership pipelines for underrepresented groups, and cultural competency training.	Aligns with *challenger safety*, where all voices—including dissenting ones—are respected in decision-making.

People Leaders should actively prioritize nurturing a culture of belonging. When individuals can express their authentic selves at work, their engagement and contributions increase (see Chapters 5 and 7). Increased belonging fosters collaboration, enhances problem-solving, and improves decision-making (see Chapter 6). When employees feel a sense of belonging, they are more willing to share ideas, express their thoughts confidently, and contribute meaningfully to the organization's success. A strong sense of belonging is key to unlocking diversity's true potential and benefits.

Promoting a sense of belonging among employees is vital under the current conditions of rapid change, constant disruption, and social unrest. People Leaders can directly implement the following strategies adapted from Cornell University (n.d.).

- **Foster intentional connections**: Fostering a sense of belonging among team members is essential for creating a positive environment. Consider how teams can be organized, how small groups can be assembled to address particular challenges, and the layout of office spaces.
- **Build trusting relationships**: Consider establishing a mentoring program, formal or informal. Such initiatives can promote significant interactions that connect individuals across differences, including age, gender, and race.
- **Invite opinions and perspectives into the conversation**: Encourage contributions and ideas from every team member while being transparent about decision-making. Leaders who actively seek input from their teams can generate better ideas, confirm their choices, and foster a sense of belonging among everyone.
- **Engage in purposeful storytelling**: Encourage team members to open up about their personal experiences. Gaining insight into someone else's narrative can break down interpersonal obstacles and reveal the various layers, dimensions, and experiences of individuals that might otherwise remain hidden. This practice fosters a sense of recognition and understanding.

The concept of belonging has gained prominence in organizational discussions, highlighting its critical role in employee engagement and satisfaction. Maxwell Huppert (2017) emphasizes that fostering a sense of belonging leads to success and has been reinforced by scholars for a long time. This aligns with Abraham Maslow's hierarchy of needs (see Chapter 7), where the need for love and belonging is a fundamental human motivation. This translates to employees feeling connected to their colleagues and finding meaning in their work, which is essential for overall job satisfaction and performance.

Furthermore, Peter Drucker (2012), a key figure in modern management, suggested that executives should treat employees like volunteers. He recognized that employees who apply their intellect to one company could just as easily lend their talents to another. To retain these individuals, companies must create a welcoming environment. Just as volunteers who stay with an organization find fulfillment, so do employees. Both groups are engaged in their work and understand its purpose, leading to a strong sense of belonging.

Many companies recognize diversity and inclusion alone are insufficient; a sense of belonging for all employees is essential. Rebekah Bastian, VP of culture and community at Zillow Group, emphasizes that the positive business outcomes linked to diverse teams can only be realized when every employee feels they belong. People Leaders actively amplify voices, remove barriers, and honor different unique backgrounds (Creary, 2019).

Exercise 9.2 MicroLabs on Fostering Belonging

Break into small groups of three, which we will call a microlab. Reflect on an experience where you felt included and belonging among a group, team, or organization. Conversely, reflect on a time when you felt excluded or did not belong in a group, team, or organization. Write down your experiences in your microlab. Share the first experience where you felt like you belonged. After each microlab member has gone, share the second experience where you felt excluded.

Consider the following questions:

1. What factors contributed to your sense of belonging?
2. What aspects were lacking that hindered feeling included?
3. How do our social identities influence perceptions of belonging?
4. How did your behavior shift when you experienced a sense of belonging or marginalization?

Leveraging Inclusive Cultures as a Competitive Advantage

Inclusive culture is not just a buzzword today but a business imperative. Specifically, leveraging a diverse workforce for competitive advantage is why many organizations invest in strategic initiatives that drive diversity, equity, inclusion, and belonging. A report by McKinsey & Company in 2020 called *Diversity Wins: How Inclusion Matters* (Dixon-Fyle et al., 2020) revealed that companies in the top quartile for ethnic and cultural diversity outperform their peers by 36% in profitability. Why? Diverse teams that function at a high level generate more dynamic solutions. Teams with multidimensional perspectives across differences can problem-solve and make decisions that have a compelling impact and are culturally in step with markets while edging out competitors who primarily rely on homogeneous groups.

Inclusive cultures are vital to innovation and profitability. Boston Consulting Group found that companies with above-average diversity scores reported innovation revenue 19 percentage points higher than those with below-average scores. This highlights the direct correlation between diversity and business success (Lorenzo et al., 2018). In the UK, companies like Diageo and Unilever have exemplified diversity in action (diageo.com & unilever.com). These organizations celebrate diverse teams and leverage diversity for greater creativity and improved decision-making, setting a benchmark for others.

For diverse companies, the likelihood of outperforming industry peers regarding profitability has increased over time, while the penalties are getting steeper for those lacking diversity (Sullivan, 2022). McKinsey & Company (2020) make the business case for inclusive cultures with their most extensive data set yet, encompassing 15 countries and more than 1,000 large companies. The report provides insights that inclusion matters, illustrating that People Leaders must pay greater attention to inclusion, even in relatively diverse industries. Those companies that were "winning" at leveraging inclusive cultures for a competitive advantage had five key components:

- Ensure representation of diverse talent,
- Strengthen leadership accountability and capability for inclusive cultures,

- Enable equality of opportunity through fairness and transparency,
- Promote openness and tackle microaggressions, and
- Foster belonging through unequivocal support for multivariate diversity.

People Leaders communicate and visibly embrace their commitment to multivariate forms of diversity. They should build connections with diverse individuals and support **employee resource groups** (ERGs) to foster community and belonging. When grounded in purpose and mission, ERGs can be assets (see Chapter 8).

Though progress generally is slow, one fast mover is Citigroup, which has gone from 8% gender diversity on its executive team in 2014 to over 30% in 2019 (McKinsey & Company, 2020). The corporation places equality of opportunity, accountability, and transparency at the center of everything it does. Business leaders at all levels are directly involved in and held accountable for advancing inclusive cultures across the organization, with scorecards presented at each board meeting where "very granular" and "very transparent" conversations are encouraged. They focus on three key areas: targeted recruitment, development and retention, and promotion paths and processes.

A gap between a company's communication and progress can significantly undermine internal and external credibility, further contributing to a lack of genuine inclusion (McKinsey & Company, 2020). Their analysis revealed that every company in their dataset that has made sustainable strides in increasing gender and ethnic diversity within its top leadership over the past five years has also made meaningful progress in fostering an inclusive workplace culture. For instance, Lockheed Martin has aimed to "create an environment where our employees feel welcomed and encouraged to bring their whole selves to work" (McKinsey & Company, 2020). Similarly, executives at Target say they are committed to building an "ecosystem" around an inclusive culture "rather than just having it as an isolated function" (McKinsey & Company, 2020). A systematic, holistic business approach is necessary to leverage inclusive cultures for a competitive advantage.

Building Multicultural Organizations

Companies that have leveraged inclusive cultures as a differentiator do so with tremendous intention. In the past, practitioners in the field of organizational development joined with experts who focused on diversity in the workplace to explore how to address cultural diversity, social justice, and systemic change in organizations. Although seemingly natural and obvious today, this union took much time to develop. Before this connection, leaders in organizations typically addressed diversity issues only as a training module or "one-off" change initiative. Diversity issues were not integrated into the organizational mission (Jackson, 2014).

Enter **multicultural organizational development** (MCOD), which embraces individuals from diverse socially defined identities, including race, ethnicity, gender, sexual identity, nationality, class, religion, and various social and cultural groups. These initiatives are rooted in social justice and aim to eliminate forms of social oppression and injustice such as racism, sexism, heterosexism, classism, and anti-Semitism.

People Leaders can pursue MCOD for several reasons: some believe it is simply the right thing to do, while others recognize that a diverse workforce and a socially just workplace can enhance the quality of products and services, boost employee productivity, and improve organizational performance. MCOD seeks to enrich organizational culture by advocating for social justice and seeing diversity as a competitive edge.

Historically, diversity practitioners viewed their role as helping organizations become more just, inclusive, and humane. This was typically achieved through seminars and training sessions that addressed individuals' exclusionary behaviors, attitudes, and limited understanding of discriminatory practices. These practitioners aimed to change individual behaviors to foster a supportive workplace culture that appreciates differences and leverages diversity as an asset.

Holvino (2014) acknowledged that while addressing individual behaviors and attitudes toward discrimination was crucial, it was insufficient for achieving substantial organizational change toward becoming a socially just entity or a multicultural organization. They theorized that to realize the vision of an MCOD, the organization itself must be viewed as the target for change. This integration of organizational development with diversity and social justice principles has led to the evolution of MCOD into a practice that continues to show promise and growth. Table 9.6 summarizes key assumptions and example action steps for practicing MCOD.

In most large organizations, divisions, departments, teams, groups, or other organizational units will be at different points on the developmental continuum regarding the strength of their affinity for (or against) the organization's MCOD goals. For People Leaders, collecting data, assessing where their respective teams sit on the MCOD continuum, and developing a change intervention plan consistent with the organization's overall mission of having an inclusive culture is essential.

Based on their work in social and racial identity development theories, Jackson and Hardiman (1989, 1997) developed the MCOD development stage model. **The MCOD development stage model** identifies six points on the developmental continuum, each describing the consciousness and culture of an organization concerning issues of social justice and diversity and where the organization is relative to becoming an MCOD (see Figure 9.1, adapted from Jackson and Hardiman, 1989, 1997).

Jackson (2014) writes in *The NTL Handbook of Organization Development and Change* that the MCOD developmental stages are still relevant today and are most useful in the assessment and planning phases of the MCOD process. The stage model presents a framework for designing assessment instruments and techniques, which can help the organization identify its stage of development and construct a beginning benchmark for MCOD initiatives. People Leaders should determine their place on the continuum before developing a change plan for the next stage.

We offer the following as possible interventions for MCOD change plans in Table 9.7.

Exercise 9.3 Practicing MCOD Change Plans

Break into groups of 4–5. Using the MCOD stage of development, identify an existing organization that a group member is a part of. Imagine being a People Leader and developing a six-point plan to move your organization toward multiculturalism on the MCOD continuum. Present your plans and discuss your approaches based on the contents of this chapter.

TABLE 9.6 Assumptions and Action for Practicing MCOD

Principle	*Description*	*Action Steps for Leaders*
Systemic Change Beyond Training	Individual awareness and training are helpful but insufficient for lasting organizational change. Policies and practices must be reformed to eliminate barriers to diversity and inclusion.	- Audit policies for bias and inequities - Align HR practices with DEI goals - Move beyond performative DEI initiatives
Organizations Exist on a Continuum	Companies are not simply "good" or "bad" regarding diversity. They exist on a developmental spectrum, from monocultural to multicultural.	- Assess where the organization currently stands - Use a diversity continuum model to track progress - Set stage-appropriate DEI goals
A Clear Vision Guides Transformation	Organizational change must be guided by a strong, shared vision of an inclusive, multicultural workplace.	- Develop and communicate a compelling DEI vision - Integrate this vision into company values and mission - Align leadership decisions with inclusive principles
Internal Assessment Establishes Reality	A structured evaluation of the organization's diversity, equity, and social justice efforts provides a baseline for change.	- Conduct regular DEI climate surveys - Collect qualitative and quantitative data - Use findings to set measurable goals
Shared Ownership Is Essential	Employees at all levels must take responsibility for driving diversity and inclusion initiatives.	- Engage employees in shaping DEI efforts - Create accountability structures across all levels - Establish diverse task forces to co-lead initiatives
Ongoing Monitoring and Commitment	Sustainable change requires long-term commitment, with continuous evaluation and alignment to organizational goals.	- Implement DEI progress tracking and reporting - Link DEI outcomes to business performance - Ensure leadership remains actively engaged

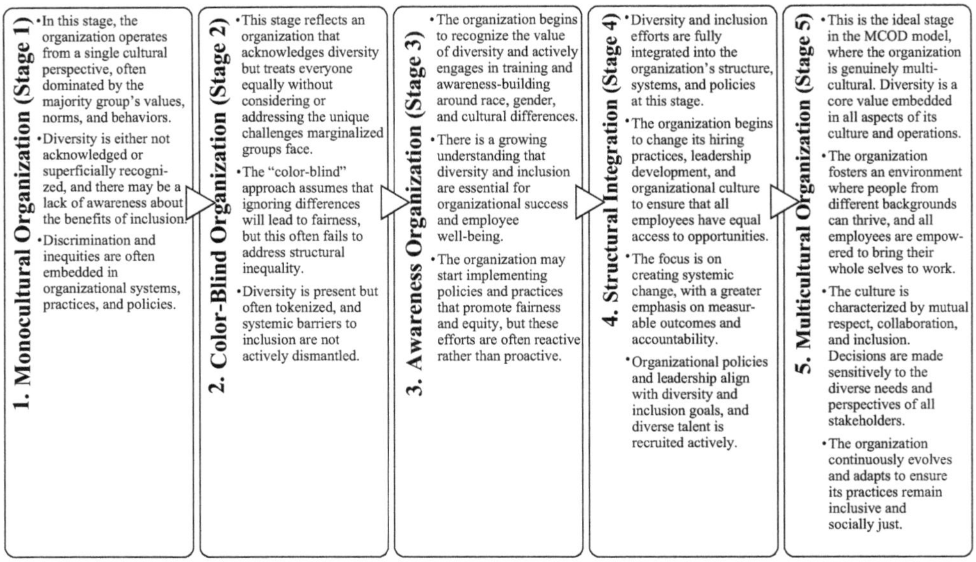

FIGURE 9.1 The MCOD Development Stage Model

TABLE 9.7 MCOD Intervention Principles and Practices

Strategy	*Description*	*Examples in Modern Business Leadership*
Diverse Recruitment Strategies	Implement recruitment practices that actively seek candidates from diverse backgrounds, ensuring a range of perspectives and experiences.	- Partnering with diverse job boards and universities - Implementing blind resume screening to reduce bias - Using structured interview processes for fairness
Inclusive Onboarding Processes	Design onboarding programs that introduce new employees to the organization's commitment to diversity and inclusion, promoting a sense of belonging from day one.	- DEI-focused onboarding sessions - Pairing new hires with diverse mentors - Including company values on diversity in onboarding materials
Employee Resource Groups (ERGs)	Establish ERGs to support, network, and advocate for underrepresented groups within the organization.	- Women's leadership networks - LGBTQ+ and BIPOC affinity groups - ERGs hosting speaker events and mentorship programs
Regular Diversity Training	Offer ongoing training and workshops on unconscious bias, cultural competence, and inclusivity to foster employee awareness and understanding.	- Annual unconscious bias training - Inclusive leadership workshops for managers - Cultural awareness education sessions

Strategy	*Description*	*Examples in Modern Business Leadership*
Mentorship and Sponsorship Programs	Create mentorship and sponsorship initiatives that connect diverse employees with leaders, helping to develop their careers and increase visibility.	- Formal mentorship programs for career growth - Sponsorship initiatives where executives advocate for high-potential employees - Reverse mentorship programs to bridge generational and cultural gaps
Flexible Work Arrangements	Provide options for flexible work hours and remote work to accommodate different needs and lifestyles, supporting a more inclusive work environment.	- Remote work policies for work-life balance - Four-day workweeks or flexible scheduling - Accommodations for caregivers and working parents
Open Communication Channels	Foster an environment where employees feel safe to share their ideas and concerns, ensuring that all voices are heard and valued.	- Anonymous employee feedback platforms - Open-door policies for leadership - Town hall meetings with Q&A sessions
Diversity Metrics and Accountability	Establish measurable diversity goals and regularly assess progress, holding leaders accountable for fostering an inclusive workplace.	- Tracking representation in leadership roles - DEI scorecards reviewed quarterly - Leadership performance evaluations, including diversity efforts
Celebrating Diversity	Organize events and initiatives celebrating different cultures, backgrounds, and perspectives, promoting employee awareness and appreciation.	- Hosting cultural heritage months (e.g., Black History Month, Pride Month) - Organizing international potlucks and storytelling events - Recognizing diverse holidays and traditions
Feedback Mechanisms	Implement anonymous feedback systems where employees can share their experiences and suggest improvements related to inclusivity and diversity.	- Regular DEI surveys with follow-up action plans - Confidential HR hotlines for reporting bias or discrimination - Employee-led focus groups to discuss workplace improvements

(*Continued*)

TABLE 9.7 (Continued)

Strategy	*Description*	*Examples in Modern Business Leadership*
Inclusive Decision-Making	Involve diverse teams in decision-making processes to ensure a variety of viewpoints are considered and integrated into outcomes.	- Establishing diverse hiring and promotion committees - Encouraging employee participation in strategic planning - Utilizing advisory boards with diverse perspectives

CONCLUSION

This chapter has offered a contemporary essential for designing culture. Specifically, healthy, functional cultures include clear directives that cultivate the inclusion of all employees in the workplace. People Leaders have tremendous influence over this process as they construct diverse teams and seek to get the best potential of each team member. The culture that teams are set in must shape connectedness, cohesion, trust, accountability, respect, and mechanisms for managing conflict if teams are to deliver and perform for the organization. Belonging adds a critical dimension to DEI initiatives today as People Leaders must foster it while removing the barriers that prevent team members from feeling included. Belonging may be a better approach to rally stakeholders due to political rhetoric and critique. Finally, all organizational units should assess and develop intervention plans to move their group toward a multicultural organization. The business case for doing so has been made. The penalty for the organizations that lag can no longer be ignored. Self and People Leadership come first in this book on purpose. Now, we get to business.

DISCUSSION QUESTIONS

1. What influences an organization's culture?
2. Why should a healthy and functional culture matter to a leader?
3. How does DEI interact with culture?
4. What does the dimension of belonging add to DEI initiatives?
5. How do inclusive cultures give companies a competitive edge?
6. What strategies are top organizations using to harness their inclusive cultures effectively?
7. What steps should leaders take to advance their teams on the MCOD continuum?
8. What does a comprehensive, organization-wide strategy for fostering an inclusive multicultural environment involve?

Key Terms

- Climate
- Culture
- Structure
- Norms
- Cohesiveness
- Standards of Excellence
- Diversity
- Inclusion
- Working Across Difference
- Intersectionality
- Equity
- Equality
- Belonging
- Multicultural Organizational Development
- MCOD Development Stage Model

CASE STUDY 9.1 HEALTHFIRST MEDICAL GROUP

Background: HealthFirst Medical Group is a mid-sized healthcare provider delivering comprehensive medical services to diverse patients. The organization is committed to patient-centered care and community health but has faced challenges in building a workforce that reflects the diversity of the communities it serves. The current staff is predominantly from similar demographic backgrounds, which has resulted in a lack of varied perspectives in patient care and service delivery.

The Dilemma: Dr. Emily Martinez, the CEO, recently recognized that the lack of diversity within the leadership team impacts the organization's ability to effectively serve its diverse patient base. She believes promoting diversity in leadership roles is essential for improving patient outcomes and fostering innovation. However, she faces resistance from the senior leadership team, which is primarily composed of long-serving members who prioritize stability and traditional practices.

During a recent leadership meeting, Emily proposed promoting two mid-level managers from underrepresented groups within the organization. Both have shown exceptional performance and commitment to inclusive care, but the senior leadership team is hesitant, citing concerns about their readiness and the potential disruption to existing team dynamics.

KEY STAKEHOLDERS

1. Dr. Emily Martinez (CEO): Dedicated to fostering an inclusive culture but facing pushback from the leadership team.
2. Rashida (Mid-Level Manager): A dedicated nurse manager who advocates for culturally competent care but often feels overlooked in leadership discussions.
3. Omar (Mid-Level Manager): A skilled health educator known for innovative outreach programs who feels marginalized within the current leadership structure.
4. Senior Leadership Team: Composed of long-tenured members focused on established practices and success metrics.

CHALLENGE QUESTIONS

1. **Evaluate the Risks and Benefits**—*What are the potential risks and benefits of promoting Rashida and Omar to leadership positions? How might their promotions influence team dynamics and the overall culture of HealthFirst?*
2. **Addressing Resistance**—*How should Emily approach the senior leadership team to alleviate their concerns about promoting Rashida and Omar? What strategies could she employ to emphasize the value of diversity in leadership?*
3. **Creating a Supportive Environment**—*What measures can Emily implement to ensure Rashida and Omar receive the support needed to excel in their new roles if promoted? How can the organization facilitate a seamless transition?*
4. **Long-Term Strategy**—*What long-term strategies should HealthFirst Medical Group adopt to cultivate a more inclusive culture and prioritize diversity in future leadership selections?*

Task: Answer the preceding questions regarding challenges and provide four comprehensive recommendations for Dr. Martinez. Connect the recommendations to key chapter concepts. Present the recommendations to a larger group for feedback and discussion.

REFERENCES

Booysen, L. A. E. (2014). The development of inclusive leadership practices and processes. In B. M. Ferdman & B. R. Deane (Eds.), *Diversity at work: The practice of inclusion* (pp. 296–329). Jossey-Bass.

Clark, T. R. (2020). *The four stages of psychological safety: Defining the path to inclusion and innovation*. Berrett-Koehler Publishers.

Cornell University. (n.d.). *Sense of belonging*. Cornell University Diversity and Inclusion. Retrieved from https://diversity.cornell.edu/belonging/sense-belonging

Creary, S. (2019, March 26). Beyond diversity: How firms are cultivating a sense of belonging. *Knowledge at Wharton*. Retrieved from https://knowledge.wharton.upenn.edu/article/belonging-at-work/?utm_source=chatgpt.com

Culture Partners (2024, April 16). *Understanding the differences: Organizational climate vs culture. Culture Partners*. Retrieved from https://culturepartners.com/insights/understanding-the-differences-organizational-climate-vs-culture/

Dixon-Fyle, S., Dolan, K., Hunt, V., & Prince, S. (2020). *Diversity wins: How inclusion matters*. McKinsey & Company. https://www.mckinsey.com/featured-insights/diversity-and-inclusion/diversity-wins-how-inclusion-matters

Drucker, P. (2012). *Management challenges for the 21st century*. Routledge.

Ferdman, B. M. (2014). The practice of inclusion in diverse organizations: Toward a systemic and inclusive framework. In B. M. Ferdman & B. R. Deane (Eds.), *Diversity at work: The practice of inclusion* (pp. 3–54). Jossey-Bass.

Herring, C., & Henderson, L. (2014). *Diversity in organizations: A critical examination*. Routledge.

Holvino, E. (2014). Developing multicultural organizations. In B. B. Jones & M. Brazzel (Eds.), *The NTL handbook of organization development and change: Principles, practices, and perspectives*. Wiley-Blackwell.

Hunt, V., Layton, D., & Prince, S. (2015). *Diversity Matters*. McKinsey & Company. Retrieved from https://www.mckinsey.com/~/media/mckinsey/business%20functions/people%20and%20organizational%20performance/our%20insights/why%20diversity%20matters/why%20diversity%20matters.pdf

Huppert, M. (2017, October 25). Employees share what gives them a sense of belonging at work. *LinkedIn Talent Blog*. Retrieved from https://www.linkedin.com/business/talent/blog/talent-engagement/employees-share-what-gives-them-a-sense-of-belonging-at-work

Jackson, B. W. (2014). Theory and practice of multicultural organization development. In B. B. Jones & M. Brazzel (Eds.), *The NTL handbook of organization development and change: Principles, practices, and perspectives*. Wiley-Blackwell.

Jackson, B. W., & Hardiman, R. (1989). Multicultural organization development: The NTL approach. In P. A. Block (Ed.), *The multicultural organization: A conceptual and theoretical framework* (pp. 1–16). NTL Institute for Applied Behavioral Science.

Jackson, B. W., & Hardiman, R. (1997). Multicultural organization development: A new vision for the 21st century. *The Journal of Applied Behavioral Science*, *33*(2), 179–206.

Laker, B. (2024, July 16). Understanding the distinctions between culture and climate. *Forbes*. Retrieved from https://www.forbes.com/sites/benjaminlaker/2024/07/16/understanding-the-distinctions-between-culture-and-climate/

Lorenzo, R., Voigt, N., Tsusaka, M., Krentz, M., & Abouzahr, K. (2018). *How diverse leadership teams boost innovation*. Boston Consulting Group.

Middlebrooks, A., Allen, S. J., McNutt, M. S., & Morrison, J. L. (2020). *Discovering leadership: Designing your success*. Sage Publications.

Myers, V. A. (2011). *Moving diversity forward: How to go from well-meaning to well-doing*. ABA Book Publishing.

Peter, S., Riemer, K., & Norman, P. (2024). *The 2025 Skills Horizon*. Sydney Executive Plus, The University of Sydney. https://doi.org/10.25910/57M8-SQ33

Streitmatter, J. (1994). *Toward gender equity in the classroom: Everyday teachers' beliefs and practices*. State University of New York Press.

Sullivan, C. (2022). Thriving Together. *Professional Safety*, 67(7), 4–4.

Talmage, C., & Knopf, R. C. (2017). Rethinking diversity, inclusion, and inclusiveness: The quest to better understand indicators of community enrichment and well-being. In P. Kraeger, S. Cloutier, & C. Talmage (Eds.), *New dimensions in community well-being* (pp. 7–27). Springer International Publishing. https://doi.org/10.1007/978-3-319-55408-2_2

PART 3

Business Leadership

The third phase of our model is uniquely situated in the 21st-century conditions today's business leaders find themselves in. *How do you expertly lead an organization when you must boldly execute strategy, effectively master the financial acumen of your role, understand and adapt to the digital transformation taking place, and still take risks with entrepreneurial know-how?* Such an inquiry mystified us like many, but we repeatedly leaned into our old and new lessons with students, clients, and communities. As mentioned in our introduction, it takes an ambidextrous leader to operate any size organization today; contemporary leadership necessitates a posture from the past and an orientation toward the future.

The collection of chapters in this section tells a story of struggles from the business sector on how to (1) enhance competitive advantage when there is so much disruption, (2) drill down to the essence of the health of a business, (3) cut out the noise from the pretenders making wild claims about the digital movement and listen to the experts, and (3) effectively create value, seize opportunity, and behave entrepreneurially amidst so much uncertainty. We challenged ourselves to craft a blueprint for meaningful discussion and guidance for application.

Business Leadership will continue to evolve but requires learning contemporary trends and topics from various scholars and practitioners. At the heart, Business Leadership accounts for the necessary knowledge and expertise to steer the ship, deliver exceptional products and services, develop the people who power the operation, and make the critical decisions to move the business forward. Within this section, strategy, finance, technology, and entrepreneurial concepts coalesce into a compelling recipe for today's business leaders to examine and iterate on.

Like each section, the Business Leadership dimension is designed for creativity, flexibility, and utility in classrooms where the work of preparing future business leaders gets done. We do not see these sections as linear or static but as comprehensive conversation starters meant to live on in the steady practice of a reader who carries these lessons into their career, applying concepts, strategies, and tools in their unique style and fashion. Those with the appetite for deepening their competencies around Business Leadership will find themselves marketable assets, competitive professionals, and high-potential talent for businesses today.

DOI: 10.4324/9781003474647-12

CHAPTER 10

Strategy

CHAPTER OVERVIEW

Business Leaders develop and execute impactful strategies that address competition and seize unique opportunities. This chapter pushes leaders to "zoom out" to grasp broader industry trends and "zoom in" on critical execution details. Using sports as an analogy, this chapter finds strategy to be an offensive method for achieving organizational goals and a defensive measure to guard against competitive threats. Historical texts and practical frameworks illustrate how a sound competitive strategy communicates unique value aligned with organizational mission, vision, and operations. Key questions help leaders define their distinct positions and make essential trade-offs when needed. This chapter overviews the vital role of strategy in achieving lasting competitive advantage and equips leaders with insights needed to navigate operational and contextual complexities.

Whenever we would teach strategy to undergraduates, the student-athletes in the room always had a better anchor than others. Strategy, we would say, is an organization's chance to play offense and score while, at the same time, working not to get exposed on defense. As a careful plan or the art of devising a plan toward a goal, strategy certainly resonates in sports contexts. In the business world, strategy needs to be part of the repertoire of a contemporary business leader, too. Strategy has existed since human competition regarding resources (i.e., capital). Many business school instructors even today still recommend (at least optionally) the 5th century AD text, *The Art of War* (孫子兵法) by Sun Tzu, or *Meditations* in the 1st century AD by Roman Emperor Marcus Aurelius to their students.

Specifically, **strategy** details distinctive approaches to competing and the competitive advantages based on those approaches (Institute for Strategy and Competitiveness, n.d.). A competitive strategy creates unique value for a distinct set of employees or clients, which we separate out in this book. Strategy positions an organization within a system of activities. In our work with students, clients, and communities, we often ask: *What defines your uniqueness? What trade-offs are you willing to make to compete? How does your strategy ensure organizational fit among your value chain activities?*

DOI: 10.4324/9781003474647-13

For Business Leaders, "the what" (mission and goals) and "the why" (vision and incentives) must align with organizational strategy ("the how") and the value network ("the who"). Competitive trends and internal and external information must reach Business Leaders swiftly, seamlessly traversing organizational levels. Business Leaders prioritize information highlighting the bottom-line impact of day-to-day choices (Neilson et al., 2008). Successful strategy articulates an organization's unique position, guiding how resources, skills, and competencies can create a competitive advantage (Porter, 2008). Porter's (2008) framework for competitive strategy (discussed next) stresses the need for a unique and valuable industry position rather than competing on the same terms as others. Readers should note the repetition of uniqueness in this chapter so far. In the previous book sections, we shared that modern business leaders must know themselves and their people; here, they must know their industries and businesses.

FIVE FORCES

Porter's (2008) Five Forces Model consists of competitive rivalry, the threat of new entrants, the bargaining power of buyers, the bargaining power of suppliers, and the threat of substitutes. These are the dynamics of competition and profitability within an industry (Porter, 2008). Business Leaders, the term we use in this section, make strategic decisions by understanding these forces to establish favorable market positions. As noted in this section of the book, strategy is at its best when it aligns mission, brand, resources, and goals, promoting cohesion across all organizational levels. Business leaders must determine how to position their products or services uniquely and leverage internal resources despite external pressures.

Strategy is an ongoing process that requires adaptability (Porter, 2008), which we covered at length in prior chapters. Strategy allows Business Leaders to anticipate market shifts and maintain a competitive edge. By aligning strategy with Porter's Five Forces, Business Leaders can more effectively navigate changes, recognize and exploit opportunities, and bolster their organizations against competitive threats while focusing on long-term vision and objectives.

ORGANIZATIONAL AND TEAM STRATEGY

There are two types of strategies. **Organizational Strategy** involves the organization's long-term direction and frequently includes the mission, vision, goals, and values. **Team Strategy** involves the team leading the organization and frequently includes performance factors and competencies. **Team Charters** can be effective as documents that define the team's purpose, how it will work, and the expected outcomes. They are "roadmaps" that the team creates at the beginning of the journey to ensure that all involved are clear about where they're heading and give direction when times get tough.

Strategy is more than definitions. Business Leaders must outline the fundamental differences between strategic thinking, decision-making, and planning to execute the proper techniques for the appropriate situations. Business leaders who prove themselves skilled at strong strategy are considered key assets to an organization. This chapter clarifies how strategic thinking, decision-making, and planning influence an organization's direction. We introduce decision-making techniques, including Drucker's strategic thinking process, Edward de Bono's Six Thinking Hats, the management science method, the Delphi method, and environmental scanning. By blending theory with practical applications, we address modern challenges such as technological disruption (see also Chapter 12) and market expansion. Lastly, we highlight the significance of effective strategic planning, focusing on employee engagement, execution excellence, and visionary leadership as components of sustained success.

STRATEGIC THINKING

Strategy thinking calls for the discovery of the novel, which can rewrite the rules of the competitive game and envision potential futures much different from the present. To gain a competitive advantage in today's business world, contemporary leaders must generate a particular brand of strategic thinking that incorporates innovative and creative ideation with business strategies. Strategic thinking is the precursor to strategic decision-making and frequently precipitates strategic planning. Productive strategic thinking can be a difference-maker in terms of executing competitive strategy. Strategic thinking is a group cognitive process, whereas the others require action (Allio, 2006; Anderson, 2024; Geier, 2024).

The dynamics of traditional strategic thinking, which equates to creating value for a company, have collided with the principles of ideation, often amounting to techniques for visioning, creating, imagining, ideating, opening, seeing alternatives, and problem-solving. Brainstorming, mind-mapping, meditation, thought clouds, scenario plans, feasibility studies, and root cause analysis are prominent when generating creative ideas that lead to determining a company's unique value. Innovative techniques can mean a cutting-edge approach and a company's forward movement when applied to strategies such as solidifying capabilities, focused opportunities, market impacts, and performance results. Rather than a division between creative and strategic thinking, the world's most agile companies understand that the key to effective design and innovation is, in fact, a symbiotic interplay between "strategic creativity" and "creative strategy" (Allio, 2006; Anderson, 2024; Geier, 2024; Roustaei et al., 2024).

In these sessions, we often asked: *How does this single big idea become many actionable small ideas? Can we constrain our brainstorming session to a fixed time frame? Does this solution use all of our existing resources before calling on anything external? How does this creative idea fit into our larger strategic vision?*

Modern strategic thinkers embrace the future, take risks, are creative, reject the status quo, are voracious learners, exercise a willingness to adapt, understand delayed gratification, and work efficiently. Today's rules are outlined precisely by Richard Shrapnel (n.d.) in *The Four Levels of Strategic Thinking in Business*:

1) Develop undefeatable strategies
2) Achieve accurate, sustainable growth
3) Create decisive competitiveness
4) Become tactically alive

What does this look like in practice? Renowned management author Peter Drucker (1954) proposed three effective techniques for strategic thinking that are still relevant today. First, leaders should ask deep questions to those who understand what is happening now and what might happen in the future. This helps them come up with strategies and consider alternatives. Second, leaders must organize situations into simple, clear ideas. This makes it easier for leaders to focus on critical items and adjust plans to keep up with the competition. Finally, leaders question assumptions underlying current perspectives in the pursuit of innovation. Business Leaders consider alternative assumptions and rigorously explore their context and strategic implications.

Strategic thinking skills can be hard to obtain, and senior executives need more than just a strategic mindset. Business leaders who bring "big picture" thinking are exciting and can distinguish professionals on their respective teams. It is a cultivated skill that requires constant attention, from analyzing opportunities and problems to taking a broad perspective and anticipating the potential impact of a company's actions on others. A distinct competency is understanding when an organization is in strategic thinking versus decision-making.

STRATEGIC DECISION-MAKING

Some decisions will be so routine that a leader can make them without much thought. Strategic decisions involve uncertainty, where many of the facts may be unknown; complexity, where there can be many interrelated factors; high-risk consequences, as the impact of the decision may be significant; alternatives, in that there may be various options, each with its own set of uncertainties and consequences; and finally, interpersonal issues in that it's hard to predict how different people will react.

Six Thinking Hats

Scholars and practitioners alike have well-documented strategic decision-making techniques. Edward de Bono (1985) created one approach: the **Six Thinking Hats**. This technique forces leaders to move outside their habitual thinking style and examine organizational situations from several perspectives, allowing them to gain a more rounded view. Table 10.1 describes the hats with examples.

Business Leaders face elevated stakes and increasingly unpredictable environments. Decision-making impacts all organizational levels, from the enterprise to specific business units and corporate headquarters. Strategic decision-making depends on various factors, including market fluctuations, opportunistic partner actions, natural disasters, and internal conflicts. These elements complicate strategic decision-making (Rahman & De Feis, 2009).

A substantial part of the literature on strategic decision-making has attended to cognitive biases. **Cognitive biases** are observer effects (e.g., statistical errors, social attribution errors, and memory errors) standard in all humans that skew the reliability of evidence (Rahman & De Feis, 2009). Due to complexity and time pressure, decision-makers may become more susceptible to cognitive bias. Strategic decision-making models and methods

TABLE 10.1 Six Thinking Hats

Thinking Hat	*Description*	*Example in Leadership*
White Hat (Data & Facts)	Focuses on gathering and analyzing available data, identifying trends, and recognizing gaps in knowledge.	A marketing executive reviews sales data from the past five years to determine which products have the highest seasonal demand before launching a new campaign.
Red Hat (Emotions & Intuition)	Encourages decision-making based on intuition, gut feelings, and emotional responses, noting how others might react.	A CEO senses tension among employees and uses their intuition to address concerns before morale declines, despite no formal complaints.
Black Hat (Caution & Risk Assessment)	Identifies potential risks and weaknesses in a decision, allowing leaders to prepare contingency plans and strengthen their approach.	Before investing in a new market, a business strategist highlights potential regulatory issues and supply chain risks to prevent costly mistakes.
Yellow Hat (Optimism & Benefits)	Encourages positive thinking by focusing on the benefits and value of an idea, even in challenging situations.	A project manager reassures their team that creative restructuring will allow successful project completion despite budget cuts.
Green Hat (Creativity & Innovation)	Emphasizes brainstorming, ideation, and thinking outside the box to find innovative solutions.	A product development team holds a brainstorming session to reimagine their best-selling product with sustainable materials, expanding into the eco-friendly market.
Blue Hat (Process & Organization)	Focuses on structuring discussions, setting the agenda, and ensuring all perspectives are considered effectively.	During a strategy meeting, the facilitator assigns different hats to participants, ensuring all viewpoints are covered before finalizing a business decision.

that guard against these key detractors in contemporary business situations offer more effective approaches.

Management Science Method

Rahman and De Feis (2009) present a collection of strategic decision-making models, such as the **management science method**, which uses sequential decision-making steps in a clear and precise way:

1. Define the problem.
2. Identify alternatives.
3. Develop some criteria.

4. Evaluate alternatives (relative to those criteria).
5. Choose an alternative.
6. Implement the decision.
7. Analyze the results.

This method involves making decisions through a series of steps, which can sometimes be completed quickly. Analysts seeking to identify how many, what size, and what dimensions would more readily be able to use this quantitative approach. Namely, it is objective, uses measurement, applies theories or models, uses experiments, and is valid and reliable. Using mathematical models, linear programming, PERT charts, and computer simulations, the management science method presents the quantitative side of management (Rahman & De Feis, 2009). However, Rahman and De Feis (2009) determined that the management science approach is an appropriate decision-making method under low complexity and time pressure.

The Delphi Method

Alternatively, The Delphi method for decision-making is an iterative process whereby the previous decisions impact each new decision. The decision process is channeled through a point person who proposes the changes in the next round of the decision process. This decision-making method consists of a structured procedure for collecting and distilling knowledge from experts, employing a series of questionnaires and interviews arranged with controlled opinion feedback (Rahman & De Feis, 2009). **The Delphi method** represents a valuable group of strategic decision-making methods with experts, facilitating the formation of a group judgment. However, due to the Delphi method's group nature, it takes longer to reach a consensus or compromise; hence, the temporal elements are not critical (Landeta, 2006).

The Delphi method works well when urgency is not of the essence because substantial time is required for the iteration process to occur. It has been developed to use experts in different locations, time zones, and cultures without permitting certain social behaviors that may occur during a regular group discussion (Rahman & De Feis, 2009). The Delphi method is an appropriate strategic decision-making method for an organizational leader under high complexity and low time pressure (Figure 10.1).

The Environmental Scanning Method

The **environmental scanning method** is the search and use of information about events, trends, and relationships in the external environment (SCIP, n.d.). This information assists Business Leaders in planning future courses of action. Business Leaders scan the environment to investigate the external forces of change and develop effective responses to improve their competitive position. The scan helps to avoid surprises, identify threats and opportunities, gain competitive advantage, and improve long-term and short-term planning (Rahman & De Feis, 2009). How well an organization can adjust to changes around

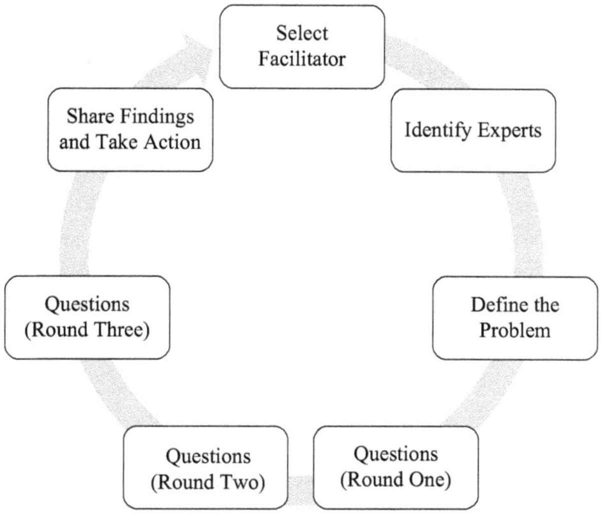

FIGURE 10.1 The Delphi Method

it depends on how well it understands and reacts to what is happening outside of it (Choo, 1999; Kiviaho & Einolander, 2023). Figure 10.2 showcases the different layers of the environment to be scanned.

Environmental scanning is a tool for organizational learning (Choo, 1999; Rahman & De Feis, 2009; Kiviaho & Einolander, 2023). It includes examining known information and identifying unknown information. Information needs refer to the aims and scope of scanning a given industry environment. Information use is usually related to decision-making or strategic planning (Rahman & De Feis, 2009). This method is highly effective under high complexity and time pressure, making it a tool for contemporary leaders.

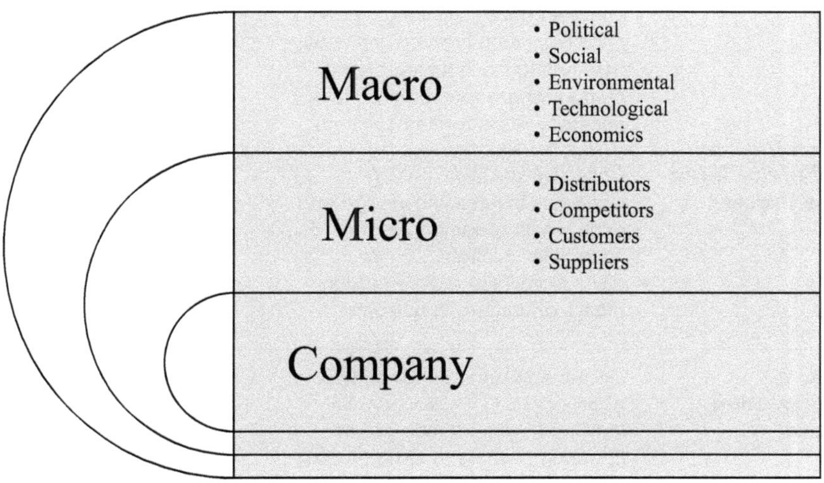

FIGURE 10.2 Macro and Micro Environments

Nominal Group Method

Rahman and De Feis (2009) recommend the **nominal group method** for strategic decision-making when time pressure is high and complexity is low. This structured approach ensures all team members have an equal chance to contribute, making it ideal for quick decisions that require diverse perspectives. Business Leaders and their teams start by brainstorming ideas individually. They then meet to talk about and prioritize them. Instead of tallying votes, the Nominal Group Method uses a scoring system to take everyone's opinions into account. This approach works well in organizations that want to be efficient and inclusive, especially during strategic planning and problem-solving, as it helps improve teamwork and decision-making.

Best Practices

Effective decision-making is a crucial business skill that impacts organizational performance (Gavin, 2020). Bain & Company surveyed over 750 businesses, revealing a 95% correlation between decision-making effectiveness and financial outcomes. The research also indicated that companies proficient in making and implementing strategic decisions achieve returns nearly 6% higher than their competitors. Further, leaders are responsible for effective strategic decision-making, and according to consulting firm McKinsey, "61% of them believe at least half the time they spend doing so is ineffective" (Gavin, 2020). This is an area that needs development across the corporate landscape. Table 10.2 (adapted from Gavin, 2020) outlines best practices to ensure strategic decision-making techniques work.

TABLE 10.2 Best Practices for Strategic Decision-Making

Best Practice	*Description*	*Key Takeaways*
Take a Process-Oriented Approach	A structured, step-by-step approach improves decision-making effectiveness by ensuring clarity and alignment. Framing the issue, assembling the right team, and managing group dynamics help generate well-informed solutions.	- Define the problem clearly. - Follow a structured multi-step process. - Align stakeholders on objectives.
Involve the Team in the Process	Collective decision-making leverages diverse knowledge and experience, leading to more innovative solutions. Group discussions help reduce hidden biases and improve outcomes.	- Engage diverse team members. - Encourage idea-sharing to uncover blind spots. - Promote inclusivity in decision-making.
Foster a Collaborative Mindset	Decision-making can follow two approaches: (1) Advocacy, where individuals defend their positions, or (2) Inquiry, where teams engage in critical thinking and open dialogue. A collaborative, inquiry-based approach leads to better outcomes.	- Promote open discussions. - Encourage critical thinking and evaluation. - Support diverse perspectives to enhance decisions.

Best Practice	*Description*	*Key Takeaways*
Create and Uphold Psychological Safety	High-performing teams thrive in environments where members feel safe to share their perspectives. Psychological safety encourages honest input and risk taking without fear of judgment.	- Build trust among team members. - Encourage respectful dialogue. - Support a culture where new ideas are welcomed.
Reiterate the Goals and Purpose of the Decision	Staying focused on the objectives prevents teams from deviating from key priorities. Clearly articulating goals at the outset and revisiting them ensures alignment.	- Define and communicate goals early. - Reinforce purpose throughout the process. - Regularly check progress against objectives.

Exercise 10.1 Strategic Decision-Making

Break into groups. Describe the scenario. Each group should analyze the device's features and decide whether to launch this product. The groups should also research trends, markets, and competitors. Finally, each group should report and share its rationale. *What are the strongest and most attractive features? Where are its weaknesses? What are larger market threats? What could the device evolve into? What could users do with the device that is not described in the following?*

The UltraFit Pro is a cutting-edge fitness tracker designed for health-conscious individuals, fitness enthusiasts, and tech-savvy users. It has advanced health monitoring capabilities, including continuous heart rate tracking with alerts for abnormal levels. The tracker also offers detailed sleep tracking, giving users insights into their sleep patterns and overall sleep quality. The tracker features blood oxygen level monitoring through SpO2 measurement and incorporates ECG functionality to detect irregular heartbeats.

The UltraFit Pro excels with its comprehensive activity monitoring. It keeps tabs on steps taken, distance traveled, calories burned, and more than 30 workout modes, including running, cycling, swimming, and yoga. The integrated GPS ensures accurate route mapping and distance tracking, making it an excellent companion for various physical activities.

The tracker is equipped with innovative features that enhance the user experience. It offers notifications for calls, messages, and app alerts, allowing users to stay connected seamlessly. Music control features enable users to manage playback directly. Compatibility with popular voice assistants, like Alexa and Google Assistant, adds another layer of convenience.

The UltraFit Pro's design and build are also noteworthy. It boasts a high-resolution AMOLED touchscreen with customizable watch faces that can reflect the user's style.

With an impressive battery life of up to 14 days on a single charge, users can enjoy extended usage without frequent recharging. The device is also water resistant, making it suitable for swimming and showering. The materials used include a durable silicone strap, a lightweight aluminum frame, and scratch-resistant glass, ensuring it can withstand daily wear and tear.

Additionally, the UltraFit Pro emphasizes health and wellness integration. It offers features for stress management, such as guided breathing exercises and tracking stress levels. Users receive hydration reminders to maintain proper fluid intake throughout the day. For women, the tracker includes menstrual cycle tracking, allowing for better monitoring of their menstrual health.

STRATEGIC PLANNING

When business leaders engage in critical strategic thinking and remain consistent with their decision-making, they often face pivotal moments in their organization's life where **strategic planning** becomes essential. These moments may include new executive leadership, organizational restructuring, industry trends to leverage, or challenges that demand significant change. Strategic planning executes an organization's unique position and provides a high-level approach to operationalizing its competitive advantage.

Classically, organizational leaders have documented their strategic plans over five-year periods. Today, there is tremendous debate about the utility of this approach. Some industries move so rapidly that a five-year plan would stagnate the organization and quickly become out of date; other industries proceed much slower and allow business leaders to develop a lengthy plan that enables them to realize incremental gains. In short, some organizations will develop five-year plans, and others will work toward a one-year plan.

Employee engagement is critical in strategic planning. Kraaijenbrink (2023) writes that for organizations, the pinnacle of good strategy is engaging all employees in the strategic planning process. The reasons are fourfold:

1. **Better Strategy**: Participation constitutes diverse perspectives, and this range of perspectives means richer input from different levels and roles in the organization. This makes the strategy more fitting, more concrete, and more relevant.
2. **Smoother Execution**: Participation means buy-in, and buy-in leads to ownership. It reduces potential resistance to strategic plans, speeding up and easing the overall strategic execution process.
3. **Competence Development**: Participation means learning by doing. The more employees engage in the process, the more they know about effective strategy, how to leverage their organization's unique position, and what it means long-term.
4. **Team Alignment**: Participation means communication, which lends to solid alignment. In a participative process, employees hear each other's perspectives, ideas, and insights, facilitating alignment across units, functions, and levels.

Strategic plans outline an implementation process's how, when, why, and who. It describes a way of doing and acting periodically to be reviewed, focused on, and executed by organization members. These plans envision the organization's future and translate this vision into broadly defined goals, objectives, and steps describing how to achieve them. Today, they frequently include elements such as a current mission statement, an updated vision statement, a statement on diversity, a set of guiding principles or values, strategic directions, goals to meet these strategic directions, areas of focus, anticipated outcomes, and then a construct of who is responsible for action items and the timetable to deliver. Organizational leaders must be clear, bold, and think ahead when developing these plans (Engel, 2024).

Traditionally, strategic plans were written documents to be shared internally, but today, they are more often animated on company websites for employees, shareholders, and customers to view.

Today, strategic plans can be public declarations of commitments to improve, grow, learn, capitalize, and compete. Business leaders who effectively implement strategic plans and produce evidence of outcomes earn their corporate credentials. They are generally highly sought after for their ability to galvanize employees and deliver on strategic directions. This is why strategic planning is essential in contemporary times.

Exercise 10.2 Strategic Planning

Craft a strategic plan outlining the strategic direction of an existing organization. Leaders of organizations generate strategic plans and often map out the organization's direction in a two-year, three-year, or four-year frame. Your plan should include (1) an Introduction with relevant context about the organization, (2) a Mission statement on the current purpose of the organization, (3) a Vision statement on where the future of the organization is going, (4) a brief Diversity statement for the organization, (5) 4–6 Strategic Directions that frame how you will strategically implement policy, positions and resources, (6) 4–6 Concrete Goals under each Strategic Direction, (7) Anticipated Outcomes if the Strategic Directions are met and (8) a Summary with future steps beyond this plan. Highlight your plan in a six-minute presentation.

SWOT Versus SOAR

SWOT is a standard tool used in strategic decision-making and planning, discussed shortly. SOAR is a modernization of SWOT. **SWOT** stands for strengths, weaknesses, opportunities, and threats and is widely used to evaluate an organization's internal capabilities and external environment (Kamkankaew, 2023). SWOT helps organizations assess their strengths and opportunities and plan to mitigate weaknesses and threats. Business Leaders pursue an optimal strategy that balances these four areas. Focusing on positive and negative factors, in balance and tethered, is especially beneficial for organizations needing a clear understanding of their competitive landscape (Pongsiri, 2023). SWOT has received criticism for being too negative and deficit-focused, devoting insufficient attention to positive assets organizations hold for creativity and innovation (Zarestky & Cole, 2017).

The **SOAR** framework (strengths, opportunities, aspirations, results) represents a more positive, future-oriented, asset-based approach to strategy. SOAR emphasizes strengths and opportunities while shifting focus away from weaknesses and threats, aligning with the principles of Appreciative Inquiry (Stavros & Hinrichs, 2019). By concentrating on aspirations and results instead of weaknesses and threats, SOAR encourages Business Leaders to examine their future potential. SOAR allows Business Leaders to craft strategies that leverage their strengths to pursue transformative growth (Stavros & Hinrichs, 2019). The SOAR framework is beneficial in environments where innovation, collaboration, and employee engagement are central to success (Kamkankaew, 2023). SOAR reifies a culture of optimism, communicating that strategic plans are feasible, aspirational, and desired.

Both are strategic tools that help businesses navigate complex environments but serve different purposes. SWOT offers a more critical, comprehensive analysis of the organization's current situation, while SOAR fosters positive change and sets a vision for the future (Pongsiri, 2023). Business Leaders who understand the strengths and limitations of both frameworks can select them strategically to meet particular needs. SWOT may be more beneficial for initial assessments, and SOAR may have more utility for inspiring growth and innovation. Thus, Business Leaders benefit from a thorough understanding of their present state while positioning themselves for future success using both frameworks (Zarestky & Cole, 2017).

BEWARE OF GROUP THINK

A business leader should strive to prevent **groupthink**. Social psychologist Irving Janis coined the term in: *Victims of Groupthink: A Psychological Study of Policy Decisions and Fiascoes* (1972). Groupthink occurs when individuals prioritize harmony within a group over sharing different ideas or opinions. This pressure to agree can lead to poor decision-making, stifling conversations, and lacking creativity and innovation. Business Leaders rely on strategic planning to avoid these issues.

The 1961 Bay of Pigs invasion offers a strong example of groupthink. President John F. Kennedy and his team backed a flawed plan to remove Fidel Castro from power in Cuba. Despite warning signs and serious risks, they failed to consider alternatives, seeing Castro's removal as the best and only possible desirable outcome. Team members stayed silent, going along with the majority, fearing that opposing views would appear disloyal. The outcome was disastrous, resulting in lives lost and political fallout. Leaders must know this hard lesson to value open discussions and independent assessments when planning strategy (JFK Library, n.d.).

CONCLUSION

Yet thinking, deciding, and planning strategically do not ensure effectiveness. Success comes from flawless execution, not breakthrough innovation. Strategy without execution is misaligned. Execution without strategy is misdirected. A decent strategy, well executed,

TABLE 10.3 Common Reasons Strategies Fail and Real-World Examples

Reason for Failure	*Description*	*Real-World Example*
Unrealistic Goals	Strategies fail when goals are overly ambitious, lack feasibility, or do not consider available resources and constraints.	**WeWork's Failed IPO (2019)** WeWork pursued rapid global expansion with unrealistic revenue projections and an unsustainable business model, leading to its failed IPO and drastic valuation drop.
Lack of Alignment	When leadership and teams are not aligned on strategic objectives, execution suffers, leading to inefficiencies and conflicting priorities.	**Yahoo's Strategy Shifts (2000s)** Frequent leadership changes and conflicting priorities led Yahoo to fail in capitalizing on search engine and social media opportunities, ultimately losing to Google and Facebook.
Little to No Accountability	Without clear ownership of strategic goals, teams lack motivation to follow through, leading to missed targets and stagnant progress.	**Kodak's Digital Camera Neglect (1990s–2000s)** Despite inventing the digital camera, Kodak failed to hold leaders accountable for adapting its business model, leading to bankruptcy in 2012.
Silo Mentality and Behavior	Departments or teams operate in isolation, limiting collaboration and preventing a cohesive strategy execution.	**Nokia's Decline in Mobile Phones (2010s)** Nokia's internal silos prevented seamless collaboration between hardware and software teams, allowing competitors like Apple and Samsung to dominate the smartphone market.
Inflexibility	Organizations that fail to adapt to market changes, consumer needs, or technological advances risk losing their competitive edge.	**Blockbuster's Resistance to Change (2000s)** Blockbuster failed to pivot to digital streaming despite Netflix's rise, ultimately leading to its downfall.

beats a brilliant plan, poorly executed. Table 10.3 contains our reasons for why strategies fail, with examples.

To implement a successful strategy, it is vital that employees clearly understand their decision-making and strategic planning responsibilities. This chapter distinguished between strategic thinking, decision-making, and planning. Business Leaders uncover and reinforce the uniqueness of their organizations despite industry and internal complexity, competition, and ambiguity. In the next chapter, we offer insights into knowing the numbers and financial acumen.

Effective strategic leadership is more pressing than ever. Strategic opportunities can arise anytime—short-term, long-term, incremental, or transformative. Business Leaders must prepare to think proactively and dynamically without falling into defensive postures. Embracing innovative techniques that enhance strategic dimensions empowers leaders to identify the initiatives that will drive their organizations forward despite challenges.

DISCUSSION QUESTIONS

1. What is the difference between strategic thinking, decision-making, and planning?
2. How can organizations play offense and capitalize on strategy during tumultuous conditions?
3. When should an organization think defensively from a strategy standpoint?
4. What kinds of conditions encourage strategic thinking within an organization?
5. Which models and tools outlined are more relevant to today's industry landscape?
6. Which criteria or tools would you leverage for a one-year or multi-year strategic plan?

Key Terms

- Strategy
- Organizational Strategy
- Team Strategy
- Team Charters
- Strategic Thinking
- Strategic Decision-making
- Six Thinking Hats
- Cognitive Bias
- Management Science Method
- The Delphi Method
- Environmental Scanning Method
- Nominal Group Method
- Strategic Planning
- SWOT
- SOAR
- Groupthink

CASE STUDY 10.1 TECHWAVE SOLUTIONS NEEDS A STRATEGY

TechWave Solutions, a tech startup founded in 2021 in San Francisco, California, specializes in a cloud-based project management tool for remote teams. With a team of 25, the company is experiencing rapid growth amidst increasing competition in the software sector and faces critical strategic decisions to ensure sustainable growth over the next three years.

The leadership team has identified market expansion as a primary objective and must choose between enhancing product features or targeting new geographical markets, particularly Europe, where demand for remote work tools is growing. Funding options are also being evaluated, such as initiating a Series A round for venture capital investment, which could accelerate growth but risk ownership dilution, or considering bootstrapping to maintain control at the expense of speed (You can explore these terms in our next chapter).

Improving customer retention is a key focus, with strategies including a loyalty program offering discounts for long-term subscriptions and a feedback loop to better align product development with user needs. The company has conducted thorough market research, including competitor analysis and customer surveys, to support these decisions, alongside financial projections and a clear understanding of the associated risks with each strategy.

Task: Provide four comprehensive recommendations for TechWave Solutions' leaders. Connect the recommendations to key chapter concepts. Present the recommendations to a larger group for feedback and discussion.

REFERENCES

Allio, R. J. (2006). Strategic thinking: The ten big ideas. *Strategy & Leadership, 34*(4), 4–13.

Anderson, T. E. (2024). *Visionary leadership: A guidebook for 21st century organizations and entrepreneurial teams*. Springer Nature.

Choo, C. W. (1999). The art of scanning the environment. *Bulletin of the American Society for Information Science and Technology, 25*(6), 21–24.

De Bono, E. (1985). *Six thinking hats: An essential approach to business management*. Little, Brown and Company.

Drucker, P. F. (1954). *The practice of management*. Harper & Row.

Engel, J. M. (2024, February 10). The second commandment of strategic planning: Think bold and think ahead. Retrieved from https://www.forbes.com

Gavin, M. (2020). 5 key decision-making techniques for managers. *Harvard Business School*. Retrieved from https://online.hbs.edu/blog/post/decision-making-techniques

Geier, M. T. (2024). Strategic thinking: theoretical development and assessment. *Journal of Strategy and Management, 17*(1), 1–21.

Institute for Strategy and Competitiveness. (n.d.). *Strategy explained*. Harvard Business School. Retrieved from https://www.isc.hbs.edu/strategy/Pages/strategy-explained.aspx

Janis, I. L. (1972). *Victims of groupthink: A psychological study of foreign-policy decisions and fiascoes*. Houghton Mifflin.

John F. Kennedy (JFK) Library. (n.d.). The Bay of Pigs. *JFK Library*. Retrieved from https://www.jfklibrary.org/learn/about-jfk/jfk-in-history/the-bay-of-pigs?

Kamkankaew, P. (2023). Current trends in strategic management: A comparative analysis of SWOT and SOAR approaches. *RMUTT Global Business Accounting and Finance Review, 7*(2), 63–78. https://doi.org/10.60101/gbafr.2023.269044

Kiviaho, A., & Einolander, J. (2023). Digital transformation, well-being, and shrinking communities: Narrowing the divides between urban and rural. *Heliyon, 9*(8). E18801. Retrieved from https://www.cell.com/heliyon/pdf/S2405-8440(23)06009-7.pdf

Kraaijenbrink, J. (2023). How to start engaging employees in strategy development. *Forbes*. Retrieved from https://www.forbes.com

Landeta, J. (2006). Current validity of the Delphi method in social sciences. *Technological Forecasting and Social Change, 73*(5), 467–482.

Neilson, G. L., Martin, K. L., & Powers, E. (2008, June). *The secrets to successful strategy execution*. Harvard Business Review. Retrieved from https://hbr.org/2008/06/the-secrets-to-successful-strategy-execution

Pongsiri, K. (2023). Current trends in strategic management: A comparative analysis of SWOT and SOAR approaches. *RMUTT Global Business Accounting and Finance Review, 7*(2), 63–78. https://doi.org/10.60101.gbafr.2023.269044

Porter, M. E. (2008). The five competitive forces that shape strategy. *Harvard Business Review, 86*(1), 78–93.

Rahman, N., & De Feis, G. L. (2009). Strategic decision-making: Models and methods in the face of complexity and time pressure. *Journal of General Management, 35*(2), 19–35.

Roustaei, A. A., Seifipour, H., & Moradi, M. (2024). Designing intelligent mind maps to develop creativity in strategy management. *Journal of Intelligent Strategic Management, 3*(4), 67–84.

SCIP. (n.d.). *Environmental scanning as information seeking and organizational learning*. SCIP. Retrieved from http://www.scipbrasil.org/docs/environmental-scanning-as-information-seeking-and-organizational-learning-4/

Shrapnel, R. (n.d.). *The four levels of strategic thinking in business*. Retrieved from https://richardshrapnel.com/thinking-strategically/

Stavros, J. M. & Hinrichs, G. (2019). *The Thin Book of SOAR: Building strengths-based strategy*. Thin Book Publishing.

Zarestky, J., & Cole, C. (2017). Strengths, opportunities, aspirations, and results: An emerging approach to organization development. *New Horizons in Adult Education and Human Resource Development, 29*(1), 5–19.

CHAPTER 11

Financial Acumen

CHAPTER OVERVIEW

This chapter highlights crucial financial acumen for Business Leaders. It breaks down essential accounting concepts to make them accessible and valuable for Business Leaders. It discusses the roles within accounting and how accounting is used to assess risk and financial health. Financial statements and their components are discussed. By understanding financial statements and the accounting equation, Business Leaders make effective decisions and ensure ethics in financial reporting, drawing on lessons from major financial scandals. This chapter equips Business Leaders with the skills to interpret and communicate financial information and navigate complex business information while ensuring transparency and accountability.

The previous chapter discussed strategy, where leaders, people, and business meet. This chapter focuses on knowing the business through financial acumen. "Knowing the numbers" is a must for Business Leaders to ensure proper monitoring, assessment, goal setting, decision-making, and strategic planning. We aim to make accounting accessible for Business Leaders, breaking down the jargon many of our students often find intimidating. If our readers can handle basic Microsoft Excel and simple arithmetic like addition, subtraction, multiplication, and division, they can navigate the accounting essentials and recognize when financial data seems off.

If people are a company's lifeblood, metrics are the necessary bloodwork. After covering accounting basics, this chapter helps Business Leaders navigate different contexts, such as talking with a seasoned executive, an entrepreneur launching a startup, or a mid-level manager aiming for promotion. Business Leaders must understand how to read financial statements and records at high levels. Those who understand financial language stand apart from others. In this chapter, comtemporary leaders will also learn how to communicate complex financial information to laypersons. Beyond terms, this chapter also explores ethical issues in financial decision-making, including lessons learned from financial scandals like FTX.

DOI: 10.4324/9781003474647-14

BASIC ACCOUNTING TERMS EVERYONE SHOULD KNOW

Accounting is often referred to as the language of business because it plays a crucial role in communicating an organization's financial health. Financial information concerns investors, employees, creditors, and government agencies. Accounting is a powerful storytelling tool depicting organizational success, challenges, and growth opportunities (Tracy & Tracy, 2022). Fear of this information, especially information that makes an organization look bad, can create problems for organizations (discussed later). Business Leaders recognize the utility and imperative of financial reporting and learn the language of accounting.

Roles in Accounting: From Bookkeepers to CFOs

Bookkeepers play a crucial role in day-to-day financial operations. They meticulously record daily financial transactions, including sales, returns, purchases, and payments. They are on the frontlines of data accuracy and entry (Tracy & Tracy, 2022). **Accountants** assume more analytical roles. They prepare financial statements to be reported and interpreted. Accountants then provide insights that aid decision-making processes, contributing to a critical understanding of an organization's financial narrative (Tracy & Tracy, 2022). **Controllers** in for-profit settings or **comptrollers** in government and not-for-profit settings oversee accounting departments (Jafri, 2023). They are accountable for the accuracy and integrity of financial reports, ensure that statements comply with applicable regulations, and provide frameworks to support organizational goals (Apostolides, 2016; Tracy & Tracy, 2022; Jafri, 2023).

The **Chief Financial Officer** (CFO) is the strategic leader overseeing all financial activities, including financial planning, risk management, and reporting. The CFO typically reports to the **Chief Executive Officer** (CEO), the highest-ranking executive who makes major corporate decisions, and the **board of directors**, who oversee the organization's activities and ensure accountability (Tracy & Tracy, 2022). The CFO strategizes to ensure financial health and accurate data for decision-making. Strong financial acumen can help Business Leaders feel comfortable in these intimidating spaces.

Financial Statements and the Accounting Equation

Financial statements are the cornerstone of accounting, and Business Leaders should understand the relationships between (1) revenue, costs, and expenses to ensure profit, balancing (2) assets, liabilities, and equity, and (3) liquid and non-liquid assets. While profit should not be the sole measure of organizational success (see Chapter 13), profit or net revenue (like in government and not-for-profit budgets) is essential to continue healthy operations that fulfill an organization's stated missions and value propositions (see Chapter 17).

Profit is a crucial indicator of a company's financial health and can be defined as **net income**. **Net income** is the remaining sales (revenue) after costs and expenses. When net income is negative, this is called **loss**. **Revenue** (also called sales and net sales) is the income generated from business activities, primarily through sales of goods or services. It can also include income from additional sources like advertising, grants, and investment returns. Consumer revenue is tantamount to for-profit organizations.

Costs typically refer to the **cost of goods sold** (COGS), which includes all expenses *directly* associated with the manufacturing and delivering products or services. This encompasses raw materials, production labor, and other necessary labor or production costs to create goods. **Gross profit** consists of sales minus COGs.

Expenses cover a broader range of operational expenditures vital for running an enterprise efficiently and can impact profitability differently. Expenses are categorized into several key areas: **Selling, general, and administrative** (SG&A) expenses include costs related to marketing, overhead, and administrative functions; **research and development** (R&D) expenses are incurred in the innovation of new products or improvement of existing ones; and **salaries and wages** cover employee compensation such as salaries, bonuses, and benefits. Other expenditures include rent, utilities, legal fees, and loan fees. Each category is critical in managing core operations and maintaining a competitive edge in the market. Organizations must also consider **taxes** (those imposed by government authorities) to ensure financial health and informed long-term strategic planning.

Business Leaders assess profitability by analyzing revenue, costs, and expenses. These components are reported on an **income statement**, also called a **profit and loss (P&L) statement** (see Table 11.1). Profit indicates whether a company is earning more than it spends, vital for sustaining operations, reinvesting in growth, and ultimately achieving

TABLE 11.1 Hypothetical Income Statement for Urban Threads, a Sustainable Fashion Company

Income Statement	*Amount*	*Notes*
Revenue	**$2,000,000**	Total sales from sustainable apparel and accessories.
Cost of Goods Sold (COGS)	**($1,000,000)**	Includes raw materials, manufacturing, and direct labor costs.
Gross Profit	**$1,000,000**	Revenue—COGS
Operating Expenses	**($700,000)**	Includes salaries, marketing, rent, utilities, and administrative costs.
• Salaries	($300,000)	Staff and leadership compensation.
• Marketing & Advertising	($150,000)	Campaigns for eco-friendly collections.
• Rent & Utilities	($100,000)	Retail space and headquarters expenses.
• Administrative Expenses	($150,000)	Software, supplies, legal, and accounting fees.
Operating Profit (EBIT)	**$300,000**	Gross Profit—Operating Expenses
Interest Expense	**($15,000)**	Interest on loans for startup capital.
Pre-Tax Income	**$285,000**	Operating Profit—Interest Expense
Taxes (20%)	**($57,000)**	Assumes a flat corporate tax rate.
Net Income	**$228,000**	Pre-Tax Income—Taxes
Dividends Paid	**($50,000)**	Paid to common and preferred shareholders.
Retained Earnings	**$178,000**	Reinvested into development and expansion.

long-term success. Business Leaders should know that most startups incur losses for their initial years due to high startup costs; however, equity and loans for cash and overall cash flow management become tantamount to ensuring the business does not fail. Business Leaders know their ways around the P&L to strategize and make informed financial decisions toward profitability.

The **accounting equation** (Assets = Liabilities + Equity) underpins the balance sheet, which provides a snapshot of financial standing. If the balance sheet is unbalanced, Business Leaders should investigate the reasons for the discrepancies rather than ignore them. The balance sheet, which can be found in Table 11.2, organizes the accounting equation. Note that most items in the balance sheet are reported as positive numbers; exceptions include depreciation.

TABLE 11.2 Hypothetical Balance Sheet for Urban Threads, a Sustainable Fashion Company

Category and Subcategory	*Amount*	*Notes*
ASSETS	**$1,283,000**	Total assets
Current Assets	**$663,000**	Liquid assets
Cash and Cash Equivalents	$483,000	Cash reserves
Accounts Receivable	$150,000	Outstanding customer payments
Inventory	$30,000	Sustainable product inventory
Prepaid Expenses	$0	Prepaid utilities, services, or other items
Non-Current Assets	**$620,000**	Long-term assets
Property, Plant & Equipment	$600,000	Equipment and manufacturing assets
Intangible Assets	$20,000	Brand value and intellectual property
Liabilities	**$955,000**	Total Liabilities
Current Liabilities	**$505,000**	Short-term obligations
Accounts Payable	$470,000	Supplier payments due
Short-Term Loans	$35,000	Loan obligations due within one year
Non-Current Liabilities	**$450,000**	Long-term debt
Long-Term Debt	$450,000	Business loans for expansion
Equity	**$328,000**	Total Equity
Common Stock	$100,000	Ownership investment
Preferred Stock	$50,000	Shares with fixed dividends
Retained Earnings	$178,000	From net income reinvested in the business
Liabilities + Equity	**$1,283,000**	

Assets are the company's resources, categorized into liquid and non-liquid assets. **Liquid assets**, such as cash, accounts receivable, and marketable securities, can be quickly converted into cash to pay off short-term bills. **Non-liquid assets**, including buildings, machinery, and inventory, take longer to convert but still represent substantial value.

Additionally, assets can be classified as short-term or long-term. **Short-term assets** (also called **current assets**) are expected to be converted into cash within one year and include cash, accounts receivable, and inventory. **Cash** refers to physical currency or funds available in checking accounts, while **accounts receivable** represent money owed to a business by its customers for goods or services delivered. **Inventory** consists of the company's goods and materials for sale or production, including raw materials, work in progress, and finished products. On the other hand, **long-term assets** are held for more than one year and include property, plant, equipment, and intangible assets like patents. Business Leaders must learn to balance short-term and long-term assets for effective financial management, controlling costs/expenses, and sustaining growth.

Tangible assets are physical items that can be touched and measured, such as machinery, buildings, and inventory. These items hold intrinsic value and can be sold or used for operations. **Intangible assets**, like patents, trademarks, and brand reputation, are non-physical resources that may still provide a competitive advantage. However, their value is more complex and subjective. **Depreciation** of assets is the accounting process that allocates the cost of a tangible asset over its useful life, reflecting its declining value over time (Apostolides, 2016; Tracy & Tracy, 2022).

Liabilities represent a company's obligations to its creditors and can be divided into short-term and long-term debts. **Short-term liabilities**, such as accounts payable and accrued expenses, are obligations to pay, usually due within a year. **Accounts payable** refers to how much a company owes suppliers for goods and services received but not yet paid for. **Accrued expenses**, such as utilities or interest on loans, are incurred but have not yet been paid. **Salaries payable** refers to the wages a company owes employees for work performed but not disbursed. **Long-term liabilities (debt)**, including loans and bonds payable, usually exceed one year. Business Leaders distinguish between these different types of liabilities to pay the bills and decrease risk (Apostolides, 2016; Tracy & Tracy, 2022).

Equity shows what is left over from a company's assets after paying off its debts. It includes things like stock and profits that the company has kept (i.e., retained earnings). **Stock** represents the ownership shares issued to shareholders, providing a claim on the company's profits and net assets. **Retained earnings** refer to the accumulated profits reinvested in the business rather than distributed as dividends. Together, equity indicates the net worth of the company and the investment made by its owners (Apostolides, 2016; Tracy & Tracy, 2022).

Business Leaders comprehend the difference between liquidity and solvency to show financial stability. **Liquidity** is the ability to quickly pay off short-term debts using available assets, ensuring the business can handle immediate expenses and run uninterrupted. Remember, cash is the most liquid of assets. In contrast, **solvency** is the capacity to meet long-term debts; a solvent company has enough assets to cover all of its liabilities (i.e., short-term obligations and long-term debt), indicating good financial health over the long term. By grasping these distinctions and tracking these via financial ratios (discussed later) based on the balance sheet, leaders can effectively evaluate their organization's stability and financial health (Apostolides, 2016; Tracy & Tracy, 2022).

The **Equity Statement** is a crucial financial document that details an owner's share of a company after all its liabilities have been deducted from its total assets. This statement reflects the owner's equity at a specific date and illustrates how that equity changes over a defined period. **Contributions from investors** represent the money or assets that shareholders put into the company. **Retained earnings** are the profits the company has reinvested in the business rather than distributed to shareholders. **Distributions to shareholders** are dividends or other forms of payouts to those holding shares in the company (Apostolides, 2016; Tracy & Tracy, 2022).

Preferred stockholders through **preferred stock** have a higher claim on assets and dividends than common stockholders, often receiving fixed and cumulative dividends before common shareholders. They also have priority in liquidation but typically lack voting rights, except in some instances, like missed dividend payments. In contrast, **common stock** represents ownership equity, granting shareholders voting rights on corporate decisions and the potential for higher long-term returns as stock values appreciate. However, common stockholders are last to receive dividends and liquidation payouts, following creditors, bondholders, and preferred shareholders (Apostolides, 2016; Tracy & Tracy, 2022).

Stocks and bonds differ. When an entity (individual or enterprise) purchases stocks, it essentially buys a piece of ownership in a company. Stockholders may receive dividends, which are portions of the company's earnings distributed to shareholders, and they can also benefit from capital appreciation, which occurs when the stock's value increases over time. **Bonds** are a form of debt. When an entity issues a bond, it borrows money from the bondholder, who receives regular interest payments over the bond's term and repays the principal amount at maturity. Bonds do not offer ownership but are considered less risky than stocks. They provide fixed interest and principal repayment, guaranteeing payment (Apostolides, 2016; Tracy & Tracy, 2022).

Dividends are payments made to shareholders out of company profits. Companies pay dividends to attract and retain investors, as consistent dividend payments can signify financial health. Dividends can be issued in cash, providing immediate returns to shareholders, or offered in stock, allowing investors to increase their ownership (Apostolides, 2016; Tracy & Tracy, 2022).

Table 11.3 contains a sample equity statement for the company. This statement shows changes between years and is the shortest of the four financial statements. Business Leaders track these changes to remain informed regarding the worth of their company to share with others.

TABLE 11.3 Hypothetical Statement of Owner's Equity for Urban Threads

Description	*Amount*	*Notes*
Beginning Total Equity	$50,000	Starting point for equity
Beginning Retained Earnings	$50,000	
Add: Net Income	$178,000	From Income Statement
Less: Dividends Paid	($50,000)	Cash dividends paid to shareholders

Description	Amount	Notes
Adjusted Retained Earnings	$178,000	Ending balance after net income and dividends applied
Add: Preferred Stock Issued	$50,000	Issued preferred stock during the year
Add: Common Stock Issued	$100,000	Issued common stock during the year
Ending Total Equity	**$328,000**	Matches Balance Sheet Equity

Cash flow is critical for financial viability, sustainability, and growth. It refers to the net amount of cash transferred into and out of a company during a specific period. Business Leaders want to ensure adequate cash flow so the business has enough liquidity to meet its short-term obligations, invest in future opportunities, and weather slow sales periods or even economic downturns. Business Leaders and their stakeholders must recognize that even businesses reporting profits can encounter dire situations if they experience poor cash flow management, leading to a liquidity crisis and potential failure (Apostolides, 2016; Tracy & Tracy, 2022).

A **cash flow statement** is an essential financial document that details a company's cash receipts and payments over a specific timeframe. **Cash receipts** refer to the cash inflow a business receives from various sources, such as sales revenue, loan proceeds, or investment income, while **cash disbursements** refer to the outflow of cash from the business for expenses like operating costs, purchasing inventory, or paying off liabilities (Apostolides, 2016; Tracy & Tracy, 2022). Table 11.4 offers the cash flow statement.

TABLE 11.4 Cash Flow Statement for Urban Threads, a Sustainable Fashion Company

Description	*Amount*	*Notes*
Operating Activities		
Cash Receipts	$1,850,000	Cash sales and paid accounts receivable
Cash Disbursements	($1,302,000)	Decrease in cash from operations payments, including interest and taxes
Net Cash (Operating Activities)	**$548,000**	
Investing Activities		
Purchase of Equipment	($600,000)	Capital expenditure
Sale of Old Equipment	$0	Proceeds from asset sale
Net Cash (Investing Activities)	**($600,000)**	

(Continued)

TABLE 11.4 (Continued)

Description	*Amount*	*Notes*
Financing Activities		
Issuance of Common Stock	$100,000	Cash inflow
Issuance of Preferred Stock	$50,000	Cash inflow
Dividends Paid	($50,000)	Cash outflow – all dividends paid in Cash
Repayment of Long-term Debt	($15,000)	Cash outflow
Net Cash (Financing Activities)	**$85,000**	
Net Increase in Cash and Cash Equivalents	**$33,000**	
Cash at the Beginning of the Year	$450,000	Opening cash balance mostly from remaining from the Long-Term Loan
Cash at the End of the Year	**$483,000**	Closing cash balance matches Balance Sheet

The cash flow statement is divided into three primary categories, each reflecting a different aspect of a company's cash-related activities: operations, investing, and financing. **Operating activities** capture the cash generated or used daily to manufacture products, deliver services, and run the business. This includes cash inflows from the sale of goods and services and outflows for operational expenses such as salaries, rent, utilities, and other costs associated with operations. **Investing activities** detail cash transactions related to the purchase and sale of long-term assets, including property, equipment, and technology, along with cash received from selling these assets. **Financing activities** reflect the cash flow of financial investments, such as issuing stock, taking on loans, repaying loans, paying dividends, and repurchasing company shares.

Business Leaders recognize that managing cash flow keeps their company financially healthy and enables growth. They spot cash flow trends, anticipate financial challenges, and plan accordingly for the future. Business Leaders who understand cash flow can better handle unexpected economic changes, invest wisely, and keep operations steady to stay competitive.

Turnover shows operational efficiency. Business Leaders monitor inventory and accounts receivable, among other assets. **Inventory turnover** measures how fast a company sells and replenishes its stock over a specific period. A high ratio signifies healthy inventory management, while a low ratio may indicate issues like overstocking or sluggish sales.

Accounts receivable turnover evaluates how quickly payments are collected. A higher ratio signifies good credit policies and efficient processes, while a lower ratio indicates difficulties in acquiring customer payments. Turnover metrics provide Business Leaders with valuable insights into operational efficiency and cash flow, enhancing resource allocation and necessary interventions for improvement (Apostolides, 2016; Tracy & Tracy, 2022).

Business Leaders can look at the efficiency and effectiveness of their organizations by looking at changes over the years. **Horizontal analysis** looks at changes between years often measured by percent change ([New-Old]/Old) as well as ratios leveraging averages, such as **inventory turnover** (Cost of Goods Sold [COGS]/Average Inventory) and **accounts receivable turnover** (Revenue [Net Sales]/Average Accounts Receivable).

Exercise 11.1 Understanding Financial Statements

Explore the P&L statement in Table 11.1. Calculate the following ratios to discuss later.

1. **Gross Margin**: Gross Profit/Revenue (Sales)
2. **Net Margin**: Net Income/Revenue (Sales)

Analyze the changes in the ratios of gross margin to net margin. Which items are consuming more revenue? Also, reflect on the dividend payout percentage. Is that reasonable?

Explore the Balance Sheet in Table 11.2 and revisit the P&L statement in Table 11.1. Calculate the following ratios to discuss later.

1. **Working Capital**: Current Assets – Current Liabilities
2. **Current Ratio**: Current Assets/Current Liabilities
3. **Quick Ratio (Acid-Test)**: (Current Assets – Inventory – Prepaid Expenses)/ Current Liabilities
4. **Debt-to-Equity Ratio**: Total Liabilities / Total Equity
5. **Return on Assets**: Net Income / Total Assets
6. **Return on Investment**: Net Income / (Total Equity + Debt)
7. **Return on Capital Employed (ROCE)** = EBIT (Earnings Before Interest and Tax)/Capital Employed (Capital Employed = Total Assets – Current Liabilities)

Reflect on the numbers generated. If the company had to pay its current bills now, could it do so? How hefty is the debt? Does the debt and stock sold appear productive? Has the company made suitable investments? Feel free to Google or utilize generative AI tools to see comparisons.

Table 11.3 offers an equity statement for a newly launched company (Urban Threads), which had a pilot year yielding $50,000 in retained earnings and received a $500,000 loan, which has been paid down to $450,000 (see Table 11.2). Urban Threads, a sustainable fashion company, had its first year of sales, offered its first year of stock offerings, and secured a loan for $450,000 before launch. To complete the calculations for this exercise, you must assume the Market Value of Shares = $500,000. You may also want to revisit Tables 11.1 and 11.2. Calculate these ratios:

1. **Dividend Yield**: Dividends Paid/Market Value of Shares
2. **Dividend Payout**: Dividends/Net Income
3. **Return on Equity**: Net Income/Total Equity

Are stockholders getting a good deal based on the dividends paid? How are the stockholders helping the company? Is the company responsibly paying out dividends, given its net income? These questions become clearer after evaluating the cash flow statement next.

Readers will need to explore Table 11.4 for Urban Threads to calculate more financial ratios, which will be discussed later. For calculations and context, readers must also look at the previous Tables 11.1–11.3.

1. **Cash Flow Margin Ratio** = Net Cash (Operating Activities)/Current Liabilities
2. **Operating Cash Flow Margin** = Net Cash (Operating Activities)/Revenue (Net Sales)
3. **Free Cash Flow** = Operating Cash Flow – Capital Expenditures
4. **Cash ROA** = Net Cash (Operating Activities)/Total Assets
5. **Cash to Debt** = Net Cash (Operating Activities)/Total Liabilities
6. **Capital Expenditure (CapEx) Ratio** = Operating Cash Flow/Capital Expenditure (CapEx). CapEx usually is calculated as: Ending Property, Plant, and Equipment (PP&E) – Beginning PP&E + Depreciation Expense – Proceeds from Asset Sales. For this exercise, just use the Purchase of Equipment in Table 11.4.
7. **Dividend Payout Ratio** = Dividends Paid/Operating Cash Flow

Reflect: *How well is the cash flowing, and are dividends high? How well are assets being used?*

Taking the average between the two years (add the two items and divide by two), calculate those ratios with the information provided in Table 11.5. Reflect on whether the turnover looks efficient and discuss where the most notable gains or shifts in income and assets have occurred. *What does this data tell stakeholders?*

TABLE 11.5 Turnover and Horizontal Analysis

Income Statement	*Year Onet*	*Year Two*	*% Change*
Revenue	**$2,000,000**	**$2,750,000**	38
Cost of Goods Sold (COGS)	**($1,000,000)**	**($1,500,000)**	50
Gross Profit	**$1,000,000**	**$1,250,000**	25
Balance Sheet			
ASSETS	**$1,283,000**	**$1,800,000**	40
Current Assets	**$663,000**	**$1,000,000**	51
Cash and Cash Equivalents	$483,000	$500,000	4
Accounts Receivable	$150,000	$200,000	33

Income Statement	*Year Onet*	*Year Two*	*% Change*
Inventory	$30,000	$50,000	67
Prepaid Expenses	—	—	
Non-Current Assets	**$620,000**	**$800,000**	29
Property, Plant & Equipment	$600,000	$750,000	25
Intangible Assets	$20,000	$50,000	150

FINANCIAL AUDIENCES DIFFER

This section shares how to communicate financial information and ratios to different stakeholders and in various contexts. The chapter then offers advice on choosing which and how to communicate financial information to different audiences based on their importance. Business Leaders often use different financial ratio analyses across years (**horizontal analysis**) and within years (**vertical analysis**) to gauge their company's performance and financial health. Both analyses are essential; however, those with strong financial acumen know which comparisons or ratios should be calculated for particular audiences (Apostolides, 2016).

Efficiency ratios, like Inventory Turnover and Accounts Receivable Turnover, help them understand how well they manage their resources. **Liquidity ratios**, including the Current Ratio and Quick Ratio, show whether a company can meet its short-term obligations, which is crucial for day-to-day operations. **Profitability ratios**, such as Gross Margin and **Return on Equity** (ROE), help improve profit productivity from sales and investments. **Leverage ratios**, like the Debt-to-Equity Ratio, indicate financial risk or stability. **Cash flow ratios**, including Free Cash Flow and Operating Cash Flow Margin, show funding capacity connecting operations and investments. Lastly, **Dividend ratios** like Dividend Yield and Payout Ratio inform investors about profitability and how much money to expect (Apostolides, 2016; Tracy & Tracy, 2022).

Business Leaders can enhance their financial reporting by understanding the particular interests of different stakeholders. CFOs focus on metrics like ROI and Free Cash Flow to guide strategic choices. To assess credit risk, lenders look at the Current Ratio and Cash to Debt. Investors prioritize ROE and Dividend Yield to evaluate growth potential, while shareholders consider dividend reliability and stock performance. Supervisors assess operational efficiency using metrics like Inventory Turnover and Working Capital. Business Leaders tailor financial information to different audiences to bolster informed data-driven decision-making.

Budgeting is an informed, data-driven decision-making process. Business Leaders create a financial plan that outlines resource allocation and expense management. For CFOs and supervisors, effective budgeting helps plan for future growth. CFOs can align financial resources with strategic goals to support expansion initiatives. Budgeting helps control costs. Supervisors can use budget data to monitor expenses, identify inefficiencies, and implement cost-saving measures. Budgeting helps measure performance. Comparing actual results to planned budgets helps all stakeholders assess the organization's performance and recommend necessary adjustments. As Apostolides (2016) highlights, budgeting is not just a financial exercise but a communication tool ensuring all organizational levels are aligned with financial goals.

Speaking Startup: Financial Terms in Startups Explained

Business Leaders will likely encounter opportunities to work for or with startup enterprises. Startups use unique jargon that may be difficult for individuals to understand. Table 11.6 offers definitions and the relative importance of each term for Business Leaders to comprehend (for more, see Burns, 2016; Kemell et al., 2020). Business Leaders who master these terms can better identify false or misleading investment pitches and partnership opportunities.

Mastering these financial insights in the startup space helps founders and entrepreneurs better navigate cash flow management, attract investment, and scale their businesses successfully (Burns, 2016; Kemell et al., 2020). Startups may eventually go public. Going public happens through an initial public offering (IPO), which is the process where a private company sells shares to the public for the first time, allowing it to raise capital from public investors. Startups may also be purchased by **private equity** firms, investment groups that buy and manage businesses. Private equity firms typically invest in companies and aim to sell them for a profit later. A startup may **bootstrap** at first. This is when a startup funds itself through the money it earns without outside investment. Such financial acumen helps Business Leaders avoid scandals and affiliations with bad actors and showcase value to the right investors.

Business Leaders learn to communicate value using concepts like value capture, value creation, and value growth. **Value capture** is when a company secures part of the value it generates, typically by monetizing its products, services, or intellectual property (Teece, 2010). On the other hand, **value creation** involves providing benefits or solutions that meet customer needs and enhance efficiency, often through innovation and leveraging unique capabilities (Porter, 1985). **Value growth** refers to a business's worth escalation over time. It is supported by rising revenues, improved operations, and enhanced market perception of its products or services, leading to better profitability and shareholder returns (Barney, 1991).

Financial Acumen for Supervisors

Business leaders in management positions must bridge strategy and execution. This section covers terms managers use in team meetings, performance reviews, and strategic planning. Table 11.7 highlights financial ratios and calculations from the financial statements that apply to supervisory roles. Supervisors explain to their team why a budget was created, met, or exceeded, proposing corrective actions or advocating for changes transparently. Supervisors must regularly compare budgeted figures to actual revenue and spending to lead their teams to meet targets and bolster company performance.

TABLE 11.6 Financial Terms in Startups

Term	*Definition*	*Why It Matters*	*Stakeholders Most Interested*
Angel Investor	An individual who provides capital to startups, usually in exchange for ownership equity or convertible debt.	Provides early-stage funding when traditional financing is unavailable.	Founders, Investors
Break-Even Analysis	Determines the point at which revenue equals expenses, meaning the business is neither making a profit nor a loss.	Provides insight into financial sustainability and cost management.	Founders, CFOs, Investors
Burn Rate	The rate at which a startup spends its cash reserves before becoming cash-flow positive.	Indicates how long a startup can operate before needing additional funding.	Founders, CFOs, Investors
Cap Table (Capitalization Table)	A document showing the ownership structure of a company, including shares, options, and equity stakes.	Essential for tracking equity ownership and dilution.	Founders, Investors, Legal Teams
Cash Flow Forecast	A projection of cash inflows and outflows over a specific period.	Helps startups plan for funding needs and operational costs.	Founders, CFOs, Investors
Churn Rate	The percentage of customers who stop using a product or service over a given period.	Measures customer retention and long-term revenue sustainability.	Founders, Marketing Teams, Investors
Convertible Notes	Short-term debt that converts into equity during a later funding round, often at a discount.	Provides flexibility for early investors and startup founders.	Founders, Angel Investors, Venture Capitalists
Customer Acquisition Cost (CAC)	The cost of acquiring a single customer includes marketing and sales expenses.	Measures the efficiency of sales and marketing strategies.	Founders, Marketing Teams, Investors
Debt Financing	Raising funds through loans or issuing bonds instead of equity.	Useful for preserving equity while accessing capital.	Founders, CFOs, Lenders
EBITDA (Earnings Before Interest, Taxes, Depreciation, and Amortization)	A measure of a startup's operating performance and cash flow.	Highlights profitability from core operations.	Founders, CFOs, Investors

(Continued)

TABLE 11.6 (Continued)

Term	*Definition*	*Why It Matters*	*Stakeholders Most Interested*
Equity Financing	Raising capital by selling shares in the company.	Helps startups avoid debt while securing funds.	Founders, Investors
Gross Margin	Calculated as (Revenue – Cost of Goods Sold) / Revenue. It measures the percentage of revenue exceeding production costs.	Indicates operational efficiency and pricing strategy effectiveness.	Founders, CFOs, Investors
Letters of Intent (LOI)	A non-binding agreement outlining the terms of a proposed deal or partnership.	Serves as a foundation for formal agreements and negotiations.	Founders, Investors, Legal Teams
Lifetime Value (LTV)	The total revenue a company can expect from a single customer over their relationship with the business.	Determines long-term profitability and customer retention value.	Founders, Marketing Teams, Investors
Profit Margin	The percentage of revenue that exceeds costs indicating profitability.	Measures the startup's ability to manage costs relative to revenue.	Founders, CFOs, Investors
Runway	The amount of time a startup can continue operating before running out of cash based on the current burn rate.	Helps founders plan funding rounds and manage spending.	Founders, CFOs, Investors
Scalability	The startup's ability to grow revenue while managing costs effectively.	Determines long-term growth potential and attractiveness to investors.	Founders, Investors
Seed Funding	Initial capital raised to start product development and initial operations.	Essential for early-stage growth and validating business models.	Founders, Angel Investors
Series A, B, and C Rounds	Successive rounds of venture funding to scale operations, grow market share, and expand product offerings.	Mark different growth milestones and funding strategies.	Founders, CFOs, Investors
Valuation	The estimated worth of a startup based on financial performance, market size, and growth potential.	Impacts fundraising terms and investor confidence.	Founders, Investors
Venture Capitalist (VC)	A professional investor or firm that invests in startups and high-growth companies in exchange for equity stakes.	Drives rapid growth and scalability for startups.	Founders, Investors

TABLE 11.7 Financial Calculations and Ratios for Different Audiences

Ratio Name	*Formula*	*Good Benchmark*	*Key Stakeholders*
Accounts Receivable Turnover	Net Credit Sales/Average Accounts Receivable	8–10 times per year (varies)	CFOs, Lenders, Supervisors
Capital Expenditure (CapEx) Ratio	Operating Cash Flow/Capital Expenditure (CapEx)	>1.0	CFOs, Investors
Cash Flow Margin Ratio	Net Cash (Operating Activities)/Current Liabilities	0.3–0.5 (30%–50%)	CFOs, Lenders
Cash ROA	Net Cash (Operating Activities)/Total Assets	5%–10%	CFOs, Investors, Lenders
Cash to Debt	Net Cash (Operating Activities)/Total Liabilities	> 0.2 (20%)	CFOs, Lenders
Current Ratio	Current Assets/Current Liabilities	1.5–2.0	CFOs, Lenders, Supervisors
Debt-to-Equity Ratio	Total Liabilities/Total Equity	Below 2.0	CFOs, Lenders, Investors
Dividend Payout	Dividends/Net Income	30%–50%	Shareholders, Investors
Dividend Payout Ratio	Dividends Paid/Operating Cash Flow	20%–50%	Shareholders, Investors
Dividend Yield	Dividends Paid/Market Value of Shares	2%–6%	Shareholders, Investors
Free Cash Flow (FCF)	Operating Cash Flow – Capital Expenditures	Positive value	CFOs, Investors
Gross Margin	Gross Profit / Revenue (Sales)	50% or higher (varies by industry)	CFOs, Investors, Shareholders
Inventory Turnover	Cost of Goods Sold (COGS)/Average Inventory	5–10 times per year (varies)	CFOs, Supervisors, Investors
Net Margin	Net Income / Revenue (Sales)	10% or higher (varies by industry)	CFOs, Investors, Shareholders

(*Continued*)

TABLE 11.7 (Continued)

Ratio Name	*Formula*	*Good Benchmark*	*Key Stakeholders*
Operating Cash Flow Margin	Net Cash (Operating Activities)/Revenue (Net Sales)	10% or higher	CFOs, Investors, Lenders
Quick Ratio (Acid-Test)	(Current Assets – Inventory – Prepaid Expenses) /Current Liabilities	1.0 or higher	CFOs, Lenders, Supervisors
Return on Assets (ROA)	Net Income/Total Assets	5% or higher (varies by industry)	CFOs, Investors, Shareholders
Return on Capital Employed (ROCE)	EBIT (Earnings Before Interest and Tax)/(Total Assets – Current Liabilities)	15% or higher	CFOs, Investors, Shareholders
Return on Equity (ROE)	Net Income/Total Equity	15% or higher	CFOs, Investors, Shareholders
Return on Investment (ROI)	Net Income/(Total Equity + Debt)	10% or higher	CFOs, Investors, Shareholders
Working Capital	Current Assets – Current Liabilities	Positive value	CFOs, Lenders, Supervisors

Supervisors must have financial acumen and understand vital concepts such as variance analysis, KPIs (key performance indicators), objectives and key results (OKRs), and cost-benefit analysis. **Variance analysis** evaluates performance, comparing actual results to budgeted figures. Discrepancies are categorized as either favorable (where actual performance exceeds expectations) or unfavorable (where performance falls short) (Garrison et al., 2018). **Key performance indicators** (KPIs) are challenging and attainable benchmarks based on industry standards, historical performance, or best practices. These measurable targets have been shown to drive better performance toward key business objectives (Parmenter, 2015). **Objectives and key results** (OKRs) are ambitious, visionary goals that organizations set to inspire and challenge their teams, pushing them beyond their comfort zones. OKRs are more "big picture" (see more on Vision in Chapter 17), and KPIs ensure day-to-day performance aligns with long-term strategic goals. Business Leaders can combine them to pursue aspirational and data-driven progress (Sabharwal, 2025). Finally, **cost-benefit analysis** (CBA) is a systematic approach to evaluate the strengths and weaknesses of alternatives. Business Leaders can use CBAs to determine the best courses of action, comparing the costs of an action to its benefits, enhancing strategic planning and decision-making (Boardman et al., 2018).

Final Financial Terms Leaders Should Know

This final section dives into three critical terms: Return on investment (ROI), net promoter score (NPS), and operating expenses (OpEx) vs. capital expenditures (CapEx). These metrics quantify performance and communicate value to different stakeholders.

Return on Investment (ROI): ROI is more than a financial statement figure; it reflects the financial return an investment generates based on cost. The formula is: ROI = Net Profit / Cost of Investment, and it is typically expressed as a percentage by multiplying the decimal by 100%. A high ROI suggests that the investment has yielded significant returns compared to its initial expenditure, which makes it a crucial measure for assessing the success of projects and for making resource allocation decisions (Brealey et al., 2020). ROI is beneficial for budgeting, analyzing marketing efforts, or evaluating projects that require substantial capital. For instance, if a marketing campaign costs $10,000 and generates an additional $50,000 in sales revenue, the ROI would be 400%. Such a tangible financial result enhances stakeholder confidence.

Net Promoter Score (NPS): NPS is used to assess customer loyalty and satisfaction. It uses feedback through questionnaires, interviews, or other survey methods, asking customers how likely they are to recommend a product or service on a scale from 0 to 10 (Reichheld, 2003). The responses are classified into three categories:

- **Promoters** (9–10)—These are loyal customers who actively endorse the brand.
- **Passives** (7–8)—These customers are satisfied but not enthusiastic.
- **Detractors** (0–6)—This group comprises dissatisfied customers who may harm the brand's reputation.

The NPS is calculated using the formula: NPS = % Promoters – % Detractors. A higher NPS signifies stronger customer loyalty. Higher loyalty is connected to long-term revenue growth. Bain & Company suggests that a score above 0% is good, above 20% is favorable, and above 50% is excellent (Reichheld, 2003). Patagonia, known for customer satisfaction, consistently achieves a high NPS, showcasing its dedication to quality and sustainability (Chouinard, 2022).

Operating Expenses (OpEx) vs. Capital Expenditures (CapEx): OpEx includes the short-term costs incurred in daily operations. **CapEx** involves long-term investments in physical assets or technology (Fernando, 2024; Kenton, 2024). We used similar terms earlier in this chapter. Business Leaders distinguish between OpEx and CapEx to properly budget and optimize resource allocation. OpEx directly influences a company's immediate profitability, as these costs are regularly deducted from revenue to calculate profit. CapEx affects long-term financial health and asset value because these investments are recorded as assets with decreasing value over time.

Walmart is a strong case to distinguish between OpEx and CapEx. Monthly lease payments for store locations are OpEx. Upgrading self-checkout kiosks is CapEx, requiring significant upfront costs to reap the benefits over time. Walmart, along with Target and Dollar General, removed self-checkout kiosks from certain locations to serve customers who prefer interacting with sales associates better (Doerer, 2024). Sometimes, CapEx does not pay off. Business Leaders can learn from Walmart how to allocate resources properly and align expenditures with strategic goals.

Price-To-Earnings (P-E) Ratio: The P/E ratio helps investors evaluate how a company's stock is valued. You can calculate the P/E ratio using the formula: P/E Ratio = Market Price per Share / Earnings per Share (EPS). A high P/E ratio usually means that investors believe the company will earn more and are willing to pay more for its stock. On the other hand, a low P/E ratio might suggest that the stock is either undervalued or that the company is going through some financial difficulties. If a company has a negative P/E ratio, it indicates that the company is not making a profit (Investopedia, n.d.). William Danoff is vice president and portfolio manager of Fidelity Contrafund ($108 billion). Mr. Danoff, in a recent presentation to our students, emphasized that when evaluating potential investments for his fund, he particularly seeks out companies with a strong P/E ratio, high profitability, and those that are founder led.

There are two main types of P/E ratios to consider. The *trailing P/E* uses earnings data from the last 12 months, while the *forward P/E* looks at expected future earnings. To better understand if a stock is reasonably priced, compare its P/E ratio with the industry average or historical figures. Typically, growth stocks have higher P/E ratios because they are expected to grow quickly, while value stocks generally have lower P/E ratios (Investopedia, n.d.).

BUILDING CREDIBILITY THROUGH METRICS, ETHICS, AND PROPER RISK MANAGEMENT

With solid financial acumen, Business Leaders can make informed decisions, engage effectively with stakeholders, and steer their organizations toward long-term growth. Transparent and accurate financial reporting builds trust and ensures regulatory compliance while serving as a foundation for strategic planning. For business leaders, financial reporting goes beyond simply presenting data; it involves communicating the narrative behind the numbers, upholding ethical standards, and implementing risk management strategies to protect the organization's integrity.

Understanding Financial Misconduct: Cooking the Books

Cooking the books is the unethical practice of modifying accounting records to exaggerate profits, obscure liabilities, or artificially boost performance indicators (Kaplan & Atkinson, 2015). Companies acting nefariously may use tricks to mislead stakeholders about their finances. They may exaggerate revenue by recording sales that are still to come or recognizing revenue too early. They might downplay expenses by postponing when costs are reported or mislabeling them. They may hide debts by temporarily moving them off the balance sheet. High-profile scandals such as Enron and WorldCom are stark reminders of the devastating impact of cooking the books. These cases underscore that financial misconduct can lead to dire consequences.

The Fraud Triangle

The Fraud Triangle, developed by criminologist Donald Cressey (1967), is a useful tool for business leaders to assess risk and deconstruct misbehavior. The triangle illuminates three critical factors contributing to misconduct: opportunity, pressure, and rationalization.

First, **opportunity** is the ease of misconduct to occur. Opportunity results from weak internal controls, insufficient oversight, or ineffective enforcement of policies. For example, a company might lack the segregation of duties, allowing one individual to handle both the cash receipts and the accounting records. Secondly, **pressure** may come from unrealistic financial targets, demanding quotas, or personal financial difficulties, which can drive individuals to make unethical decisions. For instance, an employee facing financial hardship might feel compelled to manipulate sales figures to secure bonuses or avoid job loss. Lastly, **rationalization** occurs when individuals justify dishonest actions by convincing themselves that their misconduct is only temporary, harmless, or necessary for survival. An employee might think, "I will pay it back later" or "Everyone is doing it, so it is okay" (Kaplan & Norton, 1996).

Financial Risk Management, Internal Controls, and Ethical Culture

Business Leaders establish strong **internal controls** to combat financial misconduct effectively. These controls include multiple signers on accounts, password protection, surveillance, job rotation, independent audits, and transparent fraud reporting systems. Internal controls minimize risk and ensure no single individual has complete control over financial transactions, while regular reconciliation of financial records helps detect discrepancies early. Additionally, fostering a culture of accountability, open communication, and comprehensive ethical training strengthens compliance, deters fraud, and reinforces stakeholder confidence (Drucker, 2008).

Financial Reporting and Accounting Standards

Financial reporting clearly shows an organization's financial activities, performance, and overall health. Critical documents like income statements, balance sheets, and cash flow statements act as essential resources for both leaders within the organization and external parties such as investors, regulators, and auditors. Financial reporting conforms to accounting standards, which include methods for valuing inventory like FIFO (First In, First Out), LIFO (Last In, First Out), and Average Cost:

1) **FIFO (First In, First Out)** is a method that assumes the oldest items in inventory are sold first. This method is often preferred when prices rise because it lowers costs for goods sold (COGS) and higher reported profits.
2) **LIFO (Last In, First Out)** is an approach that assumes the most recently purchased items are sold first. During periods of inflation, LIFO tends to increase COGS, which can lower taxable income and taxes owed. However, this method can distort profit margins and the reported inventory value on the balance sheet.
3) **The Average Cost** method calculates the cost of inventory based on the average price of all goods available for sale throughout the accounting period. While it helps to even out price changes, it may not accurately represent inventory costs during price volatility.

Business leaders should be cautious about switching methods unless for the right reasons; they should not switch to avoid manipulating tax bills or misleading investors (Brealey et al., 2020).

Exercise 11.2 Leading with Integrity—Learning from High-Profile Failures

Background and Purpose: Leaders often face intense pressure to meet financial expectations, manage growth, and satisfy shareholders. Yet ethical leadership and sound financial practices must take precedence over short-term gains. This exercise explores four cautionary tales—Enron, Theranos, Wells Fargo, and FTX—to examine how the **Fraud Triangle** (opportunity, pressure, and rationalization), internal controls, and financial acumen shape outcomes.

Scenario: You are the CFO of a growing clean-energy company facing mounting debt, declining liquidity, and pressure from your CEO to delay expenses and inflate revenues to appease investors. You recall the Enron scandal, where CFO Andrew Fastow concealed debt through special-purpose entities, leading to the company's collapse and the creation of the Sarbanes-Oxley Act (Carreyrou, 2018).

Like in the Theranos case, where flashy promises and vague projections misled investors, some board members in your company are inexperienced and haven't questioned the numbers. Your auditors raise concerns about discrepancies in capital expenditures—red flags similar to those ignored at Theranos (Carreyrou, 2018).

Meanwhile, your CEO reminds you of Wells Fargo's middle managers who faced impossible quotas, resulting in millions of fake accounts created under pressure (Corkery, 2016; Eisen, 2023; Wells Fargo, 2017). You know internal controls were weak there, and whistleblowers were ignored.

Most recently, the FTX scandal shows how a lack of oversight (opportunity), intense market pressure, and rationalizations for unethical behavior led to misappropriating customer funds, violating financial norms and trust (Berwick & Wilson, 2022; Morrow, 2022).

TASKS

1. Do your own research on the Wells Fargo, Theranos, and Enron scandals.
2. Using the Fraud Triangle, identify the pressures, opportunities, and rationalizations present in your company's current situation.
3. Recommend internal controls and oversight mechanisms that could prevent unethical financial decisions.
4. Explain why accurate financial ratios (e.g., current ratio, debt-to-equity) are crucial early warning signs (like HorizonTech's poor liquidity and high debt).
5. In a small group, draft a 2-minute pitch presenting your ethical strategy for the quarterly earnings call. Focus on transparency, long-term trust, and sustainable financial recovery.

CONCLUSION

Financial reporting and accounting practices should always adhere to ethical principles such as integrity, transparency, and accountability. Ethical leadership plays a crucial role in establishing financial stewardship and mitigating risks associated with fraud and misconduct within organizations. Organizations should cultivate a culture that emphasizes ethical decision-making to prevent ethical breaches. This can be achieved by providing continuous training on financial ethics and reporting standards, encouraging the establishment of whistleblower protections, and implementing a strict zero-tolerance policy for retaliation. When leaders prioritize ethics and transparency, they lay the groundwork for sustainable, long-term success and credibility.

Business leaders should reflect on how their organization ensures adherence to ethical standards in financial reporting, the presence and regular evaluation of internal controls, and how greater transparency could enhance stakeholder trust in financial practices. Financial acumen—enhanced by ethical reporting, effective risk management, and strong internal controls—fosters trust and drives organizational success. Business leaders must maintain a vigilant and proactive approach by consistently applying accounting standards, providing valuable financial information, and addressing vulnerabilities. Financial acumen extends beyond merely understanding financial data; it encompasses applying that knowledge with integrity and a steadfast commitment to long-term value creation.

DISCUSSION QUESTIONS

1. Why is it essential for organizational leaders to understand the language of business even if they are not directly in a financial role?
2. What are the big three financial statements, and what do they do?
3. What are the various financial audiences discussed in this chapter?
4. What financial terms should every supervisor understand?
5. What should you do when you notice a discrepancy in your financial statements?
6. What is the fraud triangle, and where can it be applied to ensure proper internal controls?

Key Terms

- Accounting Equation
- Accounts Payable
- Accounts Receivable Turnover
- Accrued Expenses
- Angel Investor
- Assets
- Average Cost
- Basic Accounting Terms
- Break-Even Analysis
- Burn Rate
- Capital Expenditures (CapEx)
- Cap Table (Capitalization Table)
- Cash Flow
- Cash Flow Forecast
- Cash Flow Statement
- Cash to Debt Ratio
- Churn Rate
- Common Stock
- Convertible Notes
- Cooking the Books
- Cost-Benefit Analysis
- Costs
- Current Ratio
- Customer Acquisition Cost (CAC)
- Debt Financing
- Debt-to-Equity Ratio
- Depreciation
- Dividend Yield
- Dividends
- EBITDA
- Equity
- Equity Financing
- Expenses
- FIFO (First In, First Out)
- Financial Acumen
- Financial Ratios
- Financing Activities
- Fraud Triangle
- Gross Margin
- Gross Profit
- Internal Controls
- Inventory Turnover
- Investing Activities
- Key Performance Indicators (KPIs)
- Objectives and Key Results (OKRs)
- Liabilities
- Letters of Intent (LOI)
- Lifetime Value (LTV)
- LIFO (Last In, First Out)
- Liquidity
- Liquid Assets
- Long-term Assets
- Net Income
- Net Revenue
- Non-liquid Assets
- Operating Activities
- Operating Cash Flow Margin
- Operating Expenses (OpEx)
- Operating Profit (EBIT)
- Preferred Stock

- Price-to-Earnings (P-E) Ratio
- Profit
- Profit Margin
- Quick Ratio
- Retained Earnings
- Return on Assets (ROA)
- Return on Equity (ROE)
- Return on Investment (ROI)
- Revenue
- Runway
- Scalability
- Seed Funding
- Series A, B, and C Rounds
- Short-term Assets
- Salaries Payable
- Solvency
- Taxes
- Valuation
- Variance Analysis
- Venture Capitalist (VC)
- Working Capital

CASE STUDY 11.1 CRAFTING A STARTUP PITCH FOR ANGEL INVESTORS OR VENTURE CAPITALISTS

Company Overview: Sustainable Snack Co. is a food-tech startup focused on revolutionizing food sustainability by producing eco-friendly, plant-based snacks derived from surplus crops obtained from local farmers. Dedicated to minimizing food waste and reducing carbon footprints, the company targets health-conscious urban professionals and environmentally aware Gen Z and Millennial consumers. Their high-protein, shelf-stable snacks come in biodegradable packaging, positioning them as affordable and tasty solutions to the pressing problem of food sustainability.

Business Model and Financial Overview: Sustainable Snack Co. operates on a direct-to-consumer (DTC) subscription model, alongside retail partnerships with eco-friendly grocery stores. The company's financial projections reveal a monthly burn rate of $25,000, providing an eight-month runway based on current funding. The startup anticipates a customer acquisition cost (CAC) of $50 and a customer lifetime value (LTV) of $500, achieving a favorable 10:1 LTV-to-CAC ratio. With a projected gross margin of 60% per product, the company is working toward profitability.

Currently, Sustainable Snack Co. is preparing for an expansion phase after three years of operation, seeking financial analysis to evaluate performance through key metrics: Return on Investment (ROI), Net Promoter Score (NPS), and a comparative analysis of Operating Expenses (OpEx) and Capital Expenditures (CapEx).

FINANCIAL DATA FOR ANALYSIS

1. Marketing Campaign
   - Cost: $50,000
   - Revenue Generated: $200,000

2. Net Promoter Score (NPS)
   - Promoters: 65%
   - Passives: 20%
   - Detractors: 15%
3. Operating Expenses (OpEx) vs. Capital Expenditures (CapEx)
   - Monthly Rent: $15,000 (OpEx)
   - Employee Salaries: $100,000 (OpEx)
   - Advanced Packaging Machinery: $250,000 (CapEx)

REFLECTION QUESTIONS

1. Given the current ROI, should Sustainable Snack Co. consider increasing its marketing budget in the next quarter? What factors should be taken into account when making this decision?
2. Given the NPS, how might Sustainable Snack Co. implement customer feedback initiatives and loyalty programs to ensure continued satisfaction and retention?
3. Comparing the monthly OpEx of $115,000 to the CapEx of $250,000, what short-term or long-term improvements can they implement to enhance financial health?
4. Which financial metric do you find most insightful for assessing the overall health of the startup, and why?
5. How can they balance achieving quick profitability while ensuring sustained growth?

Conclusion: As Sustainable Snack Co. prepares for its next phase, strategic evaluation of its financial metrics and customer engagement initiatives will be essential in navigating the competitive landscape and securing future funding opportunities. Addressing the posed reflection questions can lead to actionable insights that foster the startup's commitment to sustainability and customer satisfaction.

REFERENCES

Apostolides, N. (2016). *Management accounting for beginners*. Routledge.

Barney, J. (1991). Firm resources and sustained competitive advantage. *Journal of Management, 17*(1), 99–120. https://doi.org/10.1177/014920639101700108

Berwick, A., & Wilson, T. (2022, November 10). Exclusive: Behind FTX's fall, battling billionaires and a failed bid to save crypto. *Reuters*. Retrieved from https://www.reuters.com/technology/exclusive-behind-ftxs-fall-battling-billionaires-failed-bid-save-crypto-2022-11-10/

Boardman, A. E., Greenberg, D. H., Vining, A. R., & Weimer, D. L. (2018). *Cost-benefit analysis: Concepts and practice*. Cambridge University Press.

Brealey, R. A., Myers, S. C., & Allen, F. (2020). *Principles of corporate finance* (13th ed.). McGraw-Hill Education.

Burns, P. (2016). *Entrepreneurship and small business: Start-up, growth, and maturity* (4th ed.). Palgrave Macmillan.

Carreyrou, J. (2018). *Bad blood: Secrets and lies in a Silicon Valley startup*. Alfred A. Knopf.

Chouinard, Y. (2022). *Let my people go surfing: The education of a reluctant businessman*. Penguin Books.

Corkery, M. (2016, September 8). Wells Fargo fined $185 million for opening accounts without customers' knowledge. *The New York Times*. https://www.nytimes.com

Cressey, D. R. (1967). Methodological problems in the study of organized crime as a social problem. *The Annals of the American Academy of Political and Social Science, 374*(1), 101–112.

Doerer, K. (2024, April 24). Walmart removes self-checkout in select stores to improve customer experience. *Retail Dive*. Retrieved from https://www.retaildive.com/news/walmart-removes-self-checkout-stores-experience/714306/

Drucker, P. F. (2008). *The essential Drucker: The best of sixty years of Peter Drucker's essential writings on management*. HarperCollins.

Eisen, B. (2023, September 6). Wells Fargo is still in fix-it mode. *Wall Street Journal*. Retrieved from https://www.wsj.com/finance/banking/wells-fargo-fake-account-scandal-aftermath-2b9b11e9

Fernando, J. (2024, June 18). *Capital expenditure (CapEx)*. Investopedia. https://www.investopedia.com/terms/c/capitalexpenditure.asp

Garrison, R. H., Noreen, E. W., & Brewer, P. C. (2018). *Managerial accounting*. McGraw-Hill Education.

Investopedia. (n.d.). *What is the difference between forward P/E and trailing P/E?* Retrieved February 12, 2025, from https://www.investopedia.com/ask/answers/050115/what-difference-between-forward-pe.and-trailing-pe.asp

Jafri, F. (2023, April 17). *Comptroller vs. controller: What sets them apart?* Monily. Retrieved from https://monily.com/blog/comptroller-vs-controller

Kaplan, R. S., & Atkinson, A. A. (2015). *Advanced management accounting* (3rd ed.). Pearson.

Kaplan, R. S., & Norton, D. P. (1996). *The balanced scorecard: Translating strategy into action*. Harvard Business School Press.

Kemell, K. K., Wang, X., Nguyen-Duc, A., Grendus, J., Tuunanen, T., & Abrahamsson, P. (2020). Startup metrics that tech entrepreneurs need to know. In Anh et Nguen-Duc, Jurgen Munch, et al. (Eds.), *Fundamentals of software startups: Essential engineering and business aspects* (pp. 111–127). Springer International Publishing.

Kenton, W. (2024, February 26). *Operating expense (OpEx)*. Investopedia. https://www.investopedia.com/terms/o/operating_expense.asp

Morrow, A. (2022, November 17). 'Complete failure:' Filing reveals staggering mismanagement inside FTX. *CNN Business*. Retrieved from https://www.cnn.com/2022/11/17/business/ftx-ceo-complete-failure/index.html

Parmenter, D. (2015). *Key performance indicators: Developing, implementing, and using winning KPIs*. Wiley.

Porter, M. E. (1985). *Competitive advantage: Creating and sustaining superior performance*. Free Press.

Reichheld, F. F. (2003). The one number you need to grow. *Harvard Business Review, 81*(12), 46–54.

Sabharwal, G. (2025). Combining OKRs and KPIs: Maximizing performance measurement. *GetJob*. Retrieved from https://www.getjop.com/blog/combining-okrs-and-kpis-maximizing-performance-measurement

Teece, D. J. (2010). Business models, business strategy and innovation. *Long Range Planning, 43*(2–3), 172–194. https://doi.org/10.1016/j.lrp.2009.07.003

Tracy, J. A., & Tracy, T. C. (2022). *Accounting for dummies* (7th ed.). Wiley.

Wells Fargo. (2017). *Report on sales practices investigation*. https://www.wellsfargo.com

CHAPTER 12

The Digital Future

CHAPTER OVERVIEW

This chapter explores the transformative impact of digital technologies on business operations and workplace dynamics. Business Leaders must be adaptable to navigate remote, hybrid, and in-person work modalities and new technologies. They must embrace lifelong learning and ethical responsibility to address the challenges technologies pose regarding collaboration and privacy. Breakthrough technologies, such as artificial intelligence, are discussed for their potential to revolutionize industries, but they also raise ethical and social concerns. Technological advancements continue to outpace regulations. Business Leaders must be vigilant in considering economic and social implications for their workplaces and communities. When adopting new technologies, Business Leaders must continue cultivating psychologically safe environments supporting productivity, collaboration, and innovation.

The digital landscape is ushering in a transformative era that fundamentally alters how businesses function, innovate, and engage with the global marketplace. The digital future also bolsters how businesses embrace changing officescapes (e.g., balancing remote, hybrid, and in-person modalities). Breakthrough technologies such as artificial intelligence (AI), blockchain, and wearable devices have benefits, but these advancements bring substantial ethical, social, and economic challenges that cannot be overlooked.

Business Leaders are lifelong learners who are building their awareness of the digital future's potential. Additionally, they need to show a strong commitment to ethical responsibility regarding their brand (see Chapter 17), environmental and social responsibility (see Chapter 18), and inclusive progress (see Chapters 5 and 9). By doing so, they will foster sustainable growth and position themselves as leaders in a future that values responsibility as much as financial viability and innovation.

DOI: 10.4324/9781003474647-15

BREAKTHROUGH TECHNOLOGIES AND THEIR POTENTIAL

The digital landscape is rapidly evolving, propelled by transformative technologies set to revolutionize traditional business frameworks, natural and built environments, and social interactions. AI empowers organizations to streamline intricate processes, extract valuable insights from enormous datasets, and foster innovation at an unprecedented pace (Brynjolfsson & McAfee, 2014). Wearable technology and bioengineering are on the brink of redefining healthcare (Tyler et al., 2020). Technologies like blockchain and the Internet of Things (IoT) transform supply chain dynamics and create smarter cities by increasing transparency (Ullah et al., 2023; Balcıoğlu et al., 2024).

However, the promise of these innovations is accompanied by a complex array of challenges. Technologies such as virtual reality (VR) and augmented reality (AR) raise pressing concerns regarding social (dis)connection (Turkle, 2011). Swift technological progress frequently outpaces existing regulatory frameworks, creating gaps in oversight and accountability that reify social inequalities or lead to unforeseen repercussions (Tufekci, 2017). Business Leaders dare to navigate this landscape despite regulatory uncertainty but are still mindful of economic, social, and environmental ramifications.

Chapter Themes and Implications

Business Leaders focus on three main areas: ethical responsibility, social equity, and economic transformation. These items are also discussed in length in other chapters (see Chapters 5, 18–21). Companies using new technologies face tough ethical questions about privacy, autonomy, and fairness. Business Leaders consider how these advancements affect society, especially regarding access and workforce dynamics. They commit to fair solutions to ensure everyone benefits from digital innovation. On the economic side, these technologies can boost growth, enhance productivity, and encourage innovation. However, if not managed carefully, this progress may increase the gap between those with access to technology and those without, particularly when these technologies are monetized and put behind paywalls.

This chapter explores complex challenges as they steer their organizations through a more digital future, offering practical insights. First, groundbreaking technologies reshaping our time are given an overview. Then, the ethical and societal consequences of these advancements are discussed, employing Asimov's Laws of Robotics and Marx's perspectives on automation. Next, attention turns to the opportunities Business Leaders can seize by leveraging technology to promote social welfare while sustaining a competitive advantage. The chapter concludes by advising Business Leaders to drive a more just and ethical digital era.

Exercise 12.1 Self-Primer on the Digital Future and Ethical Reflection

The Example: This exercise encourages a critical examination of the ethical implications of emerging technologies through the lens of Netflix's *Black Mirror* episode "Nosedive" (Brooker, 2016). In this episode, society operates within a pervasive rating system where individuals are judged based on social scores that influence various aspects of their lives, such as housing and travel options. Reflect on how this rating system parallels current trends in digital platforms and social media. Consider corporate responsibility in designing platforms that minimize stress and avoid exclusionary practices. Real-world examples that have led to social inequities or mental health challenges can be discussed, such as social media's impact on women's body image.

The Task: Your team is in charge of a new digital professional networking platform. Based on Table 12.1, design a new networking platform and consider balancing features that engage users with mechanisms that promote mental well-being and prevent exclusionary behaviors.

Alone or with a group, share your values and principles around technology and explore various perspectives on designing digital systems that are fair and inclusive. Then, sketch out your new digital professional networking platform by drawing or writing it out.

Looking for More: Consider reading "The Machine Stops" by E.M. Forster (1909), which envisions a dystopian future dependent on a centralized machine, highlighting the perils of technological reliance and human disconnection. Kurt Vonnegut's "Harrison Bergeron" (1961) critiques extreme measures of enforced equality and the suppression of individuality. Both are available through Project Gutenberg and various public domain sites. Additionally, explore Zeynep Tufekci's essays on *Medium* for more on social media and algorithms or delve into Shoshana Zuboff's (2019) analyses of surveillance capitalism found in interviews and article summaries. **Surveillance capitalism** is an economic framework in which personal data is systematically collected, commodified, and used to predict and influence individual behavior, often raising serious concerns about privacy and autonomy (Zuboff, 2019), which has substantial ethical implications. These resources offer rich critiques of the impact of technology on society.

TABLE 12.1 Project Requirements for a Professional Networking Platform

Project Requirements	*Description*
Prioritize User Mental Health and Well-Being	Ensure your platform supports users' mental health by implementing features that promote positive interactions and mitigate stress.
Foster Inclusive Community Interactions	Create environments where all users feel welcome and valued, encouraging diverse voices and perspectives.
Implement Transparent Algorithms	Use algorithms that promote fairness and transparency, allowing users to understand how their data is used and connections are made.
Encourage Genuine Connections	Focus on facilitating authentic relationships over superficial metrics, such as follower counts or likes.

MAPPING THE DIGITAL LANDSCAPE

This section will explore various innovative technologies driving change. Topics include AI, blockchain, and the IoT. Business Leaders will recognize their functionalities, applications, benefits, and ethical dilemmas.

Artificial Intelligence (AI): Analytical and Generative

AI technologies are transforming society, specifically **analytical** and **generative AI**. Analytical AI focuses on data-driven insights, using techniques like machine learning to identify patterns, predict outcomes, and optimize operations. Generative AI creates new content via text, images, designs, and more, opening up previously unimaginable possibilities for innovation. Both AI forms transform industries, drive productivity, and inspire new business approaches.

Analytical AI remains a cornerstone of many business operations and business analytics (Mortaji & Shateri, 2023). With analytical AI, Business Leaders can empower their organizations to streamline processes, improve customer interactions, and accurately forecast trends. Predictive analytics and recommendation systems have become ubiquitous in retail, logistics, and finance. Business Leaders make data-informed decisions that enhance efficiency and customer satisfaction. Tools like IBM Watson, Tableau, and Google Analytics exemplify how Business Leaders can leverage analytical AI to extract insights and optimize strategies. Analytical AI's ability to derive actionable insights from vast (big) datasets makes it a powerful tool for improving operational excellence.

Generative AI goes beyond analysis, actively shaping the future by creating new possibilities. According to Thomas Davenport (2024) of Babson College, companies embracing generative AI perform better across key metrics. Generative AI can help businesses design new products, craft personalized marketing strategies, and create immersive virtual customer experiences. Tools such as OpenAI's GPT and Google's Gemini models, DALL·E for image generation, and Adobe Firefly for creative tasks illustrate the potential of generative AI to revolutionize industries and enhance innovation. Davenport (2024) notes that generative AI tools excel at augmenting how employees complete tasks, improving productivity; however, he cautions against using them for automation due to issues with accuracy.

Davenport (2024) highlighted seven critical challenges to effectively deploying generative AI during the GCEC 2024 conference:

1. Lack of awareness and understanding.
2. Contention for ownership within organizations.
3. Unprepared or insufficient data.
4. Limited controlled experiments to test AI capabilities.
5. Difficulty in driving user behavior changes.
6. Challenges in measuring value.
7. Integration with existing technologies.

To overcome these challenges, Davenport (2024) advises leaders to "think big, start small, and experiment widely—not tinker." He also stresses that generative AI performs best when augmenting human work rather than automating it entirely. This distinction ensures that AI complements creativity, judgment, and empathy rather than replacing them.

As Erik Noyes (2024) of Babson College stated at the same conference, "AI is the single most important technological, societal, ethical, and business innovation issue of our time." The transformative potential of AI brings notable responsibilities. Analytical AI's use in decision-making and generative AI's role in creating content raises ethical concerns for Business Leaders. Across our chapters, we have noted the importance of transparency and accountability to avoid bias, promote fairness, and bolster authenticity. Business Leaders balance the promise of AI with its societal impact. For instance, while generative AI can amplify productivity and creativity, it also poses risks of misuse and depersonalization in communications (see Chapter 17). Other risks include creating deceptive content or exacerbating inequalities in access to technology. Additionally, the reliance on large datasets introduces privacy challenges, requiring organizations to implement sufficient data governance frameworks (Zuboff, 2019).

Davenport's (2024) framework promotes experimentation while ensuring alignment with organizational goals. Business Leaders promote AI within existing workflows, invest in training employees to work alongside AI, and foster a culture of innovation that supports ethical responsibility. Generative AI represents a pivotal opportunity for Business Leaders to reimagine their industries, but its potential can only be realized when applied thoughtfully and responsibly.

Recent research by Girotra et al. (2023) highlights that while AI assistance can generate more ideas and improve their quality compared to human ideation without AI, it does not necessarily produce more novel ideas. In their study, one group of workers had access to AI assistance, while another group did not. The findings revealed that although the AI-assisted group generated more ideas and higher-quality output, the ideas generated by humans tended to be more original. While AI can augment the creative process, unique human insights and originality are irreplaceable. AI offers excellent opportunities for innovation and expression, but Business Leaders must carefully navigate its ethical and operational challenges to ensure a more equitable digital future.

Exercise 12.2 Analytical and Generative AI—Benefits, Risks, and Ethical Safeguards

Analytical AI leverages data to improve decision-making, streamline operations, and predict future outcomes. In the context of the Netflix *Black Mirror* episode "White Christmas," consider how analytical AI could enhance the services depicted, such as using real-time data to optimize household management or improve societal efficiency. However, analytical AI also poses risks, such as loss of privacy, data misuse, or the creation of systems that reinforce biases. Reflect on the episode's portrayal of digital replication—specifically, the ethical implications of using "cookie" technology to analyze and control human behavior. Identify safeguards to mitigate these risks, such as transparent data practices, privacy-first AI frameworks, and stringent ethical data collection and use standards.

Generative AI, in contrast, creates new content and ideas, which could revolutionize interactions and experiences in scenarios similar to those in "White Christmas." Imagine how generative AI might enhance or disrupt the technologies depicted in the episode, such as creating autonomous digital assistants capable of interacting seamlessly with human users. While this opens possibilities for innovation, it also introduces risks of manipulation, misinformation, and loss of autonomy, as seen in the episode's interrogation of a replicated consciousness. Consider safeguards like transparency in AI outputs, limitations on generative AI's control over human-like entities, and frameworks for respecting user autonomy and consent. Drawing from the episode, propose ethical boundaries that generative AI developers should adopt to prevent misuse or harm.

ACTIVITY STEPS

1. Compare the benefits and risks of analytical and generative AI to themes in Netflix's "White Christmas" or substitute E.M. Forster's short story, "The Machine Stops."
2. Brainstorm practical safeguards for addressing the risks you identified, focusing on both types of AI.
3. Share your thoughts on how these safeguards could align with ethical principles and promote user trust.

BLOCKCHAIN: ENHANCING TRANSPARENCY AND SECURITY

Blockchain technology functions as a decentralized digital ledger that keeps track of transactions across a network of computers, making it nearly impossible to alter or tamper with. Think of it as a public digital notebook where entries are visible to everyone, but once written, they cannot be erased or modified (Nakamoto, 2008). Blockchain is progressively being adopted in finance, healthcare, and supply chain management to enrich data security and optimize processes. The unchangeable nature of blockchain enables financial institutions to minimize fraud, allows healthcare providers to safeguard sensitive patient information, and helps supply chain managers monitor goods with remarkable precision (Akram et al., 2020).

Blockchain technology faces challenges like high energy consumption, dependence on large networks for transaction validation, and scalability issues. Solutions such as **proof-of-stake** (PoS) and sharding are emerging to address these problems. PoS is a consensus method that selects validators based on the number of cryptocurrency coins they hold and are willing to stake, which reduces energy use compared to **proof-of-work** (PoW) systems. In contrast, PoW requires miners to solve complex problems to validate transactions and secure the network. Sharding enhances scalability by breaking the blockchain into smaller shards that can process transactions independently (Hasibuan et al., 2024). Business Leaders should grasp these concepts to leverage blockchain technology where appropriate.

Cryptocurrency uses the blockchain to facilitate decentralized transactions. Leading examples include Bitcoin, Litecoin, and Ethereum, along with meme coins like Doge and Shiba Inu. These digital currencies allow for operations without traditional intermediaries, lowering costs and speeding up transactions. However, they also come with risks like market volatility, regulatory uncertainty, and potential misuse (e.g., the dark web). Business Leaders consider how principles of cryptocurrency—such as transparency, decentralization, and security—can enhance trust and efficiency in their organizations and communities. Similarly, **non-fungible tokens (NFTs)** represent unique digital assets on the blockchain, offering new ways of customer engagement, gamifying interactions, and optimizing transactions.

Internet of Things and Smart Cities: Efficient Urbanization and Improved Living

The **Internet of Things (IoT)** refers to a network of interconnected devices, ranging from household appliances to industrial sensors, that collect, share, and analyze data, hopefully in real-time. This feedback can be transformative. In **smart cities**, IoT technologies integrate these connected systems with urban infrastructure to optimize resources, enhance public services, and improve local quality of life. Cities can operate their public services more intelligently and sustainably (Holler et al., 2014). IoT offers Business Leaders vast opportunities to optimize supply chains, reduce operational costs, and contribute to sustainable development. However, these technologies also present challenges, including data privacy risks, cybersecurity vulnerabilities, intercompatability of devices, and infrastructure costs (Whig et al., 2022).

IoT helps smart cities optimize services. Smart cities can improve energy efficiency through smart grids that optimize real-time power distribution, reducing waste and improving sustainability (Zanella et al., 2014). Additionally, IoT facilitates smart transportation systems that enable dynamic traffic management, effectively alleviating congestion and lowering emissions via interconnected vehicles and intelligent traffic solutions (Song et al., 2022). These technologies also contribute to better air quality by integrating pollution monitoring systems, which provide critical data for managing urban environments (Alahi et al., 2023). Furthermore, water management is streamlined through smart water meters and leak detection systems, which help prevent resource wastage and reduce operational costs for municipal services (Di Nardo et al., 2021). Lastly, public safety is enhanced by deploying surveillance cameras, emergency response sensors, and connected devices that offer greater security and facilitate more rapid responses (Papadakis et al., 2021).

Cities like Singapore, Amsterdam, and Barcelona exemplify the transformative potential of IoT–driven initiatives, achieving improved living standards, resource efficiency, and reduced environmental impacts (Anthopoulos, 2019). IoT's connectivity and efficiency gains are notable; however, data privacy and security concerns persist with its vast amounts of collected data being vulnerable to cyberattacks and unauthorized access, threatening citizen privacy. Moreover, unequal access to IoT technologies risks exacerbating social inequalities within urban settings (Braun et al., 2018; Huang et al., 2024). Business Leaders in smart cities can address these challenges by investing in cybersecurity protocols, establishing standards for device interoperability, and promoting digital inclusion.

Business Leaders can use IoT–enabled solutions, such as real-time supply chain tracking and energy-efficient systems for smart buildings. In the healthcare sector, remote monitoring technologies can facilitate better patient care and resource management. To maximize these benefits, they must prioritize cybersecurity to protect sensitive data, foster cross-sector collaborations to spur innovation, promote employee digital literacy, and adopt scalable IoT solutions that can evolve with technological advancements. These strategies pave the way for more intelligent business practices and partnerships (Kranz, 2016; Hamdan & Braendle, 2024).

Through **data transparency**, clearly describing how data is collected, stored, and analyzed, they can build trust with citizens, employees, shareholders, and other stakeholders, fostering positive engagement. They can empower individuals to control their data and safeguard privacy through proper internal controls (see Chapter 11). They must take decisive steps to prevent surveillance overreach and protect civil liberties. Business Leaders can leverage IoT to enhance social responsibility (see Chapter 18), shared value (see Chapter 19), employee engagement (see Chapters 7 and 15), competitive advantages, and multiple bottom lines (Chapter 18).

Wearable Sensors: Well-Being in Real-Time

Wearable technology is revolutionizing how Business Leaders approach workforce management by seamlessly integrating personal well-being monitoring with real-time data analytics. **Wearable sensors** such as Wi-Fi or BlueTooth connectable watches, pedometers, rings, and fitness trackers enable continuous oversight of vital health indicators, equipping individuals and organizations with immediate insights into employee health and productivity. With the right approaches, Business Leaders can incorporate wearable technologies to foster a culture of well-being within their teams. Nonetheless, this integration brings forth significant concerns regarding body autonomy, privacy, surveillance fears, and other ethical considerations that must be thoughtfully addressed. Types of sensors with applications are listed in Table 12.2.

TABLE 12.2 Types of Wearable Sensors with Applications

Sensor Type	*Definition*	*Real-World Application*
Flexible Triboelectric Sensors	Convert mechanical energy (e.g., body movement) into electrical signals for real-time health monitoring (Mao et al., 2023).	Used in remote patient monitoring to reduce in-person visits and healthcare costs. Helps detect falls and track movement in elderly patients.
Spectroscopy-Based Sensors	Use light analysis to measure hydration and other physiological data (Belabbaci & Alam, 2024).	HydroTrack smartwatch monitors hydration with 95% accuracy, aiding athletes and workers in high-heat environments.
Electrocardiogram (ECG) Sensors	Measure heart activity, stress, and heart rate variability (Luo et al., 2020; Mary Mammen et al., 2024; Zainab et al., 2024).	Used in workplace wellness programs to monitor stress in high-risk jobs like air traffic control, reducing insurance costs.

Wearable technology links personal health to real-time analytics, providing opportunities for continuous health monitoring and proactive healthcare management. However, reliance on these devices for accurate health measurements, particularly in diagnostics, requires caution. The constant data collection can lead to challenges, such as data entry errors and missing information, which undermine the reliability of health monitoring systems (Van Der Donckt et al., 2024). Wearable devices raise ethical concerns, as continuous monitoring can infringe on privacy and lead to discomfort among users. The potential for unauthorized access to sensitive health information poses significant risks. In workplaces, monitoring employee health behaviors can create an environment of over-competitiveness and shaming, detrimentally affecting morale (Adeghe et al., 2024). Business Leaders recognize the need for comprehensive guidelines to protect individual rights and ensure the responsible use of wearable technology.

VR, AR, and Officescapes: Redefining Interactivity and Reality

Virtual reality (VR) and **augmented reality (AR)** are digital environments reshaping human interactions and business operations. VR provides a fully immersive experience, transporting users into entirely virtual spaces (often via headsets). VR can facilitate virtual meetings, high-stakes training simulations, and collaborative design projects. Companies like Meta (formerly Facebook) utilize VR for immersive team meetings in virtual spaces such as Horizon Workrooms, fostering a sense of presence and collaboration that traditional video conferencing often lacks (Carvalho & Morgado, 2022).

AR enriches perceptions of the real world by overlaying real-world imagery with digital information. It can aid tasks such as remote equipment maintenance, as seen with tools like Microsoft's HoloLens, which allows technicians to visualize schematics and receive real-time support while repairing machinery. More popularly, Pokémon GO offers an AR experience, allowing users to utilize their phone cameras through the app to locate digital creatures in everyday environments. Players compete in battles at nearby virtual gyms, often at community landmarks or gathering spaces (Carvalho & Morgado, 2022).

Research indicates that VR and AR can enhance spatial understanding and task performance while boosting efficiency across multiple industries (Adams et al., 2021); however, this research is still emerging. For today's Business Leaders, grasping the practical uses of VR and AR technologies is essential. VR can potentially train and onboard new employees by replicating real-life scenarios. AR can streamline operational workflows by offering immediate access to real-time information and guidance.

Business Leaders must approach VR and AR with a healthy dose of skepticism to not succumb to the allure of the latest trend. These technologies often come with a hefty price tag that must be considered regarding return on investment (ROI, see Chapter 11). In terms of inclusivity (see Chapter 9), these technologies should strive to enhance accessibility and not exclusively benefit those already advantaged.

The **digital officescape** refers to virtual work environments replicating traditional offices in the digital realm. Platforms like Horizon Workrooms by Meta, AltspaceVR, and Spatial pioneer immersive digital settings that enable employees to collaborate effectively. These workspaces address remote work challenges, such as isolation and a lack of spontaneous collaboration, by fostering a sense of presence and interaction in shared spaces (Ramirez, 2021). However, adoption has lagged despite their potential due to a cultural and technological gap between traditional video conferencing tools and fully immersive environments. While initial excitement surrounded the ***metaverse***, many businesses depend on conventional tools like Zoom, WebEx, and Microsoft Teams (Hoover, 2024). Nevertheless, virtual worlds present opportunities; platforms like Roblox, Fortnite Creative Mode, and VRChat showcase persistent virtual spaces' cultural and economic potential, serving as hubs for community building, content creation, and virtual entrepreneurship. They offer Business Leaders new venues for product launches, conferences, and interactive marketing campaigns.

Second Life, one of the earliest digital world platforms, is a historical case study. Launched as an expansive, user-driven digital world, it initially attracted millions of users. However, it struggled to maintain momentum due to technical limitations, governance issues, and unclear business use cases (Ramirez & LaBarge, 2018). The concept of the metaverse—a persistent, shared digital space integrating VR, AR, and real-world interactions—has gained significant attention in recent years. Popularized in science fiction, particularly in Ernest Cline's (2011) *Ready Player One*, the metaverse envisions a fully immersive world where individuals live, work, and socialize through digital avatars. The film adaptation further amplified the idea of digital worlds as parallel societies where economic transactions, education, and recreation coexist seamlessly (Spielberg, 2018). The current state of metaverse platforms diverges from this utopian vision, with critics noting a fragmented landscape lacking interoperability and practical use cases (Ramirez, 2021). Further issues such as digital fatigue, expensive hardware, and concerns about data privacy have hindered widespread adoption. The digital officescape may take off, but many are still skeptical.

VR, AR, and digital worlds present significant ethical concerns that Business Leaders must address for responsible adoption in workplace environments. One major issue involves privacy and surveillance; continuous monitoring of user interactions in these digital spaces raises critical concerns about employee privacy and the potential misuse of behavioral data (Ramirez, 2021). Additionally, accessibility and inclusivity are vital; digital environments must incorporate features that allow users with varying abilities to participate fully (Adams et al., 2021). Psychological effects are associated with prolonged immersion in virtual spaces, which may lead to issues like simulation sickness, cognitive fatigue, and a blurring of reality boundaries (Ramirez & LaBarge, 2018). Lastly, digital inequity poses a pressing concern, as do the high hardware and internet bandwidth costs.

VR, AR, and digital officescapes hold promise, especially as hardware accessibility, user interfaces, and interoperability increase across digital platforms. Business Leaders can consult Table 12.3 for advice on best integrating these technologies. With thoughtful approaches, they position themselves to harness the power of digital spaces and tools responsibly and effectively.

TABLE 12.3 Best Practices for Integrating VR, AR, and Digital Officescapes

Key Principle	*Advice for Business Leaders*
Balance Innovation with Ethics	Ensure clear guidelines protect user privacy and prevent exploitative surveillance practices.
Promote Inclusivity	Develop virtual spaces accessible to users with diverse needs and capabilities.

Key Principle	*Advice for Business Leaders*
Foster Transparency	Communicate how user data is collected, analyzed, and used in virtual environments.
Encourage Experimentation	Support pilot programs and innovation hubs to explore VR and AR applications in low-risk environments.
Prioritize Training and Education	Offer comprehensive training to employees for using VR and AR tools effectively and confidently.
Invest in Scalable Infrastructure	Invest in technology and platforms that can scale as business needs evolve.
Address Psychological Well-Being	Monitor and mitigate potential psychological impacts like digital fatigue or simulation sickness.
Evaluate ROI Regularly	Regularly assess the ROI to ensure alignment with organizational goals.

Exercise 12.3 Design an Ethical Employee Wellness Program Using Wearable Technology

The Purpose: This exercise aims to help Business Leaders critically evaluate and design an employee wellness engagement program (EWEP)—a comprehensive initiative to promote employees' physical and mental well-being through various activities and resources. This EWEP must effectively utilize wearable technology while addressing ethical dilemmas such as privacy, surveillance concerns, ingroup vs. outgroup dynamics, and overall employee well-being.

The Case: As the Chief Wellness Officer at WellTech Corp, you are tasked with spearheading the implementation of an EWEP that incorporates wearable devices. This initiative aims to enhance employee health outcomes, lower healthcare expenditures, and cultivate a competitive yet supportive culture through health challenges like step counts, hydration goals, and heart rate improvements. Each employee will receive a company-sponsored smartwatch with sensors for tracking various health metrics. The primary objectives of this program include reducing long-term healthcare costs by enabling early detection and prevention of health issues, fostering a healthier, more productive, and engaged workforce, and creating a fun and collaborative atmosphere through team wellness competitions.

However, employees have raised several concerns regarding several issues. These concerns include privacy and surveillance, with many expressing anxiety about ongoing monitoring and the potential misuse of personal health data. Additionally, you have received emails sharing worries about data security due to fears of leaks or inappropriate use of sensitive health information by external entities. Another substantial concern pertains to ingroup vs. outgroup dynamics, as employees fear potential divisions between high-achieving participants and those facing chronic health challenges. The terms **body shaming**—judging or criticizing someone based on their physical appearance—and **mental health stigma**—negative stereotypes and discrimination that discourage open discussion and support for mental health issues—have been mentioned as negatively impacting company culture. Thus, employees worry about being judged based on health-related behaviors or outcomes.

The Task: Consider the following leadership tasks. First, outline two essential wellness program features that promote ethical participation, such as ensuring opt-in–only participation and implementing anonymized health dashboards. Next, propose two specific strategies to safeguard employee health data and maintain privacy. Additionally, suggest one method to alleviate perceptions of intrusive surveillance while enabling the extraction of valuable health insights for organizational benefit. Finally, describe one approach to mitigate ingroup/outgroup dynamics and reduce the risks associated with excessive competition or health-related shaming.

Reflection: Consider how transparent communication can alleviate employee apprehensions regarding surveillance and privacy. Discuss the role of voluntary participation and **data anonymization**—removing identifying information from collected data—in building trust within the organization. Lastly, contemplate the potential long-term effects of reliance on wearable technology on workplace culture, fears of surveillance, interpersonal connections among employees, and overall employee well-being.

Manufacturing Innovations to Watch: 3D, Nanotech, Bioengineering, and More

Recent developments in bioengineering (also called biotech), nanotechnology, and additive manufacturing fundamentally change the production landscape across numerous sectors. Business Leaders must stay informed about these innovations to seize opportunities and uphold a competitive advantage. **Bioengineering** applies biology and engineering principles to create new materials and technologies, improving product performance and enhancing environmental sustainability (Kotche et al., 2020; Rai & Dhar, 2022). **Nanotechnology** involves manipulating matter at the molecular or atomic level. This technology is instrumental in developing advanced materials that often surpass traditional capabilities (Kotche et al., 2020; Rai & Dhar, 2022). **Additive manufacturing**, commonly known as 3D printing, is redefining manufacturing practices by allowing for the creation of intricate and customized products while minimizing material waste (Jadhav & Jadhav, 2022). **Digital twins** are virtual representations of physical systems that enable real-time monitoring, analysis, and optimization. They can enhance decision-making processes in manufacturing (Onaji et al., 2022). These technologies offer opportunities to improve manufacturing efficiency, quality, safety, and adaptability, especially coupling AI and robotics. These, among others, are featured in Table 12.4, which offers manufacturing innovations to watch.

TABLE 12.4 Manufacturing Innovations to Watch

Innovation Area	*Description*
Nanotechnology-Enabled Biomedical Engineering	Nanotechnology enables the development of advanced materials and devices for use in medicine, particularly in areas like targeted drug delivery and enhanced diagnostic methods. These innovations work at the molecular scale, leading to better patient outcomes and minimized side effects.
Organ-on-Chip and Genome Editing	These cutting-edge innovations enhance the precision of disease modeling and facilitate the creation of customized therapies, speeding up the drug development process.
Advancements in Additive Manufacturing Processes	Advancements like high-speed sintering and continuous liquid interface production significantly boost the efficiency and scalability of 3D printing, paving the way for its use in mass manufacturing. These enable the creation of complex designs and expand the range of industrial applications.
Integration with Industry 4.0	**Industry 4.0** represents a significant shift toward digital transformation, characterized by enhanced automation and personalized production. It plays a crucial role in decentralized manufacturing and on-demand production, fundamentally transforming supply chains and facilitating more agile production processes.
Sustainable Manufacturing Practices	Manufacturing processes progressively embrace environmentally friendly practices, including efforts to reduce waste, implement closed-loop systems, and design for energy efficiency. These initiatives aim to lessen environmental impact and support global sustainability objectives.
Digital Twins in Manufacturing	Digital twin technology allows for the creation of virtual models that mirror physical manufacturing processes or systems. This innovation facilitates real-time observation, optimization, and predictive maintenance, ultimately reducing costs and improving operational efficiency.
Smart Materials	Smart materials are designed to respond to environmental factors like temperature and pressure changes. This adaptability enhances their durability and energy efficiency, making them valuable in various manufacturing sectors, including aerospace and construction.
Collaborative Robotics (Cobots)	Collaborative robots, known as cobots, are engineered to operate alongside human workers in manufacturing settings. They boost productivity, improve safety, and enhance precision by automating repetitive tasks while facilitating smooth collaboration between humans and robots.

Modern Business Leaders must pay attention to the evolving connections between emerging technologies. AI and **organoid intelligence** (OI) are coming together to create a concept known as **living intelligence**. This innovative approach combines digital computing with biological components to tackle complex challenges. OI involves using lab-created tissues, such as small structures resembling human brain tissue formed from stem cells. These tissues mimic the brain's structure and functionality, allowing biological computing. While AI provides sophisticated computational and predictive abilities, OI offers flexible, biologically inspired systems that can learn and adapt over time. A notable example is Cortical Labs' DishBrain, which employs an organoid system that learns and improves through interactive activities like playing Pong. The fusion of these technologies can transform industries such as healthcare and biotechnology, uniting the precision of AI with the adaptability of organoid systems (Webb, 2025).

TOWARD AN ETHICAL DIGITAL FUTURE

This chapter has covered numerous emerging technologies in place in modern workplaces to varying degrees. This chapter stressed that augmentation of the human experience over automation is preferred in high-stakes decision-making settings. While this chapter has highlighted many benefits of these technological innovations, it has also sought to outline the ethical landscapes of implementing these innovations. The chapter concludes with some final advice for Business Leaders.

Find an Ethical Grounding

Business Leaders undergird technological use and pursuits with ethical foundations. They draw on various ethical frameworks, including utilitarianism, deontology, pragmatism, and virtue ethics, without needing to be experts. Early thinkers like Isaac Asimov and Karl Marx provide valuable insights for today's digital age. Their perspectives help address operational challenges while aligning technological advancements with enhancing human dignity and societal welfare.

Business Leaders can draw valuable insights from Isaac Asimov's Three Laws of Robotics, which offer a framework for ethical considerations in technological innovation and deployment. Asimov created a universe where robots created by US Robots and Mechanical Men helped humans; however, they were later expelled from Earth for many reasons. These reasons included, but were not limited to, fear that their intelligence would surpass humans, they might impersonate humans, and human interactions with robots would erode their humanity (e.g., willingness to solve their own problems). Asimov's First Law states that a robot may not injure a human being or, through inaction, allow a human being to come to harm. The Second Law asserts that a robot must obey the orders given to it by human beings, except where such orders would conflict with the First Law. The Third Law maintains that a robot must protect its existence as long as such protection does not conflict with the First or Second Laws. The Zeroeth Law, introduced later, posits that a robot may not harm humanity or, by inaction, allow humanity to come to harm (Asimov, 1950, 1985).

These laws can pertinently connect to digital technologies. For instance, AI systems used in healthcare must prioritize patient safety and adhere to ethical guidelines that reflect Asimov's First Law. This means ensuring that decisions made by AI–driven diagnostic tools do not inadvertently harm patients, showing the need for transparency and accountability in AI algorithms. The Second Law can be interpreted in the context of AI governance, where AI applications should follow specified protocols while being flexible enough to prevent adverse outcomes. The Zeroeth Law adds a broader ethical dimension; AI technologies should not only safeguard individual users but also promote societal well-being, ensuring that the deployment of AI in healthcare results in systemic improvements for communities at large. Asimov allows dilemmas to be discussed in each of his novels, and Business Leaders should do the same.

Similarly, Karl Marx's (1867) "Fragment on Machines" offers a critical perspective relevant to today's technological advancements. Marx (1867) argued that technological development should enrich human capability and societal welfare rather than facilitate exploitation or perpetuate inequality. This perspective can be applied to modern technologies, such as automation and machine learning, which can displace jobs and create opportunities for innovation and economic uplift. Business Leaders can harness automation to relieve workers from mundane tasks, allowing them to engage in more creative and strategic roles. However, Marx's (1867) principles call for carefully considering how these technologies are implemented. Business Leaders must advocate for models that prioritize efficiency and ensure workers' rights, offering pathways for skill development and equitable job distribution.

CONCLUSION

Business Leaders recognize the potential of these technologies to improve the world. For instance, ethics-driven AI training, such as the frameworks proposed by Gemini 1.5 (Google DeepMind, 2024), emphasizes transparency, accountability, and fairness in algorithmic decision-making. This includes mitigating biases, ensuring diverse representation in training datasets, and avoiding opaque AI systems that perpetuate inequalities.

Business Leaders know the purpose and limits of digital technology are equally essential for maximizing productivity while mitigating unintended consequences. Studies by Dell'Acqua et al. (2023a, 2023b) and Otis et al. (2024) highlight the uneven impact of AI on labor markets, revealing that while AI can enhance efficiency and productivity in specific domains, it may exacerbate inequalities when poorly implemented. Business Leaders remain cautious about assuming technology is a panacea and instead focus on human-centered design principles. Technology, for the most part, should augment human labor rather than replace it. Business Leaders should resist the temptation to build organizational cultures driven by surveillance capitalism, eroding trust and autonomy. Still, they should always ensure transparent governance practices where privacy, consent, and accountability are non-negotiable. Finally, they should push for inclusive innovation, going beyond profit-driven motives and aligning technological advancements with broader societal goals. Business Leaders can create company cultures where emerging technologies serve as tools for empowerment, not exclusion. Harnessing technology for societal good is not simply a technical challenge but a moral imperative for all leaders.

DISCUSSION QUESTIONS

1. How are this chapter's emerging technologies transforming our ways of work and living?
2. What are the risks and benefits of these emerging technologies?
3. What do Business Leaders need to know about the current digital landscape?
4. How can we apply Isaac Asimov's three laws of robotics to today's emerging technology?
5. How can Business Leaders harness digital technology for societal good?

Key Terms

- Surveillance Capitalism
- Analytical AI
- Generative AI
- Blockchain
- Cryptocurrency
- Proof-of-Stake
- Proof-of-Work
- Sharding
- Non-Fungible Tokens (NFTs)
- Internet of Things (IoT)
- Smart Cities
- Data Transparency
- Wearable Sensors
- Flexible Triboelectric Sensors
- Spectroscopy-Based Sensors
- Electrocardiogram (ECG) Sensors
- Body Shaming
- Mental Health Stigma
- Data Anonymization
- Virtual Reality (VR)
- Augmented Reality (VR)
- Digital Officescapes
- Metaverse
- Second Life
- Bioengineering
- Nanotechnology
- Additive Manufacturing
- Digital Twins
- Industry 4.0
- Organoid Intelligence
- Living Intelligence

CASE STUDY 12.1 SMARTMDTECH—NAVIGATE THE ETHICAL FRONTIER OF HEALTHCARE INNOVATION

Background: SmartMDTech, a mid-sized leader in healthcare technology, is committed to revolutionizing patient care and resource management through cutting-edge innovations. However, as the company races to integrate transformative technologies like AI, blockchain, and wearable technology, it faces significant ethical dilemmas that could undermine its mission.

Issues: First, integrating wearable health trackers into wellness programs raises critical data privacy and surveillance concerns. The accumulation of sensitive health data creates fears of exploitation and breaches of patient trust. Additionally, as technological benefits become more pronounced, the risk of exacerbating health inequalities looms extensive, igniting debates over the accessibility of advanced healthcare tools for all socioeconomic groups. Moreover, the introduction of AR tools for training has led to reports of digital fatigue among employees, prompting questions about the balance between innovation and mental well-being. Environmental concerns are linked to blockchain's energy consumption, and the cost of progress becomes a primary ethical consideration.

New Initiative, Response, and Effects: SmartMDTech launched Project EquiHealth, focusing on integrating technology with ethical responsibility. The initiative includes ECG–enabled wearables for chronic patients, AI–driven predictive analytics to anticipate health crises, and blockchain for secure medical records. While these innovations have led to a notable decrease in emergency hospital visits, they have also ignited concerns over patient autonomy and the extent of AI's influence on critical health decisions.

While early successes highlight enhanced patient outcomes and reduced inequities through collaborations aimed at broadening access, the transparency of data use remains an obstacle to trust. Additionally, the transition from proof-of-work to proof-of-stake for blockchain demonstrates the company's commitment to sustainability. Yet, fundamental questions linger about balancing productive innovation and ethical stewardship.

Task: Provide four comprehensive recommendations for SmartMDTech leaders. Connect the recommendations to key chapter concepts. Present the recommendations to a larger group for feedback and discussion.

REFERENCES

Adams, H., Stefanucci, J., Creem-Regehr, S., Pointon, G., Thompson, W., & Bodenheimer, B. (2021). Shedding light on cast shadows: An investigation of perceived ground contact in AR and VR. *IEEE Transactions on Visualization and Computer Graphics*, *28*(12), 4624–4639.

Adeghe, E. P., Okolo, C. A., & Ojeyinka, O. T. (2024). A review of wearable technology in healthcare: Monitoring patient health and enhancing outcomes. *OARJ of Multidisciplinary Studies*, *7*(01), 142–148.

Akram, S. V., Malik, P. K., Singh, R., Anita, G., & Tanwar, S. (2020). Adoption of blockchain technology in various realms: Opportunities and challenges. *Security and Privacy*, *3*(5), e109.

Alahi, M. E. E., Sukkuea, A., Tina, F. W., Nag, A., Kurdthongmee, W., Suwannarat, K., & Mukhopadhyay, S. C. (2023). Integration of IoT-enabled technologies and artificial intelligence (AI) for smart city scenario: recent advancements and future trends. *Sensors*, *23*(11), 5206.

Anthopoulos, L. (2019). *Smart city emergence: Cases from around the world*. Elsevier.

Asimov, I. (1950). Runaround. In I. Asimove (Ed.), *I, Robot* (pp. 41–58). Gnome Press.

Asimov, I. (1985). *Robots and empire*. Doubleday.

Balcıoğlu, Y. S., Çelik, A. A., & Altındağ, E. (2024). Integrating blockchain technology in supply chain management: A bibliometric analysis of theme extraction via text mining. *Sustainability, 16*(22), 10032.

Belabbaci, N. A., & Alam, M. A. U. (2024, July). HydroTrack: Spectroscopic Analysis Prototype Enabling Real-Time Hydration Monitoring in Wearables. In *2024 46th Annual International Conference of the IEEE Engineering in Medicine and Biology Society (EMBC)* (pp. 1–4). IEEE. Retrieved from https://arxiv.org/pdf/2407.11997

Braun, T., Fung, B. C., Iqbal, F., & Shah, B. (2018). Security and privacy challenges in smart cities. *Sustainable Cities and Society, 39*, 499–507.

Brooker, C. (2016). Nosedive (Season 3, Episode 1). In *Black Mirror*. House of Tomorrow.

Brynjolfsson, E., & McAfee, A. (2014). *The second machine age: Work, progress, and prosperity in a time of brilliant technologies*. W.W. Norton & Company.

Carvalho, F. D., & Morgado, L. (2022). Can we escape the metaverse?: Should we? *Innovation, 2022*, 118–127. https://repositorioaberto.uab.pt/bitstream/10400.2/12807/1/Fausto%20and%20Morgado%20-%20Innovaction%202022.pdf

Cline, E. (2011). *Ready player one*. Crown Publishers.

Davenport, T. H. (2024). Generative AI: Transforming business models and customer behaviors. Presentation at the *GCEC 2024 Conference*, Babson College.

Dell'Acqua, F., Kogut, B., & Perkowski, P. (2023a). Super Mario meets AI: Experimental effects of automation and skills on team performance and coordination. *Review of Economics and Statistics*, 1–47. Retrieved from https://doi.org/10.1162/rest_a_01328

Dell'Acqua, F., McFowland III, E., Mollick, E. R., Lifshitz-Assaf, H., Kellogg, K., Rajendran, S., Krayer, L., Candelon, F., & Lakhani, K. R. (2023b). Navigating the jagged technological frontier: Field experimental evidence of the effects of AI on knowledge worker productivity and quality. *Harvard Business School Technology & Operations Management Unit Working Paper*, (24-013). Retrieved from https://www.iab.cl/wp-content/uploads/2023/11/SSRN-id4573321.pdf

Di Nardo, A., Boccelli, D. L., Herrera, M., Creaco, E., Cominola, A., Sitzenfrei, R., & Taormina, R. (2021). Smart urban water networks: Solutions, trends, and challenges. *Water, 13*(4), 501.

Forster, E. M. (1909). *The machine stops*. Project Gutenberg.

Girotra, K., Meincke, L., Terwiesch, C., & Ulrich, K. T. (2023). Ideas are dimes a dozen: Large language models for idea generation in innovation. *Available at SSRN 4526071*. Retrieved from https://papers.ssrn.com/sol3/Delivery.cfm?abstractid=4526071

Google DeepMind. (2024). *Gemini 1.5: Unlocking multimodal understanding across millions of tokens of context*. https://arxiv.org/abs/2403.05530

Hamdan, A., & Braendle, U. (Eds.). (2024). *Harnessing AI, machine learning, and IoT for intelligent business* (Vol. 1). Springer. https://doi.org/10.1007/978-3-031-67890-5

Hasibuan, M. A. A., Kurniawan, A., Nugraha, F. P., Kahfi, F., & Syahputra, B. D. (2024). Advancements in Blockchain Technology: Enhancing efficiency and scalability in cryptocurrency systems. *Journal of Advanced Technological Innovations, 1*(3), 113–126.

Holler, J., Tsiatsis, V., Mulligan, C., Avesand, S., & Karnouskos, S. (2014). *From machine-to-machine to the Internet of Things: Introduction to a new age of intelligence*. Academic Press.

Hoover, A. (2024, July 14). The metaverse was supposed to be your new office. You're still on Zoom. *Wired*. Retrieved from: https://www.wired.com/story/metaverse-virtual-reality-office-work-slow-growth/

Huang, C., Chen, Q., Lin, Z., Su, W., Zhang, Z., & Liu, S. (2024). The economic impact and application challenges of IoT technology in smart home and infrastructure. *Journal of Innovation and Development*, *6*(1), 35–39.

Jadhav, A., & Jadhav, V. S. (2022). A review on 3D printing: An additive manufacturing technology. *Materials Today: Proceedings*, *62*, 2094–2099.

Kotche, M., Felder, A. E., Wilkens, K., & Stirling, S. (2020). Perspectives on bioengineering clinical immersion: history, innovation, and impact. *Annals of Biomedical Engineering*, *48*, 2301–2309.

Kranz, M. (2016). *Building the internet of things: Implement new business models, disrupt competitors, and transform your industry*. John Wiley & Sons.

Luo, H., Lee, P. A., Clay, I., Jaggi, M., & De Luca, V. (2020). Assessment of fatigue using wearable sensors: A pilot study. *Digital biomarkers*, *4*(Suppl 1), 59–72.

Mao, J., Zhou, P., Wang, X., Yao, H., Liang, L., Zhao, Y., Zhang, J., Ban, D., & Zheng, H. (2023). A health monitoring system based on flexible triboelectric sensors for intelligence medical internet of things and its applications in virtual reality. *Nano Energy*, *118*, 108984.

Marx, K. (1867). *Capital: Critique of political economy* (Vol. 1). Penguin Classics.

Mary Mammen, P., Zakaria, C., Molom-Ochir, T., Trivedi, A., Shenoy, P., & Balan, R. (2024). WiSleep: Smartphone-driven sleep population monitoring with unsupervised learning. *ACM Journal on Computing and Sustainable Societies*. Retrieved from https://dl.acm.org/doi/pdf/10.1145/3705722

Mortaji, S. T. H., & Shateri, S. (2023). Harnessing the power of business analytics and artificial intelligence: A roadmap to data-driven success. *International Journal of Innovation in Engineering*, *3*(3), 1–27.

Nakamoto, S. (2008). Bitcoin: A peer-to-peer electronic cash system. *Satoshi Nakamoto*. Retrieved December 10, 2024 https://www.poritz.net/jonathan/past_classes/winter16/CCatRU/BitcoinOriginalPaper.pdf

Noyes, E. (2024). Keynote Address on AI and Innovation. *GCEC 2024 Conference*, Babson College.

Onaji, I., Tiwari, D., Soulatiantork, P., Song, B., & Tiwari, A. (2022). Digital twin in manufacturing: conceptual framework and case studies. *International Journal of Computer Integrated Manufacturing*, *35*(8), 831–858.

Otis, N. G., Haas, B., Cranney, K., Delecourt, S., & Koning, R. (2024). *Global evidence on gender gaps and generative AI* (No. h6a7c). Center for Open Science. https://www.hbs.edu/ris/Publication%20Files/25-023_d09f0b39-4d4b-4828-b13e-df5dce799de0.pdf

Papadakis, N., Koukoulas, N., Christakis, I., Stavrakas, I., & Kandris, D. (2021). An IoT-based participatory antitheft system for public safety enhancement in smart cities. *Smart Cities*, *4*(2), 919–937.

Rai, R., & Dhar, P. (2022). Biomedical engineering aspects of nanocellulose: A review. *Nanotechnology*, *33*(36), 362001.

Ramirez, E. J. (2021). *The ethics of virtual and augmented reality: Building worlds*. Routledge.

Ramirez, E. J., & LaBarge, S. (2018). Real moral problems in the use of virtual reality. *Ethics and Information Technology*, *20*(4), 249–263.

Song, J., He, G., Wang, J., & Zhang, P. (2022). Shaping future low-carbon energy and transportation systems: Digital technologies and applications. *IEnergy, 1*(3), 285–305.

Spielberg, S. (Director). (2018). *Ready player one* [Film]. Warner Bros. Pictures.

Tufekci, Z. (2017). *Twitter and tear gas: The power and fragility of networked protest*. Yale University Press.

Turkle, S. (2011). *Alone together: Why we expect more from technology and less from each other*. Basic Books.

Tyler, J., Choi, S. W., & Tewari, M. (2020). Real-time, personalized medicine through wearable sensors and dynamic predictive modeling: a new paradigm for clinical medicine. *Current Opinion in Systems Biology, 20,* 17–25.

Ullah, Z., Naeem, M., Coronato, A., Ribino, P., & De Pietro, G. (2023). Blockchain applications in sustainable smart cities. *Sustainable Cities and Society, 97,* 104697.

Van Der Donckt, J., Vandenbussche, N., Van Der Donckt, J., Chen, S., Stojchevska, M., De Brouwer, M., Steenwinckel, B., Paemeleire, K., Ongenae, F., & Van Hoecke, S. (2024). Addressing data quality challenges in observational ambulatory studies: Analysis, methodologies and practical solutions for wrist-worn wearable monitoring. *arXiv preprint arXiv:2401.13518*. Retrieved from https://arxiv.org/pdf/2401.13518

Vonnegut, K. (1961). *Harrison Bergeron*. Public domain sources.

Webb, A. (2025, January 6). Why "living intelligence" is the next big thing. *Harvard Business Review*. Retrieved from https://hbr.org/2025/01/why-living-intelligence-is-the-next-big-thing

Whig, P., Kouser, S., Puruhit, K., Alam, N., & Velu, A. (2022). Security and privacy for IoT-based smart cities. In Keshav Kaushik, Susheela Dahiya, Akashdeep Bhardwaj, & Yassine Maleh (Eds.), *Internet of things and cyber physical systems* (pp. 231–251). CRC Press.

Zainab, H., Khan, A. H., Khan, R., & Hussain, H. K. (2024). Integration of AI and wearable devices for continuous cardiac health monitoring. *International Journal of Multidisciplinary Sciences and Arts, 3*(4), 123–139.

Zanella, A., Bui, N., Castellani, A. P., Vangelisti, L., & Zorzi, M. (2014). Internet of things for smart cities. *IEEE Internet of Things Journal, 1*(1), 22–32.

Zuboff, S. (2019). *The age of surveillance capitalism: The fight for a human future at the new frontier of power*. PublicAffairs.

CHAPTER 13

Entrepreneurial Mindset vs. Behavior

CHAPTER OVERVIEW

This chapter examines the vital distinction between entrepreneurial mindset and behavior, asserting that while an entrepreneurial mindset is valuable for Business Leaders, the actions stemming from this mindset genuinely drive success. Entrepreneurship is a transformative force for economic, social, and environmental innovation. This chapter argues that ideas without corresponding actions lead to stagnation, while proactive behaviors are essential for fostering change and innovation. The chapter leverages real stories to show how bold actions and resilience can turn visionary concepts into impactful enterprises. Five theory-based areas are introduced for Business Leaders to enhance their entrepreneurial approach: Knightian Uncertainty Bearing, Schumpeterian Disruption, Kirznerian Equilibration, Veblenian Institutional Thinking, and Social Entrepreneurship. The chapter concludes that a strong entrepreneurial mindset with decisive actions empowers Business Leaders to create meaningful change and bolster long-term success.

Entrepreneurship is a dynamic force that drives economic, environmental, and social innovation, and it is essential for Business Leaders. While discussions about entrepreneurship often highlight the importance of mindset, the debate about whether mindset or behavior holds greater significance remains lively. This chapter argues passionately that although possessing an entrepreneurial mindset is undoubtedly valuable for Business Leaders, the real driving force behind entrepreneurial success lies in the actions leaders take—their behaviors.

Business Leaders pursue an entrepreneurial mindset primed for opportunity recognition, resilience, and creativity. Ideas and intentions without corresponding actions lead to stagnation, while proactive behaviors catalyze change and drive innovation. The entrepreneurial mindset is demonstrated through entrepreneurship behaviors. These behaviors offer the most evidence of success (and failure) and provide better feedback for Business Leaders to pivot their strategies.

Consider successful entrepreneurs like Oprah Winfrey (O Network), Sara Blakely (Spanx), Blake Mycoskie (Tom's Shoes), Ted Turner (CNN), and Hamdi Ulukaya (Chobani).

DOI: 10.4324/9781003474647-16

Their journeys showcasing bold, calculated steps, facing challenges head-on, and adapting to feedback can transform visionary ideas into thriving enterprises. Despite adversity, they persevered dramatically, impacting organizations, industries, and communities.

Business Leaders maximize the synthesis and distribution of data-driven feedback from their employees, organizational units, clients, communities, and themselves. When individuals realize that success in entrepreneurship means moving beyond mere ideas to implement strategies actively, they empower themselves to create meaningful change. Combining a robust entrepreneurial mindset with decisive actions paves the way for lasting influence and success.

This chapter offers Business Leaders five theory-based areas in which to explore how to bolster their entrepreneurial mindsets and exhibit entrepreneurial behaviors: (1) Knightian Uncertainty Bearing, (2) Schumpeterian Disruption, (3) Kirznerian Equilibration, (4) Veblenian Institutional Thinking, and (5) Social Entrepreneurship. These five areas are not all-inclusive of the field of entrepreneurial leadership, nor of the many tools to enhance a person's entrepreneurial mindset. Instead, these five areas offer pathways and perspectives for Business Leaders to discover themselves and empower their teams to be entrepreneurial.

ENTREPRENEURIAL MINDSET: OVERHYPED FOUNDATION OR NECESSARY PRECURSOR?

Entrepreneurs display a prevalence of particular psychosocial qualities and advantages, which many consultants, educators, researchers, and practitioners have come to debate as an entrepreneurial mindset (McGrath & MacMillan, 2000). This entrepreneurial mindset is often presented as trait-based and includes resilience, creativity, and risk tolerance. This internal focus frequently elevates the individual's perception of opportunities and challenges (McGrath & MacMillan, 2000; Liao et al., 2022). While mindsets provide a framework for decision-making, they often remain static if not translated into actionable behaviors.

Entrepreneurs are primarily shaped by situational and familial influences rather than by inherent genetic predispositions. They exhibit unique traits that enhance their capacity to navigate complex challenges and seize opportunities. A heightened perception of opportunity allows entrepreneurs to recognize possibilities where others see obstacles, often fueled by optimism and a strong inclination toward decisive action (Schumpeter, 1934). Their belief in personal efficacy, or confidence in their ability to achieve goals, compels them to take calculated risks and adopt proactive strategies in ever-changing environments (Bandura, 1997). This is a modern-day essential for Business Leaders.

Innovativeness further delineates entrepreneurs as they generate creative ideas and solutions that drive progress (Drucker, 1985). Additionally, a pronounced need for achievement and independence underscores their motivation to succeed on their terms (McClelland, 1961). Complementing these traits, empathy and a strong sense of responsibility (i.e., emotional intelligence) enable entrepreneurs to understand and address the needs of others, particularly in social and collaborative contexts (Goleman, 1995). These characteristics collectively shape the entrepreneurial mindset and guide entrepreneurial behavior.

Entrepreneurial Mindset Components

The entrepreneurial mindset comprises three interrelated components: cognitive, behavioral, and emotional. While each component is unique, the synergy of the components firmly grounds entrepreneurial action (Kuratko et al., 2020). The entrepreneurial mindset manifests as a dynamic interaction of thinking, doing, and feeling, reifying the strengths of each aspect to drive entrepreneurial success (Kuratko et al., 2020). Business Leaders work on all three components and also work on their synergy to drive innovation and practical impact.

The **cognitive** aspect involves mental processes used to identify and pursue opportunities. Business Leaders with entrepreneurial mindsets constantly refine perception, decision-making, and problem-solving. They utilize mental models to combine various pieces of information to develop new, innovative products or solutions. Research highlights the importance of cognitive adaptability, or the ability to shift thought patterns despite uncertainty. Such mental flexibility enables Business Leaders to better frame tasks to adjust to evolving issues (Haynie et al., 2010).

The **behavioral** component is reflected in the proactive steps Business Leaders take to capitalize on opportunities. They translate their thinking into real results by identifying opportunities, allocating and activity resources, and creating ventures (Bird & Schjoedt, 2009). They often adopt a "hustle" mentality, swiftly taking unconventional actions to address immediate issues amid uncertain conditions and results (McMullen & Shepherd, 2006; Fisher et al., 2020).

The **emotional** aspect explores how feelings influence and are influenced by entrepreneurial action. Emotions like passion and resilience can be strong motivators that encourage perseverance in overcoming challenges, which we have discussed in our other chapters. But stress and risk tolerance are needed in decision-making during high-uncertainty situations. Business Leaders leverage positive emotions to inspire stakeholders and address obstacles. However, unchecked emotions, such as overconfidence, can result in serious misjudgments and erosion of credibility and trust (Cardon et al., 2009, 2012). Business Leaders demonstrate high emotional awareness and regulation (see Chapter 4 on emotional intelligence).

The three components' dynamic synergy drives the entrepreneurial mindset's self-reinforcing cycle (Kuratko et al., 2020). Cognitive processes help recognize and frame opportunities, while behaviors turn insights into actions. Emotions bolster motivation and resilience during uncertainty. Business Leaders demonstrate this synergy through proactive behaviors that show initiative and adaptability to exploit new opportunities despite adversity or uncertainty. They create and rely upon feedback loops to uphold the self-reinforcing cycle so one component is not neglected. Business Leaders hone their mindsets to achieve future success.

Action over Ideation

Actions transform ideas into impactful innovations and ventures. Theories of entrepreneurial action emphasize that behavior, more than mindset, determines the tangible impact on economic and social systems. For example, Liao et al. (2022) highlight that entrepreneurial education fosters the competencies and attitudes necessary for individuals to engage in productive entrepreneurial activities; however, Talmage et al. (2022) note unproductive and destructive activities can also be regarded as entrepreneurial.

Entrepreneurial behavior involves the capacity to overcome challenges through innovative solutions (McGrath & MacMillan, 2000). Therefore, while the entrepreneurial mindset provides cognitive scaffolding and emotional bolstering, behavior marked by risk-taking, proactivity, and innovation drives measurable outcomes. This is our primary reason for positioning a chapter on entrepreneurial mindset versus behavior within *Essentials for Contemporary Business Leadership*.

Exercise 13.1 Reflecting and Applying the Entrepreneurial Mindset

Given the three components of entrepreneurial mindsets (see helpful questions in Table 13.1), reflect on how entrepreneurs think, act, and manage emotions (Part 1). In Part 2, assess strengths and areas for growth. Then, in Part 3, apply the entrepreneurial mindset to a real-life challenge or opportunity by identifying actionable steps, analyzing potential outcomes, and preparing strategies for emotional regulation. Finally, reflect on the process to deepen your understanding of how these components drive entrepreneurial success (Part 4). Use Table 13.1 as a roadmap.

TABLE 13.1 Entrepreneurial Mindset Exercise

Exercise Part	*Key Activity*	*Cognitive Component*	*Behavioral Component*	*Emotional Component*
Part 1: Understanding	Summarize the cognitive, behavioral, and emotional components of the entrepreneurial mindset.	How do entrepreneurs think about identifying and framing opportunities?	How do entrepreneurs act to translate ideas into outcomes?	How do emotions influence entrepreneurs, and how do they manage these emotions?
Part 2: Assessment	Reflect on your strengths and growth areas in each mindset component.	How do I process complex information and adapt to uncertain situations?	How effectively do I turn ideas into actions and manage resources?	How do I handle stress, maintain motivation, and inspire others?
Part 3: Application	Choose a personal challenge or opportunity and plan actionable steps using the mindset components.	What opportunity or challenge can I address?	What three actionable steps can I take?	What emotions might arise during this process, and how will I manage them?
		What solutions can I brainstorm? How can I analyze risks and benefits?	How will I execute my steps?	How will I sustain positive emotions and manage stress or setbacks?

Exercise Part	*Key Activity*	*Cognitive Component*	*Behavioral Component*	*Emotional Component*
Part 4: Reflection	Reflect on the exercise and identify takeaways for strengthening the entrepreneurial mindset.	How did cognitive processes contribute to identifying and framing opportunities?	How did actions translate cognitive ideas into measurable outcomes?	How did emotional regulation and motivation influence my ability to follow through?

TYPES OF MINDSETS AND BEHAVIORS: THEORETICAL PERSPECTIVES

This next section summarizes and applies the groupings of the major theories in entrepreneurship. Table 13.2 showcases these comparisons across dimensions. Please note the core thinking at the heart of entrepreneurship concerns *who the entrepreneur is, what entrepreneurship is, and what constitutes success (and failure)*.

Knightian Uncertainty Bearing: Decision-Making Amid the Unknown

Business Leaders, as entrepreneurs, often excel in uncertain environments. They see challenges as opportunities to succeed, and their tolerance for unpredictability helps them find new ideas and rapidly adjust to change. For example, Airbnb started during the 2008 financial crisis, when the economy was unclear. The founders saw a chance in the short-term rental market, even with vague rules and market needs. Their ability to deal with uncertainty shows how entrepreneurs can turn challenges into opportunities for success (Ries, 2011).

Frank Knight's (1921) seminal work on uncertainty distinguishes between risk, which can be calculated and managed, and genuine uncertainty, which cannot be quantified. Hébert and Link (2009) suggest three layers: (1) **risk**—known factors with calculable probability distributions; (2) **uncertainty**—known factors without calculable probability distributions; and (3) **radical uncertainty**—unknown factors without calculable probability distributions. These distinctions are crucial for entrepreneurs who often operate in realms where outcomes are inherently unpredictable (Knight, 1921).

Business Leaders make decisions with incomplete information, which sets effective leaders apart from their peers. Richard Cantillon (c. 1680–1734), widely regarded as the founder of entrepreneurship theory, noted that entrepreneurs circumscribe their uncertainty (Cantillon, 1931), drawing boundaries between what they know and do not know before any action (Hébert & Link, 2009). Elon Musk's approach to developing SpaceX showcases radical uncertainty. Looking to launch rockets at a fraction of the cost of competitors, Musk boldly decided to innovate on existing technologies, like reusability,

TABLE 13.2 Comparisons of Mindsets and Behaviors

Aspect	*Knightian Uncertainty Bearing*	*Schumpeterian Disruption*	*Kirznerian Equilibration*	*Veblenian Institutional Thinking*	*Social Entrepreneurship*
Core Concept	Decision-making under radical uncertainty.	Innovating and disrupting established markets.	Restoring equilibrium by identifying market inefficiencies.	Addressing social and systemic values within economic actions.	Solving systemic social issues through innovative practices.
Focus	Handling uncertainty and risk through judgment.	Creative destruction and market transformation.	Opportunity discovery and resource allocation.	Institutional structures and their societal impact.	Addressing inequities and scaling solutions.
Key Behavior	Willingness to act despite ambiguity and lack of information.	Introducing revolutionary products or processes.	Exploiting unnoticed or overlooked opportunities.	Designing non-invidious innovations that benefit communities.	Implementing scalable, transformative social models.
Mindset	Risk-tolerant and decisive.	Visionary and innovative.	Alert and opportunistic.	Socially aware and ethically driven.	Empathetic and justice oriented.
Economic Role	Providing stability through risk absorption.	Driving growth and change via innovation.	Facilitating efficient market functioning.	Aligning economic actions with community and cultural values.	Balancing social impact with economic sustainability.
Examples of Impact	Entrepreneurs in speculative ventures like startups in new tech.	Tech disruptors are disrupting industries using AI, robotics, and other new tools.	Arbitrageurs optimizing resource use.	Sustainable practices in agriculture benefiting communities.	Organizations like Camfed empower education in Africa.
Primary Outcome	Reducing uncertainty for broader market activities.	Overturning old systems and creating new industries.	Balancing supply and demand dynamics.	Equitable solutions benefiting society and institutions.	Empowering marginalized populations through innovation.
Critique	Focus on judgment may overemphasize the individual's ability.	Disruption may lead to social upheaval or inequality.	Overreliance on equilibrium may ignore structural barriers.	Slower to respond to immediate economic challenges.	Risks of mission drift when scaling operations.

despite radical uncertainty (Vance, 2015). Business Leaders tolerate ambiguity and actively forge new opportunities. Knight (1921) notes entrepreneurs navigate uncertainty, making sound decisions without needing to predict every variable at play.

The behaviors exhibited during the decision-making process under uncertainty hold paramount importance and often outweigh mere tolerance for ambiguity. Evidence suggests that business leaders willing to engage with uncertainty and effectively assess risky situations can drive innovation and economic growth (Kahneman, 2011). This critical alignment of behavior and mindset empowers Business Leaders to act confidently amid chaos. Their success stories highlight the value of decisiveness in navigating the unknown and reinforce that embracing uncertainty is a vital skill in entrepreneurial ventures, not just a personality trait. Additionally, Business Leaders determine their tipping point for action, balancing their assessments of risk and potential reward. Knight's (1921) insights into uncertainty remain relevant, emphasizing that the entrepreneurial journey requires individuals to confront, interpret, and act in the face of the unknown (Hébert & Link, 2009). This also applies to Business Leaders today.

Schumpeterian Disruption: Creative Destruction

Disruptors embody a mindset defined by forward thinking and a remarkable capacity to identify and leverage unique opportunities within their markets. This visionary outlook allows them to transcend conventional boundaries, positioning them to challenge established norms and address gaps that others may overlook. Such individuals often possess a deep understanding of their industries and are eager to embrace uncertainty, viewing it as an essential catalyst for innovation. By fostering a culture of experimentation and creative problem-solving, disruptors drive change and inspire others to reconsider the possibilities within their respective fields (Hébert & Link, 2009; Shockley & Frank, 2011; Talmage & Gassert, 2020).

Business Leaders leverage Schumpeter's (1934) **new combinations** to redefine industries through innovative products and processes that disrupt social and economic equilibriums. New combinations include a new good, production method, market, supply source, organization, or monopoly. Companies like Tesla exemplify this notion by reshaping the automotive sector by introducing electric vehicles while altering consumer perceptions regarding sustainability and performance. This process reflects Schumpeter's (1934) **creative destruction** concept, where the old equilibrium is incessantly replaced by the new, compelling competitors to adapt or risk obsolescence (Hébert & Link, 2009; Shockley & Frank, 2011; Talmage & Gassert, 2020).

Creative destruction requires **novel intuitions**. These refer to original or innovative insights and understandings that arise from a fresh perspective or unusual thought processes that others think are unlikely to succeed (Schumpeter, 1934; Shockley & Frank, 2011; Talmage & Gassert, 2020). They can lead to unique new combinations that differ from conventional thinking. Thus, while novel intuitions remain vital to innovation, disruptive actions—rooted in the theories of creative destruction—catalyze transformative change within the marketplace (Hébert & Link, 2009; Shockley & Frank, 2011; Talmage & Gassert, 2020). Schumpeter (1934) asserts that innovation and the entrepreneurial spirit are essential drivers of economic advancement that shape the modern economic landscape, and the entrepreneur is the mere instrument of change. When applied more broadly in business, so too is the contemporary leader.

Kirznerian Equilibration: Alertness and Discovery

In entrepreneurship theory, Israel Kirzner's concept of **entrepreneurial discovery** plays a pivotal role in understanding how entrepreneurs navigate the marketplace; in fact, the role of the entrepreneur is to discover (Kirzner, 1973; Shockley & Frank, 2011; Talmage & Gassert, 2020). Kirzner's (1973) discovery consists of **alertness** and **surprise**. **Alertness** is an inherent capacity to recognize opportunities that others may overlook, often described as a form of heightened awareness of economic environments (Kirzner, 1973). This alertness enables Business Leaders to discover untapped profit opportunities. Kirzner (1973) posits that this quality empowers individuals to seize possibilities not readily apparent to their competitors, thereby engaging in proactive decision-making and strategic risk-taking (Kirzner, 1973; Shockley & Frank, 2011).

Kirzner (1973) emphasizes the importance of **surprise** in the entrepreneurial discovery process. Opportunity often comes unexpectedly, somewhere between pure search and sheer ignorance. Surprise can trigger a cognitive, emotional, and behavioral response that leads Business Leaders to undertake entrepreneurial action (Kirzner, 1973; Shockley & Frank, 2011; Talmage & Gassert, 2020). Business Leaders act upon these unexpected discoveries while others remain silent.

Rivalrous competition refers to competitive interactions among firms where each entity strives to outperform others by attracting customers and gaining market share (Kirzner, 1973). Rivalrous competition is the greatest compliment to the entrepreneur; success is rewarded through competition. Rivalrous competition drives Business Leaders to stay vigilant and proactive. They must continuously adapt to changing market conditions (Shockley & Frank, 2011; Talmage & Gassert, 2020).

Veblenian Institutional Thinking: Navigating Social Valuation

Thorstein Veblen (1898, 1899) understood economic activities as rooted in cultural and institutional contexts. He argued that entrepreneurial actions should go beyond mere profit-seeking to align with broader societal progress and communal values. Veblen (1898, 1899) critiqued profit-driven behavior that led to **pecuniary emulation** or **exploitation**. Innovation and improvement should benefit society. Veblen's (1898, 1899) institutionalist perspective considers how culture and institutions shape entrepreneurship and hold insights regarding societal needs and ethical issues for Business Leaders (Stanfield & Talmage, 2024).

In this light, Business Leaders should adopt **non-invidious innovation** to advance societal welfare rather than profit maximization. For example, sustainable business strategies that resonate with Veblenian ideals prioritize community benefits and address environmental concerns. They should also avoid exploitative practices often associated with traditional economic models (Stanfield & Talmage, 2024). These strategies could involve community-supported agriculture, ethical sourcing, or equitable labor practices, all strengthening local economies and fostering a sense of collective well-being.

Business Leaders exhibit socially oriented entrepreneurial behavior that addresses imbalances within economic systems and helps cultivate a more inclusive landscape where community needs and interests are prioritized (Stanfield & Talmage, 2024). They work to shape a more equitable economic landscape that moves beyond profit as the sole indicator of success. They integrate social impact into core strategies to foster community well-being and drive sustainable growth.

Social Entrepreneurship: Transforming Equilibriums

Business Leaders looking to enhance their mindsets and behaviors could consider social entrepreneurship as a framework. The field of social entrepreneurship will be discussed at length in Chapter 20. Social entrepreneurs often embody a profound **empathy** alongside a visionary outlook aimed at tackling deep-rooted systemic injustices (i.e., **unjust social equilibriums**). Unjust social equilibriums include poverty, food insecurity, water contamination, and social disparity. This combination of attributes drives the ambition to improve unfair systems and transform them to get *beyond* better (Martin & Osberg, 2015). Martin and Osberg (2015) note the need for innovative solutions that do more than just improve existing conditions; they strive for **transformative change** within communities and societies (see also Talmage, 2021).

Social entrepreneurs play a pivotal role in driving significant social impact. They engage in transformative initiatives, such as developing scalable models and establishing impactful social enterprises, which are crucial for fostering real change in communities. Camfed (Campaign for Female Education) uses educational programs to address and break down social inequalities, especially those affecting women and girls (Camfed, n.d.). Camfed empowers through education. Their programs help young women directly and involve local communities to ensure solutions are sustainable and fit well with the local context. Camfed shows how focused educational efforts can lead to broader social change and grow in their impact.

While an empathetic mindset is undeniably advantageous, the genuine measure of impact lies in executing these ideas through tangible actions. Martin and Osberg (2015) offer models for social entrepreneurs to enhance or create value and control or decrease costs (see Chapter 20). Social entrepreneurship provides blueprint replication and scaling processes vital for unlocking social entrepreneurship's transformative potential (Talmage, 2021). These behavioral implementations allow the vision for a more equitable society to be realized, driving change far beyond superficial improvements. Social entrepreneurship will be explored in greater detail in a later chapter.

Exercise 13.2 Self-Reflection on Mindsets and Behaviors

Before you begin this exercise, familiarize yourself with the five key concepts: (1) Knightian Uncertainty Bearing, (2) Schumpeterian Disruption, (3) Kirznerian Equilibration, (4) Veblenian Institutional Thinking, and (5) Social Entrepreneurship. The questions in Table 13.3 will help you: (1) identify acceptable risks and uncertainties; (2) find areas where innovation can thrive and explore new technology combinations; (3) seek opportunities for improvement and act quickly; (4) reflect on how your actions can improve lives and address social injustices; and (5) consider the broader implications of your entrepreneurial actions.

TABLE 13.3 Questions to Ground Entrepreneurial Mindsets and Behaviors

Knightian Uncertainty Bearing	*Schumpeterian Disruption*	*Kirznerian Equilibration*	*Veblenian Institutional Thinking*	*Social Entrepreneurship*
What risks do I know?	Which areas have grown stagnant?	Where are the substantial sources of disequilibrium?	How can I enhance quality of life, not just profit?	Where are unjust social equilibriums?
What uncertainty will I bear?	What possible technologies could be combined?	Where can I act swiftly to take action?	How can I ensure I do not reify exploitation?	Where can I exhibit greater empathy?
What's my tipping point for action?	What are the ramifications of potential disruption?	What will bring out rivals based on positive actions?	What are the broader implications of my actions?	What does it take to scale impact?

Document your reflections to clarify your mindset and guide your future actions. Use these insights to create a plan that addresses the identified opportunities and challenges. This will help you develop an entrepreneurial mindset that enhances your leadership skills.

CONCLUSION: RECONCILING MINDSETS AND BEHAVIORS

Business Leaders transform ideas into thriving ventures. They make good decisions while adapting to changing circumstances. Emphasizing collaboration and open communication with people, communities, and clients enhances innovation and the overall impact of initiatives. Business Leaders accept uncertainty and adapt their behaviors to meet challenges. They make a meaningful impact in contemporary business, communities, and society. Mindsets alone are insufficient to drive change.

Theoretical frameworks such as Knightian Uncertainty, Schumpeterian Disruption, Kirznerian Equilibration, Veblenian Institutional Thinking, and Social Entrepreneurship offer Business Leaders a comprehensive understanding of entrepreneurship. Entrepreneurship is a dynamic force that shapes personal growth, the professional world, and societal progress. Business Leaders epitomize the intersection of mindset and behavior. The entrepreneurial mindset lays the groundwork, yet true success is measured by executing these ideas—marked by proactive engagement, calculated risk-taking and uncertainty-bearing, and pattern-breaking innovation.

Actionable behavior is paramount to entrepreneurial success. Business Leaders actively immerse themselves in their environments, converting visionary ideas into strategic actions and navigating uncertainties with unwavering confidence. They can achieve meaningful, sustainable impact, driving innovation and creating enduring value for both communities and markets. This blend of mindset and behavior will pave the way for the next wave of transformative business endeavors.

DISCUSSION QUESTIONS

1. What are the qualities of an entrepreneurial mindset?
2. Why do these qualities have relevance today?
3. What are the components of entrepreneurial behavior?
4. What is the difference between mindset and behavior?
5. Why do the various entrepreneurial frameworks hold value for current Business Leaders?
6. What should Business Leaders consider when they shift from ideation to action?

Key Terms

- Entrepreneurial Mindset
  - Cognitive
  - Behavioral
  - Emotional
- Uncertainty Bearing
  - Risk
  - Uncertainty
  - Radical Uncertainty
- Schumpeterian Disruption
  - Novel Intuitions
  - New Combinations
  - Creative Destruction
- Kirznerian Equilibration
  - Discovery
  - Alertness
  - Surprise
  - Rivalrous Competition
- Veblenian Institutional Thinking
  - Pecuniary Emulation / Exploitation
  - Non-Invidious Innovation
- Social Entrepreneurship
  - Unjust Social Equilibriums
  - Transformative Change
  - Empathy

CASE STUDY 13.1 THE RESILIENT INNOVATOR—SOPHIE'S SOLAR SOLUTIONS

A recent engineering graduate, Sophie Ramirez, grew up in a rural community facing frequent power outages and high energy costs. While attending college, Sophie developed a passion for renewable energy, particularly solar power. After graduation, she returned to her hometown with a vision: to create affordable solar solutions tailored to underserved rural communities. Despite her technical expertise, Sophie quickly realized that launching and scaling a business required more than technical knowhow; it demanded an entrepreneurial mindset and decisive actions.

The Challenge: Sophie's Solar Solutions aimed to provide modular solar panels that were affordable and adaptable to various terrains and weather conditions. However, Sophie faced several challenges:

1. **Uncertainty**—Sophie could not guarantee community buy-in or long-term profitability. Would rural customers trust her product? Could she compete with larger, established solar companies?
2. **Market Gaps**—Sophie's research revealed inefficiencies in the rural energy market, including a lack of accessible financing options for low-income households.
3. **Social Responsibility**—Sophie wanted to ensure her venture aligned with communal values and avoided exploitative practices.

Task: Provide four comprehensive recommendations for Sophie. Make sure to connect the recommendations to key chapter concepts. Present the recommendations to a larger group for feedback and discussion.

REFERENCES

Bandura, A. (1997). *Self-efficacy: The exercise of control.* W.H. Freeman.

Bird, B., & Schjoedt, L. (2009). Entrepreneurial behavior: Its nature, scope, recent research, and agenda for future research. In Malin Brännback & Alan L. Carsrud (Eds.), *Understanding the entrepreneurial mind* (pp. 327–358). Springer.

Camfed. (n.d.). Campaign for Femail education. Retrieved December 3, 2024 from https://www.camfed.org

Cantillon, R. (1931). *Essai sur la nature du commerce en general,* edited and translated by H. Higgs. Macmillan.

Cardon, M. S., Foo, M. D., Shepherd, D., & Wiklund, J. (2012). Exploring the heart: Entrepreneurial emotion is a hot topic. *Entrepreneurship Theory and Practice, 36*(1), 1–10.

Cardon, M. S., Wincent, J., Singh, J., & Drnovsek, M. (2009). The nature and experience of entrepreneurial passion. *Academy of Management Review, 34*(3), 511–532.

Drucker, P. F. (1985). *Innovation and entrepreneurship: Practice and principles.* Harper & Row.

Fisher, G., Stevenson, R., Neubert, E., Burnell, D., & Kuratko, D. F. (2020). Entrepreneurial hustle: Navigating uncertainty and enrolling venture stakeholders through urgent and unorthodox action. *Journal of Management Studies, 57(*5), 1002–1036.

Goleman, D. (1995). *Emotional intelligence: Why it can matter more than IQ.* Bantam Books.

Haynie, J. M., Shepherd, D. A., Mosakowski, E., & Earley, P. C. (2010). A situated metacognitive model of the entrepreneurial mindset. *Journal of Business Venturing, 25*(2), 217–229.

Hébert, R. F., & Link, A. N. (2009). *A history of entrepreneurship.* Routledge. https://doi.org/10.4324/9780203877326

Kahneman, D. (2011). *Thinking, fast and slow*. Farrar, Straus and Giroux.
Kirzner, I. M. (1973). *Competition and entrepreneurship*. University of Chicago Press.
Knight, F. H. (1921). *Risk, uncertainty, and profit*. Houghton Mifflin.
Kuratko, D. F., Fisher, G., & Audretsch, D. B. (2020). Unraveling the entrepreneurial mindset. *Small Business Economics, 57*(4), 1681–1691. https://doi.org/10.1007/s11187-020-00372-6
Liao, Y. K., Nguyen, V. H. A., Chi, H. K., & Nguyen, H. H. (2022). Unraveling the direct and indirect effects of entrepreneurial education and mindset on entrepreneurial intention: The moderating role of entrepreneurial passion. *Global Business and Organizational Excellence, 41*(3), 23–40.
Martin, R. L., & Osberg, S. (2015). *Getting beyond better: How social entrepreneurship works*. Harvard Business Review Press.
McClelland, D. C. (1961). *The achieving society*. Princeton University Press.
McGrath, R. G., & MacMillan, I. C. (2000). *The entrepreneurial mindset: Strategies for continuously creating opportunity in an age of uncertainty*. Harvard Business Press.
McMullen, J. S., & Shepherd, D. A. (2006). Entrepreneurial action and the role of uncertainty in the theory of the entrepreneur. *Academy of Management Review, 31*(1), 132–152. https://doi.org/10.5465/amr.2006.19379628
Ries, E. (2011). *The lean startup: How today's entrepreneurs use continuous innovation to create radically successful businesses*. Crown Business.
Schumpeter, J. A. (1934). *The theory of economic development: An inquiry into profits, capital, credit, interest, and the business cycle*. Harvard University Press.
Shockley, G. E., & Frank, P. M. (2011). Schumpeter, Kirzner, and the field of social entrepreneurship. *Journal of Social Entrepreneurship, 2*(1), 6–26.
Stanfield, K. C., & Talmage, C. A. (2024). Detecting light amid dark: A Veblenian refinement of dark-light entrepreneurship theory. *Journal of Economic Issues, 58*(3), 871–881.
Talmage, C. (2021). Social entrepreneurship: A needed tool for contemporary community development education. *International Journal of Community Well-Being, 4*(2), 227–243.
Talmage, C. A., Boyl, K., & Gassert, T. A. (2022). Toward a theory of misfit entrepreneurship: Insights from alternative enterprises and misfit entrepreneurs. In M. M. Mars & H. Schau (Eds.), *How alternative is alternative? The role of entrepreneurial development, form, and function in the emergence of alternative marketscapes* (pp. 1–27). Emerald Publishing Limited.
Talmage, C. A., & Gassert, T. A. (2020). Unsettling entrepreneurship by teaching dark side theories. *Entrepreneurship Education and Pedagogy, 3*(3), 316–345.
Vance, A. (2015). *Elon Musk: Tesla, SpaceX, and the quest for a fantastic future*. Ecco.
Veblen, T. (1898). Why is economics not an evolutionary science? *The Quarterly Journal of Economics, 12*(3), 373–397. https://doi.org/10.2307/1882952
Veblen, T. (1899). *The theory of the leisure class*. Macmillan.

PART 4

Client Leadership

Leadership is inherently a communal, relational process that most certainly extends to the external relationships between business leaders and their buyers, customers, and clients. Leaders who master the nuance and depth of client relationships will produce critical outcomes for their organizations. This **Client Leadership** section explores theory and application for service excellence, client behaviors, managing change, and communicating brand. While comprehensive and concrete, we had to decide which chapters to include in this section. This was not easy.

While customer-focus and client-centricity are buzzworthy terms in today's business circles, our approach to Client Leadership sequenced a future leader's efforts by establishing the importance of (1) setting standards of excellence in their organization's service culture, (2) recognizing and responding to drivers of client behaviors, (3) planning for evitable change in this distinct period, and (4) distinguishing one's brand from industry rivals. Components of the People Leadership section actively play a role here, and we seek to guide students in developing key client relationships. Still, success in these external engagements is a distinct and practiced skill.

This section would benefit future account managers who are essential contributors to an organization's client management portfolio. We further wanted to influence the students who will take straightforward roles as business leaders with significant responsibilities to drive service culture, predict buying behavior, manage change for clients, and tell their brand's story to compete in the marketplace. While we tried not to get tied up in the labels of buyers, customers, or consumers, our aim was nurturing long-term relationships between clients and companies. These relationships hold resiliency to withstand disruption, upheaval, change, and reinvention.

Elements of Self Leadership chapters resonate here, too, where leaders need to lean into their authenticity, identity, and style to make the complex process of developing client relationships their own. At this stage, our model acts like a flywheel with small learning wins accumulating over time, creating momentum that keeps businesses (and the reader) growing. Client Leadership's signature qualities are employees who can repeatedly articulate the brand's story and clients who buy the organization's unique value. The bridge, so often, is the business leader who sets the stage for the relationships.

DOI: 10.4324/9781003474647-17

CHAPTER 14

Customer Service Excellence

CHAPTER OVERVIEW

This chapter distinguishes between customers and clients to position modern Business Leaders to create lasting relationships. This discussion examines the concept of client leadership and its essential role in converting one-time purchasers into loyal clients. Loyal clients are assets for long-term revenue, competitiveness, and resilience. Insights from industries renowned for strong relational foundations are explored to demonstrate customer service excellence in delivery. This chapter provides a framework for current leaders to develop strategies to exceed client expectations and foster a service culture focused on long-term loyalty. Through theoretical exploration and practical application, this analysis equips Client Leaders with the tools to create meaningful interactions that resonate with clients for the long term.

Readers might wonder why a chapter on customer service excellence opens with a section on client leadership. Although these populations have distinct meanings, today's definitions conclude that clients are customers who develop relationships with an organization's brand and make repeat purchases. Clients would be considered an organization's best customers, and we do not mean simply "cash cows." Not all customers turn into clients, but those who do represent significant revenue opportunities. As authors, we lean into the term "client" because it postulates a key relationship that can be nurtured with a buyer. We look to develop client leadership as an essential skill, if not mindset, for contemporary business leaders that helps them convert customers into long-term clients.

Clients and **customers** are individuals who engage in business transactions with companies. They are buyers who purchase goods or services. Learning the differences between these two groups will help professionals tailor their sales and marketing strategies to meet their target consumers' needs. Applying the client relationship–oriented behaviors toward a customer can significantly benefit an organization. Conversely, implementing what we know about customer service excellence in a client relationship can also have transformative effects. We will not use them interchangeably; instead, we will operate with the mindset that customers should be converted into clients. We borrow client leadership as a concept from sectors like construction, law, and therapy, noting that these sectors epitomize relationships based on strong foundations, building, maintenance, development, and growth.

DOI: 10.4324/9781003474647-18

This chapter examines the customer service experience, perceived value, and service excellence to strengthen customer relationships so that they might qualify as recurring clients. Client Leadership includes all activities, internally and externally, that allow organizations to exceed their clients' expectations. Building on historical insights into serving customers with excellence will provide contemporary leaders with the necessary know-how to maximize these critical relationships with individuals who purchase products and services from them.

CUSTOMER SERVICE EXPERIENCE

The **customer service experience** can be described as a phenomenon. Before applying a phenomenological lens to it, it is worth examining existing perspectives that can assist a leader in understanding it. Until the end of the last century, the marketing field traditionally viewed customers primarily as rational decision-makers due to its roots in neoclassical economics (Addis & Holbrook, 2001).

In the 80s, scholars renewed focus on the phenomenological nature of the customer service experience, which emerged following Holbrook and Hirschman's (1982) seminal article "The Experiential Aspects of Consumption: Consumer Fantasy, Feelings, and Fun." Holbrook and Hirschman (1982) defined the experiential view of consumption as phenomenological in spirit, which viewed "consumption as a primarily subjective state of consciousness with a variety of symbolic meanings, hedonic responses, and aesthetic criteria" (p. 132). The experiential view of consumption focuses on the nonutilitarian aspects of consumption, such as customer context, emotions, and symbolism, which may or may not be goal-directed (Frow & Payne, 2007, p. 91). Within this perspective, customers become active seekers of meaning, sometimes independent of the customer service experience context proposed by the company, rather than just passive buyers or users of products or services (Carù and Cova, 2007, p. 5). This perspective remains highly relevant today.

Customer service experience describes how customers feel after interacting with a business across every touchpoint. That includes direct and indirect support communication, customers' journeys toward a purchase, and repeat interactions. The customer service experience is all customer interactions with an organization's brand (Silva et al., 2021). Scholars and practitioners have parsed the margins between good and exceptional customer service experiences. Organizations should shift from service-dominant perspectives to customer-based approaches. Still, as authors, we would offer that a deep understanding of customer-perceived value is critical and essential for client leaders. Exercises 14.1–14.3 can help this pursuit.

Exercise 14.1 Role Play Customer Service Experience Scenarios

Purpose: Customer service builds relationships, loyalty, and brand reputation. Consider the key elements contributing to an excellent customer service experience, such as empathy, active listening, and effective problem-solving. We covered these concepts in our previous chapters.

Setup: Divide into small groups of four to five individuals. Each group should receive pre-prepared scenario cards that present different customer situations, such as a customer unhappy with a product seeking a refund, a customer confused about a service needing clarification, a customer complaining about a long wait time, or a customer expressing gratitude for excellent service. Briefly discuss the assigned scenario before moving into role-playing.

Role-Playing Activity: Each group selects one person to act as the customer, while the others take on the role of customer service representatives. Each group has ten minutes to enact their scenario, allowing all participants to experience each perspective. Then, switch roles so each person can practice interacting as a customer and serving as a representative. Discuss experiences to identify what went well and areas for improvement. Focus on tone of voice, body language, and responsiveness. Where appropriate, provide constructive criticism to peers.

Conclusion: Share insights from the role-playing experience with the larger group, discussing common challenges and practical strategies that emerged during the activity. Consider what participants learned about customer service, how to create an excellent service experience, how empathy and active listening can enhance customer interactions, and which specific techniques they plan to apply in real-world situations.

CUSTOMER PERCEIVED VALUE

Customer perceived value indicates how much a customer is prepared to pay to purchase a product or service. This is determined by a product or service's ability to meet the customer's specific needs and desires, especially in comparison with competitors. Almquist et al. (2016) identified 30 elements of customer perceived value. The 30 elements are organized in a Maslow-type pyramid (see Chapter 7). These researchers realized that what customers truly value is challenging and goes beyond comparing prices. Their approach to aspects of value extends to Maslow's Hierarchy of Needs by analyzing why a customer categorizes a specific product or service as convenient, time-saving, or luxurious, for example. The four kinds of needs they identified in which the 30 elements sit were Social Impact, Life Changing, Emotional, and Functional (Almquist et al., 2016). This explains the dynamic contexts between customers and their perceived product or service value.

Customer perceived value has become an overused and often misused concept in social sciences (Sánchez-Fernández & Iniesta-Bonillo, 2007; Wu et al., 2023). Sánchez-Fernández and Iniesta-Bonillo's (2007) systematic review identifies two research positions. The first, widely accepted in marketing, views customer perceived value as a unidimensional construct (e.g., Monroe, 1979; Bolton & Drew, 1991). Research in this stream often takes a cognitive approach, focusing on how customers perceive value primarily through its utilitarian and economic dimensions, suggesting that organizations embed value in their offerings while customers merely consume them (Graf & Maas, 2008; Helkkula & Kelleher, 2010). However, these unidimensional perspectives are criticized for being overly simplistic.

The second research stream identified customer perceived value as a multidimensional construct (e.g., Mathwick et al., 2001), which may also include hedonic (e.g., Batra & Ahtola, 1991; Holbrook, 1994, 2006) and social value (e.g., Sheth et al., 1991a, 1991b) in addition to utilitarian value (e.g., Batra & Ahtola, 1991). Consumer behavior and psychology align with recent research approaches, recognizing customer perceived value as a highly complex, ambiguous, cognitive-affective, and higher-level construct (Graf & Maas, 2008). Due to this cognitive-affective, multidimensional nature of customer perceived value, it is essential to evaluate it from the perspective of the individual's customer service experience (Helkkula & Kelleher, 2010). While the organization can create and communicate value propositions, the customer, not the organization, creates desire and fulfills needs through dynamic, situational, specific value-creating processes (Holbrook, 2006; Grönroos, 2008). This is a contemporary essential.

Apple's iPhone exemplifies how customers perceive value beyond just price and functionality. Customers appreciate exceptional hardware, smooth iOS experience, and seamless integration with other Apple devices despite higher costs than competitors. The iPhone signals prestige and security, and it also has accessibility features. Furthermore, Apple's commitment to sustainability and ethical practices attracts socially conscious consumers. Separated to mirror Almquist et al.'s (2016) approach, the perceived value of the iPhone is in its:

- **Functional Benefits**—Exceptional hardware quality, a smooth iOS interface, and seamless connectivity with the Apple ecosystem (including Mac, iPad, AirPods, etc.).
- **Emotional Benefits**—Possessing an iPhone can evoke feelings of prestige and security.
- **Transformative Benefits**—Features designed for accessibility, such as voice control and assistive touch, improve usability for individuals with disabilities.
- **Social Responsibility Value**—Apple's focus on sustainability, privacy, and ethical sourcing attracts consumers who prioritize social consciousness.

Value is not solely about efficiency; it includes emotional and social dimensions that shape customer identity (see Almquist et al., 2016). Client Leaders recognize the many facets of customer value. They prioritize personalization and convenience, as seen in successful brands like Amazon and Netflix. In Chapter 17, readers will explore this more with our productivity star. Across the chapters, we have noted that trust and ethical considerations are increasingly important. Consumers favor brands that align with their values. Client Leaders must integrate functional, emotional, and social elements into their strategies to resonate with customers and gain a competitive edge to evolve into strong client leaders.

Service-Dominant Logic

S-D Logic, or Service-Dominant Logic, is a framework for understanding value creation in economic exchanges. Developed by Stephen Vargo and Robert Lusch, it shifts the focus from goods as the primary exchange unit to services and relationships. In S-D logic, customers are seen as being inextricably involved in the entire open-ended value cocreation process, including pre-and post-consumption of a product or service (Vargo & Lusch, 2004; Ballantyne & Varey, 2006; Vargo & Lusch, 2008a). While value is experienced and cocreated (Prahalad & Ramaswamy, 2004; Vargo & Lusch, 2008b), limited attention has been paid to the relationship between customer service experiences and value creation and cocreation practices. Such an examination is vital as customer perceived value and the meanings of particular products and service experiences are no longer fixed and linked to product and service attributes and characteristics (Levy, 2006). This branch of research offers much to consider for Client Leaders.

Helkkula and Kelleher (2010) explore the relationship between customer service experiences and customer perceived value using **narrative inquiry technique**. Narrative inquiry allows researchers to examine experience holistically (Grayson, 1997; Autio et al., 2009; Rahmanian, 2021). In their analysis of the customer narratives, Helkkula and Kelleher (2010) view such narratives as being socially co-constructed, which means that the storytellers (i.e., customers) are self-reflective and embedded in a social context. This enables interpretations between social events and individual customer service experiences built on multiple truths, shifting identity positions concerning customer perceived value and the customer service experience (Rogers, 2007, p. 102). Their findings are telling.

Pettigrew (1997) defines a lived process in terms of cycles of deduction and induction, in which "a sequence of individual and collective events, actions and activities unfold over time in context" (p. 338). The lived critical events analyzed in various blog postings suggest that **circular interrelationships** exist between customer service experience and customer perception of value (Helkkula & Kelleher, 2010). Specifically, their research found that events recounted within iPhone customers' narratives tended to unfold in a chronological or other type of order, which was not necessarily linear. iPhone customers' lived experiences and customer perceived value tended to be circularly constructed through inner social dialogues (Helkkula & Kelleher, 2010). Consumers may appear habitual, but they still have a comprehensive understanding of their products and reappraise product value, even with iPhones (Helkkula & Kelleher, 2010).

Zaman (2020) conceptualizes new iPhone releases as seasonal crops constantly trying to align product value with perceived value. Such narrative inquiries accurately reflect the complex ties between customer service experience and customer perceived value.

This relationship can evolve unconsciously, much like the dynamics discussed in the People Leadership section. Customer engagement, therefore, requires continuous nourishment through excellence and connection. More recently, the focus has turned to value cocreation in service ecosystems (Kaartemo & Helkkula, 2024), which has implications as business leaders and customers embrace the digital future, including AI (see Chapter 12).

Customers are not simple decision-makers; they are complex individuals responding to various cognitive, emotional, and physical signals when purchasing. Strong client relationships can lead to cocreation of value (Kaartemo & Helkkula, 2024). This intricate relationship between experience and value emphasizes fostering brand loyalty (see Chapter 17), maintaining openness to change, building resilience, addressing service failures, and enhancing engagement. To transform customers into loyal clients, Business Leaders must focus on the factors that distinguish ordinary customer service experiences from exceptional ones.

Exercise 14.2 Customer Journeys for Understanding Customer Perceived Value

Understanding **customer perceived value** requires analyzing the **customer journey**, including every interaction with a business, from initial awareness to post-purchase engagement. A **customer persona**—a fictional representation of a target customer based on research—helps companies to anticipate needs, preferences, and pain points. Personas typically include key demographic information, motivations, frustrations, and buying habits.

To begin, work in small groups to create a **customer persona** based on a real-world brand or an assigned customer type. Outline the customer journey stages, including awareness, consideration, purchase, usage, and post-purchase interactions. Within each stage, identify touch points—moments when customers interact with the brand, such as seeing a social media ad, visiting a website, or speaking with customer service.

Once the journey is mapped, assess the perceived value at each touchpoint, considering functional, emotional, and social dimensions. Use color coding to differentiate positive, neutral, and negative experiences, helping pinpoint improvement areas. Then, brainstorm how to enhance perceived value, process efficiency, personalization, and customer engagement.

Present the customer journey map and share insights and recommendations. Make sure any points surpass price, including experiences, emotional connections, and trust-building strategies. Client leaders can enhance loyalty and stay competitive by understanding how customers interact with a brand (see Chapter 17) and where value is created or lost.

Customer Service Excellence

By definition, **customer service excellence** refers to the ability of an organization to meet but, more often, exceed customers' expectations consistently. This implies that the true meaning of customer service excellence is relative to the experience itself and customers' expectations, which also means that the burden of providing excellent customer service falls most decidedly on the organization. Perhaps no industry has encapsulated the pursuit of customer service excellence more than hospitality. As authors, we turn to the **Ritz-Carlton Gold Standards** to separate good versus great organizations in this area. Table 14.1 contains the elements of their Gold Standards (adapted from Michelli, 2015; Schaefer, 2015; Ritz Carlton, 2024).

Michelli (2015) examined what sets the Ritz-Carlton apart and how they have emerged as best-in-class customer service providers. With unprecedented access to executives and staff, they distilled key principles Ritz-Carlton has constantly honed and improved upon that any company can use to provide an exceptional customer service experience. They are:

- Understanding the ever-evolving needs of customers
- Empowering employees by treating them with the utmost respect
- Anticipating customers' unexpressed needs and concerns
- Developing and conducting an unsurpassed training regimen

The lessons from years of customer service excellence by the Ritz-Carlton can be applied across industries and in today's contemporary environments. Trust, transparency, and responsiveness are crucial to successful customer and client relationships. By aligning

TABLE 14.1 Ritz-Carlton Gold Standards Elements

Gold Standard Element	*Description*
Motto	"We are Ladies and Gentlemen serving Ladies and Gentlemen." Employees are expected to treat both guests and colleagues with dignity and professionalism.
Credo	Ritz-Carlton pledges to provide exceptional personal service and facilities, creating a warm, refined ambiance. Employees must anticipate and fulfill unexpressed guest needs.
Twelve Service Values	Employees commit to long-term hospitality excellence through values such as innovation, problem ownership, and professional demeanor.
Three Steps of Service	(1) Warm, sincere greeting with guest's name, (2) Anticipate and fulfill needs, (3) Fond farewell with name acknowledgment.
Service Values	Employees are the company's greatest asset. The Employee Promise focuses on trust, honesty, respect, integrity, and commitment to talent development.
Employees	Ritz-Carlton meticulously selects candidates based on sociability, passion for service, and willingness to learn. Employees act as brand ambassadors.
Training	Minimum of 250 hours of annual training per employee. Training includes coaching, online learning, classroom instruction, and week-long seminars.
21-Day Strategy	On the 21st day, employees are certified in their roles and participate in a forum to discuss challenges and successes, ensuring engagement and retention.

We recognize the gendered nature of this phrasing but the focus really is on sophistication and elevation, thus perhaps sophisticates or gentlepersons may be better wordings toward inclusivity.

company communication, marketing, and sales strategies with these principles, leaders can create a foundation for long-term client satisfaction and loyalty. Further, we would offer that drawing concepts from our People Leadership section, where leaders learn how to manage and treat their employees effectively, is essential for succeeding with customers and clients. Happy employees make for positive customer and client experiences.

The Ritz-Carlton employs a practical framework for continuous improvement, utilizing the *Baldrige Excellence Framework*, as highlighted by Schaefer (2015). According to Jamey Lutz, improvement manager at The Ritz-Carlton Hotel Company, this framework is a guideline for achieving lasting success. Lutz emphasized that the Baldrige framework helps elevate organizational performance (Schaefer, 2015).

Baldrige is a nonprescriptive framework that empowers organizations to reach their goals, improve results, and gain a competitive advantage. It incorporates proven practices on current organizational issues into questions that help leaders manage their company's components as a unified whole. Its core values are found in Table 14.2, which contains lessons for Client Leaders.

TABLE 14.2 Baldrige Framework Adapted and Applied

Core Value	*Description*	*Lessons for Modern Business Leaders*
Systems Perspective	Organizations should function as a unified whole, integrating key processes, goals, and performance measures.	Leaders should align departments, technology, and strategy to ensure all components work cohesively toward a shared vision.
Visionary Leadership	Strong leadership fosters a clear mission, inspires people, and drives performance excellence.	Business leaders must articulate a compelling vision, set high standards, and motivate teams through clarity and purpose.
Customer-Focused Excellence	Organizations must prioritize customer needs, experiences, and relationships.	Companies should continuously gather customer insights, personalize experiences, and adapt offerings to enhance satisfaction and loyalty.
Valuing People	Employees are an organization's most valuable resource and should be engaged, respected, and developed.	Invest in workforce training, well-being, and inclusion to drive productivity, innovation, and long-term retention.
Agility and Resilience	Organizations must be flexible and resilient in adapting to change and uncertainty.	Leaders should embrace digital transformation, prepare for disruptions, and foster a culture of adaptability.
Organizational Learning	Continuous learning and improvement drive long-term success.	Encourage data-driven decision-making, cross-functional collaboration, and ongoing employee development.
Focus on Success and Innovation	Long-term success is linked to innovation and sustained performance improvements.	Foster a culture of innovation by investing in R&D, embracing emerging technologies, and rewarding creative problem-solving.
Management by Fact	Decisions should be based on data, evidence, and sound analysis.	Use key performance indicators, analytics, and market research to inform strategic decision-making.
Societal Contributions	Organizations should contribute to community well-being and sustainability.	Corporate social responsibility initiatives, environmental sustainability, and ethical practices should be core business strategies (see Chapter 18).
Ethics and Transparency	Integrity, fairness, and trust are fundamental to leadership and organizational success.	Maintain ethical governance, clear communication, and accountability at all levels of the organization.
Delivering Value and Results	Organizations should measure success based on stakeholder value and tangible outcomes.	Set clear performance goals, measure impact consistently, and refine strategies to optimize business and customer outcomes.

The Baldrige Framework provides a structured approach for organizations to assess and improve their processes by focusing on key dimensions of performance excellence. These dimensions—Approach, Deployment, Learning, Integration, Levels, Trends, Comparisons, and Integration of Results—help leaders analyze their strategies, refine operations, and drive continuous improvement. By systematically evaluating these areas, Business Leaders can enhance efficiency, increase competitiveness, and foster innovation. Table 14.3 outlines each dimension along with lessons for modern business leaders to apply effectively (Baldrige Performance Excellence Program, 2024).

Lutz highlighted that using the Baldrige framework is highly effective and offers benefits beyond just receiving its esteemed national award. According to him, the framework helps organizations "establish a baseline of where you are as a company" (Schaefer, 2015). Customer service excellence is a "marathon, not a sprint" (Schaefer, 2015). "It has to be

TABLE 14.3 Prompts and Questions to Leverage the Baldrige Framework

Dimension	*Description*	*Lessons for Modern Business Leaders*
Approach	How an organization accomplishes its work, including the effectiveness and consistency of key processes.	Develop *clear, structured workflows* that align with business goals, ensuring efficiency and accountability.
Deployment	The extent to which key approaches are applied consistently across the organization.	Foster *organization-wide adoption* of best practices by ensuring training, communication, and leadership buy-in.
Learning	Continuous improvement through evaluation, knowledge sharing, and innovation.	Implement a *culture of continuous learning*, encouraging employees to refine processes and share insights.
Integration	How well approaches align with organizational needs and contribute to broader goals.	Align all business functions and operations with *long-term strategic objectives* to drive cohesive performance.
Levels	Measuring current performance using meaningful metrics.	Use *key performance indicators* to track efficiency, customer satisfaction, and operational effectiveness.
Trends	Analyzing whether performance is improving, stable, or declining.	Monitor *performance trends* to identify strengths and areas needing proactive intervention.
Comparisons	Benchmarking against competitors and industry leaders.	Conduct *competitive analysis* to understand industry standards and position the organization effectively.
Integration of Results	Using performance data to make informed decisions.	Ensure *data-driven decision-making* by integrating key insights into strategy development and daily operations.

built and reinforced from the highest levels of the organization. It's an ongoing, unrelenting commitment to excellence, and it never ends" (Schaefer, 2015). Client Leaders invest substantial financial, human, and operational resources in customer service excellence.

Consistent follow-ups and prompt resolution of concerns are essential for building lasting, mutually beneficial partnerships with customers who evolve into clients. Strengthening relationships through transparent communication, reliability, and a dedication to enhancing the client's goals further supports service excellence. Each client—indeed, every person—has four specific needs they continuously seek to fulfill: visual, emotional, functional, and financial. Modern leaders must integrate these elements into their business systems to address these needs effectively. The Ritz-Carlton provides a valuable model for creating and maintaining customer service excellence that other organizations can adapt.

Exercise 14.3 Role Play Service Failure

Roleplay a service failure. One partner will play the disappointed customer. One partner will play the customer service rep. One partner will be the observer.

SCENARIO #1: CATERING SERVICE INQUIRY

Customer: Hello, I'm calling to inquire about the catering service I booked for next month's wedding. I'm concerned because I haven't received any confirmation or details about the menu.

Customer Service Representative (CSR): Thank you for contacting me, and I apologize for any inconvenience. Let me look into this for you. Could you please provide me with your name and your wedding date?

Customer: My name is Sarah Smith, and the wedding date is April 15th.

CSR: Thank you, Sarah. Let me check our records ... I'm terribly sorry, but I can't seem to find any booking under your name for that date.

Customer: What do you mean? I booked the catering service months ago and paid a deposit. I have the confirmation email right here.

SCENARIO #2: DISAPPOINTMENT WITH DELIVERABLES

Client: Hello, I wanted to discuss the recent deliverables you sent over. Frankly, I'm quite disappointed with the quality of the work. It doesn't meet the standards we agreed upon, and several errors need to be addressed.

Account Manager (AM): I'm sorry to hear that you're not satisfied with the deliverables. Can you please provide me with specific details about the issues you've identified so that I can address them accordingly?

Client: Where do I start? First of all, the content lacks depth and originality. It feels like a rehash of generic information that's readily available online. Second, numerous grammatical errors and typos exist throughout the document. It's unacceptable for work of this caliber.

AM: I apologize for the oversight. I understand the importance of delivering high-quality work that meets your expectations. Please allow me to thoroughly review the content and identify areas for improvement. I'll coordinate with our team to ensure these issues are addressed promptly.

Client: Frankly, I'm not sure if this is a one-time lapse or indicative of a larger problem with your team's capabilities. We're investing a significant amount of resources into this project, and we expect nothing but the best results.

CONCLUSION

This chapter has built a complex relationship between the customer service experience, the customer perceived value, and customer service excellence. Though nuanced and varied, their interdependence is profound, constituting thoughtful attention from today's contemporary Business Leaders and investment from modern organizations. Understanding each element and appreciating how they are entwined together allows Client Leaders to perform the critical work of converting customers into responsive clients.

The phenomenology lens that allows leaders to unlock the customer service experience, along with narrative inquiries that afford a deep understanding of the multidimensional construct that dictates the customer's perceived value, contributes to an organization's collective efforts to achieve customer service excellence. This ongoing, relentless process is not a one-time, transactional interaction with a customer but a culture positioned with a purpose and fortified by systemic alignment, visionary commitment, continuous learning, employee development, and unparalleled, if not unreasonable, customer focus.

In higher education, relationship-rich experiences with multiple touchpoints for students to know they are supported in their educational journeys have become popular parlance (Felten & Lambert, 2020). Faculty and staff across all levels, including janitorial services, food services, financial aid, admissions, campus life, classroom instruction, IT support, and health services, all impact the student experience. This relationship-richness resonates with Guidara's (2022) concept of *Unreasonable Hospitality* and the FX Hulu series, *The Bear* (Fox, 2022). Guidara (2022) emphasizes creating extraordinary, memorable customer experiences by exceeding their expectations. It parallels the show *The Bear*, where the restaurant's chaotic, service-driven environment transforms to embrace deeper emotional connections and relationships with customers. Both the book and the show demonstrate how Client Leaders can shift from a service-dominant logic, which prioritizes efficiency, to client-centric approaches rooted in personalization, empathy, and tailored experiences to build loyalty and long-term success.

The upcoming chapters on Client Leadership explore client-centric frameworks for influencing client behaviors, managing organizational change, and effectively communicating brand value. These concepts enhance a leader's ability to connect, engage, and retain customers, transforming them into long-term clients. While many organizations emphasize customer focus, client centricity, and relationship management, we aim to deliver practical insights that lead to tangible results in the real world.

DISCUSSION QUESTIONS

1. What is the difference between a client and a customer?
2. Why should organizations want to convert customers into clients?
3. How does the phenomenological lens help us understand the customer service experience?
4. Why is the customer perceived value complex and nuanced?
5. What is the relationship between the customer service experience and customer perceived value?
6. How does S-D Logic elevate our understanding of customer perceived value?
7. How can we transfer the Ritz-Carlton Gold Standards elements to other industries for successful customer service excellence?
8. How should you handle a customer service failure?
9. What can we learn from applying the Baldridge Excellence Framework in other organizations?

Key Terms

- Client
- Customer
- Customer Service Experience
- Customer Perceived Value
- S-D Logic
- Narrative Inquiry Technique
- Circular Interrelationships
- Customer Journey
- Customer Persona
- Customer Service Excellence
- Ritz-Carlton Gold Standards
- Baldrige Excellence Framework

CASE STUDY 14.1 CSE CONSULTING: REPUTATION AT RISK

CSE Consulting is a mid-sized firm that specializes in strategic management consulting for small and medium enterprises. While the firm has experienced consistent growth due to its strong reputation for high-quality services, its leadership team recognized the need to enhance client relationships to differentiate itself in a competitive market.

Despite having a solid framework for customer service excellence, many consultants viewed clients as mere projects, which hindered the development of trust and engagement. To address this issue, CSE Consulting aimed to cultivate a client-centric culture focused on building long-lasting relationships.

To implement this strategy, the firm organized client engagement training for all consultants. This training emphasized empathy, active listening, and effective communication, with role-playing scenarios that allowed consultants to practice responding to client needs.

Additionally, CSE Consulting created a system for individualized communication to monitor client preferences and gather feedback. They also established quarterly client advisory councils for key clients, providing a platform for sharing insights and suggestions. This feedback helps consultants adjust their service offerings and better address client pain points.

Task: Provide four comprehensive recommendations for CSE Consulting to enhance the strategy. Make sure to connect the recommendations to key chapter concepts. Present the recommendations to a larger group for feedback and discussion.

REFERENCES

Addis, M., & Holbrook, M. B. (2001). On the conceptual link between mass customization and experiential consumption: An explosion of subjectivity. *Journal of Consumer Behaviour, 1*(1), 50–66.

Almquist, E., Senior, J., & Bloch, N. (2016). The elements of value: Measuring—and delivering—what consumers really want. *Harvard Business Review*.

Autio, M., Heiskanen, E., & Heinonen, V. (2009). Narratives of 'green' consumers: The antihero, the environmental hero, and the anarchist. *Journal of Consumer Behaviour, 8*(1), 40–53.

Baldrige Performance Excellence Program. (2024). *Baldrige excellence framework*. U.S. Department of Commerce. Retrieved 12 February 2025 from https://www.nist.gov/baldrige

Ballantyne, D., & Varey, R. (2006). Creating value-in-use through marketing interaction: The exchange logic of relating, communicating, and knowing. *Marketing Theory, 6*(3), 335–348.

Batra, R., & Ahtola, O. T. (1991). Measuring the hedonic and utilitarian sources of consumer attitudes. *Marketing Letters, 2*(2), 159–170.

Bolton, R. N., & Drew, J. H. (1991). A multi-stage model of consumers' assessments of service quality and value. *Journal of Consumer Research, 17*(4), 375–384.

Carù, A., & Cova, B. (2007). Consuming experiences: An introduction. In A. Carù & B. Cova (Eds.), *Consuming experience* (pp. 3–16). Routledge.

Felten, P., & Lambert, L. M. (2020). *Relationship-rich education: How human connections drive success in college*. Jhu Press.

Fox, C. (Creator). (2022). *The Bear* [TV series]. FX Networks.

Frow, P., & Payne, A. (2007). Towards the 'perfect' customer experience. *Journal of Brand Management, 15*(2), 89–101.

Graf, A., & Maas, P. (2008). Customer value from a customer perspective: A comprehensive review. *Journal für Betriebswirtschaft, 58*(1), 1–20.

Grayson, K. (1997). Narrative theory and consumer research: Theoretical and methodological perspectives. *Advances in Consumer Research, 24*(1), 67–70.

Grönroos, C. (2008). Service logic revisited: Who creates value? And who co-creates? *European Business Review, 20*(4), 298–314.

Guidara, W. (2022). *Unreasonable hospitality: The remarkable power of giving people more than they expect*. Penguin.

Helkkula, A., & Kelleher, C. (2010). Circularity of customer service experience and customer perceived value. *Journal of Customer Behaviour, 9*(1), 37–53.

Holbrook, M. B. (1994). The nature of customer value: An axiology of services in the consumption experience. In R. Rust & R. L. Oliver (Eds.), *Service quality: New directions in theory and practice* (pp. 21–71). Sage Publications.

Holbrook, M. B. (2006). ROSEPEKICECIVECI versus CV. In S. L. Vargo & R. F. Lusch (Eds.), *The service-dominant logic of marketing: Dialog, debate, and directions* (pp. 208–223). M.E. Sharpe Publishing.

Holbrook, M. B., & Hirschman, E. C. (1982). The experiential aspects of consumption: Consumer fantasy, feelings, and fun. *Journal of Consumer Research, 9*(2), 132–140.

Kaartemo, V., & Helkkula, A. (2024). Human–AI resource relations in value cocreation in service ecosystems. *Journal of Service Management*. Advance Online Publication. Retrievedfrom:https://www.emerald.com/insight/content/doi/10.1108/josm-03-2023-0104/full/html

Levy, S. (2006). How new, how dominant? In S. L. Vargo & R. F. Lusch (Eds.), *The service-dominant logic of marketing: Dialog, debate, and directions* (pp. 57–64). M.E. Sharpe Publishing.

Mathwick, C., Malhotra, N., & Rigdon, E. (2001). Experiential value: Conceptualization, measurement, and application in the catalog and internet shopping environment. *Journal of Retailing, 77*(1), 39–56.

Michelli, J. (2015). *The new gold standard: 5 leadership principles for creating a legendary customer experience courtesy of the Ritz-Carlton hotel company*. McGraw-Hill.

Monroe, K. (1979). *Pricing: Making profitable decisions*. McGraw-Hill.

Pettigrew, A. M. (1997), What is a Processual Analysis?, *Scandinavian Journal of Management, 13*(4), pp. 337–348.

Prahalad, C. K., & Ramaswamy, V. (2004). *The future of competition: Co-creating unique value with customers*. Harvard Business School Publishing.

Rahmanian, E. (2021). Consumption narratives: Contributions, methods, findings, and agenda for future research. *Spanish Journal of Marketing-ESIC, 25*(1), 46–84.

Ritz Carlton. (2024). *Foundations of our brand*. The Ritz-Carlton Leadership Center. https://ritzcarltonleadershipcenter.com/about-us/about-us-foundations-of-our-brand/

Rogers, A. G. (2007). The unsayable, Lacanian psychoanalysis and the art of narrative interviewing. In D. J. Clandinin (Ed.), *Handbook of narrative inquiry: Mapping a methodology* (pp. 99–119). Sage Publications.

Sánchez-Fernández, R., & Iniesta-Bonillo, M. A. (2007). The concept of perceived value: A systematic review of the research. *Marketing Theory*, 7(4), 427–451.

Schaefer, C. (2015). *Ritz-Carlton practices for building a world-class service culture*. The Official Baldrige Blog. Retrieved 12 February 2025 from https://www.nist.gov/blogs/blogrige/ritz-carlton-practices-building-world-class-service-culture

Sheth, J. N., Newman, B. I., & Gross, B. L. (1991a). Why we buy what we buy: A theory of consumption values. *Journal of Business Research*, 22(2), 159–170.

Sheth, J. N., Newman, B. I., & Gross, B. L. (1991b). *Consumption values and market choices: Theory and applications*. South-Western Publishing Co.

Silva, J. H., Mendes, G. H., Cauchick Miguel, P. A., Amorim, M., & Teixeira, J. G. (2021). Customer experience research: intellectual structure and future research opportunities. *Journal of Service Theory and Practice, 31*(6), 893–931.

Vargo, S. L., & Lusch, R. F. (2004). Evolving to a new dominant logic for marketing. *Journal of Marketing, 68*(1), 1–17.

Vargo, S. L., & Lusch, R. F. (2008a). Service-dominant logic: Continuing the evolution. *Journal of the Academy of Marketing Science, 36*(1), 1–10.

Vargo, S. L., & Lusch, R. F. (2008b). Why "service"? *Journal of the Academy of Marketing Science, 36*(1), 25–38.

Wu, D., Guo, K., He, Q., & Zhang, J. (2023). The impact of live streamers' improvisational responses to unexpected events on their entrepreneurial performance. *Journal of Retailing and Consumer Services, 70*, 103163.

Zaman, R. (2020, July 26). *Evolution of iPhone as a seasonal crop: Why does Apple keep releasing better versions?* The Waves. Retrieved from https://www.the-waves.org/2020/07/26/evolution-of-iphone-as-seasonal-crop-why-does-apple-keep-releasing-better-versions/

CHAPTER 15

Drivers of Client Behaviors

CHAPTER OVERVIEW

This chapter explores the drivers of client behaviors and the landscape of client relationships in modern business. It offers concepts such as attentional filtering, emotional primacy, and coherence. The chapter highlights how these factors affect purchasing decisions and loyalty. Organizational strategies must align with client needs and desires to foster long-term relationships beyond mere transactions. This chapter presents practical strategies for enhancing client engagement. This discussion establishes a foundation for effective Client Leadership. It shows the need to build and maintain personalized connections. The chapter also sets the stage for a return to authenticity, reinforcing the significance of enriching client relationships in the chapter and subsequent chapters.

Why do clients do what they do? Why do customers buy what they buy? Or why do they buy again? These questions challenge, if not haunt, many business leaders. In Chapter 7, we focused on motivation theory as an essential skill set for People Leadership. This chapter offers new foundations and additional motivation theories to strengthen ties between companies and clients.

Like organizations, clients have been subject to upheaval, disruptions, and rapid change in recent years. Their loyalty and trust have been challenged, leading to new opportunities and remarkable growth patterns, when realized, for future-forward organizations. Contemporary business leaders must examine and understand the key drivers of client behavior. This chapter explores attentional filtering, emotional primacy, and coherence, using examples to understand each driver's impact on client behavior.

Additionally, we will examine buyer influence and red flags from a strategic sales position. This chapter will help contemporary leaders align their organization's strategy with clients' needs and desires. Finally, we continue building upon the previous chapter, focusing on the developmental relationships between customers and companies through Client Leadership as the mantra to follow. In the next chapter, we return to authenticity, discussed in Chapter 2, focusing on enriching client relationships to bolster client leadership.

DOI: 10.4324/9781003474647-19

CLIENT RELATIONSHIPS

The frequent questions in our discussions regarding client relationships are *"What kind of relationship do we as a company want to have with our clients?" "How retainable are the clients?" "How do we 'remember' clients?" "How is the client feedback fed back into the business?"* Hundreds of our students and workshop participants have moved into professional positions across various industries, often with the title of "account manager," signifying a key responsibility: **client relationships**. Effectively navigating the critical relationship with buyers of products and services (i.e., clients) lies at the heart of Client Leadership and is essential for the success of organizations.

Readers have learned that leadership is inherently a relational process. In the People Leadership section, we surveyed the implications of supervisor-employee relationships. Similarly, we approach the account manager-client relationship with nuance and depth. Many professional roles directly interact with clients, while others operate more indirectly. An organization's financial viability, feasibility, and sustainability heavily rely on its ability to build and maintain strong client relationships. This relationship-building is not merely intuitive but a skill that must be practiced and refined over time.

This constitutes a tailored approach. To paraphrase what Thimothy (2021) wrote in *Forbes*: since clients are unique individuals, and no one is alike, understanding the client's market, competitors, practices, business model, and short- and long-term goals is essential when building a business or managing accounts. While platforms like LinkedIn make it easier than ever for business leaders to research and connect with clients, there is no substitute for preparation before an engagement, whether virtual or in-person.

Once a leader has done their background research, Thimothy (2021) recommends giving relevant advice to a client. Client leaders leverage internal and external expertise to engage in meaningful problem-solving conversations with clients, foster long-term relationships, and communicate a product or service's value (Thimothy, 2021). Through ongoing communication, this iterative process ensures alignment with client goals, needs, and challenges. Client leaders establish a productive and timely cadence through email, Zoom, Microsoft Teams, WebEx, or in-person strategy sessions, distinguishing themselves from competitors by fostering relationships beyond mere business transactions (Thimothy, 2021). They foster personal connections with clients, employing skills discussed previously, such as active listening and constructive feedback.

DRIVERS OF CLIENT BEHAVIOR

Several factors influence client behavior, including psychological, social, cultural, personal, and economic factors. Contemporary leaders must understand how these factors impact the buying process to understand what turns a prospective lead into a buying client. Client behavior is shaped by psychological factors like perception and attitudes, social factors like family and roles, cultural factors like traditions and values, personal factors like lifestyle and age, and economic factors like income and spending patterns. Each one offers insight into predictable client behavior when engaged in business relationships.

Motivational Theories Redux

Contemporary business leaders must deeply understand various motivational theories to engage and retain long-term clients. Four core theories were briefly mentioned in Chapter 7 on Motivation: **expectancy theory**, **self-efficacy theory**, the **theory of planned behavior and reasoned action model**, and **goal setting theory**. These theories may be essential for understanding how clients make decisions and how those decisions are influenced by their experiences with the company. These theories offer practical insights into the drivers of client behavior. Client leaders can align their strategies with client motivations based on these insights.

Expectancy theory, proposed by Vroom (1964), asserts individuals are motivated to act if those actions are perceived to lead to desired outcomes. This theory explains why clients engage with a service or product. For instance, if a client perceives that investing in a product or service will lead to a specific reward—such as increased efficiency, profit, or satisfaction—they are more likely to purchase. For example, clients might choose a software solution because they believe the product will save time or increase profitability, reinforcing the value of clearly communicating product benefits. Modern business leaders know how to enrich their clients' expectancy so that they can believe in themselves and the value of their actions to make purchasing decisions that are best for both parties.

This aligns with attentional filtering (discussed in the following subsection), where clients focus on information that signals potential rewards while disregarding what they perceive as irrelevant. Business Leaders can apply this theory by ensuring that their offerings match client expectations and demonstrate how those products or services can lead to tangible, beneficial outcomes. Businesses can increase the likelihood of positive client behavior by ensuring clients understand the link between effort, performance, and reward (Vroom, 1964).

Self-efficacy theory, developed by Bandura (1986), focuses on individuals' beliefs in their ability to succeed in specific situations. Client confidence is integral for decision-making to occur. If clients doubt their team's ability to implement a new technology, they may hesitate to buy it. To boost their self-efficacy, client leaders can provide training, demos, and testimonials from successful peers. Again, confidence is essential for a positive customer experience and encourages clients to engage and commit for the long term. Demonstrating ease of use, providing transparent onboarding processes, and ensuring strong customer support systems are all ways to leverage self-efficacy theory to improve client retention (Bandura, 1986).

The **theory of planned behavior** and **reasoned action model**, proposed by Ajzen (1991) and Fishbein and Ajzen (1975), suggests that behavior is determined by intentions influenced by attitudes, subjective norms, and perceived behavioral control. A client's attitude toward a product—shaped by their beliefs, experiences, and social influences—determines whether they will take the desired action, such as purchasing. For instance, if a potential client perceives a product as practical (positive attitude), sees other industry peers using it (subjective norm), and believes they have the resources to implement it (perceived behavioral control), they are more likely to move forward with the purchase. In contrast, negative perceptions may hinder action. Business leaders can effectively influence client behavior using social proof, case studies, or peer endorsements to enrich subjective norms, and providing training and resources enhances perceived behavioral control (Fishbein & Ajzen, 1975; Ajzen, 1991).

Environmental concern is particularly significant in shaping consumer behavior regarding the purchase of eco-friendly products, as highlighted in the theory of planned behavior and the theory of reasoned action (refined to the reasoned action model). Consumers with environmental awareness develop better attitudes toward green products, which boosts their intention to buy them. For example, consumers who care about the environment usually have positive views on sustainable products driven by social norms that support eco-friendliness. Moreover, how easy it is to access these green products also influences their buying choices. Thus, environmental concerns intersect with psychological drivers; leaders can tailor their strategies to meet the rising demand for sustainable options (Ajzen, 1991; Wandani et al., 2024). In our community leadership section, we dive more into environmental concerns and sustainability.

Goal Setting Theory emphasizes the power of clear, specific, and challenging goals in motivating individuals. Clients are likelier to engage in behavior that helps them achieve specific and measurable objectives (Locke & Latham, 1990). Modern business leaders impact how clients set goals for their success, whether improving operational efficiency, increasing sales, or reaching other key performance indicators.

By aligning products and services with these goals, client leaders enhance client motivation to engage with and achieve desired results. For example, a company selling marketing software may set a goal for clients to increase web traffic by 20% within six months. Clients are more likely to engage with products and services when they can track their progress toward specific goals. Client leaders help clients set realistic yet challenging goals. They provide them with the necessary tools to build long-term relationships beyond just transactions. Success in this approach depends on clear goals and ongoing constructive feedback (Locke & Latham, 1990).

With these motivational theories (among others in Chapter 7), contemporary business leaders can better understand their clients' motivations and behaviors. Expectancy theory highlights the importance of aligning client expectations with engagement outcomes, while self-efficacy theory underscores the need to provide clients with the confidence and tools to succeed. The theory of planned behavior and reasoned action model emphasize the role of attitude, social norms, and perceived control in shaping client intentions. The goal-setting theory illustrates the motivational power of clear, measurable objectives and ongoing feedback.

Attentional Filtering

But what about the unpredictable? Further examination of the psychology of behavior is necessary to gauge what a unique client might do in a particular situation. As authors, we offer the concept of **attentional filtering**, which is to focus and sustain one's attention on a specific item to filter out the others that aren't relevant in a given moment. Specifically, attentional filtering helps us understand why one focuses on some things while simultaneously ignoring others. Though not a new concept, its relevance today cannot be overstated in a world where clients receive a barrage of stimuli through media, often through multiple electronic devices, from competitors both large and small in a chaotic cycle of marketing, prospecting, and solicitation campaigns designed to earn their business. The noise is deafening for many clients, and creating the essential relationship that leads to purchasing requires that a leader *speak* to the client's attentional filtering.

Two theories of attention build on each other: **Broadbent's (1958) filter model and Treisman's (1969) attenuation model**. Broadbent's research led to the early selection model, where he claimed that the filter eliminates the unattended information right at the beginning of the flow of information. Since that research, psychologists have added layers of sophistication to Broadbent's original idea of how attention operates, claiming that instead of a filter, which barred unattended inputs from ever entering awareness, it was an attenuation process.

Attenuation is the process of reducing value or effect. Attenuation theory, also known as Treisman's attenuation model, is a framework of selective attention proposed by Anne Treisman (1969). It is seen as a revision of Broadbent's (1958) work. Treisman (1969) proposed attenuation theory to explain how unattended stimuli were often processed more rigorously. Treisman (1969) states that the attenuation of unattended stimuli made extracting meaningful content from irrelevant inputs difficult but not impossible, so long as stimuli still possessed sufficient "strength" after attenuation to make it through a hierarchical analysis process.

Treisman's (1969) model is meaningful because it suggests that audiences (i.e., clients) display tremendous agency in their choice, interpretation, and retention of messages. To effectively leverage clients' agency, we turn to **emotional primacy**, which indicates stimuli characterized by a greater persuasion because it reaches one of our primary emotions. Using primacy ensures that emotions are at the forefront of concerns and messaging (see Chapter 17 for more on messaging). The primary emotions vary but often include fear, anger, joy, sadness, disgust, contempt, and surprise. Some also include shame, shyness, and guilt. The primacy of these emotions hit popular media in Pixar productions like *Inside Out* (Docter, 2015) and *Inside Out 2* (Docter, 2024). Continuously, business leaders recognize that stimuli that have sufficient strength with clients are those that invoke one or more of these human-centric emotions (Roberts, 2009).

Roberts (2009) emphasizes the superior effectiveness of emotional advertising over rational messaging in influencing critical business outcomes. Table 15.1 summarizes these findings.

Client Leaders understand that emotional primacy significantly enhances attentional filtering. To capture a client's attention in a crowded market, client leaders must use strategies that connect emotionally. Personal touches in communication are crucial. For

TABLE 15.1 Key Findings on Emotional Primacy

Key Findings	*Summary*
Emotional vs. Rational Advertising	Emotionally based campaigns outperformed rational ones across all business measures (sales, market share, profit, etc.).
Profit Generation	Emotional appeals are nearly twice as likely to generate substantial profit gains as rational appeals.
Impact of Emotion	The more emotion dominates, the more significant the business impact; the most effective ads minimize rational content.
Price Sensitivity	Emotional advertising reduces price sensitivity.

example, remembering a client's last vacation, their children's names, recent health concerns, or their interests can help the client leader get noticed, build relationships, and earn trust. While campaigns that use tools like ChatGPT are standard for efficiency, client leaders ensure they add that personal touch to emails.

We emphasize the importance of **coherence** in effective client leadership, as it significantly influences client behavior. Coherence refers to the alignment between the customer experience and the brand. Leaders maintain this coherence, and their ability to do so directly affects all customer relationships. This framework aims to describe and deliver an exceptional experience tailored to specific customer segments. The objective is to transform customers into long-term clients. Modern business leaders excel at delivering consistent messages that convey value to clients, and their organizations consistently fulfill these promises.

Maintaining coherence is crucial in client leadership. For example, a tech company launching a new product might confuse potential clients if they receive mixed messages about the products and brand. This inconsistency erodes trust. Client Leaders weave coherence into every interaction by utilizing various channels and approaches to avoid confusion. They must meticulously manage interactions to build trust and ensure clarity in messaging.

As noted, Client Leaders recognize how attentional filtering, emotional primacy, and coherence influence client behavior. By applying these concepts systematically throughout the organization, Client Leaders can foster a culture of client-centricity that is currently highly sought after. They can continue to promote practical strategies that lead to real improvements and build strong client relationships. These are learned skills and essential components of success.

Exercise 15.1 Writing an Email Campaign

Sample Email
Subject Line: "See How [Product Name] Can Change Your Team Dynamics"
Body:

Hi [First Name],

Last week, we discussed enhancing your team's collaboration. Today, we will examine [Product Name]'s key features that make it a game-changer.

(Attentional Filtering) *We know you're busy, so we'll keep it brief: here's how [Product Name] directly addresses your needs.*

(Emotional Primacy) Imagine your team effortlessly working together, where every member feels valued and empowered. Miscommunication and frustration will be a thing of the past.

(Coherence) Here's what you can expect:

- **Real-Time Updates**—Stay informed with instant notifications.
- **Integrated Tools**—All the apps you need work in harmony.
- **Customizable Workflows**—Adjust the platform to fit your unique needs.

Curious to see these features in action? Book your demo today.

Best,
[Your Name]
[Your Position]
[Your Company]

Review the sample email. Then, research a company and its signature product. Imagine you are an account manager charged with targeting a new client through an email campaign. How could you use attentional filtering, emotional primacy, and coherence in your unique email campaign? Share with a partner.

BUYER INFLUENCE

While this chapter focuses on client leadership, particularly client behaviors, it is essential to address sales, which often play a central role in client relationships. In many cases, sales can be the primary objective of such relationships. To gain further insight into client leadership from a sales perspective, we turn to Miller et al.'s (2011) *The New Strategic Selling*.

Miller et al. (2011) examine client leadership in today's business environment, where change, disruption, and uncertainty are constants. They focus on **complex sales**, which they define as sales processes in which multiple stakeholders must approve or provide input before the deal is finalized (Miller et al., 2011, p. 37). Their strategy equips sales professionals to effectively identify and engage all key players necessary to achieve their sales objectives. Crucially, they emphasize the importance of focusing on roles rather than titles, urging professionals to avoid distractions that may arise from job positions (Miller et al., 2011, p. 37). According to their framework, every complex sale involves four key buying influences.

Table 15.2 summarizes key roles in the buying process, each with a distinct impact on whether a sale is approved. Identifying all four key buying influences and creating

TABLE 15.2 Key Roles in the Buying Process

Role	*Description*
Economic Buying Influence	Due to their financial decision-making power, this individual can approve or veto a sale. They often have the final say.
User Buyer Influence	This role assesses the impact of the product or service on job performance. The individual's success is tied to the product's effectiveness, as they will be responsible for supervising and using it.
Technical Buying Influence	This person screens out suppliers by evaluating how well a product or service meets specific criteria. While they can't make the final decision, they can reject suppliers who don't meet the necessary standards.
Coach	The coach helps the client leader by guiding them to the right buyers and providing helpful information to effectively position their product or service. This role can be found within or outside the client organization and aims to assist in making the sale.

relationships with them is the foundation of Miller et al.'s (2011) concept of strategic selling. Miller et al.'s (2011) work resonates with us as they are after satisfied customers, long-term relationships, repeat business, and good referrals (2011, p.41). Much like ours, their philosophy advocates for client leaders to look beyond the single transaction and to manage the account and the relationships it includes skillfully. Miller et al. (2011) encourage win-win scenarios with clients where "you both come out of the sales feeling satisfied, knowing that neither of you has taken advantage of the other, and that both of you have profited, personally and professionally, from the transaction" (p. 41). This is essential for client leaders.

Consumer behavior is a dynamic process shaped by various economic, psychological, and cultural factors affecting how clients engage with products and services (Czinkota et al., 2021). Understanding buyer behavior is essential for client leadership, particularly in addressing consumer needs and fostering long-term relationships. Building on Miller et al.'s (2011) work, Czinkota et al. (2021) advocate for understanding the buyer within the broader context of marketing management, illustrating how client behavior guides purchasing decisions.

Buyer needs are not solely dictated by rational thinking but are also influenced by emotional and social drivers (Czinkota et al., 2021), similar to emotional primacy discussed by Roberts (2009). Failure to account for these influences can result in misaligned marketing efforts. These lessons can be carried forward to Chapter 17 on organizational brand. Client Leaders must tailor their approach to meet the nuanced desires of clients, balancing emotional resonance with functional needs. Combining emotional and rational factors, this holistic view of buyer behavior provides critical insights for client leadership in ever-changing markets.

Exercise 15.2 Mapping Buying Influence

Complete Table 15.3. In groups or individually, answer the following:

- What is the strategy for engagement with each buying influence role?
- How does influence differ across the roles?
- Who comes to mind when viewing these roles?
- Which roles might be the most complex or most straightforward to work with?

TABLE 15.3 Mapping Buying Influence Activity

Role	*Description*	*Influence Level*	*Key Responsibilities*	*Potential Strategies for Engagement*
Economic Buying Influence	This key player has the financial authority to approve or veto a sale, often having the final say.	High	- Approves budget allocations - Reviews proposals	

TABLE 15.3 (Continued)

Role	*Description*	*Influence Level*	*Key Responsibilities*	*Potential Strategies for Engagement*
User Buyer Influence	This role evaluates the product/service's impact on job performance and has personal stakes tied to its success.	Medium	- Tests and assesses products - Provides feedback	
Technical Buying Influence	Responsible for screening suppliers and recommending how well offerings meet specified criteria.	Medium	- Evaluates technical specifications - Conducts product comparisons	
Coach	A guide who helps the client leader navigate the buying process, often providing insights and connections to other influencers.	Variable	- Shares knowledge of the organization - Introduces key stakeholders	

RED FLAGS

While we have outlined drivers that influence client behavior in a positive direction, Miller et al. (2011) highlight red flags or signs when the relationship is in trouble. They use the term **red flag** because it is used in everyday language as a signal for "warning" or "danger," which is exactly how a client leader should regard these common mishaps that can derail a relationship (2011, p. 72). Often, these mishaps present as incomplete or uncertain areas in a sales strategy where the objective is for the client to make a purchase. On the surface, the client relationship seems fine, but when the leader examines it closely, there are holes, gaps, or "fuzzy" information (Miller et al., 2011, p. 72). These are immediate red flags (see Table 15.4).

While numerous items can derail a client relationship, Miller et al. (2011) focus on five prevalent red flags (summarized in Table 15.4). First, they highlight missing information. What they do so well is help sales professionals construct a strategy to identify key players with buying influence (2011, p. 73). As client leaders engage with multiple stakeholders within corporate structures, they must understand who will most influence sales. When this information is missing, they cite this as a major red flag or sign that the sale is in danger (2011, p. 73). It could also indicate that the leader's relationship is superficial instead of solid.

Second, Miller et al. (2011) draw a distinct difference between scenarios with a lack of information versus uncertainty of relevant data. Uncertainty is generally worse, but both situations warrant red flags. As Miller et al. (2011) describe:

TABLE 15.4 Red Flags

Red Flag	*Description*
Missing Information	When key information about buying influences is missing, the sale is at risk, and the relationship may be superficial.
Uncertainty of Relevant Data	Uncertainty occurs when incomplete or conflicting data is present, making it difficult to assess the sale accurately.
Uncovered Base	Failing to contact or engage all relevant decision-makers creates uncertainty in the sales process.
Turnover in Key Players	Changes in key positions introduce new buying influencers, which can disrupt the relationship and affect the sale.
Reorganization	Reorganization can drastically alter the buying influence landscape, requiring a reorientation of the account and sales strategy.

> At least when you know you're missing a piece of the puzzle, you can take steps to track it down. When you have a piece that 'looks right' but doesn't quite fit, you risk force-fitting what you already 'know' into your analysis and ignoring what you need to know.
>
> (p. 73)

This can put the sale at risk and harm the client relationship. When faced with uncertainty, it's important to reexamine the account and closely consider buying influence roles.

Third, Miller et al.'s (2011) strategy is often used in complex sales where there are multiple key players behind layers of an organization that the client leader must penetrate. Therefore, their third prevalent red flag is the client with buying influence that has not been contacted. Miller et al. (2011) call this "an uncovered base," using a baseball metaphor. They explain further, "You can field a team without one or more of your key players, and you can close a complex sale without contacting all the relevant buying influences. But you'll do so under conditions of extreme uncertainty" (Miller et al., 2011, p. 74). While it might not be a practical approach to contact all persons with buying influence individually, arranging contact with everyone by someone is the principal responsibility of the client leader as the "strategic orchestrator" (Miller et al., 2011, p. 74). Failure to do so can mean the sale is not a lock.

Fourth, Miller et al. (2011) reference that turnover in key players can be a red flag and jeopardize a client relationship. As a client leader, it is essential to prepare for this prevalent scenario where a key player has moved on elsewhere, and there is a new face in their old position. Miller et al. (2011) explain, "Ignoring a new buying influence like this is always the wrong way to manage a complex sale" (p. 74). Further, Miller et al. (2011) describe this new buying influencer as a threat until the client leader clearly understands their role and how they feel about the leader's proposal (2011). Engaging them early and often is essential to restoring the relationship and moving forward with the sale.

Finally, a clear red flag that is frequent in business is reorganization. This is even more difficult to manage than turnover with key players, as a client leader's map of buying influence might shift drastically due to reorganization at the company (Miller et al., 2011). As this text has described, the business world is constantly in flux. Miller et al. (2011) add, "Whenever you encounter hirings, firings, promotions, consolidations, or expansions, in fact, anything that alters your decision-makers' organizational structure, you should reach immediately for your red flags" (p. 75). In this era of mergers and acquisitions, reorganizations are often easy to spot. The remedy is a deep dive into the account, almost to start again, to reorient and then map the new key players with buying influence.

Exercise 15.3 Reengaging with a Client After a Merger

Get into groups of 4 or 5. An account manager faces several challenges when a client has recently gone through a merger. Develop six key re-engagement strategies for the account manager whose client has gone through a merger. Present a plan and discuss approaches for re-engagement. Table 15.5 contains the key challenges faced regarding re-engagement.

TABLE 15.5 Key Challenges in Re-Engaging

Category	*Issue*	*Description*
Changing Organizational Structure	Role Confusion	New roles and responsibilities may lead to uncertainty about who the key decision-makers and influencers are.
	Integration of Teams	Different company cultures and processes can complicate collaboration and decision-making.
Evolving Priorities and Goals	Shifts in Strategic Focus	Mergers often result in new business objectives that may not align with previous priorities, requiring the account manager to adapt their approach.
	Resource Allocation	Budget and resource shifts may affect the client's ability to invest in ongoing projects or new initiatives.
Relationship Management	New Stakeholders	Establishing rapport with new contacts and understanding their perspectives takes time and effort.
	Loss of Established Relationships	Existing contacts may leave or change roles, making it necessary to rebuild trust and understanding.

Category	*Issue*	*Description*
Communication Challenges	Inconsistent Messaging	With multiple teams merging, communication can become fragmented, leading to misunderstandings or mixed signals.
	Cultural Differences	Merging organizations may have different communication styles and practices, complicating interactions.
Resistance to Change	Internal Resistance	Employees may resist new processes or changes in strategy, affecting buy-in for new initiatives.
	Navigating Power Dynamics	The merger might create rivalries or power struggles that complicate the account manager's role.
Need for Strategic Realignment	Adapting Solutions	The account manager may need to adjust their offerings or solutions to better suit the new organizational structure and goals.
	Reassessing Value Proposition	Understanding how to communicate the value of their services in light of the merger's impact on the client's needs.

CONCLUSION

This chapter has concentrated on theories and practices that foster strong client relationships. To enhance client relationships, Client Leaders understand the factors influencing behavior and incorporate practical strategic selling principles. This chapter highlights five key red flags that client leaders should watch out for. While various situations can jeopardize a relationship, these common scenarios can guide client leaders in knowing when to reassess their account, realign buyer influences, and implement a more effective strategy to improve outcomes. Sales are essential, but relationships are the foundations for long-term sales.

Client Leaders skillfully manage the drivers of client behavior through customized approaches, open communication, and data-driven insights. They can respond more effectively when they recognize the factors influencing client behavior. Attentional filtering, emotional primacy, and coherence are critical to client relationships and strategies for managing them. Like many others we have taught and mentored, we look forward to seeing our readers step into roles where they can notably impact their organization's success with clients.

DISCUSSION QUESTIONS

1. What are the best techniques for a first meeting with a client?
2. How should client leaders maintain the relationship with a client?
3. What essentials drive clients' behaviors?
4. How can client leaders apply the concepts of attentional filtering, emotional primacy, and coherence to client relationships?
5. How can organizational leaders transfer a client-centric culture into a company?
6. How can strategic selling help client leaders?
7. What red flags are common during the sales process?

Key Terms

- Client Relationships
- Expectancy Theory
- Self-Efficacy Theory
- Theory of Planned Behavior and Reasoned Action Model
- Goal Setting Theory
- Environmental Concern
- Attentional Filtering
- Broadbent's Filter Model
- Treisman's Attenuation Model
- Attenuation
- Emotional Primacy
- Coherence
- Complex Sales
- Economic Buying Influence
- User Buyer Influence
- Technical Buying Influence
- Coach
- Red Flag

CASE STUDY 15.1 CREATIVE SOLUTIONS MARKETING IN CRISIS

Creative Solutions Marketing, a digital marketing agency in an urban center, was tasked with developing a marketing strategy for Tech Innovations Inc.'s new software aimed at small businesses. However, the project faced challenges due to Tech Innovations' unclear expectations. While they had a general idea of their goals, the lack of specificity led to assumptions-based strategies that resulted in rework and wasted resources, frustrating the agency team and slowing project progress.

Another challenge was the client's tendency to micromanage. Tech Innovations frequently requested updates and involved themselves in every decision, which created bottlenecks and stifled the agency's creativity. This micromanagement made the creative team feel undervalued, impacting their motivation and productivity.

Midway through the project, Tech Innovations shifted its focus from small businesses to larger enterprises, necessitating a complete overhaul of the marketing strategy. This sudden pivot increased costs and caused delays, as the agency had to adjust its content, targeting, and outreach strategies to align with the new priorities.

Finally, communication styles between the client and the agency added to the tension. Tech Innovations' abrupt communication often led to misunderstandings and frustration within the team, making it difficult to receive positive feedback. This hindered collaboration and problem-solving, complicating the project's overall progress.

Task: Provide four comprehensive recommendations for Tech Innovations leaders. Connect the recommendations to key chapter concepts. Present the recommendations to a larger group for feedback and discussion.

REFERENCES

Ajzen, I. (1991). The theory of planned behavior. *Organizational Behavior and Human Decision Processes, 50*(2), 179–211.

Bandura, A. (1986). *Social foundations of thought and action: A social cognitive theory*. Prentice-Hall.

Broadbent, D. E. (1958). *Perception and communication*. Pergamon Press.

Czinkota, M. R., Kotabe, M., Vrontis, D., & Shams, S. M. R. (2021). Understanding the buyer. In M. R. Czinkota, M. Kotabe, D. Vrontis, & S. M. R. Shams (Eds.), *Marketing management: Past, present and future* (pp. 135–176). Springer. https://doi.org/10.1007/978-3-030-66916-4_4

Docter, P. (Director). (2015). *Inside Out* [Film]. Walt Disney Pictures, Pixar Animation Studios.

Docter, P. (Director). (2024). *Inside Out 2* [Film]. Walt Disney Pictures, Pixar Animation Studios.

Fishbein, M., & Ajzen, I. (1975). *Belief, attitude, intention, and behavior: An introduction to theory and research*. Addison-Wesley.

Locke, E. A., & Latham, G. P. (1990). New directions in goal-setting theory. *Current Directions in Psychological Science, 15*(5), 265–268.

Miller, R. B., Heiman, S. E., & Tuleja, T. (2011). *The new strategic selling* (Revised 3rd ed.). Miller Heiman Group.

Roberts, K. (2009). Emotional primacy. *American Association of Advertising Agencies*. https://krconnect.blog/2009/11/emotional-primacy.html

Thimothy, S. (2021, October 4). Putting customer retention first. *Forbes*. https://www.forbes.com/councils/forbesagencycouncil/2021/10/04/putting-customer-retention-first/

Treisman, A. M. (1969). Strategies and models of selective attention. *Psychological Review, 76*(3), 282–299. https://doi.org/10.1037/h0027242

Vroom, V. H. (1964). *Work and motivation*. Wiley.

Wandani, F. T., Widodo, A., Rubiyanti, N., & Silvianita, A. (2024). Analysis of the influence of environmental concern, theory of planned behavior, and theory of reasoned action on purchase intention: A conceptual paper. *International Journal of Scientific Multidisciplinary Research, 2*(5), 499–508.

CHAPTER 16

Managing Change in the Client Landscape

CHAPTER OVERVIEW

This chapter helps Client Leaders understand and respond to global and industry shifts by being adaptable. It introduces skillsets, frameworks, and practices that empower leaders to manage change and uncertainty. The discussion interconnects external factors (e.g., economic shifts, social norms, and environmental challenges) with client behavior. The chapter's insights surpass traditional topics like product quality or pricing. Through proactive engagement and strategic foresight, leaders can build resilient client relationships and foster a collaborative organizational culture. This chapter encourages leaders to synthesize insights from the World Economic Forum's Global Risks Report and develop innovative approaches to mitigate emerging threats. This chapter guides contemporary business leaders to thrive amidst complexity and lead their clients toward a sustainable and shared vision.

Rapid advances in technology, geopolitical crises, ethnocentrism trends, political polarization, the residual effects of the pandemic, and climate change effects have accelerated the pace of change today's leaders must manage. Additionally, today's leaders face increased uncertainty instead of risk, which can be easily named and predicted. Client-focused leaders need to build new toolkits to manage in these settings. This chapter will equip leaders with the key skill sets, frameworks, and practices to lead themselves and their clients in an increasingly complex world.

This chapter overviews the current client landscape, highlighting the need for Client Leaders to address significant global and industry shifts and lead change. This chapter offers frameworks for effectively managing change. Finally, the chapter focuses on adaptive leadership, teaching leaders to navigate high uncertainty through intentional and focused approaches with clients.

THE CURRENT CLIENT LANDSCAPE

The business world and the **client landscape** are irrevocably entwined. A contemporary leader is immersed in the work of being both a business leader and a client leader. Factors

DOI: 10.4324/9781003474647-20

like the environment, economic shifts, social norms, technological developments, talent pool changes, laws and regulations, market trends, growth, and public health crises (among others) impact business. We also refer to this as the client landscape. More importantly, leaders must understand how these contexts determine client behavior even more than the quality, delivery, or price of a platform, product, or service. By recognizing these factors, Client Leaders can proactively act and react better to client movements.

Client Leaders operate and thrive under conditions of uncertainty, even amid significant threats. The World Economic Forum's *Global Risks Report 2025* highlights several apparent threats on the horizon. While some regions indicate economic recovery and digital progress, many remain burdened by financial instability, conflict, and climate-related crises. For example, disparities in access to life-saving medicines and slow economic recovery are reflected in unfavorable conditions like income inequality and hindered global stability. The report also highlights concerns such as state-based armed conflicts and rising extreme weather events impacting supply chains and trade. Mis/disinformation and amplified societal polarization are additional threats (World Economic Forum, 2025). Client Leaders acknowledge the urgent need to mitigate the effects of climate change and the need to build resilience and foster adaptability. The global risk landscape is clear: challenges require foresight and collaboration across borders and sectors.

Exercise 16.1 **Synthesize the Current Client Landscape**

Divide into small groups of four to five individuals. Explore a theme from the most recent Global Risks Report published by the World Economic Forum, such as economic recovery, technology and innovation, sustainability, or social inequality. Discuss the data or statistics that support the theme and recommendations found in the report. Discuss opportunities given threats posed. Reflect on how to apply these opportunities in client relationships, mitigating threats.

Following the discussion, visually summarize the discussions using a whiteboard or flipchart. This visual representation can include statistics or data points, charts, graphs, and bullet points. Be creative, utilizing colors, drawings, or icons to make presentations more engaging. As a larger group, come up with a five-minute pitch to a potential client in a relevant industry.

MANAGING CHANGE

Some business leaders think managing change is a discipline that only applies internally to their people, processes, and products. As described previously, the current client landscape requires leaders to frequently implement change to meet their clients' evolving needs. Adaption, pivots, innovation or reinvention, and all constituents' principles and conditions are related to **change management**. Traditionally, leaders who have been the drivers of successful change have been lauded as creative, risk-takers, calculating, strategic, genius, or pioneering. It is increasingly evident that all contemporary leaders must skillfully and adeptly manage change to effectively steer their organizations and thrive in these highly uncertain times.

Client Leaders recognize barriers to change, such as resistance from team members or misalignment with organizational values, and proactively address these challenges. They craft thoughtful and tailored change strategies that build client relationships, foster resilient company culture, and align team efforts with long-term goals. Client Leadership is about guiding others toward a shared vision, which inherently involves transitioning from the current state to a more desirable future (Middlebrooks et al., 2019). Leaders who embrace this opportunity for growth and transformation will find more success. Table 16.1 highlights real examples of the levels of change discussed next.

Most leaders assume roles that require them to affect and manage change locally or globally. We often ask students and workshop participants, "*Think of a personal change you want to make. What makes personal change so difficult?*" The responses are revealing.

Personal change can catalyze a confluence of emotions, including fear of the unknown, anxiety about the future, embarrassment when unsuccessful, and disruption to routine. Examining the barriers to personal change can help business leaders who are trying to implement broader organizational change. Table 16.2 describes these emotions and how to address them.

TABLE 16.1 Levels of Change with Examples

Type	*Description*	*Example*
Personal Change	Personal change involves shifts in an individual's mindset, habits, or behaviors. It is often the starting point for broader change, requiring self-reflection, discipline, and a commitment to growth.	Steve Jobs' transformation was key to Apple's success. After being ousted from the company he founded, Jobs returned with a new approach focused on innovation, design, and simplicity. His ability to change personally and professionally laid the foundation for Apple's most successful products, such as the iPhone, by fostering a culture of creativity and resilience.
Incremental Change	Smaller efforts or initiatives that build upon existing processes or structures. These changes are often gradual and require trust-building to gain the confidence of stakeholders.	Toyota's Kaizen approach to continuous improvement, where small incremental changes in manufacturing processes led to long-term operational excellence.
Strategic Change	Change that involves significant shifts in the way an organization operates, such as changing processes, systems, or structures. It requires coordination, strategic vision, and communication.	Apple's transition from primarily a computer company to a leader in consumer electronics required a shift in product strategy, operations, and marketing to align with new market demands.
Transformational Change	Large-scale, fundamental shifts that redefine the organization's culture, mission, or long-term vision require a complete overhaul and are often driven by external pressures or innovations.	Netflix's shift from a DVD rental service to a global streaming giant required a complete overhaul of business models, content delivery systems, and organizational culture.

TABLE 16.2 Emotions and Actions

Emotion	*Description*	*Possible Actions to Take*
Fear of the Unknown	Fear arises when the outcomes of change are uncertain, leading to hesitation and avoidance of necessary steps.	Leaders should start by seeking clarity on the potential outcomes and setting a clear vision of the change, reducing fear and increasing confidence.
Anxiety About the Future	Anxiety about the future emerges from worries regarding the long-term impact of change, especially when facing large-scale transformation.	Developing a roadmap with realistic goals and timelines can reduce anxiety while encouraging open discussions about the potential challenges.
Embarrassment	Embarrassment occurs when leaders fear public failure or feel insecure if their efforts to change are unsuccessful.	Leaders should embrace vulnerability, openly acknowledge mistakes, and view failures as learning opportunities rather than permanent setbacks.
Frustration	Frustration is common when the change process becomes complicated, slow, or unclear, often causing the leader to feel stuck or ineffective.	Frustration can be alleviated by breaking the change into smaller, manageable steps and celebrating incremental progress to maintain momentum.
Disruption to Routine	Disruption of routine can cause discomfort as personal and professional habits are altered, demanding new skills and approaches.	Establishing new routines gradually and providing adequate support can help ease the disruption and encourage adaptability in daily operations.
Resistance	Resistance is a natural response to change, particularly when the leader or others feel the new approach challenges their values or role.	Leaders should address resistance directly by explaining the benefits of change, involving team members in the process, and offering opportunities for input.

These emotions that prevent personal change increase exponentially when the change is large-scale across an organization. People generally struggle with change and often dislike it. The established methods are familiar and efficient, while new approaches demand learning and practice. Change can lead to frustration and discomfort; even when employees understand the change is beneficial, they may resist it. Clients also experience similar emotions when faced with change. If they view the change as an improvement, they will adapt; however, if the change is poorly implemented or seen as a setback, clients may express their dissatisfaction strongly. When managing change, a leader can be overwhelmed by these powerful emotions, internally and externally, thus requiring a modern toolkit for change.

Contemporary business leaders are **change agents**. They shape and guide organizational change. People look to their leaders to set the tone and guide how to navigate change (see our previous chapters on followership). A leader can either demonstrate openness to change or exhibit resistance. Their actions can communicate a purposeful, goal-oriented focus or a disorganized, hesitant approach lacking a clear vision. According to Middlebrooks et al. (2019), change involves becoming different from oneself or fostering differences in others or things, which is essential for facilitating transformation. To successfully innovate within an organization, leaders must first embrace change. If leaders are unable or unwilling to change, inspiring others within and outside the organization becomes challenging.

Incremental change refers to smaller efforts or initiatives that still require focus to build effective working relationships for gaining the confidence of those with whom the organization's future success depends. Harking back to the relationship-building chapter, here is where trust pays dividends with followers, making the leader more influential. That influence will be necessary to persuade others that a specific change is worth the effort (Middlebrooks et al., 2019), even when the change is only incremental. During volatile times, incremental changes allow others to test change and validate that they will have the proper support and resources to make the change. To paraphrase Middlebrooks et al. (2019): *What gradual adjustments can leaders implement to prepare their followers for more enormous transformations? How can a leader emphasize the significance and benefits of these minor modifications?*

Microsoft's evolution under CEO Satya Nadella illustrates incremental change. The company transitioned from conventional software sales to a subscription-centric model. This evolution commenced with the launch of Office 365 in 2011, which provided users with a subscription option for the Office suite. Following this, Microsoft introduced Azure, its cloud computing platform, a substantial revenue generator. These shifts over time enabled Microsoft to build client trust and reshape company culture to prioritize customer insights and needs. This methodical approach has played a vital role in sustaining Microsoft's success within a fiercely competitive landscape (Fourie, 2023).

Conversely, **large-scale change** is a more complex process that requires integrating a strategic vision into change initiatives that redirect attention to entirely new processes, systems, or structures (Middlebrooks et al., 2019). Large-scale change requires a more extensive level of innovation, coordination, and communication. For example, reducing the hierarchy levels in an organization, designing an entirely new product line, or initiating a work-sharing practice reflects large-scale innovative processes (Middlebrooks et al., 2019). Client leaders use frameworks to innovate systematically through strong relationships and a healthy company culture.

Under Elon Musk, Tesla changed its focus from just making electric cars to becoming a leader in sustainable energy access. Tesla expanded its product lines to include electric vehicles, solar energy products, and energy storage solutions. Tesla adopted new manufacturing methods to support this shift. This transformation required hefty investment and strong leadership, setting Tesla apart from its competitors. Although the approach was risky, Tesla disrupted the automotive and energy sectors. Post COVID-19, Musk and Tesla's strategy regarding work-from-home and flexibility arrangements is changing. This illustration tethers large-scale vision to large-scale innovation (Lacey, 2024).

Strategic change is a substantial but less radical shift compared to transformational change. It entails processes, systems, or structures alterations to better align with the organization's long-term objectives or external conditions. While **transformational change** often completely redefines the company's culture, mission, or market position, strategic change optimizes existing frameworks to improve efficiency or adapt to market shifts. A clear example of strategic change can be seen in Apple's evolution from primarily a computer company to a leader in consumer electronics. In response to industry changes,

Apple shifted its product strategy, expanded its operations to include mobile devices, and revamped its marketing strategies to be a lifestyle brand, inspiring a generation of consumers to this day to question, "Am I a PC or a Mac person?" This shift required a thorough reevaluation of its operational models and new product lines (.e., iPhone, iPad, & Apple Watch), which paid off in spades (DocuSign, 2023).

As demonstrated by Apple, strategic change is targeted and surgically focuses on improving aspects of the company (DocuSign, 2023). Client Leaders must be able to reorganize existing structures or refine processes to compete better or meet new needs. Client Leaders leverage transformational change, like Netflix's shift from DVD rental by mail to streaming, to fundamentally alter operations, if not completely overhaul the business model (Kobiruzzaman, 2022). Transformational change is typically more disruptive, reshaping the organization's core functions and future trajectory, while strategic change is more about refining and optimizing what already exists to maintain relevance and competitiveness in the market.

Change often comes suddenly and can be debilitating if leaders are unprepared. Fortunately, leaders can take many approaches to anticipate change. Contemporary business leaders must continuously learn about modern trends, following events and movements worldwide. If this toolkit is applied with precision and skill, disruption can serve as an opportunity for change. The entrepreneurial leader disrupts balance when stasis becomes untenable or brings balance during crucial moments of imbalance (Talmage, 2021). Next, we outline frameworks for change.

CHANGE FRAMEWORKS

Change can evoke intriguing reactions in those who appear to be losing control over their work life. One reaction is to continue to do those tasks the way they have always been done and to undercut the change process. This individual will likely resist change and make their coworkers uncomfortable about accepting any change. Others may desire to accelerate change by setting new goals and work routines to adjust to new conditions. Similarly with clients, if leaders have developed strong relationships, managed expectations, and engaged their clients in the steps to change, their acceptance of the change is much more likely.

This section explores the multifaceted nature of change and how leaders can effectively guide individuals and organizations through its various stages. Change often elicits emotional responses, from resistance in the form of denial or anger to a desire for progress. Readers might revisit our previous chapters on motivation and emotion.

Client Leaders can apply the stages of change, inspired by Kübler-Ross's grief model and Prochaska's Model of Change, to manage transitions within their teams or organizations. Change is emotional, and Client Leaders must seek to foster confidence, optimism, and resilience. They must demonstrate clear communication, emotional support, and strategic guidance to navigate each phase successfully. They need to focus on maintaining momentum after the change has been implemented. Prochaska's and ADKAR's models can help sustain change, reinforcing new behaviors well beyond the initial shift. Planning and feedback in tandem help client leaders embed an affinity for change into organizational culture, bolstering long-term success. This section provides client leaders with the essential tools to drive effective change.

Stages of Change

Client Leaders understand the stages of change to help leaders guide their teams and clients through transitions. Middlebrooks et al. (2019) adapt the stages of grief model created by Kübler-Ross (1969) to reflect the change process. We modify this model to help Client Leaders facilitate positive transformation within their organizations and communities (see our next section on Community Leadership).

The first stage, often described as **shock or denial**, occurs when individuals or teams feel perplexed and may start blaming others for the changes around them. This is typically followed by a stage of **anger**, where feelings of anxiety, frustration, and embarrassment emerge (Middlebrooks et al., 2019). Next comes the **depression** stage, characterized by feelings of overwhelm and helplessness. This is where effective leadership is crucial. As individuals or teams move from depression to **dialogue**, they become more open to exploring alternatives, leading to **acceptance**. Engaging in conversations with friends, colleagues, and mentors allows them to transition to a stage where they can accept the need for change and begin developing new plans (Middlebrooks et al., 2019).

Client Leaders navigate their teams through these stages by fostering confidence, optimism, resilience, and engagement. Client Leaders display these qualities during times of change and uncertainty. Instead of resisting or avoiding change, they lead by example. Table 16.3 offers examples of actions leaders can take during each stage.

TABLE 16.3 Stages of Change and Actions for Leaders

Stage	*Description*	*Actions Leaders Can Take*
Shock or Denial	Individuals or teams feel perplexed and may start blaming others for the changes around them.	Provide clear, transparent communication to address concerns and reassure those uncertain about the changes.
Anger	Feelings of anxiety, frustration, and embarrassment arise, often fueled by rapid, disruptive changes.	Acknowledge feelings of frustration and offer support through problem-solving discussions or stress-reducing activities.
Depression	Feeling overwhelmed and helpless when individuals or teams struggle to cope with the change.	Offer emotional support, encourage self-care, and help employees break the change process into manageable steps.
Dialogue	Individuals or teams become more open to exploring alternatives through conversations and engaging with others.	Foster open dialogue through feedback sessions, create opportunities for idea-sharing, and build a collaborative environment.
Acceptance	Individuals begin accepting the need for change and developing new plans or strategies.	Encourage forward thinking, highlight small wins, and provide ongoing guidance and resources regarding new strategies.

Prochaska's Model of Change

Middlebrooks et al. (2019) also offer a proactive model of personal behavior change called **Prochaska's Model for Change** (see also Prochaska & DiClemente, 1983; Norcross et al., 2011). This model is based on research on changing health behaviors (e.g., smoking in Prochaska & DiClemente, 1983). It provides a practical guide for addressing individuals' thoughts and feelings during the change process. The stages are described in Table 16.4.

The change process consists of several stages, and two often overlooked stages in leadership are pre-contemplation and maintenance. In the pre-contemplation stage, individuals may not recognize the need for change, which can hinder progress (Middlebrooks et al., 2019). Leaders should highlight the possibilities for change and showcase different perspectives on what could be improved, refined, or adjusted. This early recognition is crucial to initiate the change process.

The final stage, maintenance, is equally important yet frequently neglected. Once individuals have moved through contemplation and preparation to implement change, they must have a strategy and context to reinforce this change consistently (Middlebrooks et al., 2019). Relying solely on individual willpower is insufficient, and even less

TABLE 16.4 Prochaska's Model of Change with Actions

Stage	*Description*	*Actions Leaders Can Take*
Pre-contemplation (Not Ready for Change)	Individuals are not yet ready for change and may not even recognize its need. They are unaware of potential improvements or tweaks.	Showcase possibilities for change that help individuals see the benefits and potential improvements and create awareness about the need for change.
Contemplation (Thinking About Change)	Individuals start considering change but have not yet made a decision. They weigh the pros and cons and begin thinking about possibilities.	Encourage and support individuals in reflecting on their current behaviors, weighing the pros and cons, and guiding them through their decision-making process.
Preparation (Preparing for Action)	Individuals begin preparing for change by gathering resources, creating plans, and seeking support to implement the change.	Help individuals develop clear plans, set achievable goals, and ensure they have the resources and support needed to initiate change.
Action (Make Change Happen)	Individuals actively engage in the change process, putting plans into action and starting to modify behaviors or strategies.	Support individuals during the action phase by providing structure, monitoring progress, and offering reinforcement to maintain momentum.
Maintenance (Maintaining the Changed Behavior)	After the change, individuals must reinforce the new behavior and ensure it becomes routine.	Secure a long-term plan reinforcing the change, providing continuous support, and helping individuals maintain the change in the face of challenges.

effective is organizational willpower. Therefore, leaders must design the change process comprehensively, from the initial awareness of the need for change to the ongoing reinforcement long after the change has been instituted (Middlebrooks et al., 2019).

ADKAR Model of Change

Organizations do not change unless the individuals within them change (Middlebrooks et al., 2019). Resistance to change at both the individual and organizational levels is a normal response, so leaders need to plan for it, expect it, and accept it as part of the change process. People only change when they are Aware of the need for change and the alternatives, Desire the change, Know how to go about changing, are Able to implement it on a day-to-day basis, and Reinforce the change to stay in place. This is called the **ADKAR model of change** (Hiatt, 2006), and many activities for successful individual and organizational change essentially follow these criteria (Hiatt, 2006; Middlebrooks et al., 2019). Table 16.5 describes stages with actions for leaders.

Interestingly, some of the most notable organizational change failures are not due to a lack of analytical skills but rather a lack of social skills among organizational leaders (Middlebrooks et al., 2019). Consider some of this text's essential components of Part 2, People Leadership. Engaging the model's Self, People, Business, and Client Leadership principles is key when implementing change. According to McKinsey & Co., just 30% of change initiatives succeed (Middlebrooks et al., 2019).

TABLE 16.5 ADKAR Model of Change with Actions

Stage	*Description*	*Actions Leaders Can Take*
Awareness	Individuals must understand why the change is necessary and know the potential alternatives.	Communicate the reasons for the change clearly, making sure individuals understand why the change is necessary and the benefits it brings.
Desire	Individuals must want to engage in the change process, fostering a personal commitment.	Inspire commitment by aligning the change with individuals' values, showing how it benefits them and the organization.
Knowledge	Individuals must know how to make the change happen, including the necessary skills and tools.	Provide training and resources, ensuring individuals have the knowledge and skills to implement the change.
Ability	Individuals need to be able to implement the change day-to-day, translating knowledge into action.	Offer support and practical tools, allowing individuals to practice the change and build the confidence to apply it consistently.
Reinforcement	Change must be reinforced to become permanent, ensuring the new behavior is sustained.	Recognize and reward those who embrace the change, providing ongoing feedback and support to reinforce the new behaviors and prevent regression.

Change models used by those in leadership roles are essential in setting the stage for how individuals will achieve something new and different. Change, by definition, requires a new system and institutionalizing new approaches for getting things done. While effective change depends on the leader's mindset, contemporary Client Leaders can select numerous models to help plan change execution. Action plans help leaders apply these models in practice.

Kanter (2004) at Harvard Business School specializes in strategy, innovation, and leadership for change. The following **Action Plan** in Table 16.6 was adapted from her Educational Toolkit.

TABLE 16.6 Adapted Action Plan

Component	*Explanation*	*Action*
Description	Describe your change. Name the problem you want to solve, the issue you wish to address, or the contribution you will make to your organization. Why is it important?	Clearly define the change you wish to bring about and explain why it is necessary, including its potential impact on your organization or community.
Stakeholders	Leadership is a relational process. To implement change, you need support from others in your community. Who are your key stakeholders? How will you get their buy-in?	Identify the key stakeholders whose support is vital for implementing the change. Develop strategies to secure their buy-in and commitment to the change process.
Action Vehicle	All good ideas need an engine. Engines are educational programs, clothing drives, petitions, or other initiatives that move the idea forward. What is the engine that will support your change? What global models, programs, or concepts could you innovate locally?	Determine the driving force or initiative that will move the idea forward. Explore local innovations or global programs that can be adapted for your context.
Quick Wins	When working with communities, collective leaders need to maintain momentum. This supports the action vehicle and inspires the group to push through challenges. What short-term goal can you reach? How can you use this goal to motivate your team?	Set short-term goals that can demonstrate progress, motivate your team, and build momentum. These quick wins will help maintain engagement and commitment to the long-term goal.
Sustainability	Significant change takes time. Collective leaders use quick wins to motivate but plan for long-term sustainability. What are your long-term goals? How will you keep your team focused?	Focus on creating a long-term plan for sustaining the change. Ensure your team remains motivated and aligned with the initiative's overarching goals.
Feedback	Good leaders don't need to be right; they want to get it right and recognize success! How will you gather and use feedback from your team? How will you know you're making an impact? How will you communicate your success and recognize your team?	Create a mechanism to collect feedback regularly, use it to adjust the change process, and communicate successes to ensure the team remains engaged and motivated.

Exercise 16.2 Apply the Action Plan

Break into pairs. Consider a problem that needs changing, whether on campus, at a job, or in a community. Using the Action Plan steps in Table 16.6, generate a multifaceted solution. Allow time for each pair to present.

Change management in this client landscape can be chaotic, stressful, and sometimes arduous. There is no guarantee that the change process a leader implements will work. Change is quite unpredictable; all the planning in the world may not prevent failure from occurring. The side effects of change are difficult to predict, maneuver and manage. But leaders can unlock the keys to effective change. One fundamental key lies in rethinking how the leader sees oneself relative to their employees—focusing on doing change with people rather than doing change to/for them (Middlebrooks et al., 2019). Still, modern business leaders must be able to adapt.

ADAPTIVE LEADERSHIP

To build a more sustainable world in an era of profound economic and environmental interdependence, contemporary leaders and modern organizations are challenged to sift through the knowledge of their heritage, take the best from their history, leave behind lessons that no longer serve them, and innovate (Heifetz et al., 2009). Not just for change's sake but to preserve the most essential values and competencies. We would be remiss if they did not advocate for applying adaptive leadership among increasing uncertainty and rapid, discontinuous change.

Increasingly, leaders need adaptive practices with new forms of improvisational expertise (Heifetz et al., 2009). Client Leaders have process expertise and know how to experiment with never-been-tried-before relationships and approaches to interaction. They help people develop solutions that build upon and surpass current knowledge. As this text has stated, organizations need distributed leadership because the solutions to these complex challenges must come from many places, with people developing **micro-adaptions** to all the different micro-environments (Heifetz et al., 2009).

Adaptive leadership is an approach to progressing on the most critical challenges leaders face in their organizations. This concept aims to help contemporary leaders mobilize people toward some collective purpose, a purpose that exists beyond their ambition (Heifetz et al., 2009). The practice of adaptive leadership, like the practice of medicine, involves two core processes: **diagnosis** first and then **action**. Those two processes unfold in two dimensions: toward the organization and the leader. The leader must diagnose what is happening in their organization and take action to address the problems they have identified (Heifetz et al., 2009). Yet, to lead effectively, they must also examine and take action toward themselves in the context of the challenge. Amid action, leaders have to be able to reflect on their attitudes and behavior better to calibrate their interventions to the complex dynamics of organizations (Heifetz et al., 2009). This is where the dimensions of Self, People, Business, and Client Leadership work together.

The process of diagnosis and action begins with data collection and problem identification (the what), moves through an interpretive stage (the why), and on to potential

TABLE 16.7 The Key Elements and Activities of Adaptive Leadership

Element	*Description*	*Real-World Examples*
Observing Events and Patterns	Leaders need to observe events, behaviors, and patterns to understand what is happening in the environment and among stakeholders.	In the 2008 financial crisis, leaders at banks and financial institutions closely observed market behaviors, customer reactions, and emerging economic patterns to understand the depth of the crisis.
Interpreting the Observation	Leaders develop multiple hypotheses about what is going on based on their observations, attempting to understand the root causes and implications of the situation.	In response to the crisis, many banks and companies in the industry interpreted the situation by considering multiple hypotheses: whether the issue was liquidity, trust, or systemic risks in the market.
Designing Interventions	Leaders design interventions based on their observations and interpretations, taking action to address adaptive challenges and refine strategies as needed.	After analysis, financial leaders intervened by implementing various strategies, such as restructuring business models, securing government bailouts, and improving customer communication to address the adaptive challenges.

approaches to action as a series of interventions into the organization (the what next) (Heifetz et al., 2009). The problem-solving process is typically iterative, moving back and forth among the data collection, interpretation, and action. This is much more reflective of the rapid, discontinuous state of change that contemporary leaders face today.

Adaptive leadership is an iterative process involving three key activities outlined in Table 16.7. Each activity builds on the one before it, making the overall process iterative. Adaptive leaders repeatedly refine their observations, interpretations, and interventions to address complex problems effectively (Heifetz et al., 2009).

Client Leaders and direct reports feel pressure to solve problems quickly to move to action (Heifetz et al., 2009). So, they minimize the time spent on diagnosis, collecting data, exploring multiple possible interpretations of the situation, and alternative potential interventions. To counteract this drive toward a quick-fix response based on a too-swift assessment of the situation, adaptive leaders spend a lot of on diagnosis ("What is really going on here?") for both the system-level and the self-level sections of the adaptive leadership process (Heifetz et al., 2009). Client Leaders use adaptive leadership to manage change under great uncertainty.

Exercise 16.3 Practicing Adaptive Leadership with Clients

This exercise explores how adaptive leadership guides clients through change or uncertainty. You will learn how to diagnose a situation effectively, engage stakeholders, manage conflict, and foster collaboration. You will propose an environment where all voices are heard, which is crucial for making decisions during uncertain times.

You will also practice strategies for helping clients navigate change, resolve differences, and work toward cohesive solutions.

Select a scenario from Table 16.8. Your firm is hired by a company facing rapid market changes. The client is anxious about an upcoming "big move," and there are conflicting internal opinions regarding the strategy. They operate in a competitive sector where innovation and market shifts are quick. Resistance to change is high. You will guide them through this uncertainty, ensuring that all stakeholder perspectives are considered and the team develops a unified strategy.

Divide into small groups to address each scenario. Each group must practice the perspectives of different stakeholders from the client organization. Stakeholders must include the key stakeholders in Table 16.8, but can also include the CEO, CFO, marketing director, customer experience manager, and product manager, each with various goals, challenges, and objectives.

Once roles are assigned, discuss the situation within your group. Your task is to understand the goals and obstacles of your assigned role while considering how these may conflict with others. Then, brainstorm adaptive leadership strategies to engage effectively with the client. Consider how you will facilitate communication, build rapport, and encourage stakeholder collaboration.

TABLE 16.8 Adaptive Leadership Scenarios

#	*Scenario Description*	*Key Stakeholders*	*Client Challenges*
1	A nonprofit organization is facing financial constraints and internal disagreements over resource allocation. The board is split between focusing on fundraising and expanding programs. Your task is to guide the board through a decision on prioritizing resources and aligning their strategy.	Board Members (split between fundraising vs. program expansion)	Lack of alignment on priorities, financial constraints, pressure from donors and board members, and uncertainty about future funding.
2	A retail company has seen a dramatic shift in customer preferences, and leadership is divided on whether to focus on revamping existing stores or investing in online shopping capabilities. You must help the leadership team navigate these options and align the team on a path forward.	Retail Leadership Team (split between revamping stores vs. investing online)	Shifting customer preferences, divided opinions on resource allocation, and difficulty assessing the long-term benefits of both options.
3	A tech start-up is experiencing rapid growth, but the leadership team is conflicted about the company's direction. One group wants to pursue international expansion, while another believes the company should first solidify its position domestically. You must help the team decide where to focus resources.	Tech Start-Up Leadership Team (split between international expansion vs. domestic market consolidation)	Rapid growth causes strain on resources, division of priorities, and uncertainty about how to approach new markets.

#	*Scenario Description*	*Key Stakeholders*	*Client Challenges*
4	A university is planning to implement a new curriculum but faces resistance from faculty members. Some faculty members are concerned about the changes to their workload, while others are excited about the potential for innovation. As a leader, you must help the administration navigate this resistance and facilitate buy-in from faculty.	University Administration and Faculty (split between support for new curriculum vs. resistance)	Resistance from faculty due to changes in workload and teaching methods, concerns about the impact of new curriculum on existing programs.

Once your group has developed a strategy, role-play a client meeting where one group member will act as the lead consultant. The consultant will guide the meeting, ensuring that each stakeholder's viewpoint is shared and that conflicts are addressed. You will use active listening, empathy, and conflict management to navigate differing opinions and facilitate decision-making. After the role-play, solicit peer feedback and undertake a debriefing session. Reflect on what strategies worked well, the challenges you faced, and how you adapted to the situation.

CONCLUSION

At its simplest, adaptation means continuous incremental improvement through small and frequent releases. Client leaders must hold similar desires to change and remember the advantages of startup modes and entrepreneurial mindsets (see Chapters 13 and 20). Bray (2017) writes, "…unlike existing organizations, (startups) lack legacy processes or technologies. Startup founders can reimagine a new way of doing business without the burden of how things "used to work" in their organization." Startups are, by definition, entities of experimentation, thriving off of the action or process of trying out new ideas, methods, or activities. These leaders are accustomed to failure, and successful leaders learn to do it cheaply, quickly, and without heartbreak or emotion. Such concepts embedded broadly within an organization's culture would generate a deep, lasting resilience under the disruptive conditions described in this chapter.

When applied to leadership principles and frameworks, there can be profound effectiveness for confronting uncertainty and change while also having "thick skin" when tackling the next shift. During times of complexity, competition, and obstacles, there is an instinct to hunker down, weather the storm, stay the course, and hold fast to what's in one's control. As described in the Business Leadership section, that mentality will lead to company complacency, which is detrimental to survival. Though it may appear counterintuitive, leaders must take calculated risks (when calculations are possible) and lean into experimentation to achieve meaningful change.

As for client relationships, this chapter has developed the repertoire of contemporary leaders for managing change in the current landscape. When change is handled poorly, an organization's connection to its clients suffers the most. While understanding the current client landscape, the various components of change, and applying adaptive leadership can improve relationships overall, the focus here trains a steady gaze on clients. Viewing them first as people experiencing various effects from the pandemic, geopolitical conflicts, and climate change can significantly enhance strategies for engaging, retaining, and strengthening client relationships.

DISCUSSION QUESTIONS

1. What are the conditions currently impacting business and clients?
2. Why is it important to be aware of the disruptions caused by the residual effects of COVID-19, current geopolitical crises, and the ongoing implications of climate change when managing relationships with clients?
3. How does understanding change management prepare leaders to guide clients through change?
4. What does effectively executed change look like?
5. What components are needed when a leader is navigating change within their organization and must communicate it externally to clients?
6. What are the benefits of change models and action plans?
7. Why do the principles of adaptive leadership apply in this current client landscape?
8. What missteps should leaders avoid in this current client landscape?

Key Terms

- Client Landscape
- Change Management
- Personal Change
- Change Agent
- Incremental Change
- Large-Scale Change
- Strategic Change
- Transformation Change
- Stages of Change
- Prochaska's Model of Change
- ADKAR model of change
- Action Plan
- Micro-Adaptions
- Adaptive Leadership
- Diagnosis
- Action

CASE STUDY 16.1 TECH INNOVATORS INC. MANAGING CHANGE IN THE CURRENT CLIENT LANDSCAPE

Background: Tech Innovators Inc. is a mid-sized technology consulting firm specializing in digital transformation and emerging technologies since its establishment in 2010. The company appeared in the wake of the Great Recession of 2008, marked by significant financial instability and business uncertainty. The recession had lasting impacts on industries worldwide, forcing many companies to rethink their operations and embrace new technologies to stay competitive. Tech Innovators Inc. capitalized on this need by helping clients integrate cutting-edge technologies into their operations. The firm quickly built a reputation for guiding clients through digital transformation, but it has faced significant challenges in recent years. Rapid technological advancements, geopolitical unrest, and shifting market dynamics have created opportunities and risks for Tech Innovators Inc. and its clients.

The company's clients, spanning industries such as retail, healthcare, and manufacturing, have been directly impacted by several forces. The COVID-19 pandemic accelerated the need for digital transformation across industries, with clients demanding more agile solutions to adapt to remote work, shifting consumer behaviors, and evolving market expectations. Emerging technologies, such as artificial intelligence, machine learning, and blockchain, are reshaping the competitive landscape, placing pressure on clients to innovate quickly or risk losing market share. Additionally, the geopolitical unrest that followed the 2008 financial crisis, particularly between major economic powers, has introduced uncertainty in global supply chains and business operations. Clients are concerned about the implications of trade policies, tariffs, and regional instability. As a result, Tech Innovators Inc. faces the challenge of helping its clients adapt to rapid technological changes, manage supply chain disruptions, navigate evolving regulations, and build resilience in a volatile environment.

Among Tech Innovators Inc.'s clients, the retail sector has struggled with supply chain disruptions and the shift to e-commerce, exacerbated by the financial instability following the Great Recession. A leading healthcare provider seeks assistance in implementing telehealth solutions amidst changing regulations. Meanwhile, a manufacturing company faces difficulties sourcing materials due to geopolitical tensions affecting its supply chains. These client challenges highlight the need for Tech Innovators Inc. to offer tailored solutions that address rapid technological changes, compliance with regulatory shifts, and organizational resilience. As the firm continues to support its clients through these challenges, it must develop comprehensive recommendations that align with the current client landscape while incorporating adaptive leadership strategies to manage change effectively.

Task: Provide four comprehensive recommendations for the leaders at Tech Innovators. Make sure to connect the recommendations to key chapter concepts. Present the recommendations to a larger group for feedback and discussion.

REFERENCES

Bray, D. A. (2017). Three meaningful strategies for managing rapid change. *MIT Sloan Management Review*. Retrieved from https://sloanreview.mit.edu/article/three-meaningful-strategies-for-managing-rapid-change/

DocuSign. (2023). *3 Lessons in Innovation from Netflix, Apple and Google*. Retrieved from https://www.docusign.com/blog/3-lessons-innovation-netflix-apple-and-google

Fourie, C. (2023, November 16). Radical vs Incremental Business Transformation: When and which matters most for CEOs? *Signium*. Retrieved from https://www.signium.com/news/radical-vs-incremental-business-transformation/?utm_source=chatgpt.com

Heifetz, R. A., Linsky, M., & Grashow, A. (2009). *The practice of adaptive leadership: Tools and tactics for changing your organization and the world*. Harvard Business Press.

Hiatt, J. M. (2006). *ADKAR: A model for change in business, government, and our community*. Prosci

Kanter, R. M. (2004). *The change leadership toolkit: A guide to the leadership competencies of the future*. Harvard Business Press.

Kobiruzzaman, M. M. (2022). *Netflix Organizational Change & Structure Case Study 2022. Kennisbank Sociale Innovatie*. Retrieved from https://wp.kennisbanksocialeinnovatie.nl/wp-content/uploads/2022/09/Netflixorganizationalchange.pdf

Kübler-Ross, E. (1969). *On death and dying*. Macmillan.

Lacey, S. (2024, May 15). Musk's extremely hardcore pivot: 'It's astonishing what's happened to Tesla'. *Latitude Media*. Retrieved from https://www.latitudemedia.com/news/carbon-copy-musks-extremely-hardcore-pivot-its-astonishing-whats-happened-to-tesla/

Middlebrooks, A., Allen, S. J., McNutt, M. S., & Morrison, J. L. (2019). *Discovering leadership: Designing your success*. Sage Publications.

Norcross, J. C., Krebs, P. M., & Prochaska, J. O. (2011). Stages of change. *Journal of Clinical Psychology, 67*(2), 143–154.

Prochaska, J. O., & DiClemente, C. C. (1983). Stages and processes of self-change of smoking: Toward an integrative model of change. *Journal of Consulting and Clinical Psychology, 51*(3), 390–395.

Talmage, C. (2021). Social entrepreneurship: A needed tool for contemporary community development education. *International Journal of Community Well-Being, 4*(2), 227–243.

World Economic Forum. (2025). *The Global Risks Report 2025*. World Economic Forum. https://www.weforum.org/reports/the-global-risks-report-2025

CHAPTER 17

Communicating Brand

CHAPTER OVERVIEW

This chapter explores the multifaceted nature of branding. It highlights the role of Client Leaders in forging authentic connections and fostering trust among stakeholders through intentional communication strategies. Client Leaders align branding with an organization's mission, vision, and core values to navigate operational changes and public perceptions. The concept of the organizational brand triangle is introduced, exploring the interrelation of value propositions, mission and vision statements, and social responsibility. The chapter also introduces the productivity star as an evolution of the productivity triangle. The chapter illustrates how effective brand management can enhance loyalty, instill confidence, and bolster reputation.

Way beyond its logo, tagline, or color scheme, a company brand tells the stories of employees, clients, shareholders, and community partners. This chapter explores how a brand can foster meaningful connections and stakeholder trust. Contemporary business leaders, as Client Leaders, leverage intentional communication strategies to ensure their brand resonates with different audiences while still true to an organization's mission, vision, and core values.

Client Leaders ensure that strategy or operational shifts are consistent with branding. Effective leadership requires guiding clients through a reflective process of understanding how change impacts not just the tactical aspects of their business but also how it resonates with their internal and external stakeholders. A core responsibility of leaders is to help their clients clearly define or refine their brand identity, ensuring that their mission, vision, and core values are communicated and authentically represented in every interaction, product, and decision.

For instance, Client Leaders work with companies to assess whether their internal operations, customer touchpoints, and public messaging align with their mission and vision statements. They may also work with individuals on their executive presence and personal brands. If a company shifts its product offerings, a leader's role is to help ensure these changes are tied to the organization's overall purpose. When tech companies change, new technologies and their features, interfaces, and other attributes must align with branding. Similarly, when clients struggle with public perception, such as crisis control

DOI: 10.4324/9781003474647-21

due to bad publicity, Client Leaders can help them adjust their branding strategies to (re) build trust and reaffirm company values. Client Leaders enable their clients to create more substantial and authentic brands for the long term.

WHY IS BRAND ALWAYS IMPORTANT?

Branding is more than just a logo or a marketing tool; it is the identity that defines how an organization is perceived internally and externally. As a Client Leader, understanding why a brand is always important is essential for guiding clients through growth, transformation, or crisis management. Brands showcase core values, mission, and vision, which we cover in this chapter. Brand primes and manages how stakeholders interact with and perceive a company.

Building a strong brand relies on clarity, consistency, authenticity, and consistent themes throughout this book. Client Leaders adopt holistic brand communication approaches so that every product, service, and client interaction mirrors mission and vision statements. Well-articulated brands instill confidence, bolster loyalty, and evoke a collective sense of purpose. In the social media, influencer, and digital era, Client Leaders must be mindful of how their personal and professional identities align with the brand. David Brier (2017) is well known for saying, "If you don't give the market the story to talk about, they'll define your brand's story for you" (Oh Design Studio, n.d.). This chapter guides Client Leaders in telling their stories strategically and effectively with clients.

This chapter introduces the organizational brand triangle—a framework emphasizing three interconnected areas: (1) value propositions; (2) mission and vision statements; and, (3) social responsibility, sustainability, and shared value. These components serve as guiding principles for aligning brand communication with the expectations of internal, external, and community stakeholders. Across stakeholder types, tailored brand communication strategies are needed.

Brand Components

A brand comprises several elements that influence its perception among consumers. Ashley Friedlein, founder of Econsultancy and CEO of Guild, is credited with the quote: "Brand is the sum total of how someone perceives a particular organization. Branding is about shaping that perception" (Oh Design Studio, n.d.). One essential aspect is **brand identity**, which includes the visual, sensory, and verbal characteristics that define the brand and set it apart from rivals. The brand identity encompasses the logo, business name, color palette, typography, and messaging. When these components work harmoniously, they create a unified and unique image of the brand. For modern businesses, a robust brand identity is critical; it not only differentiates them from competitors but also promotes customer loyalty and helps establish a trustworthy reputation in the marketplace (Creative Soup, n.d.).

Conversely, **brand image** refers to how current and potential customers perceive the brand. This image consists of consumers' beliefs, thoughts, and impressions based on interactions with the brand and various environmental influences. While **brand identity** is deliberately designed and controlled by the company, brand image is shaped by consumers' perceptions and experiences. Client Leaders develop strong brand identities to ensure consumer perceptions align with intended company perceptions (Key Differences, n.d.). **Brand familiarity** is how much consumers recognize a brand. Higher levels of brand familiarity can enhance trust and preference, leading consumers to favor brands that they are familiar with. Client Leaders cultivate and maintain brand familiarity through consistent branding efforts tied to quality products or services (Vaia, n.d.). Table 17.1 contains a complete list of brand concepts that Client Leaders know when communicating with stakeholders.

TABLE 17.1 Essential Brand Concepts for Client Leaders

Brand Concepts	*Definition*	*Why it Matters*	*Example*	*References*
Brand Identity	The visual, sensory, and verbal elements that represent a brand, including logo, colors, typography, and messaging.	Differentiates the brand, fosters loyalty, and builds recognition.	Apple's sleek design and minimalist logo reinforce its brand identity.	Aaker (1996)
Brand Image	Brand perceptions are based on experiences, beliefs, and associations.	Aligns customer perceptions with brand intentions, building trust and credibility.	Coca-Cola is often associated with happiness and celebration.	Keller (1993)
Brand Awareness	The extent to which consumers recognize or recall a brand, including brand recognition and brand recall.	Increases customer trust, market visibility, and sales conversions.	Nike's swoosh is instantly recognizable worldwide.	Keller (1993)
Brand Familiarity	The degree to which consumers are aware of and comfortable with a brand.	Encourages trust and repeat purchases through familiarity.	Starbucks' familiarity with customers builds trust in their coffee quality.	Aaker (1996)
Brand Equity	The value a brand adds to a product or service beyond its functional benefits.	Allows brands to charge premium prices and reduces competition vulnerability.	Apple can charge premium prices due to substantial brand equity.	Aaker (1996)
Brand Loyalty	The degree to which customers consistently choose one brand over competitors.	Increases customer retention, repeat purchases, and word-of-mouth advocacy.	Starbucks' rewards program enhances brand loyalty.	Oliver (1999)

(Continued)

TABLE 17.1 (Continued)

Brand Concepts	*Definition*	*Why it Matters*	*Example*	*References*
Brand Trust	The confidence customers have in a brand's reliability, honesty, and ability to deliver on promises.	Reduces perceived risks, builds loyalty, and fosters long-term relationships.	Patagonia's transparency fosters deep customer trust.	Delgado-Ballester and Munuera-Alemán (2005)
Brand Reputation	The collective perception of a brand's credibility, reliability, and responsibility over time.	Attracts customers, talent, and investors; mitigates crisis impacts.	Johnson & Johnson's Tylenol crisis management built a brand reputation.	Fombrun and Van Riel (2004)
Brand Experience	Customers' sensory, emotional, cognitive, and behavioral responses to a brand.	Strengthens emotional connections and drives customer loyalty.	Disney parks create magical customer experiences.	Brakus et al. (2009)
Brand Positioning	The unique space a brand occupies in customers' minds relative to competitors.	Differentiates the brand in competitive markets, aligning it with target audiences.	Volvo is positioned as the leader in automotive safety.	Ries and Trout (2001)
Brand Authenticity	How much consumers perceive a brand as genuine, transparent, and consistent with its values.	Builds emotional connections, reduces skepticism, and drives loyalty.	Ben & Jerry's activism reinforces their brand authenticity.	Beverland (2005), Beverland and Farrelly (2010), Carroll et al. (2022), and Dwivedi and McDonald (2018)
Brand Engagement	The behavioral and emotional interaction consumers have with a brand.	Encourages repeat interactions and brand advocacy.	Nike Run Club fosters ongoing brand engagement.	Hollebeek et al. (2014)
Brand Advocacy	Customers or employees who actively promote and recommend the brand to others.	Amplifies brand messaging and attracts new customers organically.	Tesla owners often advocate for the brand online and offline.	Bickart and Schindler (2001)

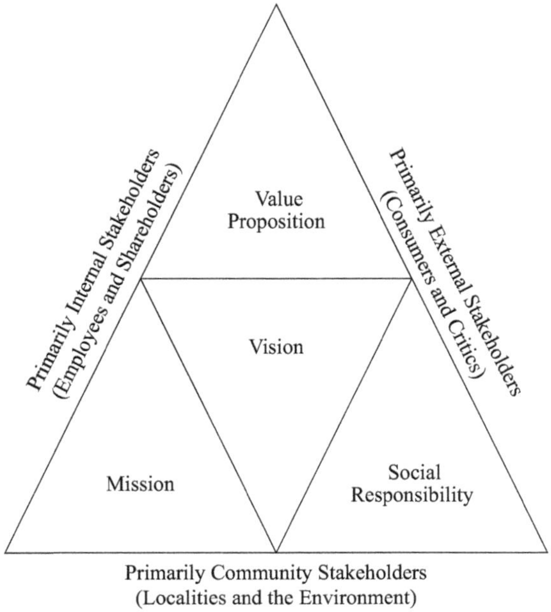

FIGURE 17.1 Organizational Brand Triangle

A strong brand significantly impacts employee satisfaction, engagement, organizational citizenship behaviors (OCB), and customer perceptions. **Employee satisfaction** reflects how content individuals are with their jobs. When employees resonate through brand identity, this enhances satisfaction and engagement. **Employee engagement** refers to emotional investment in the organization; engaged employees promote the brand and excel in their jobs. Client Leaders ensure a clearly defined brand identity to inspire and motivate staff, fostering a sense of belonging and purpose. Moreover, **OCBs** are the voluntary actions employees take that benefit the organization beyond their essential duties, and a strong brand connection encourages these behaviors, fosters teamwork, and boosts workplace morale (Asha & Jyothi, 2013).

The connections between brand identity and the elements in Table 17.1 underscore the importance of organizations developing a strong brand presence externally and internally (see also Figure 17.1), ensuring employees feel valued and engaged. Client Leaders leverage these interconnected elements to influence client behavior, employee engagement, and change initiatives. They create a powerful brand that resonates with consumers and distinguishes itself from the competition. Client Leaders map these elements across the four arenas discussed next.

MAPPING AN ORGANIZATIONAL BRAND TRIANGLE

Mapping an organizational brand triangle is a strategic exercise that helps Client Leaders understand the alignment between a company's internal culture, external messaging, and market positioning. This visual tool helps Client Leaders assess how well company values and promises are reflected across various client touchpoints. Client Leaders map this triangle to identify gaps between internal and external perceptions so adjustments can be made toward consistency and authenticity. This section discusses how to bolster the brand triangle to strengthen client brands.

A brand is not confined to slogans or advertising—it is integrated into every company layer. For contemporary leaders, this chapter offers three areas that make up the brand triangle with two dimensions: internal and external stakeholders, all of which form a cohesive brand identity. Client Leaders tackle the **organizational brand triangle** (see Figure 17.1) across its three interconnected areas: (1) value propositions, (2) mission and vision statements, and (3) social responsibility, sustainability, and shared value.

At the apex of this brand triangle, **value propositions** articulate the unique benefits a company offers its customers and stakeholders. The value proposition is robust if it distinguishes the company in the marketplace as different from competitors or of more substantial value to consumers. **Mission statements** often define a company's core purpose and values, which reflect the larger mission. Value propositions specifically highlight the products, services, and platforms offered. They detail how these offerings alleviate customer pain points and create desired gains.

To craft strong value propositions that effectively resonate with customers, Client Leaders must focus on understanding their customers' jobs, pains, and gains. **Customer jobs**, such as eating, shopping, or commuting, guide businesses to tailor solutions that directly meet these needs. **Customer pains**—frustrations or obstacles—prompt companies to proactively address these issues within their offerings. **Customer gains**—benefits or improvements—enable companies to articulate the value of their products and services effectively (Osterwalder et al., 2015). Osterwalder et al. (2015) emphasize mapping out these elements to ensure alignment between what customers need and what the company offers. **Customer context**—when, where, and why—is essential when designing new products, services, and platforms.

Client Leaders create resonating value propositions. While these value propositions often align with the **productivity triangle**—illustrating how businesses innovate products to be better, faster, or cheaper (Hanlan, 2004), ethical leaders recognize that achieving all three facets of productivity may not be feasible; however, these three facets are limited. We propose the **productivity star** found in Figure 17.2 instead of the triangle to help Client Leaders align their client's brand with mission, vision, and social responsibility (see Chapter 18). The productivity star adds sustainability (Chapter 19) and coolness factors.

Exercise 17.1 Mapping the Organizational Brand Triangle

Rationale: This exercise helps master the concept of the organizational brand triangle by analyzing a well-known company or a local business. Explore the company's official website, sustainability reports, public statements, and customer perceptions from reviews and social media. Identify unique insights for each of the dimensions of the brand triangle. Discuss the cohesiveness of these components and look for alignment or inconsistencies, such as instances of greenwashing or unfulfilled promises.

Tasks: Readers should undertake the following tasks to reinforce learning and strive toward mastering how to map the organizational brand triangle:

1. **Select a Company**—Choose a well-known or local business to analyze.
2. **Research Value Propositions**—Visit the company's official website and other reputable sources to identify its value propositions and document how they are communicated to customers.
3. **Analyze Mission and Vision Statements**—Locate the company's mission and vision statements on its website or in corporate publications, and reflect on whether they are clear and aligned with its actions and market presence.
4. **Investigate Social Responsibility Initiatives**—Research the company's initiatives related to corporate social responsibility (CSR), shared value, and sustainability, and gather information from sustainability reports, press releases, and third-party evaluations.
5. **Collect Customer Perceptions**—Explore customer reviews on platforms like Google, Yelp, or social media to gauge public perception of the company and summarize key themes and sentiments expressed by customers.
6. **Map Insights to the Brand Triangle**—Organize and identify unique insights gathered into the three dimensions of the brand triangle: value propositions, mission and vision statements, and social responsibility.
7. **Assess Cohesiveness**—Analyze the alignment between the different elements of the brand triangle, leverage the different brand concepts in Table 17.1, and look for any inconsistencies, such as instances of greenwashing or unfulfilled promises.
8. **Reflect on Communication**—Evaluate how effectively the company communicates its brand elements to stakeholders and note any strengths and weaknesses in its communication strategy.
9. **Discuss Improvements**—Discuss potential improvements and strategies for enhancing brand alignment and consider creative approaches to strengthen brand image.
10. **Summarize**—Compile the findings and reflections into a summary report or presentation, highlighting the key insights and recommendations identified during the analysis.

Completing these tasks will help Client Leaders recognize the complexities of brand management and the critical interplay between company values and public perceptions.

A compelling value proposition that prioritizes customer satisfaction and social good attracts customers and fosters loyalty and trust in a competitive environment. By integrating these essential elements into their value propositions, companies can enhance their relevance, distinguish themselves in a crowded market, and enrich their missions and visions.

Mission and vision statements are essential to define company identity and bolster stakeholder engagement and are found at the shared base of the organizational brand

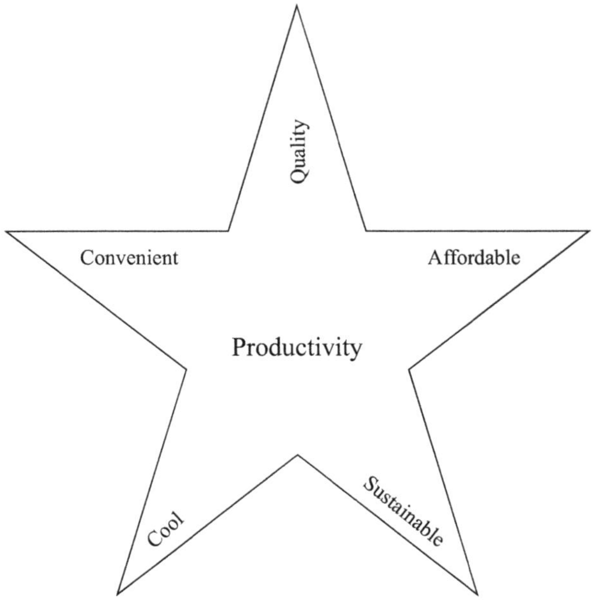

FIGURE 17.2 Productivity Star

triangle. These statements are essential for Client Leaders to articulate an organization's purpose, values, and aspirations. A mission statement is compelling if it answers, "*Why do we do what we do?*" Best practices suggest it should be purpose-driven, customer-centric, action-oriented, concise, and values-aligned, resonating with the organization's core values and commitments to social responsibility and sustainability (Beehive, 2024). A mission statement conveys a commitment to the customer, social impact, and shared value (see Chapters 18 and 19). As shown in Table 17.2, mission statements can be simple or complex, but even when unadorned, they can powerfully cover what needs to be said to stakeholders.

TABLE 17.2 Simple and Complex Mission Statements

Company	*Mission Statement*	*Why it Stands Out*	*Citations*
Simpler			
Google	"To organize the world's information and make it universally accessible and useful."	Straightforward and globally relevant.	Google (n.d.)
IKEA	"To create a better everyday life for the many people."	Simple yet deeply relatable to everyday life.	IKEA (n.d.)
LinkedIn	"Connect the world's professionals to make them more productive and successful."	Directly speaks to professional goals and productivity.	LinkedIn (n.d.)

Company	*Mission Statement*	*Why it Stands Out*	*Citations*
Nike	"To bring inspiration and innovation to every athlete in the world."	Explicit and motivational appeals to a broad audience.	Nike (n.d.)
Tesla	"To accelerate the world's transition to sustainable energy."	Focused on environmental transformation.	Tesla (n.d.)
More Complex			
Amazon	"To be Earth's most customer-centric company, where customers can find and discover anything they might want to buy online."	Customer obsession and broad scope.	Amazon (n.d.)
Microsoft	"To empower every person and every organization on the planet to achieve more."	Ambitious and universally inclusive.	Microsoft (n.d.)
Patagonia	"Build the best product, cause no unnecessary harm, use business to inspire and implement solutions to the environmental crisis facing our planet."	Balances product excellence, environmental responsibility, and purpose.	Patagonia (n.d.)
Starbucks	"To inspire and nurture the human spirit—one person, one cup, and one neighborhood at a time."	Strong emotional appeal and localized impact.	Starbucks (n.d.)
TED	"Discover and spread ideas that spark conversation, deepen understanding, and drive meaningful change."	Focuses on transformative global impact through ideas.	TED (n.d.)

The **vision statement** focuses on the future, articulating the long-term aspirations of the organization. Client Leaders ensure their vision statements are ambitious and motivational. Client Leaders paint a vivid picture of future success and over what timeframe. Vision statements should connect social responsibility and shared value in the communities impacted by a company. Following are three very impactful but short vision statements (Moy, 2024):

1. Microsoft: "To help people and businesses throughout the world realize their full potential."
2. LinkedIn: "To create economic opportunity for every member of the global workforce."
3. Patagonia: "To save our home planet."

These vision statements are impactful because they articulate each organization's purpose and inspire a shared mission. They motivate employees and stakeholders to work toward a common goal that resonates personally and globally. Patagonia's vision connects with social responsibility and climate change, which is discussed hereafter and in Chapter 20.

Client Leaders focus on core values. These beliefs ground actions and align with larger goals for organizations, communities, and the world. As Client Leaders craft the mission and vision statements discussed, they should use active language to convey the intended impact and paint a picture of what will come. Conciseness helps make them memorable and easy to communicate. After drafting mission and vision statements, Client Leaders should revisit and refine them to ensure accuracy and integrity regarding social and environmental promises.

Social value statements reflect a company's commitment to positive societal and environmental impact. They may help drive profit and perceptions but can go beyond profit aims. Client Leaders find social responsibility a core element of strategy, so long as company values and mission are not compromised. Social value statements communicate shared value, benefiting businesses, the planet, and society, which can enrich a company's reputation. In this light, Client Leaders prioritize transparency and demonstrate a genuine commitment to sustainability and meaningful community engagement, which will be discussed in the book's next section. They ensure alignment across the brand triangle to better communicate with stakeholders.

Patagonia is a leading example of alignment across the organizational brand triangle. Patagonia's (n.d.) mission seamlessly connects with its value proposition of delivering durable, environmentally friendly outdoor gear. This mission is embedded in social responsibility initiatives, including the "1% for the Planet" program, which commits 1% of sales to support environmental causes. Patagonia's dedication to sustainability is also evident in the Worn Wear program, which encourages the repair and reuse of clothing. Patagonia illustrates that alignment across the brand triangle is possible and successful (Chouinard & Stanley, 2022).

Unilever is a global leader in consumer goods. Their vision is "To make sustainable living commonplace" (Unilever, 2021). Their Sustainable Living Plan integrates environmental and social aspects into core strategies. For instance, Dove brand's "Real Beauty" campaign promotes social equity, body confidence, and well-being. Unilever commits to sustainable sourcing, including palm oil certified by the Roundtable on Sustainable Palm Oil (RSPO) (Modreanu et al., 2022); however, the company has been accused of greenwashing (see Chapter 19), which threatens its brand. They have been accused of exaggerating or misrepresenting their environmental commitments and actions, and their commitments have been called vague (Gruet, 2023). Post-critique, the company made changes and asked to be audited for its claims (Reuters, 2024), but it still faces criticism, especially regarding plastic pollution (Greenpeace, 2024). Client Leaders can learn from Unilever to prevent incidents like these from getting out of hand and becoming persistent threats to organizational well-being.

COMMUNICATING BRAND TO INTERNAL, EXTERNAL, AND COMMUNITY STAKEHOLDERS

Client Leaders know that an authentic and transparent brand is essential for maintaining consistency and engagement among internal, external, and community stakeholders (discussed here). This section offers clarity and examples to bolster their success as they leverage the organizational brand triangle and craft messaging around the brand.

Internal Communication

Internal stakeholders include employees and shareholders; they hold critical perspectives on the organization's long-term objectives and are invested in its success. The company mission and vision are vital to employees and leaders, and the value proposition must remain competitive for continued shareholder investment.

Internal communication should do more than just relay information; it should cultivate an environment where stakeholders feel heard and valued. Creating inclusive forums is essential to achieving this. When employees and shareholders perceive that their efforts align with the company's mission, value proposition, and overarching goals, it lays the groundwork for loyalty, accountability, and a collective commitment to the organization's success. Table 17.3 features advice on aligning brand identity with internal communications.

External Communication

When engaging with **external stakeholders**—including consumers, who are typically the end-users of products and services, and critics, who may include industry analysts, journalists, and advocates—organizations must focus on their most noticeable attributes, such as their value propositions and commitment to social responsibility. These stakeholders form their perceptions based on direct interactions with the company's offerings and public

TABLE 17.3 How to Communicate with Internal Stakeholders

Theme	*Summary Description*
Empowerment to Raise Concerns	Create an environment where employees feel safe to voice concerns about safety, ethics, or strategy without fear of retaliation. Use anonymous feedback systems and regular check-ins to encourage transparency and trust.
Growth Through Mistakes	Promote a growth mindset by viewing mistakes as opportunities for learning and development. Foster reflection, collaborative problem-solving, and resilience through training and workshops.
Alignment with Organizational Mission	Ensure employees understand how their roles contribute to the organization's mission and long-term goals. Use team meetings, performance reviews, and success stories to reinforce this connection.
Clarity Through Open Communication	Establish open communication channels through regular feedback sessions, town halls, and Q&A forums. Leaders should practice transparency in decision-making and organizational updates.
Authentic Team Connections	Encourage collaboration across teams to break down silos and build authentic relationships. Use team-building activities and shared success stories to foster a sense of collective purpose.

TABLE 17.4 How to Communicate with External Stakeholders

Theme	*Summary Description*
Authentic Engagement	Prioritize genuine interactions with customers, partners, and media to build trust and convey corporate values. Foster long-term relationships that go beyond transactional exchanges.
Transparent Messaging	Communicate corporate goals, actions, and areas for improvement without jargon or coded language. Transparency helps external stakeholders see the alignment between value propositions and social responsibility.
Social and Environmental Commitment	Highlight concrete examples of social and environmental initiatives to demonstrate a commitment to broader societal goals. Stakeholders value visible, measurable outcomes.
Visible Accountability	Take responsibility when commitments are not met. Acknowledge shortcomings, communicate corrective actions, and demonstrate a dedication to continuous improvement.
Proactive Participation	Engage actively in public discussions, industry events, and forums. Position the organization as a thought leader while addressing external stakeholder concerns and sharing the corporate vision.

communications, often prioritizing these elements over the organization's internal strategic objectives. Clients and consumers may need buy-in regarding understanding the company mission, vision, and overall brand (see our Client Leadership chapters for more).

Company vision may be less apparent to these audiences unless explicitly conveyed through branding and public messaging. Client Leaders can utilize the insights presented in Table 17.4 to tailor communication strategies that highlight the company as good for society and industry.

Community Stakeholders: Localities and the Environment

Organizational brand alignment is crucial for **community stakeholders** (discussed in the book's next section). These stakeholders are often directly impacted by the decisions made by Client Leaders. Client Leaders must acknowledge their influence on local communities and the wider environment, particularly climate change and environmental degradation. Table 17.5 presents ways for community engagement that align with organizational brand identity; however, more in-depth information on meaningful community engagement is provided in Chapter 21.

Client Leaders push to align company missions and values with the needs of local communities to create a respectable brand identity rooted in sustainability and community buy-in (Mallin, 2009). This alignment is essential as businesses face the challenges of climate change and environmental degradation. They can contribute to a more sustainable and resilient future for the planet and the communities they serve (Garriga & Melé, 2004). When community stakeholders observe tangible, lasting benefits from a company's presence, such as improved infrastructure, environmental stewardship, or local economic growth, they are more likely to trust the organization's intentions and support its long-term goals. However,

TABLE 17.5 Responsible Community Engagement Strategies Aligned with Brand Identity

Theme	*Summary Description*
Long-Term Community Partnerships	Develop partnerships with local organizations and public agencies to address specific community needs. Collaborate with environmental groups to implement tailored initiatives that enhance resilience and sustainability.
Sustainable Environmental Practices	Adopt sustainable practices such as zero waste, carbon neutrality, and renewable energy usage. These measures reduce environmental harm and support local economies.
Alignment with Local Needs	Support programs and initiatives that bridge corporate goals with community priorities, such as renewable energy education or community gardens promoting food security.
Two-Way Community Communication	Foster open, two-way communication with local leaders and environmental advocates. Use community forums to address concerns collaboratively and build trust.
Visible, Impactful Projects	Invest in visible projects like reforestation or habitat restoration that align with the organization's mission. These initiatives deliver tangible local benefits and reinforce corporate responsibility.

for many communities today, corporate social responsibility often feels like an unreachable ideal or myth, particularly regarding real economic growth and the enhancement of community well-being (Sharma & Sathish, 2022; see also Community Leadership chapters).

Client Leaders prioritize authenticity in brand communication to foster trust and clarity. They seek to empower employees to contribute openly and take ownership of their roles. They see community engagement as an ongoing partnership rather than a mere transaction (see Chapter 21). By being consistent, reliable, and transparent, they can strengthen ties with external stakeholders, ensuring their efforts resonate on a broader scale. Chapters 18 and 19 offer different frameworks aimed at internal and external stakeholders to assist in measurements and communications of impact. A cohesive brand emerges when communication strategies align seamlessly with the organization's mission, vision, and social responsibility (see again Figure 17.1). Client Leaders enhance organizational credibility and create powerful narratives with a measurable commitment to the greater good.

AUTHENTICITY ENSURES ETHICS IN BRANDING

Authenticity in branding builds trust among consumers and nurtures lasting relationships. Client Leaders should align their offerings with their core mission and values. Authenticity helps uphold ethical standards in branding. It is about crafting a compelling story and staying true to core values and promises. This section highlights ethical branding and why genuine brand communication can drive long-term success.

Products and Perceptions Over Slogans: Tangible Brand Value

Client Leaders demonstrate their commitment to stated values and establish genuine connections in their brands and messages. Research indicates consumers perceive brands as more authentic when the quality of products aligns with the promises made (Fritz et al., 2017). Furthermore, by prioritizing long-term community impact over immediate profits, business leaders can reinforce this authenticity and foster a sense of loyalty among consumers. For instance, leaders who choose to disengage from ethically questionable projects or partnerships uphold their brand integrity and build increased consumer trust and loyalty, essential in today's increasingly conscientious marketplace (Morhart et al., 2015).

Brand identity is often reflected in slogans used in advertisements. These slogans should drive consumers to buy products and services and utilize platforms on which others may place ads, further diversifying company revenue. While many of these slogans may be catchy, some may not communicate their main offerings or showcase oxymoronic or ironic aspects of their company, which does no favors for the business. Table 17.6 showcases examples of companies whose recent slogans may appear oxymoronic to individuals with negative experiences or perceptions already.

TABLE 17.6 Oxymoronic Company Slogans

Company	*Slogan*	*Why It Appears Oxymoronic*
Amazon	*Work Hard. Have Fun. Make History.*	Worker mistreatment and burnout undermine the motivational tone.
BP (British Petroleum)	*Beyond Petroleum*	Despite renewable energy efforts, revenue largely comes from fossil fuels.
Chevron	*The Human Energy Company*	An oil and gas company framing itself as "human energy" feels contradictory given its environmental impact.
Coca-Cola	*Open Happiness*	Health and environmental concerns challenge the cheerful promise of happiness.
De Beers	*A Diamond Is Forever*	Historical concerns about blood diamonds contrast with romantic messaging.
ExxonMobil	*Powering Progress*	Substantial historical contributions to carbon emissions contrast with "progress."
Facebook (Meta)	*Bringing the World Closer Together*	Privacy breaches and misinformation concerns contradict the unifying message.
H&M	*Fashion and Quality at the Best Price in a Sustainable Way*	Waste, labor exploitation, and greenwashing conflict with sustainability claims.
McDonald's	*I'm Lovin' It*	Fast food's health effects and environmental concerns clash with the upbeat slogan.

Company	Slogan	Why It Appears Oxymoronic
Nestlé	*Good Food, Good Life*	Controversies over water privatization and child labor undermine the wholesome message.
Philip Morris (Altria Group)	*Our Mission Is to Transition to a Smoke-Free Future*	A cigarette company pledging a smoke-free future feels inherently contradictory.
Shell	*Make the Future*	Fossil fuel dependency undermines the forward-looking slogan.
Uber	*Move the Way You Want*	Driver exploitation and fare transparency issues clash with empowerment messaging.
United Airlines	*Fly the Friendly Skies*	Incidents of passenger mistreatment undermine the friendliness implied.
Walmart	*Save Money. Live Better.*	Labor practices and impacts on small business entities challenge the "Live Better" promise.

Clear and Simple: The State Fair Analogy

Drawing from various US state fairs, where straightforward offerings like a "Pickle on a Stick" or "Shirt World" attract patrons, brands that embrace clarity and simplicity in their messaging and product lines often achieve greater consumer appeal. When a brand communicates its value propositions—how its products, services, and platforms alleviate customer pains, foster gains, and hold desired features—in a straightforward manner, it not only differentiates itself in a crowded market but also fosters a deeper connection with stakeholders. Client Leaders push for clarity in messaging to enhance consumer appeal and help avert unnecessary criticism. It minimizes misunderstandings and sets clear expectations about the brand's offerings.

Client Leaders appreciate simplicity and transparency in branding as it can lead to higher perceived authenticity (Schallehn et al., 2014). Authenticity is paramount, especially for business leaders striving to connect with various stakeholders, including consumers, local communities, shareholders, and employees (Sweeney & Soutar, 2001). As consumers become more skeptical of complex marketing strategies and insincere messaging, a commitment to clarity and simplicity emerges as a powerful strategy (Dwivedi & McDonald, 2018). By prioritizing straightforward communication and eliminating unnecessary jargon, business leaders can build genuine trust with their stakeholders (Beverland & Farrelly, 2010). When stakeholders perceive a brand as authentic, transparent, and relatable, they are more likely to engage with and advocate for that brand (Carroll et al., 2022). Transparent and communicative brands instill confidence in shareholders, who are increasingly drawn to companies that openly discuss their goals and strategies (Freeman, 2010). Simplicity and clarity in their messaging enhance brand appeal, creating a ripple effect that positively influences multiple stakeholders (Kotter, 2012). Table 17.7 provides advice on ethically communicating an authentic brand.

Exercise 17.2 State Fair Brand Pitch—Creating an Authentic Brand Experience

Background and Preparation: Design and pitch a new product or enterprise to be showcased in a state fair booth. The focus is on creating an authentic brand experience that aligns with the principles of clarity and sustainability. Work individually or in small teams of 2–4 people.

Tasks: Select a product or service that fits well within a state fair setting, such as a unique food item, craft, tech gadget, or an engaging service like an educational workshop. The chosen concept should embody authenticity and simplicity, reflecting the values discussed in the chapter. Define the brand identity by creating a name, conceptualizing a logo, and drafting a brief mission statement lasting one or two sentences. Identifying the target audience—families, teens, or environmentally conscious visitors—is also crucial to this process.

Then, craft a value proposition statement highlighting what makes their offering distinct and how it addresses a specific need or problem for the audience. For example, "Our eco-friendly lemonade stand offers locally sourced organic drinks served in reusable mason jars to reduce plastic waste while refreshing visitors on hot fair days." Identify three key messages demonstrating their commitment to genuine practices to emphasize authenticity. These might include statements like "We use locally sourced produce," "A portion of our profits goes to community food initiatives," or "We handcraft every product on-site." For fun, design a booth layout on paper or digitally, including features like signage, product placement, interactive elements, and any sustainability initiatives, such as recycling bins or compostable materials.

Deliver a 90-second pitch articulating the product, booth design, and brand values. Highlight how the offering reflects authenticity and long-term value. Consider how clarity and simplicity influenced the branding decisions, how the product or service showcases authenticity, and how the booth design supports brand identity and message. Think about what would make consumers stop at the booth when they visit the fair.

TABLE 17.7 How to Communicate an Authentic Brand

Theme	*Summary Description*
Let Products Reflect Brand Identity	Ensure your offerings embody your brand's mission and values, providing tangible evidence of your commitments through consistent quality and sustainable practices.
Stay True to Brand Values Amidst Trade-offs	Maintain adherence to ethical standards, even when facing decisions that may affect short-term profits. Uphold brand integrity by avoiding questionable partnerships or practices.

Theme	*Summary Description*
Prioritize Simplicity and Follow-through	Adopt clear, straightforward communication strategies and consistently deliver on promises. Build trust with stakeholders by being transparent, relatable, and aligned with brand values.
Authenticity Through Transparency	Be open about successes, failures, and ongoing challenges. Transparency builds stakeholder trust and reinforces the authenticity of brand communication.
Long-Term Impact Over Short-Term Gains	Focus on long-term sustainability and value creation rather than short-term profits. Decisions should prioritize enduring positive impacts on communities and stakeholders.
Empower Employees as Brand Ambassadors	Empower employees to represent the brand's mission and values in their interactions. Provide training and support to help them act as authentic brand advocates.
Consistency Across All Touchpoints	Ensure uniformity in messaging, values, and brand experience across all platforms, departments, and stakeholder interactions.

PERSONAL BRANDING AND EXECUTIVE PRESENCE

Personal branding and executive presence are closely interconnected. They relate to how leaders command confidence and demonstrate credibility. This section shares how Client Leaders may support executives in developing a strong personal brand to help their clients be perceived better internally and externally.

Personal branding involves the intentional process of crafting and managing how one is perceived by others, highlighting unique strengths, values, and expertise to create a distinctive identity (Rampersad, 2009). **Executive presence** is characterized by the capacity to act with decisiveness and dignity, encompassing confidence, communication skills, appearance, authenticity, composure, and emotional intelligence (Gallo, 2016). Personal branding is about how individuals want to be seen, while executive presence manifests that brand in practice (Heimann, 2020).

Personal branding transcends mere titles; it is found in leadership actions, communication styles, and engagement, including professional networks like LinkedIn and social media (Day & Harrison, 2007). Online, leaders who embody integrity and courage reinforce their allegiance to a company's mission and values (Brown & Treviño, 2006). Client Leaders help clients be aware of their online presence and ensure that their communications reflect their professional personas and do not contradict their employer's values.

For example, the American Lung Association prohibits smoking by its employees. Employees seen smoking on social media showcase an inauthenticity that misaligns with the nonprofit's brand. Additionally, Client Leaders help their clients balance professionalism versus personal expression. They caution against sharing too much or inappropriate personal information, which can undermine authenticity. They do not want their clients to risk overexposure or misrepresentation that can arise in influencer culture. Table 17.8 offers business leaders advice on their personal brand.

TABLE 17.8 Personal Brand Advice

Category	*Dos*	*Don'ts*
Authenticity and Transparency	Be honest and transparent in your communication. Show humility and remain approachable.	Overpromise or present an overly polished image that feels insincere.
Social Media Presence	Use social media platforms like LinkedIn professionally. Share meaningful content aligned with your brand and organizational mission.	Share inappropriate or overly personal content on social media. Avoid engaging in public disputes online.
Alignment with Organizational Values	Regularly reinforce alignment between your personal brand and organizational values. Act as a role model for ethical leadership.	Make public statements or engage in partnerships that conflict with your organization's mission or values.
Mentorship and Professional Growth	Actively mentor team members and create opportunities for professional growth.	Ignore opportunities to guide or mentor team members, focusing only on self-promotion.
Handling Mistakes	Take responsibility for mistakes, address them openly, and communicate corrective actions.	Deflect blame or hide failures to protect your image.
Consistency Across Platforms	Maintain a consistent tone, style, and messaging across all platforms and communications.	Send mixed messages across platforms, creating confusion and distrust among stakeholders.

CONCLUSION

Brand management is multifaceted. This chapter examined how Client Leaders guide clients in building, maintaining, and communicating a brand that reflects the internal culture and external expectations. Brand transcends logos or slogans; it is intricately woven into every company decision, project, and interaction. Client Leaders understand that to resonate with their audiences, they must cultivate their brand from the inside out. From brand authenticity to personal leadership presence, Client Leaders navigate changes and enrich relationships for the long term.

Brand identity is a holistic concept that goes beyond visual elements. It illustrates the importance of integrating brand values into every facet of a business. It advocates for a cohesive approach that ensures all employees and stakeholders are aligned with the company's organizational brand triangle. Finally, authenticity in leadership and brand go hand in hand at all times. Client leaders will remember this as they work with clients and communities.

DISCUSSION QUESTIONS

1. What qualities go into communicating an organization's brand effectively?
2. What do the mission statements of the organizations included in this chapter reflect about their brand?
3. What does the organizational brand triangle tell business leaders about communicating brand?
4. What should business leaders take into account when they are communicating their brand to their internal audiences?
5. What should business leaders take into account when they are communicating their brand to their external audiences?
6. How should an organization's brand influence product development?
7. How should business leaders communicate their personal brand?
8. How should environmental and social responsibility affect an organization's brand?

Key Terms

- Brand Identity
    - Brand Image
    - Brand Awareness
    - Brand Familiarity
    - Brand Equity
    - Brand Loyalty
    - Brand Trust
    - Brand Reputation
    - Brand Experience
    - Brand Positioning
    - Brand Authenticity
    - Brand Engagement
    - Brand Advocacy
- Employee Satisfaction
- Employee Engagement
- Organizational Citizenship Behaviors
- Organizational Brand Triangle
- Value Propositions
    - Customer Jobs
    - Customer Pains
    - Customer Gains
    - Customer Context
    - Productivity Triangle
    - Productivity Star
- Mission Statements
- Vision Statements
- Social Value Statements
- Personal Branding
- Executive Presence

CASE STUDY 17.1 HYPOTHETICAL CASE OF ECOGLOW

Background: EcoGlow is a sustainable beauty brand celebrated for its eco-friendly packaging and cruelty-free product lines. It rose to prominence with a compelling mission: *To illuminate beauty responsibly, one sustainable product at a time*. The company built its reputation on transparency, environmental stewardship, and community engagement. Its value proposition emphasized clean ingredients, biodegradable packaging, and partnerships with ethical suppliers. EcoGlow has offered a nearly clean record on its published sustainability reports to gain consumer trust and outline its future commitments to ethical sourcing and environmental responsibility. However, a whistleblower exposed that one of EcoGlow's top-selling products, the Radiance Serum, contained palm oil from suppliers linked to illegal deforestation and labor exploitation. The revelation triggered widespread backlash from customers, environmental organizations, and media outlets, who accused EcoGlow of greenwashing and ethical hypocrisy.

THE BRANDING CRISIS

- **Internal Stakeholders**—Employees felt blindsided and demoralized, questioning leaderships commitment to sustainability values.
- **External Stakeholders**—Customers expressed outrage on social media, many demanding refunds and vowing to boycott the brand. Influencers publicly severed partnerships.
- **Community Stakeholders**—Environmental advocacy groups launched petitions and campaigns regarding accountability and compensation for the affected communities.

Navigating the EcoGlow Scandal: Assume the role of EcoGlow's leadership team and develop a crisis communication and rebranding strategy. The team must prepare a 5-minute presentation summarizing findings, including a detailed communication strategy, revised brand triangle elements, and long-term recovery steps. To address the branding crisis, leverage critical thinking, strategic problem-solving, and a nuanced understanding of stakeholder communication.

Tasks: Sketch out the following for the team.

1. **Diagnose the Problem**. Identify failures in EcoGlow's brand triangle (Value Propositions, Mission and Vision Statements, Social Responsibility) and evaluate compromised trust among internal, external, and community stakeholders.
2. **Crisis Communication Plan**. Draft a public apology for external stakeholders, create an internal memo for employees detailing the following steps, and propose an engagement strategy for rebuilding community trust.
3. **Rebranding Initiative**: Refine EcoGlow's value proposition, suggest updates to its mission and vision statements, and propose new social responsibility initiatives that align with stakeholder expectations.
4. **Action Plan**. Outline corrective actions (e.g., supplier audits or third-party certifications) and develop a timeline for transparency measures and public progress reporting.
5. **Reflection Questions**. What communication channels are necessary for each stakeholder group? How can EcoGlow align its mission with operations long-term? What measures or strategies can prevent future crises?

REFERENCES

Aaker, D. A. (1996). *Building strong brands*. Free Press.

Amazon. (n.d.). *Our mission*. Retrieved from https://www.amazon.com

Asha, C. S., & Jyothi, P. (2013). Internal branding: A determining element of organizational citizenship behaviour. *Journal of Contemporary Management Research, 7*(1), 37–57.

Beehive. (2024, July 22). *Purpose, mission and values alignment: Beehive's guide to driving meaningful strategic growth*. Beehive. Retrieved from https://beehivepr.biz/purpose-mission-values-alignment/

Beverland, M. B. (2005). Crafting brand authenticity: The case of luxury wines. *Journal of Management Studies, 42*(5), 1003–1029. https://doi.org/10.1111/j.1467-6486.2005.00530.x

Beverland, M. B., & Farrelly, F. J. (2010). The quest for authenticity in consumption: Consumers' purposive choice of authentic cues to shape experienced outcomes. *Journal of Consumer Research, 36*(5), 838–856.

Bickart, B., & Schindler, R. M. (2001). Internet forums as influential sources of consumer information. *Journal of Interactive Marketing, 15*(3), 31–40. https://doi.org/10.1002/dir.1014

Brakus, J. J., Schmitt, B. H., & Zarantonello, L. (2009). Brand experience: What is it? How is it measured? Does it affect loyalty? *Journal of Marketing, 73*(3), 52–68. https://doi.org/10.1509/jmkg.73.3.52

Brier, D. (2017). *Brand Intervention: 33 Steps to Transform the Brand You Have into the Brand You Need*. Dbd International, Ltd.

Brown, M. E., & Treviño, L. K. (2006). Ethical leadership: A review and future directions. *The Leadership Quarterly, 17*(6), 595–616.

Carroll, R., Cadet, F. T., & Kachersky, L. (2022). Authenticity attracts authenticity: The impact of brand authenticity and self-authenticity on brand loyalty. *Journal of Brand Strategy, 10*(4), 377–388.

Chouinard, Y., & Stanley, V. (2022). *The Responsible Company: What We've Learned from Patagonia's First 50 Years*. Patagonia Books

Creative Soup. (n.d.). Components of a strong brand identity. Retrieved from https://creativesoup.io/blogs/news/components-of-a-strong-brand-identity

Day, D. V., & Harrison, M. M. (2007). A multilevel, identity-based approach to leadership development. *Human Resource Management Review, 17*(4), 360–373.

Delgado-Ballester, E., & Munuera-Alemán, J. L. (2005). Does brand trust matter to brand equity? *Journal of Product & Brand Management, 14*(3), 187–196. https://doi.org/10.1108/10610420510601058

Dwivedi, A., & McDonald, R. (2018). Building brand authenticity in fast-moving consumer goods via consumer perceptions of brand marketing communications. *European Journal of Marketing, 52*(7/8), 1387–1411.

Fombrun, C. J., & Van Riel, C. B. M. (2004). *Fame & fortune: How successful companies build winning reputations*. FT Press.

Freeman, R. E. (2010). *Strategic management: A stakeholder approach*. Cambridge University Press.

Fritz, K., Schoenmueller, V., & Bruhn, M. (2017). Authenticity in branding–exploring antecedents and consequences of brand authenticity. *European Journal of Marketing, 51*(2), 324–348.

Gallo, C. (2016). *The Storyteller's Secret: From TED Speakers to Business Legends, Why Some Ideas Catch On and Others Dont*. St. Martin's Press.

Garriga, E., & Melé, D. (2004). Corporate social responsibility theories: Mapping the territory. *Journal of Business Ethics, 53*(1), 51–71.

Google. (n.d.). *About Google*. Retrieved from https://www.google.com/about

Greenpeace. (2024, April 2). *Unilever greenwash investor briefing*. Retrieved from https://www.greenpeace.org.uk/resources/unilever-greenwash-investor-briefing

Gruet, S. (2023, December 12). *Dove and Marmite maker Unilever faces an investigation into green claims*. Retrieved from https://www.bbc.com/news/business-67658043

Hanlan, M. (2004). *High-performance teams: How to make them work*. Bloomsbury Publishing USA.

Heimann, N. (2020). Achieving executive presence: Integrating the seven dimensions of leadership intelligence. *Leader to Leader, 2020*(96), 58–64.

Hollebeek, L. D., Glynn, M. S., & Brodie, R. J. (2014). Consumer brand engagement in social media: Conceptualization, scale development, and validation. *Journal of Interactive Marketing, 28*(2), 149–165. https://doi.org/10.1016/j.intmar.2013.12.002

IKEA. (n.d.). *Our vision and business idea*. Retrieved from https://www.ikea.com

Keller, K. L. (1993). Conceptualizing, measuring, and managing customer-based brand equity. *Journal of Marketing, 57*(1), 1–22. https://doi.org/10.1177/002224299305700101

Key Differences. (n.d.). Difference between brand identity and brand image. Retrieved from https://keydifferences.com/difference-between-brand-identity-and-brand-image.html

Kotter, J. P. (2012). *Leading change*. Harvard Business Review Press.

LinkedIn. (n.d.). *About us*. Retrieved from https://www.linkedin.com

Mallin, C. A. (Ed.). (2009). *Corporate social responsibility: A case study approach*. Edward Elgar Publishing.

Microsoft. (n.d.). *Our mission*. Retrieved from https://www.microsoft.com

Modreanu, A., Andrișan, G. N., Sârbu, A. M., & Grădinaru, C. (2022). Corporate Social Responsibility, a Strategic Tool for Sustainable Value Creation: A Case Study of Unilever's Sustainable Living Plan. In *BASIQ 2022 International Conference on New Trends in Sustainable Business and Consumption* (pp. 575–582).

Morhart, F. M., Malär, L., Guèvremont, A., Girardin, F., & Grohmann, B. (2015). Brand authenticity: An integrative framework and measurement scale. *Journal of Consumer Psychology, 25*(2), 200–218.

Moy, R. (2024, January 2). Vision statement examples and how-to guide. Retrieved from https://ramp.com/blog/vision-statement-example

Nike. (n.d.). *Our mission and vision*. Retrieved from https://www.nike.com

OH Design Studio. (n.d.). *Branding quotes for business inspiration*. Retrieved from https://www.ohdesignstudio.com/blog/branding-quotes-for-business/

Oliver, R. L. (1999). Whence consumer loyalty? *Journal of Marketing, 63*(4_suppl1), 33–44. https://doi.org/10.1177/00222429990634s105

Osterwalder, A., Pigneur, Y., Bernarda, G., & Smith, A. (2015). *Value proposition design: How to create products and services customers want*. John Wiley & Sons.

Patagonia. (n.d.). *Our mission*. Retrieved from https://www.patagonia.com
Rampersad, H. K. (2009). *Authentic Personal Branding: A New Blueprint for Building and Aligning a Powerful Leadership Brand*. AuthorHouse.
Reuters. (2024, November 6). *UK regulator ends probe into Unilever's environmental claims*. Retrieved from https://www.reuters.com/world/uk/uk-regulator-ends-probe-into-unilevers-environmental-claims-2024-11-06/
Ries, A., & Trout, J. (2001). *Positioning: The battle for your mind*. McGraw-Hill Education.
Schallehn, M., Burmann, C., & Riley, N. (2014). Brand authenticity: Model development and empirical testing. *Journal of Product & Brand Management, 23*(3), 192–199.
Sharma, E., & Sathish, M. (2022). "CSR leads to economic growth or not": An evidence-based study to link corporate social responsibility (CSR) activities of the Indian banking sector with economic growth of India. *Asian Journal of Business Ethics, 11*(1), 67–103.
Starbucks. (n.d.). *Our mission statement*. Retrieved from https://www.starbucks.com
Sweeney, J. C., & Soutar, G. N. (2001). Consumer perceived value: The development of a multiple-item scale. *Journal of Retailing, 77*(2), 203–220.
TED. (n.d.). *Our mission*. Retrieved from https://www.ted.com
Tesla. (n.d.). *About us*. Retrieved from https://www.tesla.com
Unilever. (2021). *Sustainable living*. Retrieved from https://www.unilever.com
Vaia. (n.d.). Brand identity: Definition & components. Retrieved from https://www.vaia.com/en-us/explanations/business-studies/operational-management/brand-identity/

PART 5

Community Leadership

As we conclude our model, we focus on **Community Leadership**, a significant subject matter with increasing importance to business leaders. Community Leadership has a rich history and was once shelved by business leaders as the responsibility of others, but not today and not in the 21st-century era of accountability and transparency. However, business leaders who want to embed community practices within their strategic priorities do so at the cost of organizational profits and company reputation if they engage without careful thought and precise intention. This section offers a decided overview, a contemporary guidebook, and a call to action.

The Community Leadership section is enriched with concepts like corporate social responsibility, multiple bottom lines, stakeholder capitalism, shared value, sustainability, social entrepreneurship, and meaningful community engagement. It offers frameworks, strategies, tools, and measurements. Bringing the concepts to life are real-world examples of organizations—many successful at bridging business and community, and just as many suffer the consequences of community leadership gone wrong. Within our classrooms, we find students learn just as much when they examine companies who model revenue objectives alongside their moral values just as much as they do by analyzing the countless public failures where companies were corrupt, frauds, or erred against the communities they served. We wanted that experience here.

Where there are many possible ways to get it wrong, how should a contemporary business leader get Community Leadership right? Engaging in the earlier components of the model, namely, knowing oneself, valuing relationships, being an expert at one's business, and attending to client needs, are excellent stepping stones. However, careful review and taking the opportunities to apply the concepts in each chapter of this section is a pragmatic method toward genuine community leadership. We wholeheartedly believe that many leaders with small and incremental implementations can lead to transformational execution on a global scale for organizations that genuinely want to benefit people simultaneously with profits and the planet.

What matters is that contemporary graduate programs training future business leaders require many of the components featured here in our Community Leadership section.

DOI: 10.4324/9781003474647-22

It is no longer a "nice to have" but a serious undertaking and necessary skill set. We are proud to produce conscientious business leaders equipped to correct social injustices, fix inequalities, spotlight moral imperatives, institute healthy practices for the earth, and bring communities together to do what's humanly right for one another. As the reader unpacks each chapter, we know one takeaway will be that there is much work to do. Yet our purpose for this section was to prompt critical discussions, generate clear action steps, and create connections among the students who take on Community Leadership.

CHAPTER 18

Social Responsibility and Multiple Bottom Lines

CHAPTER OVERVIEW

This chapter explores the role of contemporary business leaders as Community Leaders going beyond the economic bottom line. Corporate social responsibility (CSR) within a framework of multiple bottom lines is a strong tool of stakeholder capitalism. This chapter overviews and critiques stakeholder capitalism in contrast to shareholder capitalism. The chapter examines CSR and measurement frameworks like the triple bottom line (3BL), which assesses organizational impact on communities. Community Leaders can adopt authentic social responsibility practices to foster sustainable and socially beneficial outcomes. The chapter calls for business leaders to integrate these principles into their careers, addressing social injustices, promoting environmental sustainability, and enhancing community well-being.

Contemporary business leaders, as Community Leaders, are well-versed in social responsibility and the language of multiple bottom lines. These terms are not merely buzzwords but have rich roots in business, management, and capitalistic systems. As discussed in the chapter on the purpose-driven workforce, social responsibility should not be undertaken lightly or as "lip service" to pad fancy websites or corporate reports. Authentic and measured social responsibility can have a lasting impact on communities, employees, and enterprise sustainability, which will be explored in another chapter as well. This chapter starts at the historical roots and impetus of social responsibility by critiquing the history of stakeholder capitalism. Then, the chapter discusses corporate social responsibility (CSR) and measurement frameworks like the triple bottom line as paths for measuring organizational impact on communities. CSR and stakeholder capitalism provide foundations for understanding how Community Leaders can leverage evolving tools such as social entrepreneurship, sustainability, shared value, and meaningful community engagement, which are discussed in other chapters.

DOI: 10.4324/9781003474647-23

STAKEHOLDER VS. SHAREHOLDER CAPITALISM

Stakeholder capitalism acknowledges that investors are not the only groups that benefit from the practices and successes of enterprises in society (Landry, 2009; Pfeffer, 2009). Stakeholder capitalism appears more attractive during times of need, such as recession and scandals (Landry, 2009; Pfeffer, 2009). Sundheim and Starr (2020) claim that stakeholder capitalism is due for a return, writing, "spurred by the alarming climate crisis and increasing social challenges such as rising inequality, the movement is gathering additional steam" (p. 2). CEOs realize purpose is needed beyond profit (Gartenberg & Serafeim, 2019).

Stakeholder capitalism runs in contrast to shareholder capitalism, in which enterprises only exist to serve (the greed of) financial investors (Pfeffer, 2009). Pfeffer (2009) summarizes:

> In the 1950s and 1960s, the stakeholder was king. CEOs saw their role as one of balancing the interests of the various groups that touched their companies—customers, employees, suppliers, shareholders, and the community at large. This reflected the executives' sophisticated understanding not only of their role as stewards of the valuable resources entrusted to them but also of their own enlightened self-interest: Each of these groups was essential for organizational success.
>
> (p. 1)

Stakeholder capitalism came and went fast. Shareholder capitalism returned to prominence in the 1970s due to faith in the "efficiency and intelligence of markets" (Pfeffer, 2009, p. 1), and Sundheim and Starr (2020) claim it reigned king for around 40 years thereafter. From a more balanced perspective, shareholder and stakeholder capitalism still coexist, but neither has changed substantially at its core since its beginnings (Springman, 2011).

At its heart, stakeholder capitalism questions incentive structures to do good and do well but likely still aims to benefit financial shareholders first (Pfeffer, 2009; Desai, 2012). Stakeholder capitalism leaves ambiguous who stakeholders are outside of workers and local communities (Landry, 2009). Concerns remain at the operational level, specifically regarding accounting social value (Govindrajan & Srivastava, 2020). Additionally, the mechanisms for balancing the desires of all stakeholders remain unclear (Landry, 2009). Gartenberg and Serafeim, 2019 write, "The primary criticism of stakeholder capitalism is that any purpose other than shareholder profits results in a lack of focus and, ultimately, corruption" (p. 3). Desai (2012) does not find stakeholder capitalism worth its risks, writing:

> Moving away from shareholder-centered capitalism toward stakeholder capitalism risks overcorrecting the excesses of the past three decades. Indeed, capitalism appears to be serving managers and investment managers at the expense of shareholders.
>
> (p. 9)

Thus, stakeholder capitalism falls flat as it fails to define stakeholders, who benefit most or first, and whether shareholders can handle not being first. Community Leaders must understand and strike this balance to excel as community leaders.

Old Wine, But in New Bottles

Since the late 1990s, stakeholder capitalism has returned and rebranded, much like old wine in new bottles, by thought leaders. This approach, which emphasizes the importance of serving the interests of all stakeholders rather than just shareholders, has been revitalized with new terminology and modern frameworks. Like transferring old wine into new bottles, rebranding does not fundamentally alter the core principles of stakeholder capitalism. It only offers fresh packaging and contemporary rhetoric to established concepts. Also, like transferring old wine into new bottles, each transfer risks corruption, contamination, and loss of character.

In 1997, the Clinton administration recognized a need to address distressed urban neighborhoods. They drew on a report titled "Community Capitalism: Rediscovering the Markets of America's Urban Neighborhoods" created by the American Assembly of Columbia University. The group and report were deemed nonpartisan and gained favor with both Democrats and Republicans. Famed Harvard professor Michael E. Porter hailed the potential positive impacts of **community capitalism**. Community capitalism made a financial case for financiers to invest in poor, urban communities. Community capitalism, like shared value (discussed in the next chapter), touted that communities and organizations benefit from shared economic growth (Brookings.edu, n.d.).

Conscious capitalism emerged in 2009 and gained traction in 2013 due to its association with John Mackey, co-CEO of Whole Foods Markets. Strong and Mackey (2009) posited that conscious capitalists could address all the world's problems. Later, Mackey and Sisodia (2013a, 2013b) described conscious capitalists and businesses as heroes. They define "conscious" as being mindful and awake, recognizing reality, being accountable for actions, understanding right from wrong, and rejecting violence in harmony with nature (Mackey & Sisodia, 2013b). "Conscious" was seen as fitting, given that capitalism seemed to need both a brain and a soul (Koehn, 2013). Over time, Mackey and Sisodia (2013a, 2013b) argued that conscious capitalism provides enterprises with higher purposes, creates value and prosperity for all, and still has positive economic bottom-line impacts.

Conscious capitalism emphasizes that businesses should serve the interests of all stakeholders, not just shareholders, and prioritize purpose beyond profit. According to Mackey and Sisodia (2013a, 2013b), conscious capitalism involves creating value for all stakeholders, including customers, employees, suppliers, the community, and the environment, while generating financial returns (Clune, 2017). Mackey and Sisodia (2013a, 2013b) explain how Whole Foods Market has embraced this concept by building strong relationships with suppliers, providing high-quality natural and organic products to customers, and creating a fulfilling work environment for employees. Whole Foods Market also prioritizes environmental sustainability and community engagement. Conscious capitalism is grounded in the belief that businesses can be a force for good in the world and that profits and purpose coexist harmoniously. By aligning with the interests of all stakeholders, companies can attain success and positively impact society.

In 2011, Al Gore and David Blood acclaimed the merits of community capitalism. To build on community capitalism, they proposed **sustainable capitalism**, calling for long-term economic thinking, better compliance and risk management, and a focus on waste reduction and energy efficiency. Invoking climate change among other global disruptive threats, Gore and Blood's (2011) manifesto proposes a financial case for the benefits and opportunities regarding sustainable capitalism to incentivize investors. The case for sustainable capitalism fits with Dominic Barton (2011) of McKinsey and Company's call for better leadership that ensures long-term success for capitalism. Thus, shareholders and business leaders remain the primary drivers, not consumers or citizens, in providing long-term social value.

Gore and Blood's (2011) manifesto for sustainable capitalism emphasizes the shift from short-term profit maximization to long-term value creation, focusing on sustainable growth that considers future generations. This manifesto broadens the stakeholders and timeframes typically included in stakeholder capitalism. It advocates for integrating **Environmental, Social, and Governance** (ESG) factors into all business and investment decisions to assess risks and opportunities related to climate change, resource scarcity, and social inequality (discussed later). It calls for greater transparency and accountability to investors and stakeholders, including disclosures of ESG performance and impacts. Innovation and efficiency are at the heart of new technologies and processes to reduce environmental impact and improve social outcomes. Sustainable capitalism requires supportive policies and regulations that incentivize better practices and create a level playing field for all companies. Its most notable additions to stakeholder capitalism are its heavy environmental emphasis on ESG, advocacy for policy changes, and focus on how investors, especially those that value ESG, can drive change.

George Tyler (2013) provided his version of stakeholder capitalism, titled **family capitalism**. Citing rising inequality and decreases in US long-term competitiveness and productivity, Tyler (2013) locates explicitly his capitalism alternative in free-market economics. Tyler's (2013) focus is highly embedded in European perspectives, specifically Germanic and Nordic countries. While he notes that family capitalism may be novel to the US perspective, he identifies eight countries that demonstrate family capitalism, which he proclaims that the United States has economically fallen behind (arranged in alphabetical order): Australia, Austria, Belgium, Denmark, France, Germany, the Netherlands, and Sweden.

Family capitalism benefits society by promoting substantial middle-class prosperity and sustainable growth for future generations (Tyler, 2013). It emphasizes the importance of workers in industry success, advocating for strong labor protections, generous benefits, and inclusion in decision-making. With its European roots, family capitalism supports robust social welfare systems and programs. It also prioritizes vocational training and continuous education to equip workers with the necessary skills, aiming for equitable wealth distribution and reducing income inequality. It expands on stakeholder capitalism by emphasizing laborers, worker ownership, and social welfare.

Andrew Yang, a 2020 Democratic primary presidential candidate, coined **human capitalism**, also referenced as human-centered capitalism (Yang, 2018; Harwood, 2019; Yang2020.com, n.d.). Human capitalism was a central focus of his book, *The War on Normal People* (Yang, 2018). His human capitalism had three tenets:

1. Humans are more important than money
2. The unit of a human capitalism economy is each person, not each dollar
3. Markets exist to serve our common goals and values.

(Yang2020.com, p. 4)

Yang finds it immoral to value capital over human welfare and recognizes the excesses of capitalism (i.e., greed), and he attempts to propose "a positive economic vision that people can get excited about" (Harwood, 2019, p. 27). Human capitalism is still stakeholder capitalism.

Yang's human capitalism is a holistic economic and social policy approach that prioritizes human well-being. It promotes **Universal Basic Income (UBI)** to ensure a guaranteed income for all adults, lifelong education, comprehensive healthcare, and policies to adapt to technological changes in the job market. The goal is to create a society where individuals can thrive professionally and personally. Yang (2018) emphasizes the importance of financial stability and work-life balance while focusing on social well-being beyond economic success.

The final rebrand is **accountable and transparent capitalism**. This concept is prominently featured in Larry Fink's 2020 annual letter to CEOs from BlackRock. The letter underscores corporate responsibility and the creation of long-term value as tied to the interests of all stakeholders (BlackRock, n.d.). Fink (2020) emphasizes the need for a sustainable and inclusive economy and recognizes BlackRock's role as a global investment steward. He highlights two critical points: "Companies, investors, and governments must prepare for a significant reallocation of capital" and "Disclosure should be a means to achieving a more sustainable and inclusive capitalism" (Fink, 2020, pp. 21, 23).[1]

Larry Fink (2020) calls for CEOs to embrace purpose and serve stakeholders, building on the themes from his previous letters advocating for diversity and positive social impact (Fink, 2019; Kramer, 2019). His 2022 letter emphasizes the need for sustainability, urging companies to integrate climate risk into their business models and invest in sustainable technologies that benefit both the environment and financial performance (Fink, 2022).

Fink (2020, 2022) acknowledges that accountable and transparent capitalism aligns with stakeholder capitalism. He highlights the importance of showcasing the impacts of business actions on all stakeholders, not just shareholders. He advocates for strategies prioritizing long-term sustainability and value over short-term gains, emphasizing transparency and accountability as core organizational responsibilities. Furthermore, he calls for policy shifts to reallocate capital and enhance disclosure requirements, urging companies and their leaders to communicate their long-term strategies and remain accountable to their stakeholders.

Each of these forms, while old wine in new bottles, has been fortified with lessons in community leadership that Community Leaders can employ in their organizations. Table 18.1 summarizes the lessons for modern business leaders as community leaders that can be carried on in CSR work and measurement frameworks that include multiple bottom lines. These lessons also apply to the other chapters regarding sustainability, shared value, social entrepreneurship, and meaningful community engagement.

TABLE 18.1 Stakeholder Capitalism Lessons for Business Leaders as Community Leaders

Lesson	*Description*
Authentically Embrace Stakeholder Interests or Needs	Recognize the importance of serving the interests or needs of all stakeholders, not just shareholders, to create long-term value and sustainability.
Promote Transparency and Accountability	Communicate long-term strategies and be accountable to stakeholders, ensuring that business practices are transparent and responsible.

(Continued)

TABLE 18.1 (Continued)

Lesson	*Description*
Focus on Long-Term Value Creation	Prioritize sustainable growth and long-term business strategies over short-term profit maximization.
Foster Meaningful Community Engagement	Invest in and engage with local communities, seeing them as assets and recognizing the mutual benefits of shared economic growth and responsible environmental utilization.
Integrate ESG Factors in Organizational Culture, Vision, and Action	Incorporate ESG considerations into business and investment decisions to address global challenges and enhance resilience.
Bolster Social Equity, Welfare, and Labor Protections	Implement policies that promote equity, provide strong labor protections, and bolster instead of tax welfare systems.
Embrace Digital Futures and Technological Changes	Prepare for and manage the impacts of technological advancements and economic shifts, ensuring employees and stakeholders are equipped with the necessary skills and support.

Exercise 18.1 Critiquing the Evolution of Stakeholder Capitalism

Examine how different forms of stakeholder capitalism—community capitalism, conscious capitalism, Sustainable capitalism, Family capitalism, Human capitalism, and Accountable and Transparent capitalism—differ from or align with traditional stakeholder capitalism. Examine the fundamental principles of stakeholder capitalism. Provide concise overviews of each type of stakeholder capitalism, noting common themes and goals. Explore how the aims and methods of each type differ from original stakeholder capitalism, their contexts, and what they add.

CORPORATE SOCIAL RESPONSIBILITY (CSR)

Corporate social responsibility (CSR) emerged in the 1960s[2] as a form of business self-regulation fitting with the aims of stakeholder capitalism. CSR activities include creating and running initiatives that may consist of corporate foundations, volunteering, charitable donations, sustainability projects, and worker retraining programs, among others, and issuing reports on their social and environmental impact (Porter & Kramer, 2006; Rangan et al., 2015; Medros, 2019). The success (and opportunities for improvement) regarding these activities can today be found in the triple bottom line, sustainability, and shared value reports, which can be featured on many outward-facing websites and resources for internal stakeholders and shareholders.

CSR proponents see its potential for improving the economic bottom line and wealth creation (Vermaelen, 2011; Cassar & Meier, 2018), which will be discussed further in the chapter on shared value. While CSR has been linked to economic bottom-line benefits, researchers like Cassar and Meier (2018) highlight that monetary and charitable incentives work very differently, especially on the employee level. "Employees care about the intentions behind companies' CSR activities, not just the positive impact those activities have on society" (Cassar & Meier, 2018, p. 4). These incentives connect with company culture and impact how to attract and retain purpose-minded employees. Economic bottom-line intentions for utilizing CSR can undermine pro-social aims, even if they are connected to CSR pursuits.

CSR reflects a moral obligation to engage in ethical practices so their enterprises can serve as better stewards of a sustainable long-term future (Porter & Kramer, 2006). Others note that social responsibility offers metaphorical insurance for an enterprise's public reputation (Porter & Kramer, 2006; Vermeulen, 2009). CSR may allow an enterprise to have better encounters with government regulators (Porter & Kramer, 2006; Frick, 2015), local communities (Porter & Kramer, 2006), and other stakeholders that might impede operations (Porter & Kramer, 2006). Still, corporations must listen to "the voice of the people" on social media and other outlets to be effective (Boynton, 2013). McPherson (2012) connects Occupy Wall Street, increases in consumer activities, accountability to social media, and resource depletion worldwide as impetuses for why enterprises should care about CSR; these reasons showcase how consumers and citizens can pay or are paying more attention. Again, these CSR motivations return to the aims and touted benefits of stakeholder capitalism.

Despite benefits, managers may find CSR projects challenging to support (Vermaelen, 2011; Hafenbraedl & Waeger, 2018), not because they disagree that CSR helps the bottom line, but likely because they have trouble understanding relevant social problems needing solutions (Hafenbraedl & Waeger, 2018). Porter and Kramer (2006) note that companies must identify where they intersect with society regarding social and environmental issues before selecting which to address. They also recommend that companies start with small initiatives with distinct and significant impacts. Furthermore, CSR efforts may need coordination or be incongruent with the larger goals of companies and may need more location within their business models (Rangan et al., 2015). In this light, companies may hire CSR managers to address issues regarding funding, implementation, and impact measurement (Rangan et al., 2015; Wickert & de Bakker, 2019); however, CSR not supported from the top and relegated to single siloed unit will fail to realize its benefits for organizations and communities. The case study of Starbucks offered in this chapter (see Case Study 18.1) provides a look at the new industry standard for CSR, at least for large customer-facing companies.

MEASURING IMPACT

Stakeholder capitalism and CSR can positively impact organizations and communities; however, company practices' positive (or negative) impact must be measured. Contemporary business leaders with high community leadership skills recognize the value of measuring and communicating impact to all stakeholders. Unfortunately, many managers and companies outsource these measurement efforts, removing the practice from company culture or managers' day-to-day. Also, many measurement rubrics and frameworks are proprietary, requiring companies to hire a consulting firm and lock them in with the same firm to have comparable year-to-year metrics. In 2021, Corvo and colleagues estimated at least 98 possible measurement instruments, models, rubrics, or frameworks for social impact. Rogmans and El-Jisr (2022) comment that the number of measurement models today has become overwhelming.

This chapter will provide three frameworks for most of today's measurement tactics. It does not explore the rich emerging field of social accounting in the public administration and nonprofit literature. These frameworks have evolved into more robust concepts, such as shared value and sustainability, which are discussed in a separate chapter. The frameworks discussed are triple bottom line, ESG, and community capitals.

Triple Bottom Line

Triple bottom line (TBL or 3BL). Over 20 years ago, Elkington coined the triple bottom line management concept (Elkington, 2018). His measurement instrument accounting for social, environmental, and economic impact would be popularized with the people, planet, and profit tagline. Two books stand out that generated its popularity: (1) *Cannibals with Forks: The Triple Bottom Line of 21st Century Business* (Elkington, 1997) and (2) *The Triple Bottom Line: How Today's Best-Run Companies Are Achieving Economic, Social, and Environmental Success—and How You Can Too* (Savitz & Weber, 2006). Table 18.2 describes the three bottom lines coined by Elkington and applied by many (e.g., Gergen & Vanourek, 2008). TBL asks businesses to look beyond short-term profits and consider long-term sustainability and ethical actions.

Elkington's 3BL would spur a plethora of other measurement instruments of social value, which have only further evolved and expanded (Corvo et al., 2021):

TABLE 18.2 The Triple Bottom Line Approach

Bottom Line	*Description*
Profit	This dimension represents the economic value created by the organization. It includes financial performance measures such as revenue, profit, and return on investment. Ensuring financial stability and profitability remains crucial as it sustains the business and allows for reinvestment and growth.
People	This aspect emphasizes an organization's social responsibility. It involves the business's impact on all stakeholders, including employees, customers, suppliers, and the community. Key considerations include fair labor practices, community engagement, employee well-being, and equitable treatment.
Planet	This component focuses on a company's environmental impact. It includes practices that reduce carbon footprint, manage waste, conserve resources, and ensure sustainable practices throughout the supply chain. Companies are encouraged to adopt environmentally friendly practices and reduce their ecological impact.

> Double and Quadruple Bottom Lines, Social Return on Investment (SROI), multiple capital models, Full Cost Accounting, ESG (...Environmental, Social and Governance factors), the Environmental Profit & Loss approach...Net Positive, Blended and Shared Value, Integrated Reporting, Impact Investment...BCG's Total Societal Impact Framework...Carbon Productivity, the Sharing and Circular Economies, or Biomimicry.
>
> (Elkington, 2018, p. 4)

Again, these frameworks reference and start with 3BL as their foundations and build from there.

Recently, Elkington (2018) issued a recall of his management concept to be retooled. He had hoped his measurement instrument of social and environmental value would catalyze system change; however, it became "just an accounting system" (p. 4). Critics push that TBL and other social accounting systems may have done more to separate bottom lines, CSR programs, and business functions rather than align the responsibility to do good for society within the overall business model (Rangan et al., 2015; Elkington, 2018). Still, managers may be tempted to use 3BL as checkboxes rather than a guiding decision-making tool for leaders (Talmage et al., 2024).

ESG

ESG has roots in the investing world compared to 3BL, going back to early notions of ethical and socially responsible investing, which are also grounded in stakeholder capitalism. Governance was a late addition to these early pushes for ethics and responsibility in investing. In the early 2000s, the foundation for the modern ESG framework started to develop. The term "ESG" was officially established in 2004 in the "Who Cares Wins" report, commissioned by the United Nations Global Compact. This report advocated for integrating ESG into capital markets, asserting that it would result in more sustainable markets and better societal outcomes. Following, the United Nations Principles for Responsible Investment were introduced in 2005. These principles offered a voluntary framework for integrating ESG issues into investment practices and gained support from a global network of investor signatories. Table 18.3 outlines and describes the components.

ESG, like any measurement approach, is limited by the data collected, transparency of results found, and use of the data for future decisions. Like 3BL, ESG should not be seen as a checkbox reporting tool. In current practice, ESG is also primarily used by outsiders (i.e., investors), and how well it is used internally to shape company culture requires more research. The role of community stakeholders in determining the right data points and objectives of ESG also needs more critical examination. Again, ESG is rooted in stakeholder capitalism.

Community Capitals

The community capitals framework provides another method for capturing impact and making data-informed decisions to improve community well-being. The community capitals framework categorizes several interconnected community asset domains, known as capitals. These include human-centered domains such as social, political, human, and

TABLE 18.3 ESG Components

Component	*Description*
Environment	This area measures a company's environmental influence and encompasses factors like carbon footprint, waste management, resource consumption, and actions to mitigate environmental hazards. The company is appraised based on its efforts to minimize pollution, responsibly manage natural resources, and adhere to environmental regulations.
Social	This area analyzes the strategies a company uses to maintain its relationships with employees, suppliers, customers, and the communities in which it operates. Significant elements encompass labor practices, human rights, community involvement, health and safety protocols, and initiatives for diversity and inclusion. Within the ESG framework, social responsibility examines how a company makes positive societal contributions.
Governance	This area examines company leadership, executive compensation, audits, internal controls, and shareholder rights. It also assesses the company's ethical conduct, transparency in reporting, anti-corruption measures, and board of directors' performance. Effective governance guarantees that the company operates with honesty, integrity, and responsibility.

cultural capitals, and material-centered domains like natural, built, and financial capitals (Emery & Flora, 2006). This framework is valuable for measuring, discussing, and guiding community efforts. Table 18.4 lays out the community capitals.

Community Leaders can adopt the community capitals framework to enhance their leadership and drive sustainable development. They can use the capitals in Table 18.4 to measure the impacts of their CSR efforts and shared value (see Chapter 19). The

TABLE 18.4 Community Capitals

Component	*Description*
Social	Social capital encompasses the networks, relationships, and norms enabling community collective action. It includes trust, reciprocity, collaboration, and cooperation among community stakeholders. This resource is vital for community cohesion and resilience, as it fosters mutual support and cooperation (Putnam, 2000; Woolcock & Narayan, 2000).
Political	Political capital refers to a community's capacity to influence and utilize political processes, policies, and resources. This encompasses the community's access to decision-makers, political networks, and advocacy groups that can further their interests and obtain essential resources. Political capital empowers communities to rally for change, acquire funding, and enact policies that enhance their welfare (Flora & Flora, 2008).
Human	Human capital refers to individuals' skills, knowledge, health, and abilities within a community. It encompasses education, training, and personal development, which enhance individuals' capacity to contribute to economic and social activities (Becker, 1994).

Component	Description
Cultural	Cultural capital comprises the values, traditions, heritage, and identity that define a community. This includes cultural expressions like art, music, language, and customs, which contribute to a community's unique character and sense of belonging. Cultural capital helps shape community identity, preserve historical legacies, and promote social cohesion. It enhances attractiveness and can drive tourism and cultural industries (Bourdieu, 1986).
Natural	Natural capital consists of the environmental assets and resources within a community, such as land, water, air, biodiversity, and ecosystems. It offers vital services like clean air and water, fertile soil, and recreational areas. Efficient management of natural capital is essential to preserve these resources for future generations and to build resilience against environmental challenges (Costanza et al., 1997).
Built	Built capital denotes the physical infrastructure and facilities that underpin community activities and development. This encompasses buildings, transportation systems, utilities, telecommunications, and public spaces (Flora & Flora, 2008).
Financial	Financial capital refers to the financial resources available within a community, such as income, savings, investments, and access to credit and funding. It is critical in enabling communities to invest in other forms of capital, support businesses, and fund public services and infrastructure. Developing financial capital involves promoting economic opportunities, improving financial literacy, and ensuring fair access to financial resources (Emery & Flora, 2006).

framework allows Community Leaders to assess how their organization affects community capital and well-being from multiple angles. The framework helps Community Leaders find the best leverage points and areas for improvement. It can also guide investing in community projects that strengthen multiple capitals and enhance a company's bottom lines.

Meaningful stakeholder engagement is another vital part of community leadership (see Chapter 21). The community capitals framework encourages open communication with diverse groups about different targeted aspects of communities. Community Leaders who embrace the framework can better promote CSR within their organizations by using its clear language. They can champion initiatives that enhance cultural capital, like supporting local arts and heritage projects, which reify community identity. They can leverage this framework to build resilient companies and communities committed to positive local economic development.

Exercise 18.2 Write Out How to Assess Impact Using SMART Goals

For this exercise, write measurable objectives using 3BL, ESG, or community capitals for an organization in your local community that employs or has employed you. Use the tables in the chapter to help you. Justify how your objectives are specific, measurable, attainable, realistic, and time-bound (SMART). Describe how you would get buy-in and input on these goals.

CONCLUSION

Stakeholder capitalism, CSR, and measurement frameworks are essential for Community Leaders' community leadership toolkits. Stakeholder capitalism remains prevalent in modern frameworks despite new terminology. Its enduring relevance and concepts covered in this chapter have merit in addressing contemporary economic and social challenges. Community leaders strive to put the well-being of everyone impacted by organizations at the outset of building companies and new initiatives. From the lessons in this chapter, Community Leaders can tackle these issues and promote sustainable CSR efforts. They help create a more inclusive, responsible, and sustainable future for businesses and their communities. The next chapter dives further into sustainability and shared value building on CSR efforts.

DISCUSSION QUESTIONS

1. How has the term "capitalism" evolved?
2. What are the specific dimensions of each capitalism term?
3. What does corporate social responsibility mean for today's business leaders?
4. How do organizations measure their CSR?
5. How can Community Leaders apply the 3BL?
6. What are the challenges of the 3BL?
7. What do the contemporary concepts of ESG require of business leaders today?

Key Terms

- Community Leadership
- Corporate Social Responsibility (CSR)
- Multiple Bottom Lines
- Stakeholder Capitalism
- Shareholder Capitalism
- Conscious Capitalism
- Community Capitalism
- Sustainable Capitalism
- Family Capitalism
- Human Capitalism
- Universal Basic Income (UBI)
- Accountable and Transparent Capitalism
- Triple Bottom Line (TBL or 3BL)
- ESG (Environmental, Social, and Governance)
- Community Capitals
- Social Capital
- Political Capital
- Human Capital
- Cultural Capital
- Natural Capital
- Built Capital
- Financial Capital

CASE STUDY 18.1 CORPORATE SOCIAL RESPONSIBILITY AT STARBUCKS

Starbucks (n.d.) has long been recognized for its comprehensive CSR initiatives. These initiatives span various areas, including ethical sourcing, environmental sustainability, community involvement, and employee welfare. These demonstrate how strategic and comprehensive initiatives can drive positive social, environmental, and economic outcomes. Starbucks enhances its brand value through CSR and contributes to global sustainability and community well-being. This case study highlights key initiatives and their impact.

Ethical Sourcing: Starbucks focuses on ethically sourcing coffee beans. The company is committed to ensuring that its coffee is sourced in a way that promotes economic, social, and environmental standards. Starbucks' Coffee and Farmer Equity (C.A.F.E.) Practices, developed in collaboration with Conservation International (n.d.), are designed to ensure that coffee is sourced to benefit farmers and their communities while protecting the environment. These guidelines include quality, economic accountability, social responsibility, and environmental leadership criteria.

Environmental Sustainability: Starbucks has made significant strides in reducing its ecological footprint. The company's goals include reducing waste, conserving water and energy, and promoting recycling. One notable initiative is Starbucks' commitment to certifying all its stores as LEED (Leadership in Energy and Environmental Design). Additionally, Starbucks aims to reduce the environmental impact of its cups by introducing reusable cup initiatives and collaborating with partners to develop recyclable and compostable cup solutions.

Community Involvement: Starbucks actively participates in various community initiatives. The company's Community Store (n.d.) program reinvests some profits into local community projects. Starbucks supports youth empowerment programs and provides grants to nonprofits focused on youth leadership, diversity, and inclusion through The Starbucks Foundation.

Employee Welfare: Starbucks strongly emphasizes employee welfare, offering comprehensive benefits and development opportunities. The company provides eligible employees with health benefits, stock options, and college tuition assistance through its Starbucks College Achievement Plan, which partners with Arizona State University. This initiative aims to help employees complete their college education and advance their careers.

Impact and Recognition: Starbucks' CSR efforts have positively impacted its brand reputation and stakeholder relationships. The company's commitment to ethical sourcing has supported coffee farmers in over 30 countries, contributing to sustainable farming practices and improved livelihoods. Starbucks' environmental initiatives have led to significant waste reduction and energy conservation. Moreover, the company's community and employee-focused programs have enhanced social welfare and provided growth opportunities for thousands of individuals.

Resources: Podcast Resource: "How to Do Good and Do Good Business with Starbucks' Howard Schulz" on Masters of Scale (2018): https://mastersofscale.com and Case Study Website: https://www.starbucks.com/responsibility/reporting-hub/

Task: Address these case study questions:

1. How do Starbucks C.A.F.E. Practices contribute to sustainable coffee farming, and what are the specific criteria in these guidelines? Evaluate the impact of these practices on the environment and farmer livelihoods.
2. Examine the impact of Starbucks' Community Store program on local communities. Provide examples of successful projects funded by this program and discuss how these initiatives align with Starbucks' broader CSR goals.
3. How does Starbucks support youth empowerment and diversity initiatives? How do these initiatives reflect its commitment to social responsibility? Evaluate the effectiveness of these programs in fostering community well-being.
4. Discuss the significance of the Starbucks College Achievement Plan for employee development and retention. How does this program benefit the company and its employees, and what other benefits and development opportunities does Starbucks offer?
5. What are the long-term benefits of its CSR efforts for the company and its stakeholders? How have these initiatives influenced the brand reputation and relationships with stakeholders? Provide measurable outcomes where possible.
6. How do its CSR practices align with the principles of stakeholder capitalism?

NOTES

1 The terms inclusive and capitalism have often co-mingled in literature and popular media; however, the origin of the term, *inclusive capitalism*, remains elusive. More recently, inclusive capitalism, as a unique concept, may be traced most concretely to the Coalition for Inclusive Capitalism (https://www.inc-cap.com/) and bottom-of-the-pyramid approaches proposed by Prahalad (2009). Inclusive capitalism rests among rebrands with less traction or wide reach, such as caring, responsible, and other (insert term) capitalism forms (Mintzberg, 2015).

2 The exact dates in which the phrase "corporate social responsibility" first appeared and was subsequently operationalized as a management concept remains unclear.

REFERENCES

Barton, D. (2011). Capitalism for the long term. *Harvard Business Review*. https://hbr.org/2011/03/capitalism-for-the-long-term

Becker, G. S. (1994). *Human Capital: A Theoretical and Empirical Analysis, with Special Reference to Education* (3rd ed.). University of Chicago Press.

BlackRock (n.d.). https://www.blackrock.com

Bourdieu, P. (1986). The forms of capital. In J. Richardson (Ed.), *Handbook of theory and research for the sociology of education* (pp. 241–258). Greenwood.

Boynton, J. (2013). How the voice of the people is driving corporate social responsibility. *Harvard Business Review*. https://hbr.org/2013/07/how-the-voice-of-the-people-is

Brookings.edu. (n.d.). Community capitalism: Rediscovering the markets of America's urban neighborhoods. https://www.brookings.edu/research/community-capitalism-rediscovering-the-markets-of-americas-urban-neighborhoods/

Cassar, A., & Meier, S. (2018). Intentions for doing good matter for doing well: The (negative) signaling value of prosocial incentives. *Management Science, 64*(1), 250–270. https://doi.org/10.1287/mnsc.2016.2583

Clune, C. (2017). Shaping corporate social responsibility management and reporting through engagement: The role of advocacy organisations. *CORE*. Retrieved from https://core.ac.uk/download/489756186.pdf

Conservation International. (n.d.). Starbucks Coffee and Farmer Equity (C.A.F.E.) Practices. Retrieved from https://www.conservation.org/

Corvo, L., Pastore, L., Manti, A., & Iannaci, D. (2021). Mapping social impact assessment models: A literature overview for a future research Agenda. *Sustainability, 13*(9), 4750.

Costanza, R., d'Arge, R., de Groot, R., Farber, S., Grasso, M., Hannon, B., … & Belt, M. (1997). The value of the world's ecosystem services and natural capital. *Nature, 387*(6630), 253–260.

Desai, M. (2012). The incentive bubble. *Harvard Business Review*. https://hbr.org/2012/03/the-incentive-bubble

Elkington, J. (1997). *Cannibals with Forks: The Triple Bottom Line of 21st Century Business*. Capstone Publishing.

Elkington, J. (2018, June 25). 25 years ago I coined the phrase "Triple Bottom Line." Here's why it's time to rethink it. *Harvard Business Review*. https://hbr.org/2018/06/25-years-ago-i-coined-the-phrase-triple-bottom-line-heres-why-im-giving-up-on-it

Emery, M., & Flora, C. (2006). Spiraling-up: Mapping community transformation with community capitals framework. *Community Development: Journal of the Community Development Society, 37*(1), 19–35.

Fink, L. (2019). Purpose & profit. BlackRock. https://www.blackrock.com/corporate/investor-relations/2019-larry-fink-ceo-letter

Fink, L. (2020). A fundamental reshaping of finance. BlackRock. https://www.blackrock.com/corporate/investor-relations/larry-fink-ceo-letter

Fink, L. (2022). The power of capitalism. BlackRock. https://www.blackrock.com/dk/individual/2022-larry-fink-ceo-letter

Flora, C. B., & Flora, J. L. (2008). *Rural communities: Legacy and change* (3rd ed.). Westview Press.

Frick, W. (2015). Do regulators go easier on socially responsible firms? *Harvard Business Review*. https://hbr.org/2015/06/do-regulators-go-easier-on-socially-responsible-firms

Gartenberg, C. & Serafeim, G. (2019). 181 top CEOs have realized companies need a purpose beyond profit. *Harvard Business Review*. https://hbr.org/2019/08/181-top-ceos-have-realized-companies-need-a-purpose-beyond-profit

Gergen, C., & Vanourek, G. (2008). The triple bottom line – one book at a time. *Harvard Business Review*. https://hbr.org/2008/12/the-triple-bottom-line-one-boo

Gore, A., & Blood, D. (2011). A manifesto for sustainable capitalism. *Wall Street Journal*. https://www.wsj.com/articles/SB10001424052970203430404577092682864215896

Govindrajan, V. & Srivastava, A. (2020). We are nowhere near stakeholder capitalism. *Harvard Business Review*. https://hbr.org/2020/01/we-are-nowhere-near-stakeholder-capitalism

Hafenbraedl, S. & Waeger, D. (2018). Most executives believe in the business case for CSR. So why don't they invest more in it? *Harvard Business Review*. https://hbr.org/2018/09/most-executives-believe-in-the-business-case-for-csr-so-why-dont-they-invest-more-in-it

Harwood, J. (2019). 2020 candidate Andrew Yang: 'The fundamentals that we assume to be true about capitalism are now breaking down'. *CNBC.com*. https://www.cnbc.com/2019/10/02/why-andrew-yang-says-human-capitalism-beats-democratic-socialism.html

Koehn, N. (2013). The brain – and soul – of capitalism. *Harvard Business Review*. https://hbr.org/2013/11/the-brain-and-soul-of-capitalism.

Kramer, M. (2019). The backlash to Larry Fink's letter shows how far business has to go on social responsibility. *Harvard Business Review*. https://hbr.org/2019/01/the-backlash-to-larry-finks-letter-shows-how-far-business-has-to-go-on-social-responsibility

Landry, J. T. (2009). Stakeholder capitalism and Chrysler. *Harvard Business Review*. https://hbr.org/2009/05/stakeholder-capitalism-at-chry

Mackey, J., & Sisodia, R. (2013a). *Conscious capitalism: Liberating the heroic spirit of business*. Harvard Business Review Press.

Mackey, J., & Sisodia, R. (2013b). "Conscious capitalism" is not an oxymoron. *Harvard Business Review*. https://hbr.org/2013/01/cultivating-a-higher-conscious

McPherson, S. (2012). Why CSR's future matters to your company. *Harvard Business Review*. https://hbr.org/2012/01/why-csrs-future-matters-to-you

Medros, A. (2019). Reskilling workers is a central part of corporate social responsibility. *Harvard Business Review*. https://hbr.org/2019/10/reskilling-workers-is-a-central-part-of-corporate-social-responsibility

Mintzberg, H. (2015). Rescuing capitalism from itself. *Harvard Business Review*. https://hbr.org/2015/12/rescuing-capitalism-from-itself

Pfeffer, J. (2009). Shareholders first? Not so fast... *Harvard Business Review*. https://hbr.org/2009/07/shareholders-first-not-so-fast

Porter, M. E., & Kramer, M. R. (2006). Strategy & society: The link between competitive advantage and corporate social responsibility. *Harvard Business Review*. https://hbr.org/2006/12/strategy-and-society-the-link-between-competitive-advantage-and-corporate-social-responsibility

Prahalad, C. K. (2009). *The fortune at the bottom of the pyramid: Eradicating poverty through profits* (5th ed.). FT Press.

Principles for Responsible Investment. (2005). The Principles. Retrieved from UNPRI. https://www.unpri.org/about-us/what-are-the-principles-for-responsible-investment

Putnam, R. D. (2000). *Bowling Alone: The Collapse and Revival of American Community*. Simon & Schuster.

Rangan, K., Chase, L., & Karim, S. (2015). The truth about CSR. *Harvard Business Review*. https://hbr.org/2015/01/the-truth-about-csr

Rogmans, T., & El-Jisr, K. (2022, January 14). Designing your company's sustainability report. *Harvard Business Review*. Retrieved from https://hbr.org/2022/01/designing-your-companys-sustainability-report

Savitz, A. W., & Weber, K. (2006). *The triple bottom line: How today's best-run companies are achieving economic, social, and environmental success – and how you can too*. Jossey-Bass.

Springman, J. (2011). A thousand days to reinvent capitalism? *Harvard Business Review*. https://hbr.org/2011/07/a-thousand-days-to-re-invent-capital

Starbucks. (n.d.). Committed to Transparency—People, Planet, Coffee. https://www.starbucks.com/responsibility/reporting-hub/

Strong, M., & Mackey, J. (2009). *Be the solution: How entrepreneurs and conscious capitalists can solve all the world's problems*. John Wiley & Sons.

Sundheim, D., & Starr, K. (2020). Making stakeholder capitalism a reality. *Harvard Business Review*. https://hbr.org/2020/01/making-stakeholder-capitalism-a-reality

Talmage, C. A., Mars, M. M., Hains, B. J., Hains, K. D., & Ashdown, B. K. (2024). Pushing against a future dark side for community development: An editorial call to action. *Community Development, 55*(3), 310–324.

Tyler, G. R. (2013). *What went wrong: how the 1% hijacked the American middle class…and what other countries got right*. BenBella Books.

United Nations Global Compact. (2004). Who cares wins: Connecting financial markets to a changing world. Retrieved from UN Global Compact. https://www.unglobalcompact.org/docs/news_events/8.1/Who_Cares_Wins.pdf

Vermaelen, T. (2011). An innovative approach to funding CSR projects. *Harvard Business Review*. https://hbr.org/2011/06/an-innovative-approach-to-funding-csr-projects

Vermeulen, F. (2009). Corporate social responsibility as insurance. *Harvard Business Review*. https://hbr.org/2009/02/corporate-social-responsibilit

Wickert, C., & de Bakker, F. G. A. (2019). How CSR managers can inspire other leaders to act on sustainability. *Harvard Business Review*. https://hbr.org/2019/01/how-csr-managers-can-inspire-other-leaders-to-act-on-sustainability

Woolcock, M., & Narayan, D. (2000). Social capital: Implications for development theory, research, and policy. *The World Bank Research Observer, 15*(2), 225–249.

Yang, A. (2018). *The war on normal people: The truth about America's disappearing jobs and why universal basic income is our future*. Hachette.

Yang2020.com (n.d.). Human-centered capitalism. https://www.yang2020.com/policies/human-capitalism/

CHAPTER 19

Shared Value and Sustainability

CHAPTER OVERVIEW

This chapter examines shared value and sustainability, highlighting their significance for modern business leaders as community leaders. Shared value is a management strategy that seeks to enhance competitiveness while addressing social and economic challenges. It distinguishes shared value from corporate social responsibility (CSR), emphasizing that shared value integrates social impact into core business strategies rather than treating it as an ancillary effort. The chapter's insights encourage readers to consider the transformative potential of shared value in redefining stakeholder capitalism; however, this chapter offers a healthy level of skepticism regarding stakeholder capitalism as a boon for success. The chapter shows how to create joint value between businesses and communities.

Contemporary business leaders must be Community Leaders who extend their talents beyond running their organizations. The previous chapter covered stakeholder capitalism, corporate social responsibility (CSR), and measurement frameworks for assessing social and environmental impact. This chapter discusses and critiques the concepts of shared value and sustainability, in which many CSR pursuits and reports are housed for sharing with inside and outside stakeholders. Modern business leaders can become strong community leaders by enriching their work with tools and theories emphasizing shared value and sustainability.

SHARED VALUE

Shared value, a management strategy developed by Michael E. Porter and Mark R. Kramer, aims to enhance a companys competitiveness in the marketplace while advancing its communities' economic and social conditions (Porter & Kramer, 2011). Pfitzer et al. (2013) expanded the concept to show how shared value shifts views of productivity in the value chain. This concept emphasizes the interdependence between societal progress and corporate success, moving beyond traditional CSR to integrate social improvement into core

DOI: 10.4324/9781003474647-24

TABLE 19.1 Key Principles of Shared Value

Principle	*Description*
Reimagining Products and Markets	Businesses can innovate products or revamp existing ones to tackle social issues and cater to new markets. For instance, companies can create new solutions to meet the needs of underserved markets, leading to both business growth and social benefits (Porter & Kramer, 2011).
Redefining Efficiency in the Value Chain	Organizations can strengthen their competitiveness by improving resource efficiency, adopting sustainable practices, and creating economic opportunities through local sourcing and employment. This cuts costs, reduces risks, and positively impacts society (Pfitzer et al., 2013).
Empowering Local Cluster Development	Companies can nurture local industry clusters to cultivate a more robust and supportive business environment. Through investments in infrastructure, supplier development, and education, businesses can establish thriving ecosystems that benefit the company and the local community (Porter & Kramer, 2011).

business strategies (Crane et al., 2014). Crane et al. (2014) highlighted that while traditional CSR often concentrates on philanthropy and addressing adverse impacts, shared value integrates social considerations directly into core business operations and strategies. Pfitzer et al. (2013) further emphasized that shared value initiatives are intended to be scalable and sustainable, aligning profit motives with social impact, thereby creating a virtuous cycle of business and social benefits. Table 19.1 shows three critical principles of shared value.

Porter and Kramer (2011) hailed shared value as a vehicle to reinvent capitalism, citing that capitalism was under siege. Their shared value moves the choice to do social and environmental good beyond trade-offs. The shared value model makes the case for better incentives consistent with the story of stakeholder capitalism. Shared value affirms that win-win thinking is best (Mulcahy, 2012). Shared value has been expanded to pricing models (Bertini & Gourville, 2012) and innovation structures (Pfitzer et al., 2013). Porter and Kramer's (2011) shared value approach asks firms not to separate bottom lines but instead look for intersections between companies and society, much like Porter and Kramer (2006) argued regarding CSR.

Shared Value versus CSR

Porter and Kramer (2011) argue that shared value and CSR are essentially different. They note the value proposition, connections to the profit maximization, and scope of impact between the two are distinct. Readers can see the comparisons in Table 19.2 (adapted from Porter & Kramer, 2011; Crane et al., 2014) to decide if shared value offers a paradigm shift in stakeholder capitalism or CSR. Readers should question what it takes to transform CSR into shared value. *Can joint value creation be realized in practice, or does one party always benefit more than the other?*

TABLE 19.2 CSR vs. Shared Value

Attribute	*CSR*	*Shared Value*
Value Proposition	Focuses on "doing good" through acts of citizenship, philanthropy, and sustainability efforts. These activities are generally seen as discretionary or responsive to external pressures.	Centers on creating economic and societal benefits relative to cost. It involves joint value creation between the company and the community, making it integral to its competitive strategy.
Connection to Profit Maximization	Typically operates separately from profit maximization. External reporting requirements and the personal preferences of corporate leaders often influence its agenda.	This is integral to profit maximization and is deeply embedded in core strategies. The agenda for shared value is generated internally and is specific to the company's goals and objectives.
Scope of Impact	The impact is limited by the company's corporate footprint and the budget for CSR activities.	Realigns the entire company budget toward initiatives that enhance quality and yield, having a broader and more profound impact.

Critiquing Shared Value

While Porter and Kramer (2011) do explicitly link social harms to internal firm costs and push for better incentives of shared value, these notions appear much like CSR rebranded. Instead of CSR initiatives, there are now shared-value initiatives (Rangan et al., 2015). Shared value remains criticized for failing to provide transformative change on the firm level and substantial, meaningful social impact (Kaplan et al., 2018). Just months after Porter and Kramer's (2011) article, Weinberger (2011) notes these limitations but critiques Porter and Kramer's potential homogenization of all pro-social interests shared. He purports that a better rallying concept is simply "Don't Be Evil."

Similarly, in critiquing the abstractness of shared value, Aaker (2011) proposes that social programs be leveraged instead of in addition to shared value initiatives. Earlier, Kramer (2007) recognized that the government still needed to address prominent social issues. Later, Kramer and Pfitzer (2016) reluctantly admit that companies must collaborate with governments, nongovernmental organizations, and rival companies to advance shared value. If shared value undermines competitiveness, can the strategy be sustainable if rivals do not follow? How might shared value be coopted as rhetoric for organizations to advocate for policies that incentivize socially good behavior and not punish socially bad behavior?

Exercise 19.1 Mini-Case Studies of Shared Value

Nestlé and Intel are two prominent organizations that leverage shared value. Based on what you know about shared value, discuss how either of the organizations showcases the concept. Then, search news reports and academic sources to critique whether the organizations are adequately practicing the shared value principles they tout.

- **Nestlé—**By working directly with small farmers to improve agricultural practices and ensure sustainable sourcing, Nestlé improves farmers' livelihoods while securing high-quality raw materials for its products (Porter & Kramer, 2011).
- **Intel—**By investing in education and digital literacy in developing countries, Intel enhances educational outcomes and expands its product market.

(Pfitzer et al., 2013)

Now, pick a different organization, which can be your own, and propose how shared value might enhance your CSR, positively impact community stakeholders, and increase your market competitiveness. Reflect on where shared value may go awry or fail to realize its promise.[1]

SUSTAINABILITY

Community Leaders interact with the interdisciplinary field of sustainability. **Sustainability** is more than a buzzword related to environmental impact; it holds unique frameworks that modern business leaders can leverage in pursuing CSR, shared value, and meaningful community engagement. Sustainability relies on many frameworks already covered in this section, such as ESG and 3BL; however, it aims to push individuals and organizations to go further in their efforts than these measurement frameworks and shared value. Whelan (2022) notes that ESG reports contain insufficient evidence to demonstrate sustainability and argues that while ESG disclosures provide broad process-oriented metrics, they often need to track actual performance and impact. Instead, companies should focus on integrating sustainability deeply into their operations to achieve competitive advantages and reflect prosocial missions or visions.

Sustainability as a modern concept emerged in 1987 in *Our Common Future* by the World Commission on Environment and Development:

> Sustainable development is development that meets the needs of the present without compromising the ability of future generations to meet their own needs.
> (World Commission on Environment and Development, 1987, p. 43)

Like the evolution of stakeholder capitalism, focusing on future generations is a significant addition to social and environmental responsibility. Today, sustainability extends beyond ecological responsibility to "people sustainability," which can include strategies to enhance employee diversity, equity, inclusion, learning and development, purpose, safety, and well-being (Bersin, 2023).

Community Leaders tangibly demonstrate the value of sustainability initiatives to employees, customers, and other stakeholders, as this visibility can drive engagement, trust, and business success (Unruh, 2024). Sustainability efforts must still be profitable or create business value, not requiring dependencies of communities on organizations that undermine resilience (Unruh, 2024). For some consumers, achieving sustainability goals and practical sustainability strategies are valued (Challagalla & Dalsace, 2022;

Reichheld et al., 2023); however, companies may need to encourage sustainable usage behaviors among consumers (Challagalla & Dalsace, 2022). Sustainability add-ons to products may need to be gradually added into existing markets (2022). Some have posited that a tipping point is coming where sustainability will become a baseline expectation of consumers in their purchase decisions (Reichheld et al., 2023). Reichheld and colleagues (2023) argue that sustainability efforts promote trust and loyalty between companies and consumers, especially younger consumers, who will eventually dominate purchasing power.

Sustainability efforts fail for many reasons. Some years ago, Bain & Company revealed that only 2% of companies achieved their sustainability goals (Lamach, 2017). Sustainability is often relegated to separate departments, away from core functions like strategy and operations, limiting its organizational influence and integration (Farri et al., 2022). Profit maximization can overpower business processes and decisions despite sustainability goals (Farri et al., 2022). Sustainability metrics are often inconsistent and lack the robustness of financial metrics (Farri et al., 2022). Sustainability-oriented cultures lack champions to shift company cultures; profit-centric paradigms are pervasive (Farri et al., 2022). Lastly, conventional management tools and frameworks are not naturally tailored toward sustainability (Farri et al., 2022). Still, Farri et al. (2022) note that success stories across industries demonstrate that overcoming these obstacles and realizing the potential of sustainability is possible.

Sustainability efforts may fail to differentiate organizations or provide a competitive advantage in the marketplace (Ioannou & Serafeim, 2019). Should modern business leaders pursue sustainability efforts if these two criteria are met? Modern business leaders as Community Leaders should remember that sustainability connects more intangibly to community stakeholders and employees, as discussed in this chapter. Furthermore, financial benefits may not be realized until younger generations have more purchasing power and the benefits of ecoefficiency (e.g., greener supply chain) and ecopreneurship (discussed later) are realized. To bolster Community Leadership regarding sustainability, Table 19.3 provides ten tips for contemporary business leaders to leverage in their sustainability efforts.

TABLE 19.3 Ten Tips for Contemporary Business Leaders of Sustainability

Tip	*Explanation*
Collaborate Across Departments	Form cross-departmental teams to design and implement people sustainability programs and integrate these goals into annual reports and stakeholder communications.
Communicate Clearly	Use marketing, press, and certifications to highlight the sustainability attributes of products, processes, and initiatives, ensuring stakeholders understand and trust your claims.
Embed Sustainability in Processes	Rethink business processes to include sustainability from the start, such as incorporating ESG criteria in product development and decision-making.
Engage Stakeholders	Highlight personal and community benefits to increase engagement and trust and involve employees, customers, and other stakeholders in sustainability efforts.

Tip	*Explanation*
Ensure Profitability or Minimize Loss	Design sustainability initiatives to be profitable or loss-minimizing, ensuring they are integrated into core business practices and can be sustained over the long term.
Highlight Transparency and Humanity	Demonstrate respect and care for all individuals and ensure easy access to transparent, detailed information about the organization's impact on communities and the environment.
Innovate and Adapt	Be prepared to adapt and innovate to make sustainability impacts more tangible. Use creative solutions and collaborations that resonate with different stakeholder groups.
Prepare for Generational Shifts	Start expanding sustainability efforts and communication strategies to align with the values of younger consumers, ensuring future customer loyalty.
Showcase Future Benefits	Engage in initiatives that demonstrate the future benefits of sustainability, such as educational programs and community projects, to make the positive impacts tangible today.
Track and Recognize Progress	Utilize tools to measure progress and recognize and reward employee contributions to foster a culture of sustainability and innovation.

Building on stakeholder capitalism covered in this book, this section discusses and critiques vital tools for contemporary business leaders, including ecoefficiency, ecopreneurship, and sustainable development goals (SDGs). Again, many other frameworks exist beyond our book; however, many are reformulated from CSR, 3BL, shared value, and other topics already covered thus far. The rest of this chapter aims to offer more foundational aspects of sustainability so contemporary business leaders can move their organizations toward or beyond shared value, become more socially innovative, and meaningfully engage with community stakeholders to create change.

Ecoefficiency and Ecopreneurship

A **circular economy** is a way of thinking about the economy that aims to reduce waste and make the best use of resources. Community Leaders seek opportunities like ecoefficiency and ecopreneurship to move companies and industries toward more circular economic practices. Unlike the traditional linear economy, which follows a "take, make, dispose" approach, a circular economy seeks to keep products and materials in use for as long as possible. More than just recycling, it focuses on getting the most value from items while using them and then recovering and renewing them when they are no longer needed (Ellen MacArthur Foundation, 2013).

Ecoefficiency is an approach to sustainability that urges businesses to enhance their environmental responsibility while improving economic performance. The concept is centered around generating more value with minimized environmental impact, focusing on efficiently using resources to reduce waste and emissions. According to the World Business Council for Sustainable Development, eco-efficiency is attained by providing

> competitively priced goods and services that meet human needs and enhance community quality-of-life and wellbeing, while continually decreasing environmental impacts and the intensity of resource usage throughout the product life cycle to a level at least aligned with the Earth's estimated carrying capacity.
>
> (World Business Council for Sustainable Development, 2000)

Ecoefficiency can lower costs, manage risks, and increase a company's positive perception in the community (Schaltegger & Burritt, 2010). Ecoefficiency can be measured using ratios to help Community Leaders assess and improve sustainability efforts. Table 19.4 contains ratios that Community Leaders can employ. These ratios range in specificity. Community Leaders can utilize these ratios to identify areas where resource use can be optimized and environmental impacts minimized, leading to cost savings and enriched sustainability efforts.

Shapiro (2009) highlights that eco-efficiency efforts must engage existing expertise inside organizations, go beyond focusing on energy, broadly network, and involve all employees. To achieve more ecoefficent and greener supply chains, contemporary business leaders can integrate environmental considerations into supply chain operations at every stage, from product design to material sourcing, manufacturing processes, delivery of the final product, and end-of-life management. A green supply chain approach aims to minimize the ecological footprint of supply chain activities while upholding economic efficiency and

TABLE 19.4 Sample Ratios for Eco-Efficiency

Ratio	*Description*
Economic Value/ Environmental Impact	This ratio measures the economic value generated per unit of environmental impact. It is calculated by dividing the economic output by the environmental burden, such as emissions or resource consumption (Huppes & Ishikawa, 2005).
Energy Efficiency	This ratio evaluates the economic value produced per unit of energy consumed. It is crucial for industries with significant energy use (Burritt & Saka, 2006).
Material Efficiency	This ratio assesses the economic value generated per unit of material used. It highlights how effectively a company utilizes raw materials in its production processes (Picazo-Tadeo et al., 2011).
Water Efficiency	This ratio measures the economic value produced per unit of water consumed, which is essential for industries that rely on water (Thanawong et al., 2014).
Carbon Efficiency	This ratio calculates the economic output per unit of carbon dioxide emissions, helping companies track their carbon footprint relative to their financial performance (Van Passel et al., 2007).

TABLE 19.5 Practical Avenues for Ecopreneurship

Avenue	*Description*
Product Innovation	Contemporary business leaders can influence the creation and advancement of products that facilitate repair, upgrading, and recycling. This involves selecting sustainable materials and developing modular products that prolong the product's lifespan (Bocken et al., 2016)
Sustainable Business Models	Contemporary business leaders can transition their business models from ownership to service-based models, such as leasing or product-as-a-service, which encourages the return and reuse of products (Tukker, 2015)
Partnerships and Collaborations	Contemporary business leaders can form partnerships with other businesses and stakeholders to create closed-loop systems that reuse waste from one process as input for another, which can enhance resource efficiency and innovation (Geissdoerfer et al., 2017)
Green Technology Investment	Contemporary business leaders can lead by investing in and adopting technologies that reduce environmental impact, such as renewable energy, efficient waste management systems, and sustainable supply chain practices (Porter & Kramer, 2011)
Advocacy and Education	Contemporary business leaders can educate employees, customers, and partners about the benefits of a circular economy and promote sustainable practices that can drive broader change. Advocacy for policies that support sustainability can also amplify these efforts (Ellen MacArthur Foundation, 2013)

competitiveness (Srivastava, 2007). Still, these efforts face challenges in measuring impact, collaborating with suppliers, and with costs and investment to make these changes (e.g., Walker et al., 2008).

Ecopreneurship (eco-entrepreneurship) is another approach contemporary business leaders can utilize within and beyond their organizational roles. While the chapter on social entrepreneurship provides guidelines for creating social change, ecopreneurship can be viewed as using pattern-breaking ideas, novel innovations or applications of technology, or environmentally enterprising behaviors to bolster a more circular economy. Table 19.5 outlines five practical avenues for Community Leaders to be ecopreneurs, reinforcing community leadership skills.

Sustainable Development Goals

Community Leaders can use the **United Nations** (n.d.) **Sustainable Development Goals (SDGs)** as guides for their sustainability efforts. The SDGs are 17 global objectives to promote a more sustainable future by 2030. They encompass global challenges, spanning poverty, inequality, climate change, environmental degradation, peace, and justice. Each goal has specific targets to be realized. Endorsed by all UN Member States in 2015, the

SDGs are integral to the 2030 Agenda for Sustainable Development. They show an international commitment to address pressing global issues collaboratively and systematically.

Community Leaders can integrate the SDGs into the core business strategy and sustainability objectives to make meaningful impacts. Community Leaders can meaningfully engage community stakeholders, employees, customers, and suppliers (see Chapter 21). The SDGs offer Community Leaders guides for transparently reporting sustainability efforts and progress toward the SDGs, bolstering trust and accountability. The SDGs provide Community Leaders with directions for future investment in sustainable and innovative opportunities.

Avoiding Faux Sustainability

This chapter has provided Community Leaders with pathways for pursuing shared value and sustainability in their organizations. Community Leaders received insights to build their community leadership skills. However, contemporary business leaders must go beyond part- or half-way in their efforts and be authentic.

Greenwashing and ESG washing refer to the deceptive practice of misleading stakeholders about ESG, green, or sustainable practices to create a falsely positive image. Misleading practices harm a company's reputation and erode stakeholder trust when uncovered. Companies engage in **greenwashing** when they make exaggerated or make false claims about their environmental practices (Delmas & Burbano, 2011). ESG washing extends the concept of greenwashing to encompass social and governance aspects, entailing the exaggeration or falsification of a company's ESG performance without substantial support or action (Parguel et al., 2011). To avoid greenwashing, Community Leaders may utilize third-party certifiers and auditors (Chen & Chang, 2013; Kim & Lyon, 2015). They must also be aware of legal risks; for instance, the UK is now criticizing and re-evaluating ESG ratings and frameworks (Parker & Fisher, 2024).

Exercise 19.2 Real World Greenwashing

Revisit the definition of greenwashing provided in this chapter. Then, research well-known greenwashing cases, such as Volkswagen's Dieselgate scandal or Nestlé's claims about sustainable palm oil sourcing, to conduct in-depth research. Table 19.6 contains multiple examples to explore. Discuss the specific allegations made by the company, the reality of its practices, and the ensuing consequences, encompassing legal, financial, and reputational impacts. Consider the tactics used for greenwashing, how the misleading claims were uncovered, the company's reaction and fallout, and the lessons that can be drawn concerning the importance of transparency and honesty in sustainability efforts. Finally, discuss the role of modern business leaders in ensuring transparent and honest communication about sustainability efforts.

TABLE 19.6 Companies Previously Accused of Greenwashing

Company	*Allegations*	*Details*
Volkswagen	Misleading emissions claims	Involved in the "Dieselgate" scandal (2015), where software was used to cheat emissions tests on diesel vehicles despite environmentally friendly claims.
Nestlé	Misleading claims on sustainability	Criticized for plastic packaging and water extraction practices, with claims of sustainability not matching actual environmental impact.
ExxonMobil	Misleading claims on renewable energy investments	Accused of greenwashing through advertising that portrayed the company as investing in sustainable energy while still focusing on fossil fuels.
H&M	Misleading sustainability claims	The "Conscious" collection was criticized for promoting sustainable materials while continuing to contribute to the fast fashion waste problem.
BP (British Petroleum)	Greenwashing in rebranding	Accused of greenwashing after rebranding itself as Beyond Petroleum despite continuing significant investments in fossil fuels.
Coca-Cola	Misleading claims about recycling and sustainability	Faced accusations of greenwashing due to claims about recyclable bottles while still contributing heavily to plastic waste.
Shell	Greenwashing in renewable energy claims	Criticized for promoting renewable energy investments while continuing to focus on oil and gas production, undermining its sustainability claims.
Unilever	Overstating the environmental benefits of some products	Accused of exaggerating the sustainability of certain products while the company continued practices with a large environmental footprint.

CONCLUSION

Community Leaders recognize the evolution of stakeholder capitalism, CSR, shared value, and sustainability. Shared value and sustainability connect societal progress and corporate success. Shared value initiatives are intended to be scalable and sustainable. They attempt to align profit motives with social impact; however, they are only as strong as the champions behind them. Sustainability can lead to innovation, efficiency, and meaningful community engagement. As this chapter outlines, Community Leaders can integrate sustainability into their decision-making processes and core business strategies. This chapter showcases why Community Leaders should accurately, not falsely, champion such endeavors. By doing so, they can fulfill their role as Community Leaders and contribute to a more sustainable and prosperous future for all.

DISCUSSION QUESTIONS

1. What are the dimensions of shared value?
2. What is the difference between shared value and CSR and critiques of them?
3. What do current business leaders need to know about sustainability initiatives?
4. Why do sustainability or "green" efforts in organizations fail?
5. What are ecoefficiency and ecopreneurship? What are their benefits?
6. How do the Sustainable Development Goals continue to guide sustainability?

Key Terms

- Shared Value
- CSR
- Sustainability
- Ecoefficiency
- Ecopreneurship
- Circular Economy
- United Nations Sustainable Development Goals (SDGs)
- Greenwashing

CASE STUDY 19.1 XYZ IS TOO AMBITIOUS

XYZ Corporation, a prominent global consumer goods company, launched an ambitious sustainability program aimed at significantly reducing its carbon footprint and promoting environmental stewardship. However, the execution faced challenges due to the company's structure and culture. While the initiative included a shift to renewable energy, waste reduction targets, and eco-friendly product promotions, it was largely confined to a dedicated department, limiting its influence and fostering a disconnect from core business operations.

The isolation of the sustainability program hindered integration across teams, as many departments continued to prioritize traditional profit-focused practices over sustainability objectives. This lack of cohesive support led to inconsistent reporting on sustainability efforts. Additionally, the entrenched profit-centric mindset of the leadership created barriers to adopting a culture that could support these new initiatives, leaving employees confused and disengaged.

As a result, XYZ Corporation faced reputational damage stemming from unmet commitments, which disillusioned customers and stakeholders regarding the company's authenticity in its sustainability claims. XYZ needs recommendations that foster cross-department collaboration and shift the company's cultural mindset toward embracing sustainable practices.

1. **Enhance Cross-Departmental Collaboration**: Break down silos by fostering a culture of collaboration between departments. Establish cross-functional teams that integrate sustainability into all aspects of the business.
2. **Align Profit Metrics with Sustainability**: Revise performance metrics to include sustainability benchmarks alongside profit measures. This alignment financially incentivizes departments to innovate while pursuing profitability and sustainability.
3. **Invest in Training and Education**: To enhance understanding and engagement, provide comprehensive training to employees on sustainability concepts, tools, and practices. Facilitating workshops and seminars can equip employees with the necessary knowledge to integrate sustainability into their daily operations.
4. **Leadership Commitment and Cultural Change**: Figure out how to actively communicate the importance of sustainability in driving long-term success and encourage an organization-wide mindset shift.
5. **Set Realistic and Incremental Goals**: Set realistic, incremental goals to foster momentum and build confidence. Celebrating small achievements motivates employees and demonstrates tangible progress, gradually leading to more changes.
6. **Transparent Reporting and Accountability**: Establish transparent reporting mechanisms to hold the company accountable for its sustainability claims. Clearly communicate progress and setbacks to stakeholders to rebuild trust and credibility.

XYZ Corporation can create a more integrated and effective sustainability strategy that mitigates the risk of greenwashing and reinforces its commitment to genuine environmental stewardship. *But which paths should it take, and which should it take first?*

Task: Provide four comprehensive recommendations for XYZ. Connect the recommendations to key chapter concepts. Present the recommendations to a group for feedback and discussion.

NOTE

1 For more, check out this podcast: https://hbr.org/podcast/2023/01/nestls-kitkat-diplomacy-neutrality-vs-shared-value.

REFERENCES

Aaker, D. (2011). Creating shared value vs. leverage social programs. *Harvard Business Review*. https://hbr.org/2011/06/creating-shared-value-vs-lever

Bersin, J. (2023, September 15). Sustainability is about your workforce, too. *Harvard Business Review*. Retrieved from https://hbr.org/2023/09/sustainability-is-about-your-workforce-too

Bertini, M., & Gourville, J. T. (2012). Pricing to create shared value. *Harvard Business Review, 90*(6), 96–104.

Bocken, N. M. P., de Pauw, I., Bakker, C., & van der Grinten, B. (2016). Product design and business model strategies for a circular economy. *Journal of Industrial and Production Engineering, 33*(5), 308–320. https://doi.org/10.1080/21681015.2016.1172124

Burritt, R., & Saka, C. (2006). Measuring eco-efficiency performance of firms. *Journal of Cleaner Production, 14*(9–11), 887–898.

Challagalla, G., & Dalsace, F. (2022, November–December). Moving the needle on sustainability. *Harvard Business Review*. Retrieved from https://hbr.org/2022/11/moving-the-needle-on-sustainability

Chen, Y. S., & Chang, C. H. (2013). Greenwash and green trust: The mediation effects of green consumer confusion and green perceived risk. *Journal of Business Ethics, 114*(3), 489–500. https://doi.org/10.1007/s10551-012-1360-0

Crane, A., Palazzo, G., Spence, L. J., & Matten, D. (2014). Contesting the value of "creating shared value". *California Management Review, 56*(2), 130–153.

Delmas, M. A., & Burbano, V. C. (2011). The drivers of greenwashing. *California Management Review, 54*(1), 64–87. https://doi.org/10.1525/cmr.2011.54.1.64

Ellen MacArthur Foundation. (2013). *Towards the circular economy: Economic and business rationale for an accelerated transition*. Retrieved from https://www.ellenmacarthurfoundation.org/publications/towards-the-circular-economy-vol-1-an-economic-and-business-rationale-for-an-accelerated-transition

Farri, E., Cervini, P., & Rosani, G. (2022, September 26). How sustainability efforts fall apart. *Harvard Business Review*. Retrieved from https://hbr.org/2022/09/how-sustainability-efforts-fall-apart

Geissdoerfer, M., Savaget, P., Bocken, N. M. P., & Hultink, E. J. (2017). The circular economy: A new sustainability paradigm? *Journal of Cleaner Production, 143*, 757–768. https://doi.org/10.1016/j.jclepro.2016.12.048

Huppes, G., & Ishikawa, M. (2005). A framework for quantified eco-efficiency analysis. *Journal of Industrial Ecology, 9*(4), 25–41.

Ioannou, I., & Serafeim, G. (2019, February 11). Yes, sustainability can be a strategy. *Harvard Business Review*. https://hbr.org/2019/02/yes-sustainability-can-be-a-strategy

Kaplan, R. S., Serafeim, G., & Tugendhat, E. (2018). Inclusive growth: Profitable strategies for tackling poverty and inequality. *Harvard Business Review*. https://hbr.org/2018/01/inclusive-growth-profitable-strategies-for-tackling-poverty-and-inequality

Kim, E. H., & Lyon, T. P. (2015). Greenwash vs. brownwash: Exaggeration and undue modesty in corporate sustainability disclosure. *Organization Science, 26*(3), 705–723. https://doi.org/10.1287/orsc.2014.0949

Kramer, M. (2007). Why Robert Reich is wrong about corporate social responsibility. *Harvard Business Review*. https://hbr.org/2007/09/why-robert-reich-is-wrong-abou

Kramer, M. R. & Pfitzer, M. W. (2016). The ecosystem of shared value. *Harvard Business Review, 94*(10), 80–89.

Lamach, M. W. (2017, October 27). How our company connected our strategy to sustainability goals. *Harvard Business Review*. https://hbr.org/2017/10/how-our-company-connected-our-strategy-to-sustainability-goals

Mulcahy, A. (2012). Finding my own path to shared value. *Harvard Business Review*. https://hbr.org/2012/10/finding-my-own-path-to-shared

Parguel, B., Benoît-Moreau, F., & Larceneux, F. (2011). How sustainability ratings might deter 'greenwashing': A closer look at ethical corporate communication. *Journal of Business Ethics, 102*(1), 15–28. https://doi.org/10.1007/s10551-011-0901-2

Parker, G., & Fisher, L. (2024, August 7). UK to introduce bill to regulate ESG rating agencies. *Financial Times*. https://www.ft.com/content/128f6f71-62b2-4cea-b0e1-32e38925b2f0

Pfitzer, M., Bockstette, V., & Stamp, M. (2013). Innovating for shared value. *Harvard Business Review*. https://hbr.org/2013/09/innovating-for-shared-value

Picazo-Tadeo, A. J., Gómez-Limón, J. A., & Reig-Martínez, E. (2011). Assessing farming eco-efficiency: A data envelopment analysis approach. *Journal of Environmental Management, 92*(4), 1154–1164.

Porter, M. E., & Kramer, M. R. (2006). Strategy & society: The link between competitive advantage and corporate social responsibility. *Harvard Business Review, 84*(12), 78–92.

Porter, M. E., & Kramer, M. R. (2011). Creating shared value: How to reinvent capitalism—and unleash a wave of innovation and growth. *Harvard Business Review*. https://hbr.org/2011/01/the-big-idea-creating-shared-value

Rangan, K., Chase, L., & Karim, S. (2015). The truth about CSR. *Harvard Business Review*. https://hbr.org/2015/01/the-truth-about-csr

Reichheld, A., Peto, J., & Ritthaler, C. (2023, September 18). Research: Consumers' sustainability demands are rising. *Harvard Business Review*. Retrieved from https://hbr.org/2023/09/research-consumers-sustainability-demands-are-rising

Schaltegger, S., & Burritt, R. (2010). Sustainability accounting for companies: Catchphrase or decision support for business leaders? *Journal of World Business, 45*(4), 375–384.

Shapiro, A. (2009, March 3). Take eco-efficiency to a higher level. *Harvard Business Review*. https://hbr.org/2009/03/take-ecoefficiency-to-a-higher

Srivastava, S. K. (2007). Green supply-chain management: A state-of-the-art literature review. *International Journal of Management Reviews, 9*(1), 53–80.

Thanawong, K., Perret, S. R., & Basset-Mens, C. (2014). Eco-efficiency of paddy rice production in Northeastern Thailand: A comparison of rain-fed and irrigated cropping systems. *Journal of Cleaner Production, 73*, 204–217.

Tukker, A. (2015). Product services for a resource-efficient and circular economy: A review. *Journal of Cleaner Production, 97*, 76–91. https://doi.org/10.1016/j.jclepro.2013.11.049

United Nations (n.d.). The 17 Goals. United Nations Department of Economic and Social Affairs. https://sdgs.un.org/goals

Unruh, G. C. (2024, March 15). Making sustainability more tangible. *Harvard Business Review*. Retrieved from https://hbr.org/2024/03/making-sustainability-more-tangible

Van Passel, S., Nevens, F., Mathijs, E., & Van Huylenbroeck, G. (2007). Measuring farm sustainability and explaining differences in sustainable efficiency. *Ecological Economics, 62*(1), 149–161.

Walker, H., Di Sisto, L., & McBain, D. (2008). Drivers and barriers to environmental supply chain management practices: Lessons from the public and private sectors. *Journal of Purchasing and Supply Management, 14*(1), 69–85.

Weinberger, D. (2011). Shared value vs. don't be evil. *Harvard Business Review*. https://hbr.org/2011/04/shared-value-vs-dont-be-evil

Whelan, T. (2022, July 27). ESG reports aren't a replacement for real sustainability. *Harvard Business Review*. Retrieved from https://hbr.org/2022/07/esg-reports-arent-a-replacement-for-real-sustainability

World Business Council for Sustainable Development. (2000). *Eco-efficiency: Creating more value with less impact*. Retrieved from https://www.wbcsd.org/Programs/Circular-Economy/Resources/Eco-efficiency

World Commission on Environment and Development. (1987). *Our Common Future*. Oxford University Press.

CHAPTER 20

Social Entrepreneurship

CHAPTER OVERVIEW

This chapter presents social entrepreneurship as a catalyst for social change and justice. Social enterprise and social innovation differ but are both forms of social entrepreneurship. Modern business leaders, as Community Leaders, can leverage innovative approaches to address systemic injustices. This chapter emphasizes that social entrepreneurship generates economic value and implements pattern-breaking ideas to disrupt unjust systems. While acknowledging social entrepreneurship's risks of harm while trying to do good, the chapter offers guidance for leaders to engage with community stakeholders, uphold ethical practices, and strive for meaningful progress. This chapter shares how social enterprising behavior can strengthen community ties, promote local sourcing, and enhance resilience during challenging times. This chapter is a resource for contemporary business leaders looking to take their skills to the next level as social entrepreneurs and community leaders who navigate the complexities of creating impactful, sustainable change within their organizations and communities.

Social entrepreneurship is a powerful driver for impactful change, promoting justice, and rectifying unfair systems. This chapter introduces social entrepreneurship to enhance strategies for contemporary business leaders as Community Leaders. It explores Martin and Osberg's (2015) social innovation approach—a model for transformational change—while distinguishing it from social enterprise, which often focuses on social accounting and incremental change. Social entrepreneurship involves implementing innovative, pattern-breaking ideas to spur substantial, sustainable shifts in unjust social and economic equilibriums (Light, 2008; Talmage, 2021). It encompasses revenue-generating activities that can bolster enterprises seeking to foster positive social impacts in their communities (Dart et al., 2010; Talmage & Gassert, 2022).

Social entrepreneurship can lead to positive change, but it risks failing to fulfill that promise and sometimes causes harm. Its less-than-positive expressions can take unproductive, destructive, or subversive forms. This chapter presents a helpful model to guide business leaders in addressing unjust circumstances, pursuing community stakeholder

DOI: 10.4324/9781003474647-25

input, leveraging ethics, and striving for transformative progress within organizations and the communities they impact.

SOCIAL ENTREPRENEURSHIP: OPERATIONALIZED

Social entrepreneurship at its heart is about leveraging innovative ideas to create social change (Talmage, 2021); however, two schools of thought (i.e., social enterprise vs. social innovation) have fragmented since its appearance in the literature (Dees & Anderson, 2006). The main differences between social enterprise and social innovation are their approaches to addressing deeply rooted social injustices. While social enterprise focuses on creating social and economic value without necessarily prioritizing the disruption or reconciliation of unjust social equilibriums, social innovation aims to bring about transformational change by rectifying unfair systems and promoting justice within organizations and communities (Talmage, 2021).

Socially entrepreneurial or enterprising behavior occurs within organizations that may not outwardly identify as social enterprises (Dart et al., 2010; Talmage, 2021). Community Leaders should prioritize social entrepreneurship, as it offers a dynamic approach to addressing societal challenges while creating economic value. Through small grassroots initiatives, social entrepreneurship fosters innovation and positive societal impact. Social entrepreneurship is a strategic behavior and skill set for Community Leaders. It can also be a competitive advantage in core business strategies.

Social Enterprises

Dart et al. (2010) highlighted the challenges in defining **social enterprises**, emphasizing their intentional or unintentional efforts to create social and economic value. At their best, social enterprises incorporate, engage, and train marginalized individuals (e.g., LGBTQIA+, socioeconomically disadvantaged persons, etc.) within their business models, driving both social impact and economic success within their organization and the communities in which they are located. While social enterprise frameworks like those presented by Dart et al. (2010) and Talmage and Gassert (2022) offer new measurement rubrics, they do not provide explicit pathways for disrupting or reconciling unjust social equilibriums.

Instead, social enterprises often align with established concepts such as corporate social responsibility, triple bottom lines, and shared value, rooted in stakeholder capitalism, which were covered in earlier chapters. Social enterprises significantly shape organizational and community well-being by promoting local sourcing, economic wealth, and environmental sustainability. They may also focus on restoring infrastructure and creating pathways for economic mobility through skill-building and job training. Furthermore, some organizations obtain certifications like Fair Trade or B Corp or even directly involve community stakeholders in their operations (Talmage, 2021). Social enterprises do not require large-scale disruption or transformation but are great contributors to community change and development. They may also be more resilient during tough times. Finally, they have different expressions or frames, as seen in Table 20.1 (Dart et al., 2010).

TABLE 20.1 Framing Social Enterprises

Frame	*Definition*
1. Value Creation	"Organizations which create both social and economic value" (p. 187).
2. Deliberate Cultivation	"Organizations which deliberately cultivate both social and economic value" (p. 188).
3. Central Strategy	"Organizations which have social and economic value creation as central to their organizational strategy" (p. 188).
4. Social Enterprise Identity	"Organizations which identify themselves as 'social enterprises'" (p. 189).
5. Social Purpose Business	Organizations that create "social and economic value by employing some group of marginalized or excluded people in quasi bona fide businesses constructed to train/employ clientele as well as be economically successful" (p. 190). (Dart et al., 2010)

Exercise 20.1 Defining Social Enterprise

Based on the principles discussed in the chapter, explore the Internet (using search engines like Google, YouTube, etc.) to identify social enterprises in your local community. Table 20.1 outlines Dart et al.'s (2010) five frames for mapping social enterprises. Find examples that fit each of these definitions. Note that some enterprises may fit multiple definitions. Analyze what makes these entities social enterprises and how they contribute socially and economically to their communities. Finally, discuss what separates these frames and why some are harder to enact or find in society than others.

Social Innovation: A Disruptive or Reconciliatory Force

The **social innovation** school focuses on disrupting or reconciling unjust social equilibriums using methods that scale (Talmage, 2021). This school of thought emerged from journalistic and organizational endeavors to identify and support exemplars of social innovation (e.g., Ashoka, Skoll Foundation, and David Bornstein's [2007] *How to Change the World*). Debatably, Muhammad Yunus and the Grameen Bank were the first significant examples that brought social innovation to the public sphere (Talmage, 2021). More recently, Martin and Osberg (2015), in *Getting Beyond Better*, outline four essential milestones for transforming unjust social equilibriums, which social entrepreneurs can harness to foster change: **understanding the world**, **envisioning a new future**, **building a model for change**, and **scaling the solution**. Martin and Osberg (2015) published the first book to truly bridge research and practice around social innovation, which Community Leaders can leverage. While not all-encompassing, Martin and Osberg (2015) provide concrete examples of innovative ideas that have led to scalable models for substantially shifting unjust social equilibriums.

Understanding the World: Community Leaders, as social entrepreneurs, know many innovations arise from dissatisfied users (Von Hippel, 2006). Social entrepreneurs can be dissatisfied stakeholders; however, they must actively seek to understand the complexities of unjust equilibriums before initiating any transformative change (Bornstein, 2007; Martin & Osberg, 2015). They question assumptions, consult community experts, and comprehend the various forces that sustain these injustices (Martin & Osberg, 2015).

Martin and Osberg (2015) note three tensions Community Leaders must navigate. Firstly, modern business leaders must abhor the unjust equilibrium while appreciating (i.e., understanding and evaluating) its root causes and the factors or forces keeping the equilibrium in place. Community members or elites (those with power and resources) in communities may resist potential change because they benefit from the current status quo. Secondly, Community Leaders balance outside expertise with community expertise, recognizing knowledge gaps and asking stakeholders for help with interpretation. Finally, they experiment with potential solutions and eventually commit to the most promising opportunities.

The Equal Justice Initiative (EJI), founded by Bryan Stevenson, is a strong example of an enterprise that balanced Martin and Osberg's (2015) three tensions. The EJI works to confront and disrupt the injustices in the American criminal justice system, mainly focusing on issues such as mass incarceration, racial inequality, and wrongful convictions. Through deep engagement with communities and extensive research, EJI has been at the forefront of challenging unjust practices (i.e., racial bias in sentencing) and advocating for criminal justice reform. Through in-depth conversations and research, they address the historical legacy of racial inequality and advocate for policy changes to create a more just and fair society. The EJI showcases deep listening as crucial to drive meaningful engagement and sustainable change.

Community Leaders encourage a culture of questioning assumptions and diverse stakeholder participation. They recognize that they are not the only experts. They actively promote openness to experimenting with potential solutions and know when to commit to action.

Envisioning a New Future: Visioning is fundamental to driving impactful change within organizations and communities (Hsia, 2020; McGrath, 2015). For Community Leaders, visioning involves creating a new and just equilibrium rather than focusing on incremental improvements (Martin & Osberg, 2015). Martin and Osberg (2015) have two requirements for visioning. First, the vision is systemic and focused, benefiting marginalized groups while still considering all stakeholders. Secondly, the vision is a compelling and sustainable future state to garner support and drive transformation. This new state must be a substantial improvement.

An exemplary case that demonstrates sustainable and large-scale transformational change through visioning is Riders for Health in The Gambia, showcasing how a vision of improved healthcare access transformed community health and well-being (Skoll.org, 2011). Riders for Health set up a fleet of motorbikes (and other vehicles) and rent them to the government. This shift allows the Gambian healthcare system to deliver medicine to rural areas and address gaps in service. Community health workers are trained to care for their assigned medical vehicles. With financial backing from a national bank in Gambia, these changes have resulted in 47 million people now having access to healthcare (Riders for Health, n.d.).

Healthy Food Financing Initiative (HFFI) is another example of sustainable, large-scale, and visionary change. The HFFI was established to improve access to nutritious food in underserved areas, addressing food deserts and community health. HFFI provides financial and technical assistance to grocery stores, farmers' markets, and other food retail outlets. They have increased access to fresh and nutritious food in low-income communities. They have not only improved the physical health of residents but have also stimulated economic development and revitalized neighborhoods, creating jobs and supporting local businesses (Reinvestment Fund, n.d.).

Community Leaders must recognize the essential role of visioning in driving impactful change within organizations and communities. Community Leaders can envision business models that can partner with organizations like these to create visionary change. Community Leaders can also ensure that their economic visions for change do not come at substantial social costs to necessary change that must occur in communities for them to thrive. Community Leaders ensure the new vision addresses the needs of all stakeholders and contributes to the betterment of the entire system. They work with others to craft a compelling and sustainable future state to garner support from stakeholders to drive transformation, adaptive but still steadfast in purpose.

Building a Model for Change: Community Leaders are crucial in shifting organizations from settling on incremental change to participating in transformational change. Social innovation holds innovative models across social entrepreneurs and their ventures, combining public and private sector practices to enhance community stakeholders' health, quality of life, and well-being (Martin & Osberg, 2015). These models focus on improving value or lowering costs and involve multiple mechanisms to achieve significant change (Martin & Osberg, 2015). The prominent examples of these mechanisms are provided in Table 20.2, sourced from Ashoka, the Skoll Foundation, and Martin and Osberg's work (2015). All organizations listed still exist and have further scaled their social and economic impacts.

TABLE 20.2 Models for Change from Martin and Osberg (2015)

Mechanism	*Description from Martin and Osberg (2015)*	*Examples*
Value Enhancement		
Transparency Standard	Implementing or achieving a transparency standard (such as a label or certification) increases a product or service's perceived value and encourages consumers to invest.	GoodWeave
Measurement Rubric	Implementing a measurement rubric for assessing equilibrium enhances government initiatives, willingness to invest, and financial commitment by effectively demonstrating value to government officials.	Pratham
Powerful Methodology	Enhancing the worth of a pre-existing asset through an innovative application of methods.	One Acre Fund

(*Continued*)

TABLE 20.2 (Continued)

Mechanism	*Description from Martin and Osberg (2015)*	*Examples*
Cost Diminution		
Borrow an Asset	Assets initially produced and employed by others for alternative reasons are now being repurposed to serve social goals.	Imazon
Investing in a Platform	A new platform has been created to address issues with scalability, cut operational expenses, and facilitate growth.	Kiva
Substitute Lower Cost Labor	Effectively and innovatively finding affordable labor to reduce operational costs.	APOPO
Create a Low-Cost Product or Service	Implementing a less expensive product or service previously impractical, unworkable, or unsustainable.	Proximity Designs

Community Leaders build models for change by adopting innovative models like those described by Martin and Osberg (2015), and they can draw on the lessons in our previous chapter on managing change (see Chapter 16). They combine public and private sector practices to improve stakeholders' lives. Community Leaders focus on improving value or lowering costs through multiple change mechanisms. Examples include labels or certifications, measurement rubrics, repurposing existing assets to serve social goals, investing in new platforms, innovations that reduce operational costs, and creating less expensive products or services previously unfeasible. These approaches can help Community Leaders drive transformational community change.

Patagonia is an excellent example of a company making a positive impact in the United States. This outdoor clothing brand focuses on the well-being of its community and is open about where and how its products are made. It shares detailed information on its website and product labels, which helps customers see the value in its goods while highlighting its commitment to environmental and social responsibility. Chobani, a popular yogurt maker, also champions transparency by sharing information about its ingredients and production methods. They use high-quality, natural ingredients and sustainable practices. This approach not only aligns with their values but also boosts the perceived value of their products, showing their dedication to social and environmental issues. Both companies have founders who are excellent examples of Community Leaders. They have firm commitments to social and environmental responsibility. They show how companies can drive positive change in their communities and remain competitive.

While a transparency standard may seem the quickest win for Community Leaders, they can again partner with local organizations to share their assets and drive substantial change. They can also work with local communities to address labor shortage issues and construct rubrics for measuring local and community well-being. Community Leaders can make a difference by effectively collaborating with local organizations and community stakeholders to leverage their assets and opportunities. Through these collective efforts, modern business leaders can continue to enhance the value and well-being of their organizations and the communities they serve, ultimately creating a positive ripple effect that benefits society. However, the final component of social innovation is that the models must change to shift equilibriums.

Scaling the Solution: Social innovation focuses on the magnitude of impact rather than the organization's size. While economies of scale are essential for cost control, growth must be slow and geared toward creating significant positive social impact. In social innovation, the effectiveness of a new equilibrium replacing the old one determines the effect, as emphasized by Martin and Osberg (2015). Open-source methods may be necessary for scaling impact, focusing on reducing costs while maintaining high value. Social entrepreneurs document their transformative change model, as highlighted by Martin and Osberg (2015), so others can leverage it in the future. Bornstein (2007) refers to this as blueprint copying.

Partners in Health in Malawi have made significant strides in addressing HIV/AIDS and poverty through comprehensive programs connecting health outcomes and economic stability. They focus on providing accessible healthcare services, such as HIV testing, treatment, disease prevention, and management education. They have developed community-based programs to alleviate poverty by promoting sustainable agriculture, vocational training, and small business development. These efforts have improved health and well-being and strengthened regional economic resilience, creating a model for integrated health and economic development interventions in resource-limited settings (RuniTravel, 2011a, 2011b).

The New Teacher Center (NTC) in the United States has effectively scaled its operations, similar to Partners in Health. NTC works to help students learn better by making new teachers and school leaders more effective. NTC started in 1998 with a small program for new educators and has grown to support schools across the United States. NTC partners with school districts and education agencies to offer strong mentoring and training for new teachers to help them improve their skills and stay in their jobs longer. Their evidence-based approach and scalable model have positively impacted educational outcomes and teacher retention (Teach Movie, 2014).

Community Leaders can draw valuable lessons from organizations like Partners in Health and the New Teacher Center. Meaningful community engagement and strategic local partnerships can lead to scalable impact. Localized approaches help to design relevant and sustainable solutions, facilitating broader adoption and scaling. Community Leaders can embrace technology and possibly open-source methods to assess community impact and scalability. Successful models reduce organizational dependency and keep costs low while positive social impact widens. Community Leaders must stay critical and vigilant as they scale to remain true to their missions.

Exercise 20.2 Finding Models for Change

Leveraging what you learned about change models in this chapter, research Martin and Osberg's (2015) examples in Table 20.2. Then, identify examples of your own. Write out how your examples fit the models and mechanisms described for better reflection. What was their unjust equilibrium? What was the vision, and how was it crafted? How can organizations from their outsets (e.g., startup mode) or even long-standing organizations shift their strategies to be more socially innovative? How might different models be combined? Which models fit better together? How did or might they scale?

CRITICAL PERSPECTIVES

Community Leaders critically examine the processes and impacts of social entrepreneurship within their organizations and for community stakeholders. Social entrepreneurship, particularly within social innovation, offers immense potential for improving organizational and community stakeholders on a large scale. Transformational change involves multiple moments where errors, unexpected outcomes, failures, and setbacks are likely. Like social entrepreneurs, Community Leaders understand the interplay between power dynamics, intentions, processes, and potential unintended consequences (Talmage & Gassert, 2020, 2022).

Community Leaders can adopt critical perspectives to scrutinize the underlying values promoted by their organizations, how their community stakeholders value their organizations, and cultivate new values as contexts and organizations evolve. Critical perspectives challenge entrepreneurs' motivations, values, and methodologies and assess their initiatives' outcomes, recognizing unintended negative repercussions can stem from well-intentioned efforts (Talmage & Gassert, 2020, 2022). Talmage and Gassert (2020, 2022) underscore how even sincere efforts can inadvertently foster irresponsible behavior, corruption, and exploitation within communities. Furthermore, Talmage et al. (2022) discuss social entrepreneurship's darker forms that undermine social well-being (e.g., predatory or parasitic NGOs) or aim to enhance it using economic subversive methods (e.g., hacking). Finally, the same strategies for doing "social good" can be used for "social bad." Canales (2013) describes drug cartels as social enterprises based on their moral codes and practices similar to legitimate social enterprises.

Microfinance provides a poignant case study for critical examination in social entrepreneurship, where good intentions can have unintended adverse outcomes. Microfinance initiatives aimed at improving the economic well-being of the poor sometimes exacerbate inequalities and reinforce unjust social structures (Karim, 2008). Moreover, the effectiveness of microfinance can vary significantly based on whether initiatives are locally driven or influenced by external NGOs (Morais & Ahmad, 2011), consistent with calls to further pay attention to the role of power dynamics in community work (Talmage et al., 2024). Community Leaders and their organizations hold powerful influences on community stakeholders' well-being. Unfortunately, social entrepreneurship sometimes fails to achieve its goals and may even harm specific individuals, negatively disrupting local systems (Islam, 2020).

Readers will find an example of failure in Case Study 20.1. Some examples of failed social enterprise experiments include Homejoy (cleaning services), Panera Cares Community Cafes (a pay-what-you-can restaurant), and One Laptop per Child (educational technology). While these enterprises had great intentions, they fell short. They are not the first and will not be the last.

CONCLUSION

This chapter highlighted how social entrepreneurship offers action-oriented approaches to enhance community leadership skills. While social enterprises significantly benefit communities, social innovation is often seen as a more transformative force for substantial change. As a school of thought, social enterprise represents an emerging "gold standard" for community leadership that Community Leaders can seek to achieve. This chapter notes that social entrepreneurship transcends CSR, the triple bottom line, and shared value approaches. It positions business leaders as Community Leaders at the forefront of social and environmental good and meaningful, transformative change. In our final chapter, we offer the ideal path of meaningful engagement as a powerful driver of change for Community Leaders.

DISCUSSION QUESTIONS

1. What is the value of social entrepreneurship in today's organizations?
2. How does it differ from social enterprise and social innovation?
3. How do business leaders operationalize social entrepreneurship?
4. How do business leaders scale social innovations?
5. What is an example of an unjust equilibrium?
6. What are the critical perspectives of social entrepreneurship?
7. How can these efforts fail?

Key Terms

- Social Entrepreneurship
- Social Enterprise
- Social Innovation
- Understanding the World
- Envisioning a New Future
- Building a Model for Change
- Scaling the Solution
- Critical Perspectives

CASE STUDY 20.1 CAUSE, A FAILED SOCIAL ENTERPRISE

In *Stanford Social Innovation Review*, Cobb et al. (2015) tell the story of the failed social enterprise, Cause. Cause was a social enterprise in Washington, D.C., operated as a "philanthropub," a unique type of restaurant and bar. Its primary business model involved donating its profits to vetted social purpose organizations. The founders envisioned a place where patrons could contribute to charitable causes simply by engaging in everyday activities like dining out. The establishment aimed to support various nonprofits by donating profits quarterly and serving as a community space to raise awareness about social issues.

Cobb et al. (2015) note that Cause failed for many reasons, typical of many enterprises. First, Cause suffered from financial mismanagement and unrealistic projections. Cause started with limited capital, relying on a $100,000 business loan and additional funds from an Indiegogo campaign, significantly less than the industry standard for new restaurant ventures. The founders projected revenues of $1.2 million in the first year with a profit margin of 10–20%, which was too ambitious for new restaurants. They took losses. Cause reported $220,000 in revenue in its first quarter but an $8,000 loss. This made it difficult to donate to nonprofits. Cause compromised their giving, counting in-kind contributions as part of their charitable giving.

Cause also had substantial operational challenges and structural issues. The business model depended on volunteers and low-cost labor, which affected staff morale and turnover, especially when pay was inconsistent and inadequate. Management of Cause showed a disconnect between the founders' visions and the operational realities. Cause's leaders were also disconnected from day-to-day operations. Cause was structured as a for-profit rather than a nonprofit to avoid complex tax issues and have greater flexibility in donations. However, this choice limited their ability to engage in capacity-building efforts and required them to maintain a lean operation. The mission of donating profits to charity was a byproduct of financial success rather than being integrated into the core operations. Overall, Cause failed because its founders were unequipped with community leadership skills, despite having plenty of business management skills.

Task: Provide four comprehensive recommendations for the leaders at Cause. Make sure to connect the recommendations to key chapter concepts. Present the recommendations to a larger group for feedback and discussion.

REFERENCES

Bornstein, D. (2007). *How to change the world: Social entrepreneurs and the power of new ideas*. Oxford University Press.

Canales, R. (2013). Rodrigo Canales: the deadly genius of drug cartels [video file]. Retrieved 24 October 2020, from: www.ted.com/talks/rodrigo_canales_the_deadly_genius_of_drug_cartels

Cobb, M., Rosser, C., & Vailakis, A. (2015). Cause for reflection. *Stanford Social Innovation Review, 13*(2), 20–25.

Dart, R., Clow, E., & Armstrong, A. (2010). Meaningful difficulties in the mapping of social enterprises. *Social Enterprise Journal*, 6(3), 186–193.

Dees, J. G. & Anderson, B. B. (2006). Framing a theory of social entrepreneurship: Building on two schools of practice and thought. *Research on Social Entrepreneurship: ARNOVA Occasional Paper Series, 1*(3), 39–66.

Hsia, C. M. (2020). *From Soul Searching to Community Building: Understanding Community Identification through Community "Jen-Tung" Process* (Doctoral dissertation, Arizona State University).

Islam, S. M. (2020). Unintended consequences of scaling social impact through ecosystem growth strategy in social enterprise and social entrepreneurship. *Journal of Business Venturing Insights, 13*, e00159.

Karim, L. (2008). Demystifying micro-credit: The Grameen Bank, NGOs, and neoliberalism in Bangladesh. *Cultural Dynamics, 20*(1), 5–29.

Light, P. C. (2008). *The Search for Social Entrepreneurship*. Brookings Institution Press.

Martin, R. L., & Osberg, S. (2015). *Getting beyond better: How social entrepreneurship works*. Harvard Business Review Press.

McGrath, M. (2015). Community visioning and strategic planning. In R. Phillips & R. H. Pittman, *An Introduction to Community Development* (2nd ed.) (pp. 125–153). Routledge.

Morais, N., & Ahmad, M. M. (2011). NGO-led microfinance: Potentials and challenges in conflict areas. *Journal of International Development, 23*(5), 629–640.

Reinvestment Fund. (n.d.). *America's Healthy Food Financing Initiative*. Retrieved February 26, 2025, from https://www.investinginfood.com/

Riders for Health. (n.d.). *Riders for Health*. Retrieved February 26, 2025, from https://riders.org/

RuniTravel. (2011a, February 1). Alvin's Guide to Good Business 7 - Partners in Health 1 of 2 - BBC Travel Documentary [Video]. YouTube. https://www.youtube.com/watch?v=Mjj6swayBbQ

RuniTravel. (2011b, February 1). Alvin's Guide to Good Business 8 - Partners in Health 2 of 2 - BBC Travel Documentary [Video]. YouTube. https://www.youtube.com/watch?v=Y2-7sM-3DyA

Skoll.org (2011, November 14). Riders for Health [Video]. YouTube. https://www.youtube.com/watch?v=P-YD9Jg4QZM

Talmage, C. (2021). Social entrepreneurship: A needed tool for contemporary community development education. *International Journal of Community Well-Being, 4*(2), 227–243.

Talmage, C. A., Boyl, K., & Gassert, T. A. (2022). Toward a theory of misfit entrepreneurship: Insights from alternative enterprises and misfit entrepreneurs. In Mars, M. & Schau, H. (Eds.), *How alternative is alternative? The role of entrepreneurial development, form, and function in the emergence of alternative marketscapes* (pp. 1–27). Emerald Publishing Limited.

Talmage, C. A., & Gassert, T. A. (2020). Unsettling entrepreneurship by teaching dark side theories. *Entrepreneurship Education and Pedagogy, 3*(3), 316–345.

Talmage, C. A., & Gassert, T. A. (2022). Enhancing social entrepreneurship education with dark side theory to frame social enterprises. *Entrepreneurship Education and Pedagogy, 5*(2), 245–263.

Talmage, C. A., Mars, M. M., Hains, B. J., Hains, K. D., & Ashdown, B. K. (2024). Pushing against a future dark side for community development: An editorial call to action. *Community Development, 55*(3), 310–324.

Teach Movie (2014, May 12). Mentoring new teachers [Video]. YouTube. https://www.youtube.com/watch?v=tVoyzliq7Ro&list=PLsaF7pmbwIYi15HV9Y_BYtJ0SVb9efxE6&index=6

Von Hippel, E. (2006). *Democratizing innovation*. The MIT Press.

CHAPTER 21

Meaningful Community Engagement

CHAPTER OVERVIEW

This chapter explores how meaningful community engagement promotes sustainable and equitable social change. It critiques traditional top-down approaches that overshadow the voices of marginalized communities. Meaningful community engagement requires genuine transformation involving stakeholders directly affected by social issues in decision-making processes. Meaningful engagement addresses root causes rather than just symptoms of inequality to create a lasting impact. Contemporary business leaders, as Community Leaders, learn to foster community connections and belonging. By adopting asset-based approaches, Community Leaders identify and mobilize local strengths and resources to nurture collaboration and enrich social cohesion and resilience. They create environments that promote mutual support and collective action toward meaningful change and a more just society.

This chapter focuses specifically on interactions with community stakeholders in those efforts. This chapter offers critical leadership insights so contemporary business leaders, as Community Leaders, can meaningfully engage with community stakeholders and not ruin their efforts toward sustainability and shared value before they begin. This chapter builds on the previous frameworks (CSR, social enterprise, sustainability, etc.) to pursue a better future.

WHY MEANINGFUL COMMUNITY ENGAGEMENT?

In Anand Giridharadas' book *Winners Take All: The Elite Charade of Changing the World* (2018), he critiques top-down approaches to social change, where elites implement market-based solutions and philanthropy, often preserving systems of inequality. Giridharadas (2018) argues that genuine change requires **meaningful community engagement**, involving those directly affected by social issues in the decision-making process to address root causes rather than symptoms. Meaningful community engagement counters the pitfalls of elite-driven (e.g., CEO-driven or thought leader-inspired) initiatives often found in modern-day CSR and shared value work. Without meaningful community engagement, existing power

DOI: 10.4324/9781003474647-26

dynamics are reified, and the needs of marginalized groups are overlooked. Therefore, meaningful community engagement is essential for achieving lasting and equitable social transformation.

Classical Readings on Meaningful Community Engagement

Many seminal works exist that undergird this chapter, which contemporary business leaders can and should explore as they continue to develop their community leadership skills professionally. Table 21.1 contains a list of classic books for modern business leaders; however, many resources

TABLE 21.1 Classic Books on Meaningful Community Engagement

Book and Author(s)	*Description*
Community: The Structure of Belonging by Peter Block (2009)	The book explores how communities can create spaces of belonging and engagement, emphasizing the importance of collective work and dialogue in meaningful change.
Deepening Community: Finding Joy Together in Chaotic Times by Paul Born (2014)	The book discusses the importance of fostering deep connections within communities and provides practical guidance on building stronger, more engaged communities.
The Tyranny of Experts: Economists, Dictators, and the Forgotten Rights of the Poor by William Easterly (2014)	The book critically analyzes the development community's dependence on technocratic solutions and highlights the importance of adopting approaches that honor the rights and autonomy of the impoverished.
Pedagogy of the Oppressed by Paulo Freire (1970)	The book emphasizes the critical significance of involving marginalized communities in their liberation process and highlights the power of inclusive educational practices.
Building Communities from the Inside Out: A Path Toward Finding and Mobilizing a Community's Assets by John P. Kretzmann and John L. McKnight (1993)	The book introduces the Asset-Based Community Development (ABCD) concept, which focuses on identifying and leveraging communities' strengths and resources to drive sustainable change.
The Abundant Community: Awakening the Power of Families and Neighborhoods by John L. McKnight and Peter Block (2010)	The book advocates for communities to thrive through local engagement and mutual support. It emphasizes that true abundance arises from the strengths and capacities of individuals and families within neighborhoods. By fostering connections and utilizing local assets, communities can establish a better quality of life.
Development as Freedom by Amartya Sen (1999)	The book argues that proper development should be measured by expanding human freedoms and capabilities rather than purely economic metrics and emphasizes the role of public participation in development.

are available in academic and industry publications. This list and other references in this chapter are a start for the Community Leadership journey.

Community Leaders can promote meaningful community engagement. According to Peter Block (2009), establishing a sense of community belonging is paramount. Business leaders can initiate and endorse local initiatives that foster community bonds, creating environments where individuals feel connected and esteemed. Born (2014) underscores that Community Leaders should nurture meaningful connections and collective joy; for example, employees should get involved in community activities. Collaborative endeavors unite people and bolster social cohesion and resilience. Community Leaders embrace an **Asset-Based Community Development** (ABCD) approach (Kretzmann & McKnight, 1993) like community capitals (Emery & Flora, 2006), identifying and mobilizing existing community strengths and resources to cultivate sustainable and influential endeavors. Community Leaders unleash the power of families and neighborhoods by promoting local entrepreneurship and endorsing family-centered community projects, enabling them to pursue meaningful community engagement that contributes to the well-being and empowerment of the communities they serve (McKnight & Block, 2010).

Community Leaders work toward inclusivity and betterment in communities. Easterly (2014) recommends that Community Leaders need solutions that honor and integrate the voices of the often marginalized. He criticizes top-down, expert-driven interventions. Community Leaders ensure community engagement efforts are participatory and inclusive of community stakeholders, going the extra mile to recruit diverse voices. Community Leaders can learn from Freire's (1970) emphasis on education as a tool for empowerment by investing in educational programs in their communities. Community Leaders should work to broaden human freedoms and capabilities to pursue new opportunities and choices in communities (Sen, 1999).

Meaningful Community Engagement and CSR

The *Harvard Business Review* has many articles on CSR, shared value, and sustainability; however, few focus on meaningful community engagement. Successful community engagement requires integrating various life domains—work, home, community, and self—rather than viewing them as separate or conflicting (Friedman, 2014). Contemporary business leaders may consider flexible working arrangements that allow employees to engage in community activities (Friedman, 2014).

As noted in other parts of this book, effective community partnerships involve equitably valuing all stakeholders and focusing on sustainable, long-term solutions. Community Leaders prioritize trust, listening, and involving local stakeholders in decision-making. They train employees and supervisors to ensure they understand local contexts and recognize the value of community engagement. Strong community partnerships help Community Leaders reduce conflict, garner buy-in for change, and ensure uninterrupted operations (Miklian et al., 2021).

Business leaders may need experimental approaches in their CSR programs, which require high levels of community engagement. Experimental approaches may be more likely to achieve meaningful impacts by continually producing and using knowledge about local effects to adapt the CSR practices. Community Leaders encourage experimentation within their CSR activities and with community stakeholders. This aim can be achieved by involving employees at all levels and promoting quality and rapid feedback from diverse stakeholders in local communities (Marti et al., 2024). Community Leaders pursue strategic partnerships with NGOs, government bodies, and other organizations to enhance the reach and effectiveness of their CSR initiatives. Collaborations can provide additional resources and expertise, helping to address complex social challenges more comprehensively (Beard & Hornik, 2011).

CAUTIONS AND PITFALLS

Community engagement can go wrong in many ways. Exploiting vulnerable community members for fundraising purposes through images or narratives can harm the dignity of the individuals and communities involved (Gibbons, 2024). To avoid damaging community relationships, Community Leaders should establish training programs that enhance cultural intelligence and community engagement skills to minimize misinformed assumptions and biases (Hains & Hains, 2024). Community Leaders embrace ABCD, prioritizing community strengths, building social capital, and entrusting the community to co-create visions and decision-making processes (Tchida & Stout, 2024). Community leaders ensure they leverage sustainability and do not leave communities worse once initiatives end (Cafer & Rosenthal, 2024).

The presence of multiple organizations working in the same area without coordination can lead to duplication of efforts, wasted resources, and confusion within the community (McConnell & Lachapelle, 2024). Establishing accountability mechanisms with community-centric grievance procedures ensures the community has a voice in engagement and issue resolution, fostering trust and transparency (Cafer & Rosenthal, 2024). Diversifying funding sources and building local capacity for self-sustenance is crucial, as dependence on external funding sources can lead to instability and unsustainable practices (Gibbons, 2024).

When planning community engagement activities, Community Leaders must ensure that the relationship is mutually beneficial and not parasitic, with both the business and community gaining from the engagement (Hains & Hains, 2024). They involve community members as co-researchers and collaborators, enabling them to participate in data collection, analysis, and reporting to ensure accurate and respectful data interpretation and empower communities to utilize findings for their advocacy (Cafer & Rosenthal, 2024).

Top-down approaches that impose external solutions without involving the community in decision-making often fail to address the community's real needs, leading to resistance and disengagement (Gibbons, 2024). To ensure ethical and beneficial community engagement, establish inclusive policies and procedures developed in consultation with diverse community stakeholders (Hains & Hains, 2024). Achieving success in community engagement depends on making a long-term commitment to nurturing and sustaining relationships, as short-term, project-based efforts frequently do not lead to enduring effects (Gibbons, 2024). Community Leaders engage in ethical and practical community engagement that empowers communities.

Major Examples of Failure

Two examples stand out regarding failures in meaningful community engagement. In 2017, Pepsi faced much criticism for a commercial featuring Kendall Jenner that appeared to downplay the work of social justice movements. In the ad, Jenner resolves a protest by giving a can of Pepsi to a police officer. Many felt that it made light of serious issues faced by protestors. Community Leaders should not simplify or exploit social movements to profit. Returning to our first section on self-leadership, business leaders need authenticity and respect to deal with serious issues. After the pushback, Pepsi pulled the ad, showing how much consumer opinions can affect a brand's image and the risks of insensitive advertising (Victor, 2017).

In 2015, Starbucks started the Race Together campaign to provoke customers to discuss critical social issues. Starbucks asked baristas to write "Race Together" on cups and discuss race with customers. The public pushback highlighted that Starbucks did not fully understand the complexities of race issues, and perhaps a coffee shop was not the appropriate place for everyone to have the conversations, especially before people drank their coffee. Again, Community Leaders dealing with sensitive social topics must think carefully about context and how to approach tough conversations (Fell, 2015).

Community Leaders must take the time to fully understand social issues by leveraging empathy, emotional intelligence, and cultural intelligence. They ensure their initiatives reflect the community's values and needs by pursuing diverse perspectives and investing in communities. Community Leaders epitomize genuine commitments to authentic engagement, recognizing the significance of their actions and how those actions meaningfully impact their communities.

Exercise 21.1 Recognizing Failures in Meaningful Community Engagement

Identify real-world examples of failures in CSR initiatives or meaningful community engagement. Evaluate the issues and lessons learned from these failures. Provide recommendations to avoid similar pitfalls in CSR efforts. Find a real-world example of a CSR initiative criticized for failures in community engagement. Failures often involve exploiting vulnerable community members and a lack of coordination, authenticity, and cultural intelligence. Offer recommendations for improvement based on findings. Finally, reflect on the lessons learned and discuss how to apply these lessons to improve future CSR practices.

CONTEMPORARY APPROACHES TO MEANINGFUL COMMUNITY ENGAGEMENT

This chapter continues by discussing contemporary approaches to meaningful community engagement. This section offers three contemporary approaches: feminist community engagement, Indigenous community engagement, and environmental justice.

Perhaps a future version of this book will add more chapters on environmental justice, an integral field of inquiry and practice (Cachlin et al., 2015; Walker, 2012). For our purposes, we see environmental justice as the systematic pursuit of reconciliation of harm to and future sustainable living for humans, animals, and ecosystems towards greater well-being for all.

Feminist community engagement (FCE) involves incorporating feminist values and methods into CSR. Community Leaders use FCE to address power imbalances and promote social justice. This approach emphasizes the importance of amplifying the voices and experiences of women and other marginalized groups. Community Leaders challenge unfair systems and encourage collective problem-solving, leveraging shared goals, trust, respect, and values. Community Leaders can apply FCE to identify strengths and areas for growth within the community, highlighting issues of power and inequality. With FCE, they can push everyone to contribute knowledge and work together toward common objectives, showcasing inclusivity. Finally, Community Leaders can infuse FCE in CSR efforts by supporting initiatives addressing the social and economic challenges that women and those marginalized face (Abbot, 2019).

Indigenous community engagement involves the collaborative and respectful involvement of Indigenous communities in decision-making processes that affect them. Community Leaders respect Indigenous communities' sovereignty, knowledge, and cultural practices. They honor Indigenous rights, traditions, and cultures by understanding their historical context and current sociopolitical landscapes (IndigenousAware, 2023). They build genuine relationships founded on transparency and trust with Indigenous communities, not just at a project's onset (Cambium Indigenous Professional Services, 2023).

Engagement should include Indigenous voices at every project stage, ensuring their perspectives and knowledge are integrated into decision-making processes and that traditional knowledge and practices are heard (National Science Foundation, 2023). Community Leaders educate their teams about Indigenous cultures and practices through cultural training, inviting local leaders to share their knowledge, participating in cultural activities, and building cultural intelligence (IndigenousAware, 2023). Finally, Community Leaders pursue shared value between companies and the Indigenous communities. Strategies are co-developed with Indigenous community input to ensure they align with community values and needs (IndigenousAware, 2023).

Community Leaders go beyond meeting regulatory requirements. They demonstrated ongoing dialogue, patience, and a willingness to listen and change (Cambium Indigenous Professional Services, 2023). Meaningful community engagement is not easy or cheap (IndigenousAware, 2023). Women and Indigenous communities are also not homogeneous in needs, values, or experiences. Community Leaders will not find one-size-fits-all approaches; they must be adaptable to challenges and opportunities (National Science Foundation, 2023). They continuously educate and train their teams, participate in cultural events, and foster respect and appreciation for marginalized cultures (IndigenousAware, 2023)

Exercise 21.2 Practice Hypothetical Example of Meaningful Community Engagement

When a company involved in manufacturing realizes through impact assessments that a local community near its factory is disproportionately affected by pollution, it could take several steps to address this issue:

- Implement cleaner production technologies to reduce emissions.
- Engage the community in monitoring air quality.

- Invest in local health clinics to address pollution-related health issues.
- Offer job training programs to enhance local employment opportunities.
- Regularly communicate with the community about steps to mitigate negative impacts and seek ongoing feedback.

Consider the following questions for reflection on the most meaningful ways to engage:

- How can the company ensure that cleaner production technologies are effective and sustainable in the long term?
- What strategies can the company use to actively involve the community in monitoring air quality and ensure their meaningful participation?
- How can the company collaborate with local health clinics to address pollution-related health issues and positively impact the community's well-being?
- How can the company tailor job training programs to highlight local needs and assets?
- What communication channels and mechanisms can promote transparent and open dialogue with the community regarding mitigating negative impacts?

CONCLUSION

Meaningful community engagement gives Community Leaders a larger ideal around which to wrap their skills and mindset. Classic literature and modern sources offer pervasive insights for Community Leaders. Community Leaders can address root causes and create equitable and prosperous communities for the future, but they cannot do it alone. This chapter guides business leaders in developing community leadership skills and creating positive change through meaningful engagement with community stakeholders.

DISCUSSION QUESTIONS

1. What does meaningful community engagement entail from a leader's perspective?
2. How can communit engagement foster social change and sustainable development?
3. How can business leaders incorporate community engagement into their organizational strategies?
4. What are the pitfalls to guard against with community engagement efforts?
5. What are the contemporary approaches to community engagement?
6. How does meaningful community engagement enhance CSR initiatives?

Key Terms

- Meaningful Community Engagement
- Asset-Based Community Development
- Feminist Community Engagement
- Indigenous Community Engagement

CASE STUDY 21.1 DAKOTA ACCESS PIPELINE (DAPL) AND THE NEED FOR CULTURAL INCLUSION

Since its announcement in 2014, the Dakota Access Pipeline (DAPL)—a 1,172-mile underground crude oil pipeline from North Dakota to Illinois—has sparked national and international controversy, particularly regarding its environmental and social impacts on the Standing Rock Sioux Tribe. Despite widespread protests and legal battles, the pipeline was completed in June 2017, becoming emblematic of environmental justice failures and community engagement breakdowns (Konyn, 2020; NRDC, 2024). Energy Transfer Partners, the company behind DAPL, and the US Army Corps of Engineers, which issued construction permits, played central roles. The Standing Rock Sioux Tribe, along with environmental and social justice organizations like the Sierra Club and Greenpeace, opposed the project, citing threats to water sources and sacred lands. Feminist and Indigenous activists further highlighted how gender, race, and Indigenous sovereignty intersect within this environmental conflict, stressing the need for inclusive governance approaches.

Concerns about oil spills, particularly near the Missouri River—a vital water source—were paramount, as was the threat to sacred burial grounds, seen as a violation of treaties. The lack of "meaningful consultation with the Standing Rock Sioux Tribe" (American Rivers, 2016) intensified resistance and underscored systemic inequities in stakeholder engagement. From a management standpoint, the controversy underscores the necessity of equitable benefit distribution and inclusive decision-making. Energy Transfer Partners reaped most benefits, while Indigenous communities bore disproportionate cultural and environmental risks. The neglect of sacred sites demonstrated a broader disregard for Indigenous heritage, emphasizing the importance of culturally sensitive planning and authentic engagement.

Restorative practices are essential in addressing historical injustices, such as restoring sacred sites and ensuring clean water access. Transparency and accountability throughout project development could have reduced mistrust and conflict. Long-term trust-building through active listening and community involvement is imperative. Moreover, the DAPL case highlights the need for sustainability and holistic corporate social responsibility, where projects align with ecological goals and community well-being. The protest movement also emphasized intersectionality: Indigenous women, often caregivers and water protectors, led the charge, drawing attention to gendered dimensions of environmental activism and the violence associated with nearby "man camps." Moving forward, recognizing Indigenous sovereignty and incorporating Indigenous leadership in decision-making is vital for fostering respect, collaboration, and equitable outcomes.

Task: Provide four comprehensive recommendations for addressing future environmental justice scenarios. First, consider researching a current scenario to discuss. How is that situation being addressed? Connect the recommendations to key chapter concepts. Then, present the recommendations to a larger group for feedback and discussion.

REFERENCES

Abbot, S. (2019, November). Feminist Community Engagement. Elon University *Center for Engaged Learning*. Retrieved from https://www.centerforengagedlearning.org/feminist-community-engagement/

American Rivers. (2016, November 3). *American Rivers statement in support of the Standing Rock Sioux Tribe's right to clean water*. American Rivers. Retrieved from https://www.americanrivers.org/media-item/american-rivers-statement-support-standing-rock/

Beard, A., & Hornik, R. (2011). It's hard to be good. *Harvard Business Review, 89*(11), 88–96. https://hbr.org/2011/11/its-hard-to-be-good

Block, P. (2009). *Community: The structure of belonging*. Berret-Koehler.

Born, P. (2014). *Deepening community: Finding joy together in chaotic times*. Berrett-Koehler Publishers.

Cachelin, A., Rose, J., & Ashcraft, C. (2015). Investigating critical community-engaged pedagogies for transformative environmental justice education. *Environmental Justice, 8*(5), 199–204.

Cafer, A., & Rosenthal, M. (2024). The dark side of moral outrage: Understanding the risks to long-term, meaningful community development work in higher learning. *Community Development, 55*(3), 339–352.

Cambium Indigenous Professional Services. (2023). Our approach to Indigenous awareness and engagement. Retrieved from https://www.indigenousaware.com/cips-approach-to-indigenous-awareness-engagement

Easterly, W. (2014). *The tyranny of experts: Economists, dictators, and the forgotten rights of the poor*. Basic Books.

Emery, M., & Flora, C. (2006). Spiraling-up: Mapping community transformation with community capitals framework. *Community development, 37*(1), 19–35.

Fell, J. (2015, March 17). Why Starbucks' 'Race Together' Campaign Backfired. *Entrepreneur*. Retrieved from https://www.entrepreneur.com

Freire, P. (1970). *Pedagogy of the oppressed*. Herder and Herder.

Friedman, S. D. (2014). Work + Home + Community + Self: Skills for integrating every part of your life. *Harvard Business Review*. https://hbr.org/2014/09/work-home-community-self

Gibbons, J. L. (2024). Problematic issues in well-intentioned interventions: Reflections of an international researcher. *Community Development, 55*(3), 439–445. https://doi.org/10.1080/15575330.2024.2339277

Giridharadas, A. (2018). *Winners take all: The elite charade of changing the world*. Alfred A. Knopf.

Hains, B. J., & Hains, K. D. (2024). Symbiotic university-community partnerships: The good, the bad, and the ugly. *Community Development, 55*(3), 407–419.

IndigenousAware. (2023). Achieving meaningful Indigenous engagement. Retrieved from https://www.indigenousaware.com/post/indigenous-community-engagement-methods.

Konyn, C. (2020, July 9). *The Dakota Access Pipeline has been ordered to temporarily shut down*. Earth.Org. Retrieved from https://earth.org/dakota-access-pipeline-ordered-to-temporarily-shut-down/

Kretzmann, J. P., & McKnight, J. L. (1993). *Building communities from the inside out. A path toward finding and mobilizing a community's assets*. Northwestern University.

Marti, E., Risi, D., Schlindwein, E., & Athanasopoulou, A. (2024). Creating a corporate social responsibility program with real impact. *Harvard Business Review*. https://hbr.org/2024/03/creating-a-corporate-social-responsibility-program-with-real-impact

McConnell, C., & Lachapelle, P. (2024). The seven deadly sins of community development. *Community Development*, 55(3), 325–336. https://doi.org/10.1080/15575330.2023.2217883

McKnight, J., & Block, P. (2010). *The abundant community: Awakening the power of families and neighborhoods*. Berrett-Koehler.

Miklian, J., Katsos, J. E., Rettberg, A., & Oetzel, J. (2021). The Power of Community Partnerships in Times of Crisis. *Harvard Business Review*.

National Science Foundation. (2023). Arctic community engagement. Retrieved from https://www.nsf.gov/geo/opp/arctic/ace/

NRDC. (2024, June 12). The Dakota Access Pipeline: What Do You Need to Know. Retrieved 5 February 2025 from https://www.nrdc.org/stories/dakota-access-pipeline-what-you-need-know

Sen, A. (1999). *Development as freedom*. Knopf.

Tchida, C. V., & Stout, M. (2024). Disempowerment versus empowerment: Analyzing power dynamics in professional community development. *Community Development*, 55(3), 389–403.

Victor, D. (2017, April 5). Pepsi Pulls Ad Accused of Trivializing Black Lives Matter. *The New York Times*. Retrieved from https://www.nytimes.com

Walker, G. (2012). *Environmental justice: Concepts, evidence, and politics*. Routledge.

CHAPTER 22

Conclusion

CHAPTER OVERVIEW

This chapter concludes the book by discussing the New Normal and the Future of Work. Modern business leaders will face profound challenges amid shifting digital and analog landscapes and significant external threats. We outline five key shifts, which underscore the need to adapt to varying generational expectations, technological advancements, and societal demands for sustainability and transparency. We call upon aspiring leaders to embrace these challenges as opportunities for impactful change, advocating for a more humane, holistic, empathetic, courageous, and innovative approach to leadership in an increasingly complex world.

In our concluding chapter, we return to our introduction, where we sketched an outline of the **New Normal** and provided commentary about the **Future of Work**. Specifically, we spoke of how both concepts were being dominated by megatrends such as digital transformation, acute climate change, accelerated globalization, residual effects of the pandemic, geo-political unrest, and shifting demographics. We emphasized that these would serve as the contextual backdrop of all the forthcoming chapters, compelling us to visit some very new topics and well-trodden subjects but with a highly contemporary twist. We are resolute in what we've provided.

As authors, we stay mindful that the task is to prepare the next generation of leaders who face profound uncertainty, ambiguity, change, and disruption. Leading has become nearly untenable because our challenges are global, multi-faceted, interconnected, generational, polarizing, and deeply ingrained in our culture. It is so much that many avoid the job. In a survey by Robert Walters (2024) called Conscious Unbossing, the following was found:

- 52% of Gen-Z professionals don't want to be middle managers
- 72% of Gen-Z would choose an individual route to advancement over managing others
- 63% of professionals think senior professionals value middle management more than their younger peers
- 69% of Gen-Z say middle management is too high-stress, low-reward

DOI: 10.4324/9781003474647-27

Contributing to these findings is a complicated set of factors, namely, standard of living, low of workplace capital, lack of power, and inability to say no to tasks, to name a few. Yet still we would be remiss if we did not say *leading is hard*. The burden is hefty; the information can be unclear, the responsibilities weigh one down, and the stress can be enormous. David Gonski, Chancellor of the University of New South Wales and Chairman of the UNSW Foundation Ltd., says, "Our leaders are going to have to be much more human than they were previously, much more caring and more innovative" (Peter et al., 2024). We would agree.

We have explained in detail *how* to lead. Now, we use our remaining words to impart reasons to the reader, likely a promising student, *why* they should lead even under today's conditions.

THIS DECADE AHEAD

Peter, Riemer, and Norman (2024) recently published *The 2025 Skills Horizon*, and they report, "The next ten years will be the most disorienting of your career. They could also be the most impactful" (p. 10). Peter et al. (2024) share **five primary shifts** to worry about in our messy future, which we depict in Table 22.1. Based on their shifts, we offer reminders for each.

1. **The values shift**: Workplaces are unprecedentedly diverse (see Chapters 5 and 9), and authenticity (see Chapter 2), adaptive leadership (see Chapter 3), and emotional and cultural intelligence (see Chapter 4) are key to navigating this shift. Additionally, a higher purpose than profit is found among employees, leaders, and clients, such that

TABLE 22.1 Leadership Worries for the Future

Shifts	*Description*	*Relevant Quotes*
Values	This shift refers to the coexistence of multiple generations in the workforce with differing values and work expectations and the fragmentation caused by political and social divides.	"How do you maintain cohesion amidst such plurality? Will productivity suffer or soar? How do you manage diverging expectations of where, when, and how to work? How do you harness differences while working towards inclusion to create a true sense of belonging?" (Peter et al., 2024, p. 11)
Technology	The transformation driven by data, AI, and cyber technology advancements will affect businesses from the front line to the boardroom.	"Data, AI, and cyber conversations are happening at every level of your organisation, and ensuing transformations will run from the front line to the board level. At the same time, technology is changing society more broadly. As these conversations move out of IT and into the C-suite, they directly impact strategy, operating models, and growth." (Peter et al., 2024, p. 12)

(Continued)

TABLE 22.1 (Continued)

Shifts	*Description*	*Relevant Quotes*
Accountability	This shift highlights how business leaders must take responsibility for issues related to sustainability and regulatory demands and answer tough questions about product origins and impacts.	"All businesses must respond to sustainability and regulatory demands: tracking the provenance of materials in their supply chains; the scope and volume of their carbon emissions; and the impact of their products on the natural, social and economic worlds." (Peter et al., 2024, p. 13)
Trust	The decline of trust in traditional institutions will increase scrutiny of businesses and their legitimacy in making important decisions, managing services, and governing.	"Trust in traditional institutions and enduring ideas like liberal democracy are in sharp decline. [...] this changes our global dynamics, creating tensions and obscuring our ability to understand geopolitical developments." (Peter et al., 2024, p. 14)
Energy	Discusses the global transition from fossil fuels to renewable energy and the challenges companies face in making this shift amidst geopolitical tensions, economic volatility, and technological changes.	"The pace of progress has slowed due to economic volatility, increased geopolitical confrontations, technological shifts, and the hottest years on record several times over." (Peter et al., 2024, p. 15)

these stakeholders call for more socially responsible (see Chapter 18) and sustainable (see Chapter 19) organizations. More-than-value orientations promote social entrepreneurship (see Chapter 20) and meaningful community engagement (see Chapter 21). *Contemporary business leaders must know themselves as tied to their values, organizations, and communities before leading.*

2. **The technology shift**: New technologies and modalities for work continue to impact industries and workplaces. Chapter 12 overviews the digital future and the relevant considerations when using technology. Multimodalities and technologies will also impact how to lead collaborative teams (see Chapters 6 and 8) and business strategy (see Chapter 10). In a highly digitally connected world, business leaders must ensure they can authentically build generative relationships (see Chapter 6). Furthermore, modalities and technologies will be essential tools and considerations when leading organizational change (see Chapter 16) and pursuing social responsibility, shared value, and sustainability (see Chapters 18 and 19). *Contemporary business leaders must be lifelong learners regarding technology and understand how to apply technology across different modalities and for larger-than-profit purposes.*
3. **The accountability shift**: Companies are accountable to all stakeholders, not just shareholders. We covered the evolution of stakeholder capitalism in Chapters 18 and 19. Authenticity (since Chapter 2) and transparency have echoed across the book. Transparency was given significant attention in Chapter 11 on financial acumen;

however, transparency is also vital to meaningful community engagement (see Chapter 21). Accountability bolsters customer service excellence (see Chapter 14). Accountability can enrich authenticity and transparency, especially as business leaders seek to boost perceptions of their organization's brand (see Chapter 17). *Contemporary business leaders see accountability as a competitive advantage and primary strategy for cultivating trust among all stakeholders.*

4. **The trust shift**: When authenticity is scarce, trust in leadership erodes. Trust is tantamount to maintaining legitimacy and social license to make decisions that impact stakeholders, governments, and communities. Trust is essential to motivate employees (see Chapter 7), drive client behavior (see Chapter 15), and lead considerable change efforts (see Chapter 16). Again, trust starts at the beginning of any endeavor (see Chapters 1 and 2) and must be repaired when it is questioned (see Chapter 17). *Contemporary business leaders actively build trust in every interaction with stakeholders.*
5. **The energy shift**: We are witnessing an uneven adoption of renewable energy, departing from fossil fuels around the globe. It is hard for today's business leaders to know whether the shift is a reality or grounded in risk for their company. Business leaders must recognize the differences between risk and uncertainty (see Chapter 13) to guide their strategy (see Chapter 10). Contemporary business leaders can leverage entrepreneurial mindsets and behaviors (see Chapter 13), even social entrepreneurial behaviors (see Chapter 20), to harness the power of the energy shift. Still, critical perspectives are necessary for a healthy level of skepticism (see Chapter 20), constantly questioning whether a new technology is sustainable (see Chapter 19) or strategically worthwhile (see Chapter 10). *Contemporary business leaders do their homework to minimize risks and uncertainty to make bold decisions that leverage new energy technologies.*

BACK TO THE MODEL

Now that we have clarified the hard truth, we invite students to use this textbook, particularly the model within (see Figure 22.1), to aid their discovery of these critical questions resulting from the shifts. Consider how a steady course of **Self Leadership** will strengthen one's core self, helping to crystalize values, beliefs, and overall purpose. Mindful reflection is necessary to constantly refine values and beliefs, which should align with purpose. Such an ongoing practice will be essential for navigating and leading others through these shifts. Development of the self, at any age, is a critical function of a leader.

Contemporary business leaders should surround themselves with solid teams with differing perspectives, backgrounds, and talents. These teams must be resoundingly united in their shared goals and be the backbone of business success going forward. With complex, multifaceted, and large-scale challenges, it will take high-functioning, psychologically safe teams to solve them. The **People Leadership** section offered multiple approaches for relationship-building, collaborating, motivating, and creating inclusive cultures. Investing in tightly formed teams is a recipe for withstanding these shifts and solving for transformative change.

No section is better timed to tackle these shifts than our **Business Leadership** dimension. This section candidly discussed solid strategy, digital futures, financial acumen, and

FIGURE 22.1 Leadership Dimensions for Contemporary Business Leaders

(Figure 1.1 repeated here for illustrative purposes.)

entrepreneurial know-how. This is an innovative response to current headwinds, including Peter et al.'s (2024) documented shifts. Contemporary business leaders will build capacity to address the shifts and leverage lessons from this book section at every level (e.g., entry-level employees to C-Suite).

Business leaders will expend just as much energy managing these shifts internally as they will externally. For this reason, we crafted a section specifically on **Client Leadership**, as business leaders must be poised and ready to usher their clients through change, disruption, and uncertainty. Relationships matter, service excellence is a differentiator, predicting client behavior makes one's strategy sophisticated, and effectively telling an organization's story through its brand means survival in a competitive marketplace.

Finally, we want to produce contemporary business leaders who serve as the consciousness of their organization, which is why we assembled the **Community Leadership** section. Several of these shifts are connected to the concepts outlined in Community Leadership, which states that sustainability, stakeholder capitalism, shared value, triple bottom line, social entrepreneurship, and meaningful community engagement must be embedded in business priorities. This circles back to the need for authentic leadership, which is found in Chapter 2 and is vital to the thoughtful implementation and steadfast practice of community leadership, which is why our model is designed circularly.

REMAINING LESSONS

When we wrote this collection of chapters and organized them into this model, we imagined the thousands of compelling discussions and breakthrough learning moments they might generate in countless classrooms. We have fortified the reader with practical knowledge from experience and expertise. As we always prompt our students, they must go forward and execute with ingenuity and style. Yet, we feel there are two more areas that leaders must master in the next decade to become more human in their leadership.

Courageous Action

Simon Sinek famously offered his Three Golden Circles concept in his book "Start with the Why" (Sinek, 2009a) and also in his TedTalk video (Sinek, 2009b), which has received almost 70 million views. He explains by drawing three concentric circles (see Figure 22.2). The innermost is the "Why," the second most is the "How," and the outermost is the "What." He says that most businesses move from the outside in, starting with the "What" and eventually getting to their "Why." However, genuinely remarkable organizations do the opposite. They start with the innermost circle, defining their "Why," and then work their way out. It is a simple but powerful display of understanding the business's core purpose. Contemporary Business leaders know their core purpose.

Exercise 22.1 Start and Find Your Why

Draw three concentric circles on a piece of paper. In the innermost, label it "Why." In the second most, label it "How." In the outermost, label it "What." From the inner circle to the outer circle, consider your "Why" or your purpose. Next, craft how you'll get there. Finally, explain what you want to do for your job or career. Share with a partner.

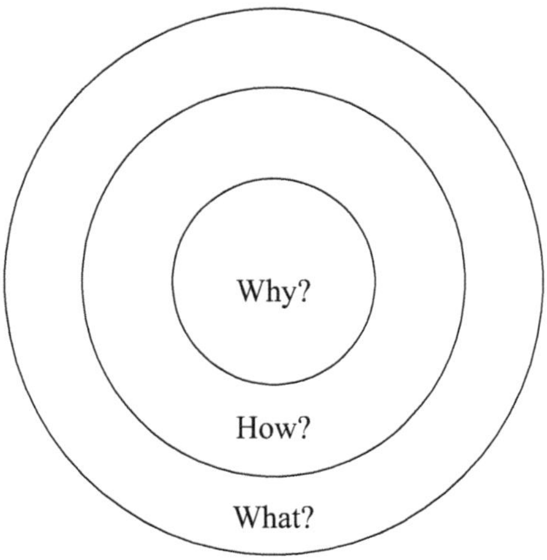

FIGURE 22.2 Why, How, and What Exercise

We frequently use this exercise with students, asking them to do it individually. Understanding their purpose or "why" first, crafting a path to get there, and finally determining what they will do with their job or career has tremendous meaning for many students, mainly when they are in school. However, many struggle with this assignment, unable to develop an apparent "why."

If we might make a suggestion, if you're a student looking for your "why," consider courage. Specifically, choose **courageous action**. Detert (2022) reminds us that courage historically was seen as a masculine trait or "tough guy" quality. These were physically strong individuals who were aggressive and infallible. Detert writes, "This is an example of what evolutionary scholars call **mismatch theory**—the idea that something that was once useful for survival has not evolved quickly enough to match the current environment" (2022). Today, courage has become a way to be more human or vulnerable as a leader.

In modern times, courageous leaders put principles first. They focus on making environments safer for others, are willing to take risks, and make difficult decisions, especially in the face of adversity and uncertainty. For example, in business, saying "I don't know" or "I need help with this" takes courage because the perception, though mistaken, is that it shows weakness. In actuality, being vulnerable draws others towards you. Similarly, when leaders dare to genuinely say, "I'm sorry, I screwed that up," they might fear it shows incompetence when in fact, Detert (2022) reports, "we see that person as more likable and more trustworthy."

In choosing this "Why," courage requires leaders to put principles first. Dertert (2022) writes, "Real leadership isn't about winning a popularity contest. It's about doing important work on behalf of others." Making difficult decisions because it's the right thing to do for other employees takes courage. Where the action takes place is often when a courageous leader must defend their principles when others disagree, sometimes vehemently. Principles such as resilience, perseverance, honesty, humility, integrity, compassion, and remaining committed to a vision and goals despite obstacles and setbacks take courageous action. We need more leaders who embody this. Principled and informed decision-making, even if unpopular, can lead to long-term success.

Demonstrating courageous action also calls for making environments safe for others. Much like our focus on psychological safety, courageous action means leaders change organizational conditions to make it safer for people to be honest, try new things, or take other prudent risks. Business leaders must model courageous action, sometimes by sticking their necks out despite legitimate fear, if they expect others to (Detert, 2022). Without courageous action, business leaders will never realize or activate the growth, transformation, or innovation necessary for survival, particularly in this decade of shifts.

So, *how does one learn courage?* By practicing it. We recommend taking initiative, speaking up, and letting go of the need to control. As a leader, should you choose this as your "why," you will become more human because you'll be exposed—vulnerable, alone, even weak. Where there is courage, tremendous learning can happen. Famously, Brené Brown said, "The courage to be vulnerable is not about winning or losing, it's about the courage to show up when you can't predict or control the outcome" (CEO Magazine, 2019). Arguably, Debbie Ford (2012) puts it best: "The greatest act of courageous action is to be and to own all of who you are, without apology, without excuses, without masks to cover the truth of who you are." *Wouldn't that be remarkable for business culture? And shouldn't all of our leaders set the example?*

Professional Resilience

In addition to courageous action, we wanted to raise another critical quality for managing these shifts: professional resilience, potentially another "why." **Professional resilience** is an individual's capacity to thrive in demanding situations. The choices one makes when responding to difficult situations and one's attitude and willingness to act demonstrate resilience. Building this muscle will be a game-changer in the decade ahead.

The Rs of resilience, found in Table 22.2, is a simple framework widely applied across domains such as business contingency, disaster management, and personal development. Table 22.2 summarizes multiple Rs from different sources and provides examples.

Often, our students ask, *how could you apply the concept of robustness to your current work? How could you use the idea of redundancy in your current roles? How could you become more resourceful in your competitive environments?* And *what are the consequences if you are not resilient?* Developing and internalizing these qualities can transfer these skills into professional careers. When one commits to this as their "why" as a leader, they must engage others in creating behavioral norms, structures, and a culture that fosters resilience.

TABLE 22.2 The Rs of Resilience

R of Resilience	*Definition*	*Examples*	*Citation*
Robustness	The ability to withstand shocks and disruptions by building strong systems, structures, and processes that resist failure.	A manufacturing company invests in high-quality cybersecurity measures to protect its supply chain from cyberattacks.	World Economic Forum (2013)
Redundancy	Implementing backup systems or alternatives to ensure business continuity in case of failures or disruptions.	A retail company establishes relationships with multiple suppliers to ensure a steady supply of goods in case one vendor fails.	Sheffi (2007)
Resourcefulness	The capacity to adapt and innovate when faced with unexpected challenges.	A logistics firm reroutes shipments using alternative transportation when primary routes are blocked due to a natural disaster.	Fiksel (2006)
Response	The ability to take immediate, effective action to mitigate damage and recover operations.	A financial services firm has a crisis response team trained to handle data breaches, minimizing downtime and reputational harm.	Holling (1973)
Recovery	The capability to restore operations and return to normal or an improved state after a disruption.	A tech company implements a post-crisis business continuity plan to rebuild operations after a major IT system failure.	World Economic Forum (2013)

Other dimensions of resilience operate at the individual and organizational levels. We would spotlight the following:

- **Mental Resilience**: The psychological strength to cope with adversity, including stress management and positive thinking.
- **Emotional Resilience**: The ability to regulate emotions and maintain balance, especially during times of stress or crisis.
- **Physical Resilience**: The health and well-being of the body, which includes nutrition, exercise, and sleep.
- **Social Resilience**: The capacity to rely on and build strong relationships with others for support and collaboration.

As professionals, what kind of value do we place on these dimensions of resilience? Often, these dimensions are where professionals suffer the most, losing focus, lacking time, being overcommitted, and not attending to, which frequently turns individuals away from the responsibility of leadership roles. Additionally, it leads to burnout, low productivity, poor morale, and the resignation of good employees, even when they have exceptional cultures. If we're not purposeful about professional resilience, it can make work miserable and a grind. Further, one will never survive budget cuts, reorganizations, product failures, mistakes large and small, or project deadlines.

Like any skill, resilience can be learned with practice. For example, Maddi and Khoshaba (2005) studied employees of a large US telecommunications company when this industry was being deregulated. The company was constantly changing, and jobs were at stake. During the 12-year study period, almost 50% of the employees lost their jobs, and two-thirds experienced remarkably stressful life events including divorce, mental health issues like depression and anxiety, and heart attacks. Despite this, one-third of the workers endured the tremendous challenge and found ways to flourish (Craig, 2019).

In *Resilience at Work: How to Succeed No Matter What Life Throws at You*, Maddi and Khoshaba (2005) reported that employees who retained their positions rose to the top, while those who lost their jobs either started their own companies or took strategic roles in other companies. *What does this study show about professional resilience?* For a start, resilience is an active, dynamic process.

Resilient employees build strong relationships with others (Davis-Laack, 2014). These high-quality connections are characterized by active listening and responsiveness to colleagues' emotions (Davis-Laack, 2014). Further, in positive workplace relationships, resilient workers will do what they can to help another colleague succeed. Professional resilience means being a team player who looks out for the well-being of their fellow employees. Finally, social support is vital in workplace resilience (Jackson et al., 2007). Developing personal and professional networks is beneficial and can guide times of stress or provide a nurturing relationship.

Critical life skills, resilience, and adaptation are key to human survival (Craig, 2019). In the decade ahead, leaders will be challenged by disruption, change, and uncertainty, and workplaces will be beset with stress. Occupational stress affects personal and performance outcomes (Rees et al., 2015). Furthermore, workplace stress is correlated with high levels of depression, anxiety, and burnout (Rees et al., 2015). Professional resilience is a must for future business leaders.

Exercise 22.2 Your Leadership Legacy

Imagine you are celebrating your 100th birthday at a fantastic party with family, friends, and former colleagues. Your favorite family member invites partygoers to reflect on who you were in your life and work. What are three things you most want partygoers to say? How could you relate this to your "why"? How can you connect this reflection to professional resilience, and courageous action? Share with a partner.

PARTING THOUGHTS

Though seasoned educators, we have so much more to say. We are reminded of the French expression "dénouer un noeud," which means it is impossible to untie all the knots. Admittedly, we have unlocked more questions than we have answered here, but we are confident that the instructors and students, as they use this text, have a strong foundation for future-forward learning and discussion. Our passion for leadership development led us through each component of this text, appreciating the skills that would never go out of style while adding some much-needed contemporary essentials.

What is compelling about leadership development from an individual perspective is that there is no mastery. Leaders commit a lifetime to learning, managing, transforming, and innovating, each situation calling for a new set of adaptations. Particularly within the coming decade, we sought to arm the next generation of leaders with skills, strategies, tools, and frameworks that they could apply on the job with the complex business scenarios coming their way. After reviewing this text, students should have a comprehensive understanding of theory and ample opportunity to apply and practice.

Peter et al. (2024) leave us with four skill "blobs" that students need to know. Why blobs? Because that's what the research suggests. "Our quartet of Blobs plays an important role in thinking about leadership upskilling. They visually embody how skills converge around key topics and perspectives that are relevant to your leadership journey and your organisation's future" (Peter et al., 2024). These areas of convergence include technology and its implications, large-scale challenges in the external environment, people and workplace issues, and the complexity and uncertainty individuals will face as leaders. Leaders will need to master new things in each of these areas (Peter et al., 2024). These coincide with many of our chapters.

Working with you, who are engaged in this text, is a privilege and honor. We wholeheartedly get behind your potential; who you are, what you value, and what you will pursue matter to us. You can show the future what a better leader, not a bad boss, looks like with discipline and practice. Societies have long positioned individuals to be the leaders that their communities need. We hope you will seize the opportunity and bring your talents, energy, and willingness to learn to the role. The world needs contemporary leaders who are confident in the self, people, business, client, and community aspects of their responsibilities. We hope to see you as a leader soon.

DISCUSSION QUESTIONS

1. How can business leaders cultivate resilience and adaptability to effectively lead in an era of uncertainty and rapid change?
2. How can leaders balance profitability with social responsibility and integrate ethical considerations into decision-making?
3. How does a leader's willingness to admit mistakes and show vulnerability influence organizational culture and employee trust?
4. What ethical considerations should leaders address when integrating AI and other emerging technologies into their organizations?
5. How can organizations and leaders foster professional resilience among employees to prevent burnout and enhance long-term leadership effectiveness?

Key Terms

- Five Primary Shifts
- Self Leadership
- People Leadership
- Business Leadership
- Client Leadership
- Community Leadership
- Courageous Action
- Mismatch Theory
- Professional Resilience
- Rs of Resilience

CASE STUDY 22.1 LEADING THROUGH CRISIS

Background: In the fast-paced and highly competitive tech industry, a prominent software company, *TechForward*, was known for its innovative products and strong market position. However, in early 2020, the company faced an unprecedented challenge when a cybersecurity breach occurred, compromising sensitive client data and leading to an immediate loss of trust among its clients. The breach, coupled with the COVID-19 pandemic disrupting operations, created an environment of chaos, uncertainty, and intense pressure on the leadership team.

At TechForward's helm was CEO Sarah Langston, a seasoned leader known for her calm demeanor and strategic foresight. However, the crisis put her leadership skills to the ultimate test. The situation demanded quick thinking, courageous actions, and professional resilience. This case study examines how Sarah navigated the crisis and emerged with the company intact but forever changed.

The Crisis: The breach was discovered when one of the company's largest financial institution clients reported unusual system access patterns. Upon further investigation, TechForward's internal security team confirmed that hackers had infiltrated the company's software infrastructure. The breach compromised sensitive data from thousands of users across several industries.

The immediate impact included:

- Loss of key client contracts.
- A sharp decline in stock value.
- Negative media coverage leads to reputational damage.
- Loss of employee morale as many staff were uncertain about the company's future.

At the same time, the COVID-19 pandemic forced the company to quickly transition to remote work, further complicating the response to the breach.

Task: Provide four comprehensive recommendations for Sarah, connecting them to key chapter concepts. Then, present the recommendations to a larger group for feedback and discussion.

REFERENCES

CEO Magazine. (2019, June 4). Exclusive interview with Brené Brown: "Failure is part of the ride". *CEO Magazine*. Retrieved from https://www.theceomagazine.com/lifestyle/interview/brene-brown/

Craig, H. (2019). *Resilience in the workplace: How to be resilient at work*. Positive Psychology.

Davis-Laack, P. (2014). Seven things resilient employees do differently. *Psychology Today*. Retrieved from https://www.psychologytoday.com/us/blog/pressure-proof/201410/seven-things-resilient-employees-do-differently

Detert, J. (2022). What courageous leaders do differently. *Harvard Business Review*. https://hbr.org/2022/01/what-courageous-leaders-do-differently

Fiksel, J. (2006). Sustainability and resilience: Toward a systems approach. *Sustainability: Science, Practice, & Policy*, *2*(2), 14–21. https://doi.org/10.1080/15487733.2006.11907980

Ford, D. (2012). *Courage: Overcoming fear and igniting self-confidence*. HarperOne.

Holling, C. S. (1973). Resilience and stability of ecological systems. *Annual Review of Ecology and Systematics*, *4*(1), 1–23. https://doi.org/10.1146/annurev.es.04.110173.000245

Jackson, D., Firtko, A., & Edenborough, M. (2007). Personal resilience as a strategy for surviving and thriving in the face of workplace adversity: A literature review. *Journal of Advanced Nursing, 60*, 1–9. https://doi.org/10.1111/j.1365-2648.2007.04412.x

Maddi, S., & Khoshaba, D. (2005). *Resilience at work: How to succeed no matter what life throws at you*. American Management Association.

Peter, S., Riemer, K., & Norman, P. (2024). The 2025 skills horizon. *Sydney Executive Plus, The University of Sydney*. https://doi.org/10.25910/57M8-SQ33

Rees, C. S., Breen, L. J., Cusack, L., & Hegney, D. (2015). Understanding individual resilience in the workplace: The international collaboration of workforce resilience model. *Frontiers in Psychology*. https://doi.org/10.3389/fpsyg.2015.00073

Robert, W. (2024, September 23). *Conscious Unbossing*. Retrieved from https://www.robertwalters.com

Sheffi, Y. (2007). *The resilient enterprise: Overcoming vulnerability for competitive advantage*. MIT Press.
Sinek, S. (2009a). *Start with why: How great leaders inspire everyone to take action*. Penguin.
Sinek, S. (2009b, September). *How great leaders inspire action* [Video]. TED Conferences. https://www.ted.com/talks/simon_sinek_how_great_leaders_inspire_action
World Economic Forum. (2013). *The Global Risks Report 2013*. https://www.weforum.org/reports/global-risks-2013

Index

Page numbers in italics denote figures, page numbers in bold denote tables, and n refers to a note.

For Product Safety Concerns and Information please contact our EU
representative GPSR@taylorandfrancis.com
Taylor & Francis Verlag GmbH, Kaufingerstraße 24, 80331 München, Germany

www.ingramcontent.com/pod-product-compliance
Ingram Content Group UK Ltd.
Pitfield, Milton Keynes, MK11 3LW, UK
UKHW050230200926
475702UK00020B/2954
* 9 7 8 1 0 3 2 7 5 5 8 2 3 *